Creatures of Attention

signale
modern german letters, cultures, and thought

Series Editor: Paul Fleming, Cornell University
Peter Uwe Hohendahl, Founding Editor

Signale: Modern German Letters, Cultures, and Thought publishes new English language books in literary studies, criticism, cultural studies, and intellectual history pertaining to the German-speaking world, as well as translations of important German-language works. Signale construes "modern" in the broadest terms: the series covers topics ranging from the early modern period to the present. Signale books are published under a joint imprint of Cornell University Press and Cornell University Library in electronic and print formats. Please see http://signale.cornell.edu/.

CREATURES OF ATTENTION

*Aesthetics and the
Subject before Kant*

JOHANNES WANKHAMMER

A Signale Book

CORNELL UNIVERSITY PRESS AND CORNELL UNIVERSITY LIBRARY
ITHACA AND LONDON

Cornell University Press and Cornell University Library gratefully acknowledge the College of Arts & Sciences, Cornell University, for support of the Signale series.

Copyright © 2024 by Johannes Wankhammer

All rights reserved. Except for brief quotations in a review, this book, or parts thereof, must not be reproduced in any form without permission in writing from the publisher. For information, address Cornell University Press, Sage House, 512 East State Street, Ithaca, New York 14850.

First published 2024 by Cornell University Press
and Cornell University Library

Library of Congress Cataloging-in-Publication Data

Names: Wankhammer, Johannes, 1982– author.
Title: Creatures of attention : aesthetics and the subject before Kant / Johannes Wankhammer.
Description: Ithaca [New York] : Cornell University Press and Cornell University Library, 2024. | Series: Signale: modern German letters, cultures, and thought | Includes bibliographical references and index.
Identifiers: LCCN 2023043873 (print) | LCCN 2023043874 (ebook) | ISBN 9781501775796 (hardcover) | ISBN 9781501775802 (paperback) | ISBN 9781501775826 (epub) | ISBN 9781501775819 (pdf)
Subjects: LCSH: Attention—Philosophy. | Subjectivity. | Aesthetics, Modern—18th century. | Autonomy (Philosophy) | Philosophy, German—18th century. | German literature—18th century—History and criticism.
Classification: LCC BH183 .W26 2024 (print) | LCC BH183 (ebook) | DDC 111/.85—dc23/eng/20240112
LC record available at https://lccn.loc.gov/2023043873
LC ebook record available at https://lccn.loc.gov/2023043874

To the memory of my father

"In dieser Welt aber rollen die Tage dahin;
die einen gehen, die anderen kommen, aber keiner bleibt."
—Said the page where the bookmark was left

Contents

Preface ix

Acknowledgments xi

Introduction: ATTENTION. Introducing a New Faculty of the Soul 1

1. SCIENCE. Attention, the New Science, and the Disembodied Mind 39

2. SUBJECT. Before the Autonomous Subject: Disciplines of Attention in the German Eighteenth Century 92

3. POETICS. Wonder and the Poetics of Attention: Poetry as Education of Attentiveness in B. H. Brockes and J. J. Breitinger 152

4. AESTHETICS. Attending to the Margins: Baumgarten's Unredeemed Foundation of Aesthetics 199

Epilogue: AFTERLIVES. Modulations of Attention
since 1800   278

Bibliography   301

Index   323

Preface

It was the first session of a writing seminar on the Enlightenment, and my students were eager to show their enthusiasm for the subject. One student was particularly vocal. As a yoga teacher, he announced, he had been on the path to enlightenment for years. Another student chimed in, reporting details of her daily meditation practice.

Sparing me the task, other students who remembered enough of their high school history classes (and had read the course description) cleared up the misunderstanding. Relieved but somewhat irritated, I wrote off the confusion as an example of how language can, à la Sapir and Whorf, shape our perception of the world. Surely, the same misunderstanding would not have occurred in a German language seminar on *Aufklärung*—although different double entendres might have come up in that course. And did the need to explain the term "Enlightenment" not perhaps also signal, more than its deplorable decline, a welcome shift from a monolithically Western-centric perspective in secondary education?

A few sessions later, class discussion turned to Descartes's *Meditations on First Philosophy*, and my yoga instructor was triumphant: so it was meditation, my student concluded, that was the key to enlightenment "in that other sense" (of the age of reason) as well? Another example, I thought, of the malignant genius of language. But the series of coincidences was indeed striking. Concerns with the imagery of illumination and with meditation are, after all, not the only overlaps between the semantic fields of Eastern spirituality and Enlightenment rationality. Attention and mental clarity are invoked in both areas, and the "eye of the mind" belongs as much to the metaphorical repertoire of seasoned yogis as to that of Descartes and Locke. What if one took these resonances seriously and considered Enlightenment "in that other sense" to be based on a form of psychophysical practice as well?

That I did not immediately dismiss this thought was in part due to the currency of the concept of "cultural techniques" in recent German media theory, which has shifted the spotlight of theoretical discussion to the practices that precede and consolidate formal systems of communication and action. Certainly, whatever practice my students had integrated into their daily routines had little in common with what Descartes described in terms of meditation. The Cartesian meditations and the paradigm shift they exemplified were certainly part of a very different "culture of attention" than that of Eastern spirituality—but a culture that could perhaps likewise be described by the way it organizes individual and collective attention.[1] Perhaps the specific difference between the cultures of attention that clashed in my seminar was the reason my students, like so many post-Enlightenment subjects, yearned for the different kinds of focus, attentiveness, and discipline promised by the practices of yoga. My teaching that day was not the most focused, but I left class with a thought that injected a fresh dose of thinking into my project. The result is the book that follows.

---

1. Assmann uses the term "culture of attention" in analogy with the phrase "memory culture" in "Die Aufmerksamkeit Gottes," 69.

Acknowledgments

Many of the influences that have shaped this book defy acknowledgment through proper names. How to acknowledge the otherworldly light of the midnight sun on a long day in Reykjavík that crystallized some of the initial ideas for this book? How to credit the structural liberties and pressures of the American research university, and the chain of contingencies that has led me to find myself in one of them? How to account for the diffuse influence of a Romantic concept of literature developed around 1800 in Northern Germany on the Southern Austrian provincial milieu where I grew up? It was there that a girl who would become my maternal grandmother spent hours locked in the outhouse of the family farm reading books to escape the confines of her world. And it was there that my young mother used the alchemy of books from a local library to transmute intolerable circumstances into a livable life and, eventually, a life well lived. This book would not exist without them, and without the complex forces that intersected in their lives.

I would like to begin by thanking Peter Gilgen, whose guidance, support, and camaraderie were instrumental in shaping the thinking from which this book eventually emerged. Nathan Taylor and Bryan Klausmeyer have been congenial interlocutors and intellectual companions along the way who have enriched both my thinking and writing; this book owes much to them. I am deeply grateful to Paul Fleming, who has been beyond generous with his time and provided indispensable intellectual and institutional support. I would like to extend my thanks to several readers who offered insightful comments on earlier versions of this material, including Florian Fuchs, Amando Jo Goldstein, Hannah Miller, Neil Saccamano, Greg Sevik, and Antoine Traisnel. My deep gratitude goes to two anonymous reviewers commissioned by Cornell University Press. At times, reading their reports afforded the pleasure of being understood as Kant thought we should strive to understand all authors—better than they do themselves. The reviewers' suggestions have made this a better book. I would also like to thank Rüdiger Campe and Jocelyn Holland, who read and commented on an earlier version of the manuscript for a virtual workshop organized by the German Department at Princeton University. Convention demands that I claim all remaining shortcomings as my own, though a contrarian impulse has me wondering: If others share some of the credit, should they not also share some of the blame? Of course, even minimal reflection proves otherwise: I can recall more than one instance when I was not able to live up to the astute feedback and suggestions offered by readers.

I thank my colleagues at the Department of German at Princeton for conversations that animated hallways, seminar rooms, cafés, cafeterias, restaurants, bars, and the winding walkways on campus: Brigid Doherty, Devin Fore, Joel Lande, Tom Levin, Susan Morrow, Adam Oberlin, Sally Poor, Jamie Rankin, Juliane Rebentisch, Joseph Vogl, and Nikolaus Wegmann. Equal thanks go to Janine Calogero, Lynn Ratsep, Fiona Romaine, and Ed Sikorski, who have provided more than merely logistical support.

Throughout the years, numerous interlocutors in conference or seminar settings have stimulated my thinking on various aspects of this book. I am indebted to Hans Adler, D. Graham Burnett, Christiane Frey, Carl Gelderloos, Alexandra Heimes, Anja Lemke, Dalia Nassar, Ross Shields, Lauren Stone, Andreas Strasser, Baeti Tebase, Evan Torner, Gabe Trop, Gernot Waldner, and David Wellbery. An early influence on my intellectual development was Günther Höfler at the University of Graz. Among my nonacademic friends, I will name only three who have been such an important part of my life that their influence is no doubt subtly present in these pages: Raphaela Haring, Hannes Grassegger, and Alex Sommer.

I thank Kizer Walker at Signale and Mahinder Kingra at Cornell University Press for their professionalism and patience throughout the publication process. All this would not have been possible without the pioneering work of Peter Uwe Hohendahl, who established the Signale series as an indispensable forum for publication in German Studies.

A substantial portion of the section on Breitinger in chapter 3 draws from a previously published article titled "On Seeing Otherwise: Johann Jakob Breitinger's Poetics of Attention," which appeared in *The Germanic Review: Literature, Culture, Theory* 95, no. 3 (2020): 162–81 (reprinted by permission of Informa UK Limited, trading as Taylor & Francis Group, www.tandfonline.com). The brief section on Lichtenberg in the epilogue is largely based on my article "The Art of Taking Note in G. Ch. Lichtenberg's WasteBooks," published in *MLN* 136, no. 5 (2021): 984–1009 (copyright © 2021 Johns Hopkins University Press).

I have saved the weightiest acknowledgments for last. Katrina Nousek has brought vibrancy to my days and continues to help me see the world with fresh eyes. I thank her with all my heart. Finally, I would like to give thanks to and for my mother, Susanne Wankhammer-Strack, my brother Alexander Wankhammer, and my grandmother Anna Winter. This book is dedicated to the memory of my father, Rudolf Wankhammer. No doubt I have unintentionally omitted names, as I am writing this up in a café in Berlin, where the sun does not quite shine until midnight but does shine long and bright on warm summer nights.

Creatures of Attention

Introduction

ATTENTION
Introducing a New Faculty of the Soul

For two millennia in the West it seemed that Aristotle's *De anima* had provided a complete inventory of what souls can do. Treatises on the mind in the seventeenth century continued to divide their subject according to the Aristotelian capacities of sensing, remembering, imagining, reasoning, and willing, even if they otherwise sided with the moderns against the authorities of ancient philosophy. Discussions of the five external senses were typically followed by chapters on the internal senses (memory and imagination) and culminated in a treatment of judgment, reason, and the will—as the so-called higher powers of cognition.[1] By the middle of the eighteenth century, however, the nature of the soul seems to have undergone a

---

1. An overview of standard topics in seventeenth-century treatises on the soul is offered in Hatfield, "Attention in Early Scientific Psychology," 6–7. The two most basic capacities Aristotle had ascribed to all living beings (including plants)—nourishment and reproduction—had dropped out of the picture by the seventeenth century.

small but momentous shift. In the 1730s and 1740s, treatises began to appear that included chapters on a mental faculty with no equivalent in the Aristotelian architecture of the soul: the faculty of attention.

This book contributes a chapter to the history of how the soul acquired this new faculty. Today, strikingly popular self-help books declare that we must "regain control" over our attention in order to lead self-determined lives. Philosophers like Bernard Stiegler call for the reeducation of attention in the digital age to recover the mature (*mündig*) subject of the Enlightenment, while others follow Walter Benjamin and Bertolt Brecht in probing the potential of collective distraction to overcome bourgeois individualism.[2] Yet self-help gurus and high theorists alike assume that the modern self is made or unmade by the ability to pay attention. Whether commentators reclaim or renounce individual autonomy, they invariably target the ability to control attention as its practical core. In the chapters of this book I offer a deep history of the links between attention, autonomy, and the modern subject that continue to limit the range of possible positions in contemporary thought. To understand how this discourse coalesced, I recover a body of philosophical and literary texts from the recognizably modern yet excitingly strange period of German and European thought from about 1650 to 1780 in which the terms "attention" and "subject" first developed their modern meanings. While the scholarship on the history of attention has focused on showing how the successive shocks of industrial modernity, mass media, and digital technology have threatened the integrity of the modern subject since the late nineteenth century, it has so far largely failed to ask how this subject became defined by attention in the first place. I address this lacuna by explaining how the link between attention and subjectivity was first forged in the service of the eighteenth-century ideal of individual autonomy—and first challenged in the emerging field of aesthetics, which I present in chapters 3 and 4 as an internal critique of the Enlightenment paradigm of strenuously focused attention.

---

2. See Stiegler, *Taking Care of Youth and the Generations*, 23–28.

My project proceeds from the premise that the Kantian watershed in European thought obscured many of the problems for which it offered a paradigmatic solution. The problem of attention is one of them. It emerged for minds confronted with a world to which tradition and theology no longer provided reliable guides. Against the background of widespread epistemological uncertainty at the threshold of modernity, honing individual attention as a tool for the conscious processing of experience promised to secure a vantage point from which the world could again be reliably known. Kant would remove this problem from the empirical struggles over attention by transcendentalizing the subject as an extra-empirical site of perceptual synthesis, moral action, and aesthetic judgment. And yet the problem of attention reemerged whenever Kant's transcendental solution faltered. In a contemporary context where the Kantian foundations of modern thought—above all, the picture he helped entrench of a human subject that gains autonomy by cutting itself off from the world—are again being widely questioned, this book rediscovers pre-Kantian thought on attention and aesthetics as a laboratory of alternative modernities.

To account for a development that traverses cultural fields, my approach is decidedly interdisciplinary: I read early modern treatises on scientific observation and pedagogical manuals alongside canonical and less canonical works of eighteenth-century philosophy and literature. The discursive coherence of the problem I explore emerges in connections between seemingly disparate fields that any study drawing on primary texts and secondary literature from a single discipline is bound to miss. Whereas my first chapter focuses on Francis Bacon and René Descartes—and all other chapters include material that attests to the international dimension of the problem—most of the texts I read are by polyglot authors from German lands, such as Leibniz (who wrote in French and Latin), Christian Wolff (who wrote in Latin and German), and Alexander Baumgarten (who mostly published in Latin). The book's relative focus on the German intellectual tradition does not simply reflect its disciplinary origins but is grounded in the fact—already noted by William James—that German rationalism's emphasis on the mind's spontaneity proved a much more fertile ground for elaborating problems of attention than British empiricism or French sensualism.[3] Although the problem of attention was by no means restricted to Germany, German thinkers were able to draw on a theory of mind that facilitated their paradigmatic articulation of a general problem of European modernity.

A Diagnosis of "Attention Deficit" in 1777

In the eighteenth century no less than today, what was meant by this new power of the mind is most evident wherever attention is said to be lacking. Deficiency of attention (*Mangel der Aufmerksamkeit*), explains a medical textbook first published in 1777 by the German "philosophical physician" Melchior Adam Weikard (1742–1803), is the inability to keep the mind focused on the same object with any intensity and for any duration of time (*länger und nachdrücklicher bey demselbigen Gegenstand verweilen*).[4] As Weikard's textbook diagnoses, those who suffer from this ailment of the soul are incapable of anything more than shallow knowledge and tend to be impetuous in their actions. Among underlying causes, Weikard includes a poor upbringing and the rampant reading frenzy (*Wut, alles zu lesen*) that had corrupted the minds of an entire generation.[5] Then as now, people were supposed to have been more attentive in the old days. On closer inspection, the disease could be traced to two disorders that are quite distinct despite their shared set of observable characteristics: a deficit of attention results either from an attention so feeble that it cannot sufficiently shield the mind from unwanted sensory stimuli, or from an overly vigorous attention so

---

3. James, *The Principles of Psychology*, 1:402.
4. Weikard, *Der philosophische Arzt*, 1799, 3:31–41, here: 36; first edition of the respective section: *Der philosophische Arzt*, 1777, 4:114–29. "Mangel der Aufmerksamkeit" is a relatively common phrase in the eighteenth-century discourse on attention, and it already played a role, for instance, in Georg Friedrich Meier's discussion of attention in his midcentury *Anfangsgründe aller schönen Wissenschaften*, 2:72 (§292), 2:93–100 (§§299–300).
5. Weikard, *Der philosophische Arzt*, 1777, 4:116, 118.

absorbed by whimsical objects that not even the most vivid sense impressions register in the mind.[6] Though distinct, these etiologies constituted a single medical diagnosis, as both insufficient attention *and* excessive attention lead the diseased to fill their minds with mere trifles or minor issues (*Nebensachen*) rather than focusing on what counts in a given context as the matter at hand.[7] In a finding that will prove generalizable for the eighteenth-century discourse on attention and its pathologies, deficiency of attention is thus the inability to keep the mind focused on what one is *supposed* to be attentive to, whether this is due to insufficient attention or an attention misplaced; it is the inability to pay a normatively sanctioned kind of attention.

Does Weikard's account constitute "the earliest reference to ADHD in the medical literature," as a German neurologist and an American psychiatrist argue in a 2012 article published in a medical journal focused on disorders of attention? Comparing what Weikard describes as *Mangel der Aufmerksamkeit* with the criteria for diagnosing attention-deficit/hyperactivity disorder (ADHD) in the *Diagnostic and Statistical Manual of Mental Disorders*, fourth edition (DSM-4; 2012), the authors observe that there is "considerable overlap" not only "with the nature of the attention problems believed to exist in ADHD as it is currently conceptualized" but even with regard to some of the suggested treatments.[8] According to the authors, Weikard's recommendation that patients be placed in distraction-free environments, abstain from stimulants like coffee, or engage in regular exercise still makes good medical sense today. Of course, the authors grant, contemporary psychology no longer recommends taking ice baths or ingesting steel powder to strengthen the nerve fibers. And confining patients, as Weikard advises, to a

---

6. Weikard, *Der philosophische Arzt*, 1799, 3:36. Weikard equates the first variety with inattention (*Unaufmerksamkeit*) and the second with distraction (*Distraktion*). In what will be a staple of eighteenth-century discussions of attention, excessive attention can thus become indistinguishable from distraction. (The explicit distinction between the two varieties only appears in the 1799 edition of vol. 3, although the underlying logic is already suggested in earlier versions.)

7. Weikard, *Der philosophische Arzt*, 1799, 3:37; 1777, 4:114.

8. Barkley and Peters, "Earliest Reference to ADHD," 628.

dark room for some salutary sensory deprivation would, of course, be "considered inhumane if not unethical" today.[9] But all this only goes to show, in the opinion of the authors, how far medical science has come since the first reference to the disorder, whose causes and cures we now understand "from our current and better scientifically informed perspective."[10]

I open this study on problems of attention in the German eighteenth century with this encounter across the annals of medical history because it throws into relief how I construct attention as the focal topic of this book. Do the eighteenth-century "philosophical physician" and modern neurologists refer to the same object? If assuming that they do would be overly naive, as historical discourse analysis has taught us, what might we make of what nevertheless seem like striking continuities in how these ailments of attention are described? Reasonably enough, historian of philosophy Gary Hatfield offers two possible explanations for what he, too, diagnoses as "significant descriptive, theoretical, and empirical continuity" between eighteenth-century psychology and modern research on attention: either such continuity is "conditioned by the basic structure of attention as a natural phenomenon" or contemporary research remains trapped in a discursive framework instituted in the eighteenth century and is therefore condemned to the "reshuffling of a few core ideas."[11]

Perhaps the alternative is not as clear-cut as Hatfield assumes. As even the brief extract from Weikard's treatise makes clear (and as our readings will repeatedly demonstrate), the psychology of attention was, already in its eighteenth-century beginnings, concerned with shaping the human mind it sets out to describe scientifically.[12] There

---

9. Barkley and Peters, "Earliest Reference to ADHD," 628.
10. Barkley and Peters, "Earliest Reference to ADHD," 628.
11. Hatfield, "Attention in Early Scientific Psychology," 3–4.
12. Compare the first sentence of Weikard's preface: "By philosophical medicine, I understand the one that is concerned with researching the faculties and afflictions of the intellect and the mind *as well as with guiding them and maintaining them in their proper state through physical and moral measures, or with restoring them to such a state if a deviation has occurred*" (Weikard, *Der philosophische Arzt*, 1799 [n. p.], my emphasis and translation). All translations from German, Latin, and French in the book are mine unless otherwise noted. The gendering of translations reflects the original texts.

is in this psychology no absolute distinction between *knowing* and *molding* this new faculty—no neat separation, therefore, between what we can loosely distinguish with Gottlob Frege as the "sense" and "reference" aspect of psychological knowledge of attention (its mode of presentation and what it is "about"). In a strict sense, to ask whether *Mangel der Aufmerksamkeit* offers an early "reference" to ADHD is to ask the wrong question, since Weikard's diagnosis is part and parcel of discursive practices that help produce the phenomenon it describes along with its specific pathologies. If there are—across a notable historical discontinuity—similarities between *Mangel der Aufmerksamkeit* and contemporary medical diagnoses, these can in part be ascribed to a certain persistence of imperatives and practices by which attention has been molded since the eighteenth century. What we are dealing with is neither the tenacity of a discursive construct unmoored from psychological reality, nor the invariability of a natural constant, but instead a relative continuity in how individual minds are shaped by historical forces. Because the training of attention in the eighteenth century was designed to fortify the mind's self-sufficiency and its distinctness from internal and external environments, it is even possible to venture that we see a relative continuity in how minds are formed *into* discrete individuals.

Was There an Eighteenth-Century Regime of Attention?

As these opening reflections suggest, I frame my study as historical and do not share the ambition of scholars who aim to harness the latest science on attentional processing to shed new light on how we read or to supplement neurological findings with phenomenologically rich, first-person accounts from literature.[13] In dialogue

---

13. For an example and a summary of readings of eighteenth-century poems informed by cognitive science, see the introduction to Koehler, *Poetry of Attention*. Natalie Phillips's study *Distraction: Problems of Attention in Eighteenth-Century Literature* shows that a reliance on neuroscience does not need to come at the expense of historical specificity and critical verve (for her suggestion on how to reconcile cognitive science and history of mind, see 21–23). Other approaches develop transhistorical concepts of attention to redescribe literary form, poetics, or narratology that are

with emerging interdisciplinary scholarship loosely grouped under "critical attention studies," I approach attention instead as a normative performance of mindedness lodged at the intersection of social and discursive practices.[14]

From the outset, any such study of attention in the eighteenth century faces a major hurdle. The work rightly identified as the foundational text of the emerging field of critical attention studies, Jonathan Crary's *Suspensions of Perception: Attention, Spectacle, and Modern Culture* (1999), proposed that the modern problem of attention did not arise before the later nineteenth century—that it, in fact, *could not* have preceded this period. According to this influential historical schema, the rise of attention presupposed the demise of older modes of subjectivity untroubled by perceptual fragmentation and represented, for Crary, by the early modern observer's effortless overview of the field of vision. Only once this solution became practically and theoretically untenable under the shocks of late nineteenth-century urban and industrial modernity did attention, according to Crary, impose itself as a problem. In his account, the concern with attention arose in the wake of various measures to produce attentiveness in a subject constantly threatened by collapse.

We can begin by noting that the claim foisted by this historical framing—that before the nineteenth century, attention had only "local importance" and remained a "marginal, at best secondary problem within explanations of mind and consciousness"[15]—simply does not hold up. As Patrick Singy has countered, "anyone familiar with eighteenth-century metaphysics, natural philosophy, or medicine will be puzzled by such a statement, to say the least."[16] (One can add aesthetics, ethics, and pedagogy to the list.) In fact, many of the features of the nineteenth-century discourse Crary identifies as evidence for its radical historical novelty (such as attention's fun-

---

not exclusively informed by cognitive science; see, for instance, Alford, *Forms of Poetic Attention*.

14. This label was proposed in Rogers, *The Attention Complex*, 4, and has since been adopted more widely. See also the introduction to Citton, *The Ecology of Attention*.
15. Crary, *Suspensions of Perception*, 17–18.
16. Singy, "Huber's Eyes," 69n18.

damentality to the cognitive apparatus, its essential selectivity, and the problem's interdisciplinary range) turn out to recycle commonplaces established in eighteenth-century discussions of attention.[17] As I will detail in chapter 1, Crary's dismissal of eighteenth-century discussions of attention rests on portraying the knowledge of the "classical" subject of the camera obscura as effortless and instantaneous self-presence of the world to the observer. Effectively, this leads Crary to adopt elements of a narrative he explicitly warns against—that of framing modern attention and distraction as a "fall" from the supposedly unfractured wholeness and stability of earlier modes of subjectivity and perception.[18] The point of my revising the dominant narrative is not just to correct the scholarly record but to challenge the genealogy of modern subjectivity this narrative has advanced. What my study shows is that the seemingly "Archimedean" vantage point of the classical observer was itself established by disciplining attention and learning to insulate the conscious mind against the vagaries of imagination and the senses. When periodically recurring crises of attention in modernity threaten

---

17. Crary, in *Suspensions of Perception* (17, 21), for instance, cites claims by nineteenth-century psychologists according to which attention "underlie[s] every other mental faculty" or is "the essential condition for the formation and development of the mind" as evidence for the unprecedented status of attention in that period. In fact, Georg Friedrich Meier had already maintained in 1754 that selective attention "underlies all other cognitive faculties" so that it is "impossible to improve any other cognitive faculty unless one has improved one's attention"—and was far from alone in making such assertions. Meier, *Anfangsgründe aller schönen Wissenschaften*, 2:48 (§283).

18. Crary, *Suspensions of Perception*, 49–51. Despite the steering effect of Crary's book on subsequent research, recent scholarship has begun to shed light on the cultural history of attention in the eighteenth century: Lorraine Daston ("The Disciplines of Attention," and other essays) and Patrick Singy ("Huber's Eyes") have restored the place of attention in the seventeenth- and eighteenth-century history of scientific observation. Studies by Natalie Phillips (*Distraction*) and Lily Gurton-Wachter (*Watchwords*) have described a vibrant concern with attention and distraction in eighteenth-century British literature. In the German context, Barbara Thums (*Aufmerksamkeit*) and Michael Hagner ("Toward a History of Attention") have begun to reconstruct the importance of *Aufmerksamkeit* as a "cultural technique" or "bourgeois virtue" in Enlightenment dietetics, whereas Matthew Riley (*Musical Listening*) has detailed the importance of attention for eighteenth-century listening practices. Carolin Duttlinger's *Attention and Distraction* appeared too late to be considered in this book.

the coherence of the subject, this subject comes undone at the very seams where it was first sutured together: it was itself a creature of attention.

Attention and Selective Perception

The foundation for eighteenth-century discussions of attention in Germany and beyond were laid by Christian Wolff (1679–1754), the eminent philosopher in Germany before Kant. In his widely read German textbook on metaphysics from 1719, Wolff provided an initial definition of the term, which helped to establish the word "Aufmerksamkeit" as the canonical loan translation of the Latin *attentio*: "We find in the soul a faculty to direct itself ... to one among the things it senses, imagines, or thinks in such a way that we are more conscious of it than of others, that is, to make one thought have more clarity than the rest: which we commonly call attention."[19] For Wolff, attention is characterized by narrowing awareness to one thought or sensation among others, thus increasing the degree of clarity of the focused representation. What motivates the idea is the assumption that, unlike the infinite mind of God, the human mind cannot consciously perceive everything all at once. Selectivity of focus, and therefore the need to pay attention, is the mark of a mind that is, like the human mind, finite; investing *one* thing with attention necessarily withdraws attention from others. Today the idea that attention is a limited resource subject to an internal economy is so widely shared that it often serves as the self-evident opening premise for theories of attention that otherwise have little in common with each other. "Capacity-limitation theories" in cognitive psychology, which explain attentional phenomena through a "bottleneck in information processing,"[20] assume this economy with the same air of ob-

---

19. Wolff, *Vernünfftige Gedancken von Gott*, hereafter cited by the conventional shorthand *German Metaphysics*, 149 (§268).
20. For an overview of different theories of attention in twentieth-century and contemporary psychology, see Mole, "Attention."

viousness with which phenomenological accounts presuppose attention's need to selectively structure the chaos of experience,[21] and with which sociological approaches construe attention as a form of social action necessitated by an oversupply of possibilities that cannot all be realized at the same time.[22] In his posthumously published sketches on a phenomenological anthropology, Hans Blumenberg pithily summarizes the premise behind these various concepts of attention as the assumption "that a subject is confronted with a world that overwhelms and inundates its informational needs."[23]

The interesting question is why, despite the apparent obviousness of the economy governing attention as a finite resource, the selectivity of attention became a focal topic of discussion only when Wolff and others began to turn their attention to attention in the early eighteenth century.[24] The sudden rise of interest in attention in the eighteenth century was not simply a matter of the progress

---

21. Bernhard Waldenfels (*Phänomenologie der Aufmerksamkeit*, 13) begins his phenomenological reflections on attention in this way. His opening idea that "whoever sees everything, sees and hears nothing," is the flipside of the economy of finitude assumed by Wolff.

22. See, for instance, Schroer, "Soziologie der Aufmerksamkeit," 200; Hahn, "Aufmerksamkeit," 25–26, 30. For a critique of the Darwinist connotations of conceiving attention in terms of selectivity, see Seitter, "Aufmerksamkeitskorrelate," 172. On selectivity as the basic operation of attention, see also Neumann, "Aufmerksamkeit."

23. Blumenberg, *Zu den Sachen und zurück*, 188.

24. The pertinent sense of economy as a closed "household" must be distinguished from recent diagnoses—based on increasing competition for consumer attention in the economic sphere of modern societies—that a growing sector of the modern information economy can be described as an "attention economy." Although there are isolated phenomena in the eighteenth century (such as *Lesewut* and the competition for attention on a fast-growing literary market) that prefigure such an attention economy, economies in the eighteenth century are generally a far cry from directly monetizing attention. Nevertheless, the connection between both senses of "economy" seems more than random. As I will suggest in the epilogue, the conception of attention as a limited quantity of identical quality that can be invested here or there conditions the modern treatment of attention as a resource. On the concept of an "economy of attention," see Franck, *Ökonomie der Aufmerksamkeit*. For a media-theoretical version of a similar argument, see Schmidt, "Aufmerksamkeit: Die Währung der Medien." For alternative conceptions of attention as a collective ecology, see Citton, *The Ecology of Attention*.

of knowledge.[25] Attentional phenomena of directing awareness had been discussed since Greek and Roman antiquity and throughout the Middle Ages (without, however, becoming a topic of the first order).[26] In a world in which the microcosm reflected the macrocosm—as in the classical *kosmos*, the medieval *ordo creationis*, or the order of resemblances that guided the Renaissance—the narrowing of focus characteristic of attention was not an urgent matter.[27] Where every particular thing reflects the entire order of being alongside it and the whole is therefore seamlessly present in the part, focusing on one thing does not come at the expense of others, as it does in the familiar "economic" view of attention.

Rather, the exacerbated sense of selectivity and partiality that defines modern attention only surfaces once the ramifications that connect any one thing to all others no longer hold. Substantial conflicts can then arise between focusing on this *or* that thing; foregrounding this *or* that aspect; seeing something one way *or* another. The result is not only a new urgency of the problem of attention but, as already indicated in the opening reflection, the possibility of distraction. Coined in the modern sense in seventeenth-century France and soon imported into German as *Zerstreuung*, distraction is discussed, in the eighteenth century, as the malady of *misusing* selective attention. Lessing interpreted this misuse as a moral failing, because we ought to be able to control where we place the focus of our attention: "Do we not have it in our power to exert, to withdraw attention as we wish? And what is distraction other than an improper use of our attention? The distracted person does think, he merely does not think . . . what he should be thinking."[28]

---

25. This is the general assumption behind much literature on (the history of) attention in psychology and analytical philosophy; see, for instance, Mole's otherwise highly instructive overview in "Attention"; or Murphy's *Historical Introduction*, 3–22.

26. For overviews, see Neumann, "Aufmerksamkeit"; Hatfield, "Attention in Early Scientific Psychology"; Waldenfels, *Phänomenologie der Aufmerksamkeit*, 15–20.

27. On the order of similitude in the Renaissance, see the pertinent sections in Foucault's *The Order of Things*, 17–45.

28. Lessing, *Werke und Briefe*, 6:322. Lessing reflects on the (for him, recent) history of the word *Zerstreuung* in a 1767 review of Regnard's *Le Distrait*, empha-

Just as attention grew increasingly threatened by distraction, an attitude of attentiveness became, however, more necessary than ever. As long-established frameworks of understanding were submitted to systematic doubt—paradigmatically, in the Cartesian project—the need for attention as a perceptual "state of exception" in which experience is scrutinized with a heightened level of awareness became imperative.[29] This imperative also can be—and famously was—interpreted optimistically, as the opening of new horizons of understanding. Once traditional frameworks of understanding are cast aside as a mere contrivance of prejudices, empty words, and arbitrary tradition (Bacon's "idols"), an unprejudiced attention would finally be free to register what a gaze clouded by false preconceptions had been unable to see, and to take note of the details and parts of which things are truly composed. No one portrayed this experience more vividly than the poet of attention Barthold Heinrich Brockes, who begins one of his volumes of poetry with an emblematic rise from a dim cave into a spring day simply to register things as they show themselves in the bright light of the sun. For Brockes, emergence from the Platonic cave simply meant perceiving the world anew with fresh and attentive eyes.[30] This tension between partiality and discovery—between the risk of missing the mark and the exuberance of marking things for the first time—defines attention in the eighteenth century.

Both poles testify to the demise of an unfractured framework of understanding in which everything possesses its preordained place.[31]

---

sizing that the play was initially met with an unfavorable reception but became a success during his time.

29. Michael Hagner has characterized attention as a "state of exception." See Hagner, "Aufmerksamkeit als Ausnahmezustand"; Hagner, "Toward a History of Attention."

30. In Brockes, the exit from the Platonic cave leads not into a beyond of immaterial ideas but into the midday sun of the physical world—as suggested by the title of his poetry collection: *Irdisches Vergnügen in Gott* (Earthly Delight in God). Brockes, *Irdisches Vergnügen in Gott*, 4:3–5.

31. The diagnosis that the rise of modern social forms went hand in hand with the destruction of traditional forms and conceptions of order is central to all classics of sociology. Synthesizing sociological and intellectual-historical approaches, Niklas Luhmann has characterized the prevalent conception of order in feudally stratified premodern societies (as opposed to functionally differentiated modern ones) as that

The rise of attention can thus be understood as the correlate, in individual and collective consciousness, of the becoming-questionable of order that theories of modernity (especially in the German tradition) have described through the analytical category of "contingency"—the awareness that things *could also be otherwise*. Paralleling the conceptual history of attention, contingency was first defined as a concept in classical philosophy but remained of rather marginal importance until the eighteenth century.[32] Specific events could be contingent—they could either happen or not happen, and were therefore possible in another way as well—but the horizon of possibility as a whole was not. As Michael Makropoulos and others have noted, *modern* contingency-consciousness marks the moment when contingency affects the horizon of possibility itself, so that whole frameworks of understanding forfeited their semblance of inevitability.[33] The risk and the exuberance of attention arose in close entanglement with such a rising awareness of the contingency of things.

Habits of the New: Attention between Innovation and Routine

Sociological approaches to the problem of attention in modernity have described modernization in terms of a "profound disruption of the established order of attention" caused by the fraying of traditional social units (such as guilds or medieval towns) that granted everyone a fixed place in the social order.[34] In response, members of modernizing societies had to cultivate an individual faculty of attention necessary for orienting themselves in an oversupply of different

---

of a "cosmos of essences"; see Luhmann, *Beobachtungen der Moderne*, 130–31. On this topic in the context of a sociology of attention, see Schroer, "Soziologie der Aufmerksamkeit," 207–8; also Hahn, "Aufmerksamkeit," 44–51.

32. As Stephen Greenblatt has shown in *The Swerve*, the full impact of the work of Lucretius, the great philosopher of contingency in classical antiquity, was only felt in the modern age.

33. Makropoulos, "Modernität als Kontingenzkultur," 65.

34. "Modernization can also be understood as a comprehensive disruption of the established order of attention" (Schroer, "Soziologie der Aufmerksamkeit," 207–8).

and ever-evolving possibilities of behavior. A remark from Christian Thomasius's *Ausübung der Sittenlehre* (Practice of ethics; 1696) documents the problem: "One cannot learn decorum through basic infallible rules, but only through continuous and meticulous attention [*Auffmerckung*] even to the smallest of details, as decorum varies every day and differs in every location."[35] The uncertainty of what is socially acceptable in the context of what Thomasius already calls "bürgerlich[e] Gesellschafft"[36] (civil/bourgeois society) demands an attitude of persistent watchfulness that must pick up on the minutest details in order to properly read a social situation. The concept of *decorum*—which for a long time epitomized what was natural and proper in sociality as well as in the arts—becomes a matter of sheer contingency for Thomasius (it has "no certain ground").[37] Bookish knowledge, he emphasizes, is of no use in understanding the fashions of the day; the only remedy is a constant exercise and refinement (*exerciren und schärfen*) of attention.[38] Thomasius offers his cautionary note in the context of a typology of ambitious individuals (*der Ehrgeizige*) who must develop a quickly adaptable attention in order to raise their status in an increasingly fluid society. *Aufmerksamkeit* emerged, as Barbara Thums has suggested, as a principal "cultural technique of modernity"—as technique necessary for flexible orientation in an age characterized, as Thomasius's prescient reference to fashion implies, by constant innovation and change.[39]

In eighteenth-century poetics, the sensibility articulated by Thomasius first surfaced with Johann Jakob Breitinger's *Critische Dichtkunst*

---

35. Thomasius, *Ausübung der Sittenlehre*, 238 (§28). *Aufmerkung* was an alternative loan translation of Latin *attentio* before the eighteenth-century terminologization of *Aufmerksamkeit*. Italics reproduce Latin print in the original. Complaints about the fickleness of decorum became common in the late seventeenth and early eighteenth century; see Disselkamp, *Barockheroismus*, 404–5.
36. Thomasius, *Ausübung der Sittenlehre*, 13 (§21).
37. Thomasius, *Ausübung der Sittenlehre*, 239 (§28).
38. Thomasius, *Ausübung der Sittenlehre*, 238–39 (§28).
39. Thums, "Die schwierige Kunst," 131; Thums seems to use *Kulturtechnik* in the broad sense of a cultural skill. Focusing on the nineteenth century, Walter Benjamin famously saw fashion's turning novelty into a constant ("the new and the ever same") as paradigmatic for a characteristically modern temporality of unending innovation that bars substantive change. See the convolute "B" in Benjamin, *Das Passagen-Werk*, 1:110–32.

(Critical poetics; 1740), which raised the *new* into the central category of poetic theory. In contrast with the neoclassical equation of decorum with the order of nature, which art was supposed to reflect and "imitate," Breitinger proposed that novelty—the source of poetic beauty—consisted precisely in *deviation* from the customs, laws, and habits familiar to an audience. Breitinger saw poetry as catering above all to the attentive needs and capacities of an audience, turning the cognitive absorption of new material into the prime source of poetic pleasure. A similar tension between innovation and routine also defines the juxtaposition of attention and habit, perhaps the most frequently invoked contrast in the eighteenth-century discourse on attention. Breitinger saw the force of habit as the reason people let the beautiful complexity of the world pass by unnoticed most of the time, and prescribed poetry's attention-inducing novelty as a cure for the malady. What Breitinger prescribed in theory, Barthold Heinrich Brockes's poems performed in practice, using detailed description as a tool to alert readers to the overlooked wonders of even the most everyday objects as they reveal themselves to the attentive gaze. Brockes's massive poetic oeuvre is, as I will argue in chapter 3, best understood as the attempt to continuously jolt readers out of their inattentive stupor, culminating in Brockes's *cri de coeur* "Laß ja Gewohnheit mir die Augen nicht verkleistern!" (May habit never clog up my eyes!).[40]

For both Breitinger and Brockes, the relationship between habit and attention will turn out to be more complicated than this clearcut opposition suggests. The opposition assumes that the default mode of perception is not natural, not fixed or given, but learned—a *habit*, therefore, of noticing and (more often) not noticing things. This means that habit is itself a form of habituated or automated *attention*—a specific pattern of taking note and disregarding—but one that is reduced to customary modes of coping with everyday challenges, and therefore blind to the slumbering complexity of the world. The same reversal takes place in the case of the exceptional

---

40. Brockes, *Irdisches Vergnügen in Gott*, 2:465. Heinz Drügh (*Ästhetik der Beschreibung*, 32) prefaces his chapter on Brockes's descriptive technique with this memorable motto.

attention evoked by poetry, whose goal turns out to be the education of a new *habit* of perception. The relationship between attention and habit is thus dialectical—a tension between what Michael Hagner has described as attention's "state of exception" and the solidification of moments of heightened awareness into new routines.[41] In the words of Walter Benjamin, "All attention must flow into habit, if it is not to blow us apart; all habit must be disrupted by attention, if it is not to paralyze us."[42] Benjamin goes on to invoke a form of habitual attention that would arrest the dialectic by cultivating an attentive receptivity that is not limited to exceptional moments of conscious awareness. Echoed today in projects as diverse as Peter Handke's decidedly highbrow celebration of literary attentiveness and the popular-psychological "mindfulness" movement, efforts of habituating attentiveness have their seeds in the eighteenth-century poetics of attention developed by the likes of Breitinger and Brockes.

Lens Technology

Beyond its broadly sociological dimensions, the concept of attention operative in the body of work I discuss is critically shaped by an epochal innovation in media technology. Breitinger's, Baumgarten's, and especially Brockes's recurrent analogies between the marvelous representations of poetry with observations through telescopes, microscopes, and magnifying glasses point to the lens technology that we still invoke when speaking of "focusing" attention as a further source of the eighteenth-century discourse on attention. Writing about the uses of microscopes for scientific experimentation, Christian Wolff reports an experience that encapsulates the effect of lens technology as concisely as Thomasius captured attention's sociological aspect: "that, after looking at something closely through a magnifying glass, one will perceive many differences with the naked eye that

---

41. Hagner, "Aufmerksamkeit als Ausnahmezustand."
42. Benjamin, "Gewohnheit und Aufmerksamkeit," 407–8, here: 407. See the translation of this passage and a contextualizing reading of Benjamin's brief text on attention and habit in Liska, "Walter Benjamins Dialektik der Aufmerksamkeit."

one had not considered before."[43] Having observed things with an optical instrument, we look at them with different eyes—but not, Wolff notes, because our physical eyes now work any differently than before. It can only be "because we now pay more attention [*acht haben*] to what we see."[44]

Wolff interprets the feedback effect of microscopic observation on the natural gaze as the increasing subtlety of an attention that can now discriminate more finely than before. The deeper experience suggested in Wolff's comments is, however, a new awareness that something mediates between things and the way they are perceived *even when no refracting lens is present*. In microscopic observation, a physical element was literally placed "in between" things and their perception, with the effect that things now appear in a different granularity. The after-image of microscopic observation gives rise to the thought that even in the absence of an actual lens, something like an "internal lens" mediates between objects and how we see them—something that, in analogy with the lens, decides how finely we discriminate, what we see and cannot see, what comes into focus and what recedes into the background. This mediator is attention; and it is because of this structural affinity of attention with optical media that, in the works I read, reflections on attention tend to morph seamlessly into reflections on prosthetic technologies of perception and vice versa.

The overall effect of lens technology and the post-Copernican world it helped to inaugurate has been described by Hans Blumenberg as the breakdown of the "postulate of visibility."[45] Once telescopes discovered previously unknown stars, and microscopes disclosed worlds of visibility inaccessible to the naked eye, the postulate of an essential fit between the structure of the world and the human perceptual apparatus—which was central to a classical metaphysics for which seeing and knowing were closely intertwined—had to be abandoned. Just as the disintegration of traditional social structure was interpreted in the eighteenth century as an opportunity to

---

43. Wolff, *Allerhand nützliche Versuche*, 3:312 (§82); parts of the German passage are also quoted in Thums, *Aufmerksamkeit*, 44.
44. Wolff, *Allerhand nützliche Versuche*, 3:312 (§82). The phrase "acht haben" is often used by Wolff and others as the verbal form of *Aufmerksamkeit*.
45. Blumenberg, *Die Genesis der kopernikanischen Welt*, 717–47, here: 746.

finally make things right—to impose, as the French revolutionaries intended, a reasonable order on the social—the emerging incongruence between reality and natural visibility was initially understood in an optimistic light: new instruments of prosthetic vision and an unprejudiced, disciplined attention would finally reveal things as they truly are. This general optimism is the default interpretation in Descartes and Wolff. In the other works I read, however, the latent contingency of perception begins to surface simultaneously as a threat to a harmonious order of creation (a threat felt poignantly by Brockes) and an opportunity for poetic representation (a dimension emphasized in Breitinger) before it finally becomes, with Baumgarten's appraisal of the loss of abstraction, a key motivating factor behind the emergence of philosophical aesthetics.

Leibniz: Attention and the Definition of Things

The metaphysical reverberations of the developments sketched above were first conceptually articulated—but ultimately also defused—in Leibniz's philosophical project. Against Descartes, Leibniz objected that even in clear and distinct cognitions, we do not perceive things as they are in themselves, or as God would know them. Rather, we only clarify them to ourselves as far as our differentiating capacities go—even though any little section of the world enfolds (as Leibniz could witness through Antonie van Leeuwenhoek's microscope) infinitely more nuances than a finite mind can perceive.[46] This idea informs Leibniz's entire philosophical outlook. Monads, the basic entities of Leibniz's metaphysics, are such essential cognitive limitations incarnate. Their unique "point of view" grants to each perceiving unit only a limited "zone of clarity," raised from a perceptual background noise that indistinctly echoes the vast expanse of the world.

The clearest exposition of the problem is provided in Leibniz's early "Meditations on Knowledge, Truth, and Ideas" (1684). In this

---

46. On the relationship between Leibniz and the microscopist Leeuwenhoek, and its influence on the *Monadology*, see Schmidt, "Leeuwenhoek," 17–18.

brief but extremely influential essay, Leibniz differentiates between two types of definitions: "nominal definitions," which list a set of characteristics sufficient to distinguish a thing from other similar things, and "real definitions," which define a thing down to its most minute differentiating features.[47] Leibniz argues that because the world is too complex for finite minds to acquire exhaustive "real" definitions of things, finite perceivers like humans must make do with nominal definitions, or notions that rely on a limited number of features to define things one way or another. Human knowers must, in other words, *give definition to* things by imposing their own measure on a world that infinitely exceeds their perceptual capacity. Leibniz's essay spells out the logic that motivates emerging conceptualizations of attention as a capacity for selective perception: attention *must* select because the world is too complex for a finite mind; attention *can* select because the lack of fit between mind and world opens up a space for the independent structuring activity of perception; and attention can select *between different possibilities* because, in the absence of a single mode of perception prescribed by and inscribed into things, multiple ways of structuring perception are always possible.

Leibniz's project of a philosophy that departs from classical metaphysics by construing the world as an assemblage of limited, partial, and individual viewpoints is famously ambivalent. In the bigger picture, the monadic points of view converge in the oversight of the divine monad—an all-seeing gaze that accommodates the viewpoints to each other and guarantees that that all take part in a cosmic harmony that constitutes, per Leibniz's most famous and infamous doctrine, the best of possible worlds. This tension between partiality and its redemption in a harmonizing providential order looms, as Leibniz's vision generally does over German eighteenth-century thought, over all the texts I discuss. Nowhere is it entirely resolved; but there are distinctive shifts of emphasis: when Breitinger, for instance, discovers the possible worlds kept latent in Leibniz's metaphysical picture as an opportunity for poets to conceive and represent things *differently* from what they are like according

---

47. Leibniz, "Meditations on Knowledge, Truth, and Ideas," 24.

to our normal conceptions; or when Baumgarten, in a foundational move of his new discipline of aesthetics, takes the essential incompleteness of cognition as an occasion to challenge the exclusivity of clear and distinct notions altogether and explore sensate perceptions in their own right.

In its identification of selective attention as the agent that *gives definition to things*—"definition" both in the sense of a "formal statement of meaning" and the "defining of contours" to make things tractable to a finite mind—Leibniz's proposal also carries methodological significance for this book. I will make Leibniz's suggestion my own and examine attention as a fundamental patterning of perception that *gives to* things their definition and therefore occurs *before* definition; in a yet-undefined space that, however, always needs to be delimited, closed, defined. Paying attention to historical forms of attention thus makes it possible to study how, in different contexts and at different times, specific features were noted as salient and others passed unnoticed; some things were invested with special significance and others ignored or disregarded; and, finally, how the lines were drawn between aspects that belonged to one (type of) thing and those that already belonged to another.[48] In the following chapters I excavate how this indefinite space of attention was shaped by attentional techniques and technologies while also tracing different conceptualizations of attention that indicate how this process of defining was itself historically understood in the eighteenth century.

My focus will necessarily be selective. Not only will I focus on a limited historical period; I will also foreground certain traits of the eighteenth-century regime of attention over others. Specifically, I will focus on how techniques and theories of attention that emerged in the methodology of the observational natural sciences and in the

---

48. The idea of attention as a *metahistorical* device is briefly entertained by Lorraine Daston in the introduction to her *Kurze Geschichte*. Studying scientific attention, Daston observes, makes it possible to study the changing ontology of scientific objects—how objects are established by investing certain things and certain differentiating criteria with significance. Daston uses the term *besetzen* in this context, suggesting the interaction of libidinal cathexis with different ways of "occupying" the perceptual field with significance (11).

context of a post-Cartesian, representationalist philosophy of mind informed the reconceptualization of poetry, poetics, and aesthetics in German letters at around the middle of the eighteenth century. Nevertheless, the specific constellation of attention at the intersection of early natural science, representationalist philosophy, and the rise of aesthetics that I will trace negotiates and condenses many of the broader stakes of the specifically modern problem of attention—including the question of how attention, as a faculty that is both voluntary and involuntary, both active and passive, articulates and disarticulates body and mind; how techniques of attention cope with a surplus of information and competing possibilities of perception and action; and how they serve, in this way, to stabilize and destabilize a "subject"—a term whose modern philosophical meaning was coined in the context of Christian Wolff's and Alexander Baumgarten's reflections on the agent of attentive perception.[49]

Methodological Questions: Rules, Techniques, Practices

Is it possible to identify or posit a common denominator underlying the panoply of problems associated with the eighteenth century's newly minted faculty of attention? And what methodological approach may be suited to explain how these problems cohere? The most prominent reference works for understanding eighteenth-century logics of knowledge, perception, and subject formation remain Michel Foucault's great studies of the "classical regime" of representation in *The Order of Things* and of disciplinary techniques in *Discipline and Punish*. While both texts continue to be important reference points for this book, the structuralist side of Foucault's concern with unearthing implicit "rules of discourse"—a grammar of power and knowledge that remains relatively consistent between the bookends of an epoch—has lent itself to hyposta-

---

49. Baumgarten's chapter "Empirical Psychology" in his *Metaphysica* is generally identified as one of the first instances where the subject/object distinction is used in a recognizably modern sense. As we will see in chapter 2, Wolff's psychological writings prefigure this usage.

tizing epistemic paradigms and breaks in a way that has produced symptomatic blind spots. Crary's blindness to the problems of attention in the eighteenth century, which is conditioned by Foucault's understanding of the classical episteme and the classical subject, is one striking example.[50]

With another side of Foucault, I will therefore prioritize a praxeological style of analysis pioneered by Marcel Mauss's influential 1934 essay, "Techniques of the Body." Mauss identifies behaviors (such as walking, swimming, or giving birth) that may seem governed by physiological processes as culturally specific ways of inhabiting the body, which are transmitted by education and training, vary between sociocultural groups, and can change dramatically over time.[51] Contrasted with the structuralist focus on implicit rules, this approach makes it possible to understand idiosyncrasy and experimentation within a given paradigm as more than nonessential variation: culturally specific manners of walking and their institutionalizations (for instance, military marching or schoolchildren walking in lines) do not eliminate differences in individual gait. Mauss further offers a generative model for understanding how biology, technology, and culture intersect in embodied techniques. New technologies like shoes fundamentally change manners of walking, and media can disseminate and shape such techniques; Parisian women, he noticed, began walking like actresses in American movies. More counterintuitively, however, techniques of the body have a prosthetic quality even where all prostheses are absent: Mauss's essay shows that we always wear our feet like "shoes." In emphasizing implicit and explicit education, Mauss finally highlights the exercises and disciplinary training necessary to in-corporate or em-body cultural forms: "I can still remember my third-form teacher shouting at me: 'Idiot! why do you walk around the whole time with your hands flapping wide open?' Thus there exists an education in walking, too."[52]

---

50. As noted above, Crary develops his account of the classical subject through an engagement with Foucault; see Crary, *Techniques of the Observer*, 25–66.
51. Mauss, "Techniques of the Body," 70–76.
52. Mauss, "Techniques of the Body," 72, 72–74, 82. Mauss's essays also played an important role in the development of the concept of "cultural techniques" in recent German media theory. See Geoghegan, "After Kittler," 71–72.

In the eighteenth century, teachers would yell at students in a similar tone to instill attentiveness in them, as documented in the admonitions of a schoolmaster Alexander Baumgarten reports to illustrate the importance of paying attention: "Concern yourself with this thing only! Consider why you are here! Pay attention! Take heed!"[53] Like Mauss's techniques of the body, attentional behaviors are instilled through implicit and explicit education, culturally preformed yet idiosyncratically variable, and amalgamated in various ways with technology and media. And yet, it would be rather awkward to describe them straightforwardly as "techniques of the body." In a pronounced sense, what is at stake in attention is a behavior of the mind. This difficulty imposes itself almost inevitably when trying to give an account of attention based on practices. With the exception of a family of concepts focused on individual self-formation developed in the wake of Pierre Hadot's work on "spiritual exercises," analytical categories developed in recent practice theory programmatically deemphasize the role of the mind in determining human behavior.[54] Recent shifts to praxeological styles of analyses in various fields—from the turn to "cultural techniques" (*Kulturtechniken*) as the condition of discourse networks in German media theory to the "practice turn" in history of science and cultural theory—all recover skillful performance, embodied know-how, and technical artifacts as the neglected "mindless" preconditions of knowing and acting.[55] Practice theory emerged precisely to counter

---

53. Baumgarten, "Philosophischer Briefe zweites Schreiben," 70.
54. For an initial overview of Hadot's concept and its reception, see Chase, Clark, and McGhee, *Philosophy as a Way of Life*. Foucault's "technologies of the self" and practices of "care of the self" belong in this category.
55. The sociologist Andreas Reckwitz describes praxeology as one among a family of "culturalist" theories that investigate the social through shared symbolic forms governing social action even in the absence of explicit normative consensus. Among culturalist theories, praxeology is distinguished from "mentalisms" like structuralism, which understand these symbolic forms in terms of the structures of an (unconscious, collective) mind, as well as from (post-structuralist) "textualisms" that locate symbolic forms in material signs and discourses external to and constitutive of the mind. Praxeologically oriented theorists—Reckwitz names (among others) Anthony Giddens, Charles Taylor, Judith Butler, Bruno Latour, and Pierre Bourdieu—locate the symbolic forms that structure the social in cultural practices, shared embodied routines that involve tacit know-how and instruments irreducible to explicit

models of human action—engrained in traditional social and cultural theory—that assume that mental processes somehow precede or steer the actions of the body or that humans act "out of" rational deliberation or explicit norms.

Although this quandary seems merely methodological, it in fact hits at the heart of the matter at hand. After all, the concept of human action attacked by different varieties of practice theory emerged at the same time and in the same contexts as the problem of attention.[56] The connection between attention and the Enlightenment ideal of deliberative action can be illustrated by Max Weber's matrix of four ideal types of social action in connection with his rationalization thesis. According to Weber, human action can be (1) "purposively rational" (determined by deliberate purposes); (2) "value-rational" (guided by conscious norms); (3) "affective" (triggered by emotion and feeling); or (4) "traditional" (settled by custom and habit).[57] It is instructive how Weber marks the contrast between the first two types of (characteristically modern) rational action and the latter two: while the rational action-types realize consciously devised or examined purposes or norms, traditional behavior is "a matter of almost automatic reaction to habitual stimuli"; affective behavior, similarly, is mere "uncontrolled reaction to some exceptional stimulus."[58] This frames the contrast between modern and premodern action-types as one between behavior that is trapped in stimulus-response loops engrained by habit or instinct and actions that are performed consciously or "attentively"

---

rules. See Reckwitz, "Toward a Theory," quotes at 249, 258. Schatzki provides an overview of praxeological approaches in sociology, philosophy, and the history of science in the introduction to Knorr-Cetina et al., *The Practice Turn.*

56. Reckwitz ("Toward a Theory") contrasts praxeological approaches with the analytical figures of the *homo oeconomicus* (which models social action as the purposive activity of individuals) as well as the *homo sociologicus* (which models the social as the result of norm-governed interaction). Both explanatory models first emerged in eighteenth-century reflection on human agency in moral philosophy and political economy.

57. Weber understands "ideal types" as categories of sociological analysis; empirical behavior will often appear as a mix of various aspects of these types. Weber, *Soziologische Grundbegriffe,* 32–33.

58. Weber, *Soziologische Grundbegriffe,* 33; translations from Weber, "Basic Sociological Terms," 37.

because they actively regulate the interface between mind and things. What distinguishes rational types of action for Weber is less the capacity for reason itself (which had defined the rational human animal since Aristotle) but a capacity for attentive self-monitoring that enforces a deliberative, "calculating" attitude in all aspects of individual behavior. Against this background, the eighteenth-century age of reason looks more like an age of attention.[59] Following Weber, attention can be understood as the mental aptitude necessary for fully rational action—the learned skill behind the "mentalist" understandings of human action that recent turns to practice have attacked. Rather than conceiving eighteenth-century techniques of attention as straightforward techniques of the body, we can conceive of them as techniques for separating the mind from the body (as that in which habits and instinct reside). By means of such techniques, the mind is fashioned into a command center that issues orders the body is meant to execute. The various ailments of attention would then attest to the difficulties of turning human body-minds into the mind-driven agents they were supposed to become.[60]

From the perspective of praxeological cultural theory, I examine attention as the acquired skill necessary to enact central epistemic and practical ideals instituted in the eighteenth century. In matters of knowledge, learning to control attention underwrote the analytical ideal of enlightened knowledge. In matters of practical conduct, it supported an ideal of rational agency that promoted deliberate purposive action over routines and affective behavior. The earliest

---

59. For the same point in a different context, see Phillips, *Distraction*, 14.
60. Methodologically, this requires a concept of practice that is capacious enough to describe the shape and structure of techniques without presupposing too much about the inherently embodied or mental, media-determined, or individual nature of actions. The broad concept of practice developed in recent praxeological cultural theory can be a first reference point: for Reckwitz, "a 'practice' (*Praktik*) is a routinized type of behavior consisting of several interconnected elements: forms of bodily activities, forms of mental activities, 'things' and their use, a background knowledge in the form of understanding, know-how, states of emotion and motivational knowledge." Elsewhere, this is shortened to "routinized body/knowledge/things-patterns." See Reckwitz, "Toward a Theory," quotes at 249, 258; and Reckwitz, "Grundelemente." In the introduction to Knorr-Cetina et al., *The Practice Turn*, Schatzki suggests "arrays of activity" as a minimal definition.

indications of the division of attention into a theoretical and a practical variety appear in Descartes's oeuvre. As I will show in chapter 1, Descartes extolls attention as the epistemic virtue necessary for the analytical clarification of confused ideas. But attention also appears in a different context, in the theory of the passions, where Descartes introduces attentional control—the ability to shield the will's rational motives from affective distractions—as the only way to ensure that action springs from well-considered reasons rather than from the impulsions of the passions. As indicated by Christian Wolff's pioneering psychology of attention, the subject of chapter 2, this dual function of attention as a prerequisite for both rational knowledge and rational agency became firmly established in Descartes's wake. This was not limited to Enlightenment philosophy of mind but extended to various fields of practice that were closely linked to this philosophy—from scientific and literary practice to applied pedagogy and models of conduct that emphasized self-reliance and rational citizenship.

"Clear and Distinct" Knowledge

The ubiquitous appeals, in seventeenth- and eighteenth-century writings on epistemology and method, to observe things "with attention" or "attentively" have rarely become the focus of scholarship because they are too easily mistaken for general exhortations to be alert and diligent. In fact, imperatives of attentiveness demand much more, and something much more specific: these appeals to attention mandate a specific routine of focusing the mind successively on the various "parts," "sides," or "aspects" of a matter until each part is clearly distinguished and the composition of the whole from parts becomes transparent to the mind. This is what having "clear and distinct" knowledge means; and a sharply focused and rigorously analytic attention is the way to achieve it, no matter whether the object is material or immaterial, animate or inanimate, or whether its parts can be distinguished with or without the help of instruments. Botanists who engage in cataloguing the distinctive features of plants enact this basic epistemic program in the same way as metaphysicians who meditate on a problem by dividing it into its constituent parts or microscopists who use lenses to enhance their focus and identify the parts of a flea.

By the early eighteenth century, Christian Wolff had codified this technique into an elaborate concept of attention as a faculty (*Vermögen*) with a fundamental role in philosophical epistemology.[61] For Wolff the perceptual labor of attention in cognition involved two levels or stages.[62] The first stage, attention proper (*Aufmercksamkeit*), focuses—as discussed above—on one feature of a compound representation at the expense of all others in order to increase the clarity of the selected part. The second stage, a protracted form of attention Wolff identifies with reflection (*Überdencken*), strings these attentive acts together into a sequence: it consists of focusing attention on one feature of a representation after another until all relevant features, as well their interconnection, can be surveyed by the mind. Once a complete inventory of the relevant component features of represented objects—their "marks" or "notes" (*Merkmale, notae*)—has been established, a representation becomes "clear and distinct" or, as Wolff defines distinctness, *clearly recognized in its parts*: "When we represent a thing ... and direct our thoughts to one of its component parts after another ... we [can be said to] reflect on the same thing, and through this continued attention to one part after another ... it becomes clear in its parts ... but distinct in itself."[63]

How foundational the methodical attention outlined by Descartes and Wolff would become for seventeenth- and eighteenth-century philosophical discourse can be gleaned from the widely ramified terminological network in this discourse centered around Latin *notare*: the mental activity of "taking note" (*notare*) identifies the features or "notes" (*notae*) that distinguish one thing from another, and that

---

61. On Wolff's pioneering concept of attention, see Adler, "Bändigung des (Un)Möglichen," 41–47; Hatfield, "Attention in Early Scientific Psychology," 4–7.
62. Wolff develops parallel accounts of attention in Wolff, *German Metaphysics*, 149–52 (§§268–73); Wolff, *Psychologia empirica*, 167–193 (§§234–64); Wolff, *Psychologia rationalis*, 286–305 (§§357–86).
63. Wolff, *German Metaphysics*, 151 (§272). In the *Psychologia empirica* (189–90 [§§259–60]) the final synopsis of parts is distinguished as a third stage of *collatio* or *comparatio*.

can then be gathered in "notions" (*notiones*)—concepts understood as collections of marks that capture the essential characteristics of a class of objects.[64] Similar resonances abound in the German terminology, where *Aufmerksamkeit* (the faculty of attention), *(Auf-) Merken* (the activity of taking note of features), and *Merkmale* (distinctive marks that typify a phenomenon) form a nexus that ties objective properties to a specific technique of perception. The structure of objects conceived by the philosophy of the time is first and foremost the structure of a particular form of attention.

Echoing a further meaning of Latin *notare* (to write), the mental notation of representations is also the basis of an arbitrary signification that was understood, at the time, as the conventional naming of features or "notes." In converting the imagistic impressions received by the senses into sets of communicable characters that can be marked and represented through signs, methodical attention is foundational to a notion of transparent signification that Michel Foucault has described as a centerpiece of the classical regime of representation.[65] Applying the Foucauldian approach to the philosophy and literary theory of the German Enlightenment, David Wellbery has argued that Enlightenment semiotics saw conventional signification as a double-edged sword that made higher-order thought possible but also led away from the ideal transparency of intuitive meaning. Poetry, Wellbery argues, took on the role of recovering the original plenitude of meaning before and beyond conventional signification.[66] We might add to this that according to the same paradigm, signification is itself contingent on a prior selection of nominable features that is accomplished by *attention*—a qualification with important consequences for understanding the function of literary works in Enlightenment culture. I propose that the stratum *before* conventional signification targeted in poetic works is not simply the locus of an ideal plenitude of meaning beyond signification: it is instead attention's

---

64. This terminology is too ubiquitous to trace it to a single source, but Leibniz's influential "Meditations on Knowledge, Truth, and Ideas" gives an overall impression.
65. On the importance of the sign in classical representation, see Foucault, *The Order of Things*, 58–63.
66. Wellbery, *Lessing's Laocoon*, 30–42, 83–84.

primary patterning of perception, which, as Breitinger and Brockes will realize, can lead to the experience of a constitutive partiality rather than an original wholeness at the bottom of signification. At the end of the period I examine, Georg Christoph Lichtenberg (1742–99) would develop a practice of writing that targets precisely this fundamental patterning of perception. He began to understand his notebooks as "Brillen für die Seelenkräfte" ("spectacles for the powers of the soul")[67]—prosthetic aids to perception that make it possible to discover new aspects of things by experimentally modulating attention in and through the act of writing.

My excavation of the problem of attention in eighteenth-century philosophical and scientific epistemology will further proceed in conversation with a tradition of scholarship—dating back as far as Hegel's recapitulation of early modern science under the heading "Observing Reason"[68]—that identifies *observation* as the paradigmatic epistemic practice of classical modernity. In the context of a poetics of knowledge that studies, in the wake of Foucault, epistemic constellations beyond or below disciplinary divisions, important work has been done in recent years to reconstruct a paradigm of observation formative for the sciences and literature in the classical age of European modernity from around 1600 to 1800.[69] As this work has shown, a paradigm of observation formed the common ground on which modern concepts of literature and science took shape, but also, eventually, the basis of their divergence into the "two cultures" we inhabit today.[70] Emphasizing *attention* over observation does not dispute the importance of observation but shifts the emphasis to the infrastructure of psychophysical techniques that underlie the paradigm of observation. This reorientation follows

---

67. Lichtenberg, *Schriften und Briefe*, 2:416 (K 96).
68. Hegel, *Phänomenologie des Geistes*, 164–232.
69. For recent examples, see Campe, Holland, and Strowick, "Observation in Science and Literature"; Hoffmann, *Unter Beobachtung*; Stadler, *Der technisierte Blick*; Crary, *Techniques of the Observer*; Singy, "Huber's Eyes"; Daston and Lunbeck, *Histories of Scientific Observation*; Zelle, "Experiment, Observation, Self-Observation."
70. This point is made in Campe, Holland, and Strowick, "Observation in Science and Literature," 372.

clues in eighteenth-century treatises on observation in the sciences, which characterize disposal over attention as the principal tool of skilled observers.[71] Diderot and d'Alembert's *Encyclopédie* only articulates common knowledge when it defines the headword "OBSERVATION" succinctly as "the mind's attention turned toward the objects nature presents."[72] Observation and attention often designated different aspects of the same epistemic activity, with observation referring to this activity's completed *objective*, and attention referring to the *means of carrying out* the objective through various techniques for attentively sifting through a wealth of phenomena to identify their characteristic features.

Self-Monitoring and Rational Conduct

In matters of practical conduct, learning to pay attention enabled a new model of rational agency. Attentiveness in acting ensures that individual actions conform to realizing the purposes that agents set out for themselves (whether these purposes are understood as "merely" instrumental or, like the ultimate purpose, "moral"). The ethics of "perfection" espoused by early eighteenth-century philosophers like Wolff or Baumgarten describes moral conduct along these lines: to act morally, it is necessary to constantly check whether all your actions contribute to realizing the ultimate purpose of your life (the realization of human perfection). As both Wolff and Baumgarten emphasize, the cultivation of attention is thus absolutely indispensable for morality. This includes not only first-order attention to phenomena of one's choosing but also a second-order

---

71. Summarizing the eighteenth-century discourse on observation in a 1775 treatise "The Art of Observation," Jean Senebier declares that "attention alone ... makes [the observer] master over the thing he is observing"; see Senebier, *Die Kunst zu Beobachten*, 1:148–49. In his 1759 *Essai analytique sur les facultés de l'ame* the Swiss naturalist Charles Bonnet similarly identified the careful or regular (*avec regle*) application of attention as the "universal spirit of observation" in the arts and sciences (134).

72. "L'attention de l'ame [*sic*] tournée vers les objets qu'offre la nature," Chambaud, "Observation."

attention that monitors which perceptions matter with regard to a purpose. To become a moral human being, Baumgarten advises, you must not only learn to pay attention but to "pay attention to what it is you pay attention to."[73] In buttressing rational moral conduct, the ability to control attention performs the self-monitoring necessary to realize a consciously chosen, premeditated goal. Attentional control keeps all powers of the mind and body focused on completing the task at hand. Above all, this ability to concentrate on realizing a purpose rests on the negative skill of suppressing distractions like inner compulsions, instinctual reflexes, or habitual automatisms that threaten to thwart the self-imposed course of action. As Wolff explains, attentive self-monitoring and suppressing irrelevant stimuli ensure that "ratio" becomes the sole motive force of the will—a term that, for him, meant "a reason" as well as "reason" in general.

The capacity for controlling attention is the bedrock of the rational subject; it is also, however, this subject's Achilles heel. Attention has, as Descartes already acknowledged, a less compliant side. Not only can one *make* oneself concentrate on things; things also *draw* attention to them, or *tug* at the attention when one is trying to focus on something else. Involuntary attention poses both a systematic and a pragmatic problem for rational subjectivity. In light of the new dualistic ontology, automatic responses to external stimuli threaten to extend the mechanical pushing and pulling that governs the corporeal world into the immaterial mind, and thus to corrode the ontological separation Descartes had posited between *res cogitans* and *res extensa*. At the pragmatic level, a subjectivity based on controlling attention threatens to become anthropologically unviable if the human mind proves incapable of sufficiently extracting itself from involuntary distractions of attention.

To ward off these threats, Descartes partially redeemed involuntary attention as a natural disposition for voluntary attention in the passion of wonder (*admiration*), which he defines as a "sudden surprise of the soul which brings it to consider with attention the objects that seem to it unusual or extraordinary."[74] Wonder occupies

---

73. Baumgarten, *Ethica philosophica*, 130 (§221).
74. Descartes, *Philosophical Writings*, I:353 (§70).

a special place among the passions because it facilitates a transition from passive affectedness to active mental scrutiny. This transition from passion to self-controlled mental activity also has an ontogenetic component: although it is "good to be born with some inclination to wonder," eventually we "must attempt to free ourselves from this inclination as much as possible" and replace it with "the special state of reflection and attention which our will can always impose ... when we judge the matter before us to be worth serious consideration."[75] To become a mature and rational self, one must acquire control over one's attention by converting what begins as an involuntary response into a deliberate activity. Descartes's comments on wonder underscore that the separation of mind and physical world presupposed by his philosophical approach—but also, as we have seen, by modern attention discourses in general—first had to be *enacted* through a form of disciplined behavior. Learning to pay attention the Cartesian way helps to *constitute* the mind as a separate entity by extracting thought from involuntary responses to external stimuli that draw it into the vagaries of the physical world. Failing to establish the necessary distance undermines the very separation of mind and matter on which the epoch-making Cartesian standpoint is based. The device for controlling attention outlined in Descartes's remarks on wonder is therefore no less than a blueprint for the education of the post-Cartesian subject.

The forms of embodied behavior negotiated and enforced by such philosophical reflections can be glimpsed in illustrations to Charles Le Brun's *The Expression of the Passions*, a treatise on painting emotions based on the Cartesian typology of the passions, which strikingly visualizes the contrast between wonder and active attention (see figure 1).[76] With wide-open eyes and a mouth gaping in astonishment, the face of wonder is visibly struck by its object, as if overwhelmed by a yet unmanageable influx of new perceptions. The face of attention, by contrast, confronts its target head-on. With

---

75. Descartes, *Philosophical Writings*, I:355 (§76).
76. On the genesis and historical influence of Le Brun's illustrated lecture course on the passions (including reproductions of Le Brun's original drawings), see Montagu, *The Expression of the Passions*.

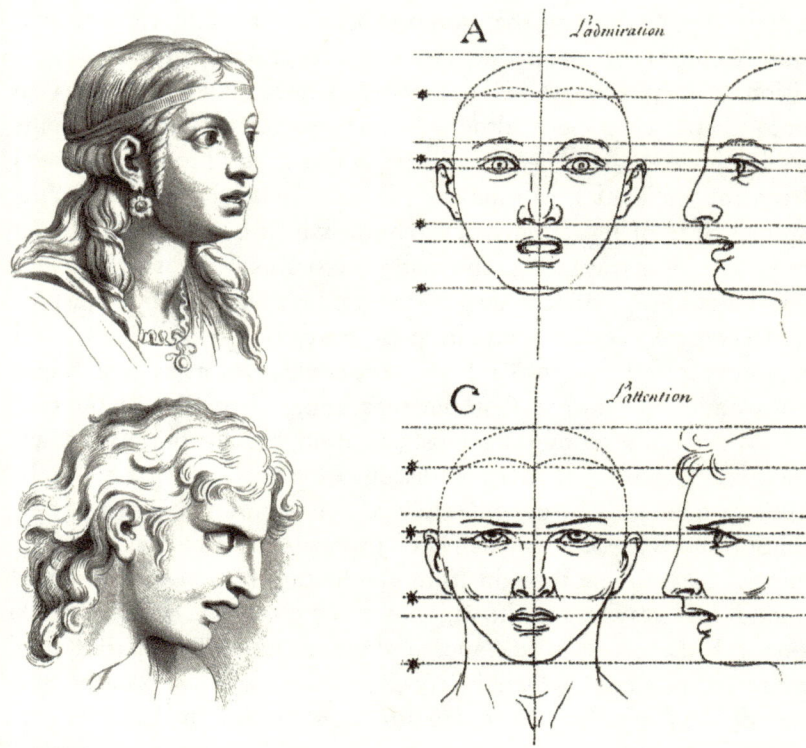

Figure 1. Illustrations of wonder (*above*) and attention (*below*) from eighteenth-century editions of Le Brun's *Expression of the Passions* (Le Brun, *Expressions des passions de l'Ame*, 2, 4; *Caracteres des passions*, n.p.).

the head tilted toward the object of attention, the pupils are ready to pierce the object with their gaze, supported by contracted eyebrows and raised lower eyelids that limit peripheral vision. Wonder, in short, is *transfixed by* whereas willful attention *fixates* its object. The hidden irony of Le Brun's appropriation of the Cartesian treatise on the soul—and perhaps the rejoinder of the artist Le Brun to the philosopher Descartes—is that he depicts wonder *as well as* attention among the *passions*, suggesting that even the successful conversion of wonder into active attention leads to the disembodied space of meditation only by ways of a strained—and conspicuously gendered—face. The gendered contrast between the passive piety of wonder and actively directed attention shaped a widespread cultural imaginary that coded voluntary attention as masculine and feminized its passive counterpart. Such imaginary contrasts were, of course, all too unimaginatively institutionalized in eighteenth-century educational practices. Women's education shaped minds in accordance with these gendered stereotypes and instilled what early feminists like Mary Wollstonecraft decried as "cognitive habits of inferiority."[77] As we will see when encountering Kant's lectures on Baumgarten in chapter 4, the obverse applied as well: Kant's male students were vehemently reminded not to "feminize" their minds but comport themselves as rational, properly focused, and self-determined subjects of attention.

Overview and Structure

I advance my argument through four chapters that are divided into two distinct parts. In chapters 1 and 2, I trace the sudden emergence of attention as a distinct mental faculty around the turn of the eighteenth century and explain how developing a capacity for attention became the hallmark of the rational subject. Here I recover attention as a linchpin concept of early modern thought and dismantle the prejudice that attention was only marginal to explanations of the mind before the late nineteenth century. In chapters 3 and 4, I offer a new account of the emergence of aesthetics in mid-eighteenth-century Germany, in which I draw on the genealogy of the rational subject presented in the first two chapters. These chapters redescribe the emergence of aesthetics in mid-eighteenth-century Germany as a response to and early critique of this subjectivity—not of its "rationality," to be sure, but of the strained form of attention that came to circumscribe what counts as rational in the eighteenth century. I close with an epilogue in which I explore the afterlives of the eighteenth-century discovery or invention of attention in later

---

77. This is Natalie Phillips's felicitous formulation in *Distraction*, 20; Wollstonecraft, *A Vindication*, 1:90–91.

German thought (Lichtenberg, Hegel, Marx) and in contemporary debates about the imperative to "regain control" over attention.

Each chapter highlights one key aspect indicated in the chapter heading. Focusing on SCIENCE, chapter 1 explores the conscious regulation of the mind's attention as the epistemic technique behind seventeenth-century reforms of knowledge. As representative reformers of scholasticism, Francis Bacon and René Descartes faulted prejudice—premature and hasty judgments—for what they saw as the corrupt state of the sciences. Their solution, however, was not to become better at judging but to cultivate attention. If observers of nature learned to process experience consciously and selectively, good judgments would inevitably follow. It was attention—not judgment or observation per se—that Descartes saw as the key to the rigorously analytical knowledge he famously dubbed "clear and distinct." In emphasizing the pivotal role of active attention, this chapter revises influential accounts of representational knowledge by Foucault and Cassirer, who ascribe an essentially passive role to the mind in the representation of external reality. I then turn from epistemic to practical matters and identify control over attention as the basis of a new concept of rational agency. However intractable the problem of mind-body union proved for Descartes's dualistic metaphysics, his psychology of the passions solved it in practice through the disciplining of attention. Descartes explained that only an attention vanquished by the will can shield the mind from impulsive reactions and ensure that it was in fact as independent from the body as Cartesian metaphysics taught. For Descartes, human beings were free to the exact extent that they controlled their attention, and unfree whenever their attention was captured by stimuli (the mechanism of nature) or blunted by thoughtless routines (the mechanism of habit). Attention became the hallmark of freedom in a defining new sense: the determination of the will by the rational mind rather than the mechanisms of habit or nature.

In chapter 2, I trace the genesis of the figure of the SUBJECT by reading Christian Wolff's influential psychology of attention as a blueprint for the modern faculty. For Wolff, learning to focus the mind suppresses disruptive associations and meaningless reverie, objectifies the contents of perception, and, in this way, generates the distance from sensation required for all higher thought. I then survey three strands of German eighteenth-century thought to show how, in each one, Wolff's theory of attention came to define a new vision of the human subject: (1) In eighteenth-century pedagogy, reformers like J. B. Basedow and J. H. Campe saw the improvement of attention as the bedrock of all further education. (2) In philosophical anthropology, voluntary attention became the defining feature of human freedom and language in contrast with nonrational animals. However, it also came to define hierarchies between the rational subject and its racialized and gendered others, who were excluded from full humanity because of their alleged fickleness of attention. (3) In moral philosophy, the capacity for attentive self-monitoring was considered the *sine qua non* of self-determined action. In critical dialogue with Foucault's account of discipline, I explore the pragmatic prehistory to the ideal of individual autonomy formulated by Kant at the end of the eighteenth century.

Turning to POETICS, chapter 3 reads the poet Barthold Heinrich Brockes and the poetic theorist Johann Jakob Breitinger as representatives of a poetics of the marvelous (*das Wunderbare*) that highlighted the power of the rare, strange, and extraordinary to captivate an audience. Literary histories typically frame this development as a poetics of wonder, but I argue that it is better understood as promoting the poetic education of attention. The poetry of the marvelous offered itself as a solution to the problem of involuntary attention that plagued the rational subject. It appealed to a passive side of the mind unmoved by the rational will and harnessed the charms of strange objects to jolt the mind into activity, thus facilitating the transition to the self-directedness that distinguished a mature human mind. As I argue by reading the early eighteenth-century poetics of attention alongside modern theories of literary defamiliarization, poetry here first acquired a function that would define literary language in modernity: the goal of marvelous poetry was no longer to imitate nature or convey moral precepts but to encourage readers to think for themselves by estranging habits of perception.

In chapter 4, I offer a new account of the emergence of AESTHETICS as a critical appropriation of the eighteenth-century discourse on attention. I demonstrate that the new discipline emerged from

Alexander Baumgarten's protest against the narrowing of attention that defined the rational subject—a figure Baumgarten was the first to systematically call *subiectum*. Against the restriction of experience to what focused attention can pin down as a distinct object, Baumgarten rehabilitated modes of attention in which the boundary between self and world is less rigidly drawn, including daydreaming, peripheral awareness, and even subliminal perception. These "extensive" modes of attention anticipate forms of attentiveness Freud would call "free-floating" (*gleichschwebend*). Yet Baumgarten's point was to explore not the individual unconscious but everything the "intensive" attention of the rational subject was supposed to keep at bay: the self's connectedness with the world through the femininely coded passive or passionate side of the mind, the senses, and an imagination that overshoots the boundaries of the self. Countering Enlightenment psychology's disparagement of such states of mind as inattention or distraction, Baumgarten insisted on understanding them in positive terms as alternative modes of attention, capable of disclosing other possible relations to the world. Art was central to this endeavor because it demonstrated to Baumgarten that even subrational states of mind were capable of cultivation or increasing "perfection." Conversely, cultivating such modes of attention became, with Baumgarten, the primary function of art in his new aesthetic sense.

1

SCIENCE
Attention, the New Science, and the Disembodied Mind

The idea that attention is a distinct faculty of the human mind only surfaced in the eighteenth century, but it has a long prehistory that includes a particularly formative episode in the epistemic ruptures of the early seventeenth century. In this chapter I excavate the seventeenth-century framing of the epistemological, psychological, and ethical questions that would coalesce in the eighteenth-century problem of attention. I will focus on two figures who have come to signify the transition to the early modern period to the point of a cliché: Francis Bacon and René Descartes, two figures either heroized as "fathers" of modern science and philosophy or vilified as the instigators of a domination of nature that afflicts the modern age.[1] In what follows, I will try to sidestep such oedipal framings of history as the legacies of good or bad fathers by reexamining the Baconian

---

1. For one paradigmatic example in the German tradition, see Heidegger's discussion of Descartes in "Die Zeit des Weltbildes."

and Cartesian oeuvres as sites of a profound transformation of knowledge practices.

In the early seventeenth century, Bacon and Descartes contributed to the widespread effort to overthrow scholasticism and gave conceptual shape to a new way of going about knowing that was emerging across Western Europe. If their works indeed possess exceptional diagnostic value for the history of knowledge, it is because they reflect and model these emergent knowledge practices with unusual clarity and vivacity. The paradigmatic force of their oeuvres explains why the two continue to be referenced even as many of their specific doctrines, such as Bacon's rigid concept of induction or Descartes's explanation of mind-body union through the pineal gland, were quickly discarded as the new method evolved.

In this opening chapter, I focus on the role of attention in solidifying a set of dualisms that became mainstays of modern architectures of knowledge: the distinction between mind and world, and the related distinction between mind and body. In the subcultures surrounding the emphatically new philosophies and new sciences emerging during the first decades of the seventeenth century, a novel way of attending to things by deliberately directing the mind's focus came to be regarded as the key to accurate knowledge of the external world. Attention was seen as capable of penetrating the illusion of false familiarity created by common and habitual notions, which only appeared to connect the mind to the world. Paying methodical attention to the particular details of which things are truly composed promised to free knowledge from such bad habits and introduce the mind to the nature of things for the first time—a nature of things that would be revealed as much stranger, but also as much more marvelous, than common notions made one believe.[2] In this epistemic constellation, effective knowledge of the physical world was a function of attending to things deliberately, slowly, and carefully—as if they were completely alien objects—while actively suppressing the attribution of mind-like qualities to things. I argue that regulating attention functioned as a simulta-

---

2. For the role of wonder and marvel in this context, see Daston, *Kurze Geschichte*, 19–35; Daston and Park, *Wonders*.

neously defamiliarizing and refamiliarizing device: in the same act, attention enforced an artificial distance between mind and world and promised to bridge this distance in a controlled and regulated manner. The systematic place of attention in this epistemic context thus lies "in between" mind and world, as an interface or intermediary that proves the essential separation of counterparts in the very act of linking them together.

One might assume (and it has certainly been argued) that the intensified split between mind and physical world shaped a new conception of the mind's intercourse with the body; that, as a consequence of a new conception of the physical world, the body, too, came to be placed in a categorically different order of being than the mind. A closer look at contemporaneous accounts of attention suggests a more complicated story. The ability to focus and direct attention at will rests on suppressing automatic responses to external stimuli that spontaneously draw the mind's attention into the physical world and obliterate the distance necessary for proper attentiveness. Ensuring attention's independence from external stimuli involved redrawing and reinforcing Descartes's dividing line between mind and body. The dualistic picture launched by Descartes hinged on claiming that all the ways in which human beings interacted automatically with the world, without the intellect's deliberate mediation—including sensory perception and instinctual responses to stimuli—were not part of the soul or mind at all. The Scholastic-Aristotelean paradigm traditionally ascribed these functions to the sensitive or "animal" part of the soul; Descartes instead incorporated all these functions into the mechanical body. Corporealizing the sensitive soul amounted to subjecting its functions to instrumental treatment. I argue that because this hierarchical relationship between mind and body is a condition for focused and deliberate attention directed at the external world, the divide between mind and body is structurally prior to the divide between mind and world, though both conceptions were certainly shaped simultaneously by emerging practices of attention.

Such conceptual reconfigurations are not merely a matter of shifting discursive signposts. Even though I focus on reading texts—and closely, at times—I approach textual phenomena as negotiating not exclusively conceptual distinctions but simultaneously questions of practice. In line with praxeological approaches developed especially in sociology and in the history of science, I treat texts as records of cultural practices rather than as documents of a culture understood as a complex of mental structures or signs. My model of reading borrows from praxeological cultural theory more broadly, and specifically from Pierre Hadot's approach to ancient philosophical texts.[3] Hadot makes a point of reading these texts as documents of "spiritual exercises" designed to transform a person's way of life rather than as merely theoretical speculations. To be sure, Hadot's approach is accompanied by the lament that modern philosophy strayed from this practice-orientation and became overly theoretical, decoupled from its embeddedness in specific forms of life. Here, I suggest that the Cartesian decontextualization of the mind from bodily and social practices itself hinged on a set of new epistemic practices. This implies that the "mentalism" of modern philosophy often identified with Descartes is itself an effect of practice—and that the practices in question are practices of attention.

Refocusing Attention

Practices of regulating and focusing attention were not invented in the seventeenth century, but they did receive a decidedly new direction during this period. The ideal of devotional attention in Christian meditational practice—influentially revived, in the sixteenth century, by Ignatius of Loyola's *Exercitia spiritualia* (1548)—demanded withdrawing attention from the world and redirecting it toward the self and, via the closely focused, undivided self, towards divine transcendence.[4] In such exercises, worldly things may serve as intermittent

---

3. See Hadot, *Philosophy as a Way of Life*, especially the chapter "Spiritual Exercises," 81–125.

4. Tracing Ignatius's spiritual exercises back to early Christian monastic practice, David Marno lucidly summarizes the ideal of devotional attention in the following way: "In the *Spiritual Exercises*, attention is relevant insofar as it signals the self's capacity to turn away from the world and attend to God. To attend, in this sense, means primarily one thing: that the self is as undivided as it can possibly be

focal objects for attention, but the inherent nature of such objects is programmatically insignificant; their function is entirely exhausted in serving as arbitrary vessels for gathering the mind's focus.[5] Such Christian meditational practices continued to flourish in and beyond the seventeenth century, and we will repeatedly encounter variations of them as they intersect with other practices of attentiveness. Yet in the avant-garde subcultures surrounding the new natural philosophy, a different ideal of attention began to emerge, one that took an interest in worldly things for their own sake. Focusing on particular objects was no longer the means to an end beyond this world; it became a tool for knowing what this world is actually like if we thrust aside all preconceptions. According to the historian of science Lorraine Daston, who has contributed much to reconstructing the import of attention for early modern science, such practices of focusing attention were instrumental to investing the natural world with new value and were responsible for a new seventeenth- and eighteenth-century "this-worldliness," a rehabilitation of nature as more than the ugly mark of a fallen world.[6]

---

and that in this unified state it is directed towards transcendence. The spiritual ideal of attention is coextensive with the lack of distraction by the world. The ideal of attention that informs Ignatius's *Spiritual Exercises* rests, then, on a crucial assumption: that the turn *away* from the world is a turn, or at least the beginning of a turn, *towards* God; that leaving behind the distractions of the world is already an act of attending to God" (Marno, "Attention and Indifference," 237).

5. The practices of attentiveness traced by Dorothea von Mücke in the opening chapter of *The Practices of Enlightenment* align with this tradition of devotional attention. I would argue that Mücke's identification of these practices as precursors of "disinterested interest" in late eighteenth-century aesthetics, however, skips the redirection of attention to the world for its own sake. From the perspective of the genealogy I trace in this book, aesthetic disinterestedness more plausibly results from a reflexive turn back to the self of attentional practices that dramatically changed through the emergence of the secular forms of attention I trace in this chapter. See Mücke, *Practices of the Enlightenment*, 1–26.

6. On the connection between attentive practices and a new valuation of nature, see Daston, "Attention and the Values of Nature." The best overview of Daston's work on attention in early modern science is her *Kurze Geschichte*; she also develops aspects of her view in a series of articles and book chapters, including "The Disciplines of Attention," "The Empire of Observation," and the relevant chapters in the collaborative volumes Daston and Galison, *Objectivity*, and Daston and Park, *Wonders*.

The rise of such attentive practices is closely associated with the beginning institutionalization of the modern natural sciences. In the middle of the seventeenth century, scientific societies devoted to a new natural philosophy appeared across Western Europe, including the Academia del Cimento, founded by students of Galilei in Florence (1657), the Royal Society of London (1660), the Académie royale des sciences (1666) in Paris, and the Academia naturae curiosorum in Schweinfurt (1652). The name of the German academy in Schweinfurt (still operating today as the Leopoldina) echoes the predilection of the new science for the "preternatural," for curious and strange objects that seemed to defy the common course of nature studied by scholastic natural science but were nevertheless attributable to natural rather than supernatural causes.[7] The pragmatic counterpart to this choice of scientific object was an attention closely focused on particulars *qua* particulars rather than as specimens of a natural order already assumed to be familiar in its general course. Early scientific societies devoted themselves to "practicing" attention on the preternatural, both in the sense of carrying out the program of focusing on unusual phenomena and in the sense of becoming increasingly skilled at the task. Promoting "disciplines of attention," in Lorraine Daston's double entendre, these societies became the sites of a massive retraining of perception to make attention capable of focusing on particular details with the necessary devotion.[8] At the

---

7. In the same journal, the co-founder of the Royal Society Robert Boyle, for instance, published both pioneering articles on the respiratory systems of mammals and lengthy discussions of "monsters" of nature, such as a misshapen calf. Leibniz dealt with topics like the arithmetic of squaring a circle side by side with the case of a dog who could allegedly bark several words in French; the only monograph Leibniz published during his lifetime is not only a pioneering study of the earth's geology but includes a detailed report and sketch of a unicorn skeleton supposedly dug up near the German city of Quedlinburg. For the first two examples, see Daston, *Kurze Geschichte*, 14; for the third, see Leibniz, *Protogaea*, 101–3.

8. Daston's formulation suggests the co-implication of disciplined habitus and emerging scientific disciplines. As she points out, "the habit of paying close attention to natural phenomena" promoted by the new natural philosophy "required a special discipline of both the senses and the mind" (Daston and Park, *Wonders*, 144). As Daston and others have shown, this habitus of a sharply focused attention produced a new *psychology of inquiry* (which revalued the "epistemic passions" of wonder and curiosity as prerequisites for sustained attention); gave rise to a distinct cultural

heart of the new way of knowing nature through its preternatural marvels was, thus, a new way of conducting perception; a "habit of paying close attention to natural phenomena ... [which] required a special discipline of both the senses and the mind."[9]

Much of what follows in this chapter probes the various elements Daston defines almost in passing as constitutive of the new regime of attentiveness: What exactly does the "closeness" of the new attention to the particular consist in, and how is it achieved? What comes into focus, and what falls out of focus, in such a procedure? What understanding of the natural world reveals itself in the light of this knowledge practice? In what precise sense does such closely focused attention rely on "habit" and "discipline"? And how do such habits and disciplines of attention enlist—and in enlisting, shape—the mind, the senses, and the relationship of one to the other? To begin with, we turn to the work of Francis Bacon, the figurehead of early scientific societies, for clues to the question of what commanded the attention to preternatural particulars of nature in the first place.

Retooling the Inquiring Mind: Bacon's *New Organon*

Although Bacon himself rarely uses the word *attention*, his attempt to articulate the logic of the new mode of scientific inquiry he saw emerging during his lifetime helps to illuminate what motivated the redirection of attentive exercises toward strange phenomena in the natural world. As Lisa Jardin remarks, Bacon did not merely formulate an abstract philosophical epistemology; his *New Organon* instead constitutes an "extraordinary attempt to *give formal shape*

---

type of the scientist (prone to paying intense attention to narrow details, thus becoming in the eyes of others an "absent-minded professor" or even a "mad scientist"); and was concomitant with a new *poetics of scientific knowledge* (involving techniques of recording and organizing isolated observations in journals, tables, lists, and such). See esp. Daston, *Kurze Geschichte*, 24–25, 45–48; Daston, "The Disciplines of Attention," 436–37; Daston and Park, *Wonders*, 303–28; as well as Adler, "Bändigung des (Un)Möglichen"; Singy, "Huber's Eyes."

9. In context, the formulation refers to the beginnings of an anti-Aristotelean "preternatural philosophy" in the late Renaissance, but it applies equally to the consolidation of this type of natural philosophy in the seventeenth century.

to a rapidly emerging (but hitherto largely problem-driven and ad hoc) new experimentally based science."[10] The title of Bacon's *Novum Organum* (1620) indicates the author's intention to replace the old *Organon*—Aristotle's writings on logic and syllogism, which were collected under that name because they provided the "tool" or "instrument" (*órganon*) of philosophical inquiry. Bacon's argument for providing a long-due overhaul of syllogistic reasoning is simple enough. The Aristotelean logic employed by scholastic natural philosophy provides thought with tools for policing the consistent use of concepts and extracting inferences from given premises. Yet it is useless and, in fact, treacherous—good only "for establishing and perpetuating errors"—if the concepts one plugs into the logical apparatus lack "reference to things" in the first place.[11] This, precisely, is Bacon's reproach to the scholastic natural philosophy of his time.[12] By his verdict, the entire edifice of scholasticism was erected on ill-informed premises, "abstracted from things without care" so that "there is nothing sound in what is built on them."[13]

The diagnosis implies the cure. By uprooting tradition and tending to the experiential roots of knowledge, the break with the old natural philosophy must be as "radical" as the errors such a philosophy perpetuated: "a new beginning has to be made from the lowest foundations."[14] Bacon's proposed toolset for a reformed natural philosophy intervenes precisely at the point he claims Aristotelean logic neglected with such disastrous results: the process of acquiring the basic data of nature in the first place. Famously

---

10. See Lisa Jardine's lucid introduction to Michael Silverthorne's new translation of Bacon's *New Organon*, xii. As Jardine notes in the introduction, Bacon was in epistolary dialogue with practitioners of the new "experimental" science across Europe.

11. Bacon, *New Organon*, 35 (aph. 11) (translation modified), 35 (aph. 13).

12. The chutzpa of Bacon's break is apparent in his swipe at the fundamental concepts of scholastic natural philosophy: "There is nothing sound in the notions of logic and physics: neither substance, nor quality, nor action and passion, or being itself are good notions; much less heavy, light, dense, rare, wet, dry, generation, corruption, attraction, repulsion, element, matter, form and so on; all fanciful and ill defined" (Bacon, *New Organon*, 35 [aph. 15]).

13. Bacon, *New Organon*, 35 (aph. 14).

14. Bacon, *New Organon*, 38 (aph. 30), 39 (aph. 31).

termed "true induction," Bacon's method promises to provide a fail-safe toolset for reliably gathering information about "actual particulars of nature" as well as their "sequences and orders," in order to then to guide the gradual formation of more general concepts and axioms on their basis.[15]

Bacon's basic point is obvious, perhaps blindingly so. What could be more sensible than to demand that knowledge should concern itself with what is "there," with what nature "really is like," in the first place? What could be more reasonable than to require that any science—if we take his objection more broadly—at least consistently "check" its concepts against phenomena, to see if they "fit" the reality they claim to describe? Yet the supposed self-evidence of Bacon's reproach masks the historical novelty and strangeness of the intuition that underlies his critique of scholastic natural philosophy. The truly radical break had already occurred by the time Bacon began to formulate the specifics of his new method.[16] Bacon's program is animated by the presumption of a lack of natural fit between common notions and things. His objections against scholastic natural philosophy only become plausible—indeed, inevitable—once one obviously knows, even before all theorizing, that mind and world are strangers to one another; that nature is not "made" to be understood by human minds, and human minds are not naturally equipped with what it takes to understand the world as it really is.

Not only does accurate perception not come naturally, but the kind of perception that merely comes naturally is, in Bacon's etiology, the root cause of all epistemic error. The aphorisms in the first, critical part of the *New Organon* converge in the admonition that all devices supposed to familiarize the mind with the world only lull the mind into a false sense of familiarity. Plagued by "dullness, limitations and deceptions," the senses are inherently defective and no

---

15. Bacon, *New Organon*, 35 (aph. 14), 40 (aph. 36).
16. Its traces are legible in the crass juxtaposition of "notions" and "actual things" in the following aphorism, which summarizes what it takes to rebuild the edifice of knowledge from the ground up: "There remains one simple way of getting our teaching across, namely to introduce men to actual particulars and their sequences and orders, and for men in their turn to pledge to abstain for a while from notions, and begin to get used to actual things" (Bacon, *New Organon*, 40 [aph. 36]).

match for the actual complexity of the world;[17] the mind has an innate tendency to "leap to generalities" on the basis of "rash" and "hasty" reasoning that passes off superficial abstractions for the actual natures of things;[18] and as a "poor and unskillful code of words" informed by faulty sense perceptions and rash abstractions, natural language, too, is no more than a deceptive construct, lodged exclusively on mind's side of the divide between thought and things.[19] Bacon's demand that science must challenge familiar notions to get acquainted with the true nature of things follows "naturally" from this intuition, much as scholasticism's belief in the mind's ability to apprehend the intelligible species of things reflected an unspoken confidence that the mind is compatible with and can access a world that corresponds to its powers.

Bacon hardly defeats scholasticism by the force of a better argument; his argument proceeds from an entirely different place.[20] In an epistemic constellation marked by the rift between human intellect and nature, the primary task of the methodological toolset of philosophy shifts from regulating the use of concepts to regulating perception, as the long-neglected interface between mind and world.[21] The artificial regulation of perception is thus the key to

---

17. Bacon, *New Organon*, 45 (aph. 50).
18. Bacon, *New Organon*, 36 (aph. 20), 38 (aph. 26), 48 (aph. 60).
19. Bacon, *New Organon*, 40 (aph. 43).
20. Bacon's text gives voice to a changed or changing background intelligibility; an emerging "horizon," "episteme," or "paradigm" of knowledge that takes the fundamental alienation of mind and world as its point of departure. If his objections against Aristotelean natural philosophy continue to resonate as all too obvious, it is only because we are heir to the historical change in "obviousness" Bacon articulates.
21. As fundamental but also fundamentally defective recording devices of data, the senses come under particular pressure in the Baconian program, simultaneously being the origin of "the greatest obstacle and distortion of human understanding" and the source "from which, if we prefer not to be insane we must derive everything." It is one of the great paradoxes of Baconian science—one it would bequeath to its successors—that it tasks the most fallible part of human nature with setting the secure foundation for the new edifice of knowledge. The presumption of a lack of natural fit between subject and object of knowledge explains both sides of the paradox. That perception is fallible also means that it is corrigible, and that the way information is processed across the gap is not determined, so that science can hope to gain knowledge about things themselves merely by artificially repairing the faults of perception. Bacon, *New Organon*, 45 (aph. 50), 18.

Baconian science, at least in its primary, data-gathering stage. Bacon's revised philosophical organon submits the senses and other faculties of perception to a rigorous disciplining program to remedy their innate faults and shape them into the reliable conduits of information they must become if secure knowledge about the natural world is to become possible. To this end, his method prescribes "assistants to the senses" in the form of methodical experiments and protocols of observation that turn perception from a haphazard process into a controlled procedure.[22] Only through avowedly artificial techniques is there a chance to regain something akin to Edenic knowledge of the nature of things—or at least to permanently compensate for its absence.

Bacon's *New Organon* thus also provided a blueprint for a metaphysics of technology and media that would come to dominate in the Enlightenment or the classical age, when calculable technologies and techniques—including, and especially, prostheses of perception—were viewed as artificial tools for *reconstituting* and *regaining* nature rather than as something at odds with it. (The widespread identification of reason with nature was only one aspect of this broader constellation.) The ideal that methodical art leads to nature (while relying on "merely" natural devices spelled corruption) was, as we shall see, critical for poetics and literary theory as well. For now, it is sufficient to note that Bacon and his followers saw techniques and technologies of perception as having a compensatory function: they were deemed capable of *removing* obstacles—defects of the senses, prejudiced notions—that would "stand between" the registering mind and things themselves. The claim to firsthand observation characteristic of the sciences that emerged in Bacon's wake thus rested on the ideal of a precarious immediacy of the second order—a kind of direct contact with things enabled by media practices that are paradoxically intended to eliminate all forms of mediation.

Across its various aphorisms, the *New Organon* propagates a fundamental readjustment of the epistemic attitude that promises

---

22. "Assistants to the senses" include experiments *as well as* methodical experience (context makes clear that artificially structured experiences or "observations" are included in the term).

to bring things *closer* by first *distancing* them, and that actively interrupts the seemingly natural intercourse between mind and world to then reestablish proper contact through a set of methodical techniques. If there is a general formula for how such perceptual devices and protocols function, it is expressed negatively in what Bacon identifies as the basic weakness of human understanding: that it is "most affected by things which have the ability to strike and enter the mind all at once (*simul*) and suddenly"—and then, on this scant basis, assumes that "everything else is just like the few things that took the mind by storm."[23] Bacon's famous "idols," various ingrained illusions that block the mind's access to nature, all reduce to this basic error.[24] The antidote he offers against this cardinal defect of human understanding is an artificially defamiliarized and decelerated mode of perception that lingers on particular details and gradually inspects their arrangements.

Bacon does not himself associate such a mode of perception with the word *attention* (though he sometimes uses verbal forms like *animum advertere, animadvertere,* and *notare* in pertinent contexts). But his admonition that what commonly passes for the world is nothing but a web of customary notions that block access to things—an access that can be restored only by a disciplined focus on particulars that circumvents the deceptive familiarity with things—betrays the underlying motivation for the focus on attention in the new science. Methodical attention became required as an intermediary between mind and world once their connection had become fundamentally problematic. The diagnosis of an opening, a fissure, or a gap between thought and things made it both necessary and possible to bridge this gap in a controlled and newly careful way.

---

23. Bacon, *New Organon*, 43 (aph. 47).
24. The phrase "idols of the tribe" refers to the innate defect of human receptivity to be overly affected by striking things; the phrase "idols of the marketplace" warns against common language as a repository of such hasty, unexamined affectations; "idols of the cave" highlights the individual confirmation bias that results from overgeneralizing a few striking things and then assuming that everything else is similar to it; and "idols of the theater" expands this confirmation bias to entire scientific schools, for which everything begins to look like a small number of striking observations. Bacon, *New Organon*, 18–19, 41–51 (aph. 41–62).

The Strangeness of the World

It is tempting to speculate on why Bacon suddenly detects a glaring omission in the method of scholastic natural philosophy where generations of scholars had not noticed a problem. The time when Bacon was writing was certainly ripe with developments that had the potential to make the world seem like a strange place. For an (undoubtedly selective) overview, it is sufficient to recall the proliferation of "worlds" in the new plural sense that cut across various areas of seventeenth-century knowledge. In the wake of Copernicus's new astronomy, a cosmological revolution was underway that Alexandre Koyré has characterized as the shift from the "closed world" of the well-ordered classical and medieval cosmos to the "infinite universe" of an acentric modern worldview.[25] New "worlds" discovered through telescopes in the heavens and through microscopes within proverbial grains of sand gave compelling evidence that the human perceptual apparatus indeed does not measure up to the vast expanse of nature. As suggested by the famous frontispiece of the *New Organon*, with its ships transcending the Pillars of Hercules, terrestrial geographies were changing as well. The discovery of what appeared to Europeans as "new worlds" with unfamiliar cultures, fauna, and flora challenged traditional orders of knowledge, while the beginning colonization of these worlds resonated eerily with Bacon's call for an epistemic conquest of the *terra incognita* of nature. Within Europe, religious, social, and political transformations in the wake of the Protestant Reformation caused civil wars across the continent, shattering the sense of a stable, divinely sanctioned social world just as new lens technologies and astronomies challenged unified order of the cosmos.[26]

---

25. Koyré, *From the Closed World*, esp. 1–57; see also Hans Blumenberg's extensive *Die Genesis der kopernikanischen Welt*.

26. Blumenberg traces the *Ordnungsschwund* to the escalating "theological absolutism" of the Middle Ages, which no longer offers an explanation for how and why things are what they are other than divine decree, the "quia voluit" of nominalism: "Der 'Ordnungsschwund' als Grund zum Zweifel an einer auf den Menschen beziehbaren Struktur der Wirklichkeit ist die Voraussetzung für eine generelle Konzeption des menschlichen Handelns, die in den Gegebenheiten nichts mehr von der

As a well-connected politician-scientist at the English court, Bacon not only witnessed these developments but was personally involved in each of them. Still, in the absence of historical meta-narratives that privilege a distinct set of phenomena as drivers of historical change, it is doubtful whether any of these developments qualify as answers to "why"-questions that demand reasons for or causes of the new preconception about the mind's place in the world. It does not necessarily follow that we have to give up explanatory efforts altogether and resign ourselves to identifying sudden mutations in the grammar of knowledge that deflect all further explanation. Focusing on what Baconian science meant in practice may not yield reasons but contributes to explaining how the rift between mind and world intensified; how, within a set of practices in early modern science, the world began to appear as emphatically different from and strange to the inquiring mind.

A curious shift in the kinds of objects on which seventeenth-century naturalists exerted their attention is instructive for tracing the effects of these practices. As we have seen, a first generation of naturalists around the middle of the seventeenth century trained their attention on preternatural phenomena that embodied the strangeness of particulars vis-à-vis the general course of nature. Once practices of attentiveness had solidified into the professional habitus of scientific observers, however, the directionality of attention and strangeness switched. By the late seventeenth century, the preferred object choice of scientists shifted from the inherently strange objects populating the walls of early modern curiosity cabinets to the likes of aphids and worms, which a professionally trained attention could reveal *as* strange and extraordinary *despite* their ordinariness and triviality to the uninitiated eye. While early acolytes relied on objects capable of eliciting the curiosity necessary

---

Verbindlichkeit des antiken und mittelalterlichen Kosmos wahrnimmt und sie deshalb prinzipiell für verfügbar hält." Blumenberg, *Die Legitimität der Neuzeit*, 150; Blumenberg, *Legitimacy of the Modern Age*, 137. Imperatives of attention mandate a surplus of vigilant consciousness that is necessary to orient human practice in the absence of natural order—or to destroy the illusion of such order once it is no longer seen as reliable; once concepts of given order are revealed to be no more than a wild conglomerate of arbitrary conventions, old habits, and confused "common notions."

to focus on particulars with the sustained attention mandated by the new science, later naturalists learned that a sufficiently close focus could reveal even seemingly familiar things as singularly curious and strange—no less eccentric to habitual notions of nature than "objectively" preternatural phenomena.[27]

The lesson of this relocation of strangeness in the eye of the attentive observer is that the alterity of the natural world to the mind—its incommensurability to common and familiar notions the mind comes by naturally—is the effect of a defamiliarizing knowledge practice. Sustained attention thus effects the very strangeness of the world it was called upon to remedy. The prevailing interpretation of this effect at the time was to consider disciplined attention not as just one knowledge technique among others but instead as a reliable truth-practice that could finally reveal the world's true nature. Accordingly, the deliberate externalization of the world does not necessarily—and certainly not initially—entail estrangement in the sense of a painful alienation. Casting a methodically artificial gaze upon things was instead seen as a condition for discovering nature's marvels—a salutary defamiliarization that finally brought to light what tradition and custom had obscured.

Attendamus! Attention and the Representational Paradigm

The epistemological breaks advocated by Descartes and Bacon, two figures commonly portrayed as figureheads of opposing rationalist and empiricist factions within early modern philosophy, have much in common, especially if one disregards the broad principles attributed to them and instead focuses on the mechanics of the cognitive and scientific procedures they devised. As part of a broader effort to overthrow scholasticism and set philosophy and science on new foundations, both proceeded from a trenchant critique of the knowledge practices of scholasticism—syllogistic reasoning, dialectical disputation—as sterile methods that yield no new insights and are

---

27. Daston, *Kurze Geschichte*, 15–35; see also Daston and Park, *Wonders*, 215–328.

prone to perpetuating errors inherent in the underlying premises. Both figures also identify the mind's tendency to get ahead of itself by relying on hasty judgments and preconceived notions as the cardinal error in epistemology.[28] Descartes, however, specifically identified the deliberate direction of attention as the antidote against such precipitate judgments. And he provided an epistemological foundation for the knowledge practices of the new natural philosophy that will frame discussions and practices of attention discussed in the remainder of this book.

The systematic function of attention in Cartesian knowledge is most evident in the *Meditations on First Philosophy*, which announces through its title that it aims to supplant Aristotelean metaphysics or first philosophy (*protē philosophía*) just as Bacon aimed to replace Aristotelean logic. The title's first word suggests that it will do so through a meditation, a sustained exercise in attentiveness. Drawing on early modern traditions of meditative exercises—such as those of Ignatius of Loyola and Teresa of Ávila—the text abounds with addresses to an "attentive reader" and exhortations to direct the mind's focus along the path laid out by the Cartesian meditator.[29] The epistemic attitude the *Meditations* aim to induce thus depends on translating the words on the page into a series of attentive acts within the "interior castle" of the mind, as Teresa of Ávila called the space of meditation—a spiritual journey propelled by the guided direction of one's mental focus. Descartes, however, repurposed the genre of meditative exercises to serve as an initiation to his *physics*, his umbrella term for his new scientific account of the natural world. The Cartesian meditations lead inward, toward the self, with the stated purpose of clearing the way for a new epistemic engagement of the self with the world outside.

---

28. Bacon termed this error the "anticipation of nature"; Descartes castigated "precipitate conclusions [*précipitations*]." Bacon, *New Organon*, 38 (aphs. 26–29); Descartes, *The Philosophical Writings of Descartes* (hereafter cited as *PWD*) I:120–22.

29. Long-overlooked parallels between Teresa of Ávila's *El Castillo Interior* (The interior castle; 1588) and Descartes's *Meditations* have recently been excavated by Christia Mercer, "Descartes' Debt to Teresa." For the *Meditations*' debt to the tradition of spiritual exercises, see Kobusch, "Descartes' *Meditations*: Practical Metaphysics."

Yet attention is not only the medium of the Cartesian meditations but also one of their focal topics. The *Meditations* first turn attention to the concept of attention in the Second Meditation, specifically during its iconic contemplation of a piece of wax, which invites readers to recognize the essential distinction between the mind and the body and the priority of the former over the latter in matters of knowledge. After discovering that the only certainty withstanding the meditator's hyperbolic doubt is the fact that he is "a thing that thinks," Descartes introduces an important claim about sense perception. When properly understood, he argues, even the kind of perception one might think of as "sensory" in fact counts among the activities performed by a thinking thing or mind. Implying a contrast with the scholastic view, which credits the lower, "animal" soul with the reception of "species" or perceptible forms emitted by things, he suggests that sensing should instead be explained as the mind's activity of "taking note of" or "turning toward" (*animadvertere*) impressions. This suggests, in turn, that the mind is undivided and does not have a distinct sensory part.[30] (Where such impressions come from is yet under the screen of systematic doubt at this point in the *Meditations*; Descartes later advances mechanical explanations.) The Aristotelean soul thus becomes the undivided Cartesian mind, without a lower floor, at one with itself—a mind whose unity with itself will become the basis for a new way of mastering the unruly multiplicity of the world.

As the Cartesian meditator admits, so abstract a claim is unlikely to jolt anyone out of the lifelong habit of thinking that nothing is

---

30. On Descartes's implicit dialogue with and rejection of the scholastic view of the mind in the Second Meditation, see Alanen, "The Second Meditation." Among the mental acts of which the meditator finds himself aware and that undoubtedly belong to him as a merely thinking thing, the meditator includes "imagining" and "sensing," set off from the rest of the list by "also" or "even" (*quoque*) as unlikely possessions of a purely thinking thing. The reason for their distinct status is that, unlike mental acts such as "doubting," "understanding" and "affirming," imagining and sensing are not fully controlled by the thinking ego: imagining can occur "even against my will" and sensory perceptions "appear to" come from without, from bodily things received through the senses. They nevertheless count among the activities in which the thinking thing is aware of itself because the criterion for inclusion is not simply control over activity but the *ego sim qui* (it is I who) that introduces all characterizations of the cogito's activities in this section.

more intimately known than corporeal things that impress themselves on the senses. The wax episode is supposed to remedy this shortcoming by demonstrating the priority of the mind even in the case of perceiving a sensory particular. All the sensory "secondary" qualities the meditator recounts about this particular piece of wax—its color, sound, texture, shape, a scent that recalls the flowers from which bees collected the material the wax is made of—change when the wax is placed close to a fire. Nevertheless, no one disputes that it remains the same piece of wax across its various permutations. A resounding *attendamus* (let us pay attention) heralds the recovery from the failed attempt to know the wax through its sensory qualities.[31] If we consider the matter attentively, we will see that the piece of wax really is something "extended, flexible, and changeable" (that is, something close to Descartes's eventual definition of a body; something whose range of possible properties is accessible only to thought).[32]

Descartes's exhortation to focus attention simultaneously announces *and* produces the switch from a "naive" mode of allegedly sensory perception to an active mental scrutiny that reveals the wax's true nature. The lesson from the thought experiment is not that one ought to abstain as much as possible from sensory perception and instead let the mind do all the work. It is that even what previously seemed like sense perception aided by imagination was exclusively the mind's doing all along—but a work sloppily performed, without the proper attention. "This inspection," he notes, "can be imperfect and confused, as it was before, or clear and distinct, as it is now, *depending on how closely I pay attention to the things in which the piece of wax consists.*"[33] What appeared to be stages of perception performed by different parts of the soul—a

---

31. Adams and Tannery, *Oeuvres de Descartes* (hereafter, by convention, cited as AT for Adam and Tannery), 7:30–31.
32. *PWD* II:20; AT 7:31.
33. *PWD* II:21. Passage modified following Donald A. Cress's translation to preserve the reference to attention in Descartes's "prout minus vel magis ad illa ex quibus constat attendo"; AT 7:31; Descartes, *Meditations on First Philosophy* (Cress translation), 22. Highlights mine.

lower "sensory" and a higher "intellectual" part—are, Descartes suggests, simply different modes of the mind's attending to things—a "proper" way of attending and a relative lapse of attention. The passage is pivotal for our story because it links the key distinction of Cartesian epistemology between "confused" and "clear and distinct" perceptions to the application of attention. It even suggests something about the type of attention that effects the transition from the confusion of so-called sensory perception to the compelling *évidence* of clear and distinct perceptions: it is an attention directed at the component parts of things (*ea ex quibus constat*) until each of them is clearly recognized by the mind.[34]

Descartes's insistence that even perceptions labeled as sensory are generated by the mind itself offers a first opportunity to identify the systematic role of attention within the paradigm of representation, which assumes that the only way the mind can access the external world is through internal images or representations.[35] As Jonathan Crary and others have argued, the representational paradigm rests on a technical-epistemological background metaphor that imagines the mind along the model of a camera obscura—a darkened box into which images of the outside world are projected through a pinhole onto a two-dimensional surface inside (see figure 2).[36]

In analogy to the camera obscura, philosophical interiority is established by walling off an interior space from the outside world—as Descartes announces in the *Meditations*, "I will now shut my eyes, stop up my ears, and withdraw all my senses"—and then admitting the outside back in under controlled conditions, in the form of orderly impressions on a wax tablet, screen, or canvas inside the

---

34. The French version authorized by Descartes makes the reference to an attention directed to component parts even clearer: "selon que mon attention se porte plus ou moins aux choses qui sont en elle, & dont elle est composée" (depending on whether my attention directs itself more or less on the things which are in it, and of which it is composed) (AT 9, 25).

35. Compare the chapter on "Representing" in Foucault's *The Order of Things*.

36. See the second chapter of Crary's *Techniques of the Observer*, 25–66. For a complementary account of epistemic inner vision in this period, see Wilson, "Discourses of Vision."

Figure 2. Model of "large portable camera obscura" from Athanasius Kircher, *Ars magna lucis et umbrae*, 806–7.

mind. These internal images, however, only attain their status as representations of external objects by virtue of their inspection by a disembodied internal observer, commonly metaphorized as the "eye of the mind." "All the knowing gets done," as Richard Rorty notes in his deconstruction of Locke's wax tablet metaphor, "by the Eye which observes the imprinted tablet, rather than by the tablet itself."[37] Descartes's meditation on the piece of wax, which identifies this mental inspection with attention, conveyed precisely this point. This equation would become canonical. Within the topology of the mind traced by the camera obscura, attention is the agency for inspecting mental images, both those produced by the senses and those recalled in the imagination.

As presented by Crary, however, the cameral model of the mind leaves one aspect of the procedure for producing representational knowledge underexposed. Crary portrays the internal observations performed by the mental eye as an effortless "mental survey of its [the exterior world's] 'clear and distinct' representation within the

---

37. Rorty, *Philosophy and the Mirror of Nature*, 143–44.

room," as if perceptions attained their evidentiary distinctness merely by passing through the orderly representational machine.[38] The unobstructed overview of the field of representation within the dark chamber would accordingly establish the "unified and homogeneous coherence" of the classical knowledge-type, which for Crary serves as a foil to the physiologically conditioned models of epistemic vision he sees arising in the early 1800s.[39] What his characterization misses is the qualification, central to various adaptations of the camera obscura model from Descartes to Locke and Leibniz, that any instantaneous survey of ideas is the privilege of an infinite mind. (And indeed, Crary comes close to identifying the supposed "infallible metaphysical eye"[40] instantiated by the apparatus with the divine eye's sovereign gaze.) The human mind, by contrast, is defined by its limited capacity to attend to ideas with the proper exactitude. The eye of the mind, in other words, has a limited focus.

Highlighting "attention" as an analytical category for understanding the logic of representational knowledge over "observation" or "mental screening" of internal images therefore signals more than a preference for one term over another. Emphasizing the role of attention in the private theater of representation reveals that the inner vision assumed by this model was subject to essential sight limitations. From this new perspective, the compensatory measures marshaled to surmount the partiality and inconstancy of attention become recognizable as defining elements of representational knowledge.

In many respects, the deficiencies of attention mark the return of the classical observer's repressed corporeality within the dark chamber of the mind. They represent all the elements we might think of as contingent anthropological conditions of knowledge—the fallibility associated with human finitude, situatedness, embodiment. Seventeenth-century thinkers usually explained these theologically, through the fallenness of human nature. A diverse tradition of scholarship from Cassirer to Foucault identified the sovereign overview

---

38. Crary, *Techniques of the Observer*, 46. The formulation occurs in Crary's discussion of two Vermeer paintings.
39. Crary, *Suspensions of Perception*, 24. For the contrast with postclassical models of vision, see Crary, *Techniques of the Observer*, 67–96.
40. Crary, *Techniques of the Observer*, 48.

over a unified table of knowledge as the ideal of knowledge in the age of representation. Foregrounding the role of attention, however, reveals the ways this ideal overview was staged, propped up by a series of indispensable supporting devices.[41] These devices included mechanical memory and linguistic signs, which—as deconstructive critiques have pointed out—Descartes simultaneously denounced as obstacles to intuitive clarity and yet conceded must be admitted as placeholders for the direct access to distinct ideas when the length of meditations exceeds even a trained mind's limited focus. Less attention has been paid to the arsenal of practical precepts, procedures, and techniques that make up the Cartesian method. The various rules Descartes developed in the early treatise *Rules for the Direction of the Mind* and in his later *Discourse on Method* provide, above all, precepts for supporting and fortifying a fallible attention in the pursuit of mental clarity.

What are the procedures the Cartesian method teaches? *Rules for the Direction of the Mind,* drafted around 1628, offers an early example. Concerned with instructing the "mind's eye" in how to "acquire the habit of intuiting the truth distinctly and clearly," the ninth rule spells out the proper direction of mental attention in analogy with the exact corporeal vision acquired by practicing a precision craft:

> If one tries to look at many objects at one glance, one sees none of them distinctly. Likewise, if one is inclined to attend to many things at the same time in a single act of thought, one does so with a confused mind. Yet craftsmen who engage in delicate operations, and are used to directing the focus of their eyes attentively to a single point, acquire through practice the ability to make perfect distinctions between things, however minute and delicate. The same is true of those who never let their thinking be distracted by many different objects at the same time, but always devote their whole attention to what is most simple and basic: they become perspicacious.[42]

This passage illustrates the background assumption that motivates the procedures prescribed by the Cartesian method and turns atten-

---

41. Foucault, *The Order of Things,* 73–76; Cassirer, *Die Philosophie der Aufklärung,* 22–28.
42. *PWD* I:33, AT 10:400–1, translation modified.

tion into a prerequisite of clear and distinct knowledge: the idea that the acuity of discernment is inversely correlated with the breadth of its focus. The narrower the focus, the clearer the discernment, and vice versa. Like the eyes, the mind can therefore only ever *see* one "part" or "side" of a particular matter with the intuitive clarity demanded by Cartesian epistemology. This does not mean, however, that knowledge is irremediably partial or one-sided. The trick of the Cartesian method is to convert the *parts* of an epistemic object into the *steps* of a procedure. By projecting the confusing simultaneity of parts onto a temporal axis, even minds with a limited focus can gain clarity about all relevant components—so long as they confront them one at a time, one after another. "Hasty" and "precipitate" judgments, contrarily, constitute the cardinal errors of thought, because they forego this sequential processing and leap to the whole "at once" without taking time to distinguish the parts.

As elaborated in *Rules for the Direction of the Mind*, concentrated attention in fact plays a dual role in this procedure. It both performs the detailed inspection of parts and watches over chains of reasoning to make sure nothing that has not been sufficiently resolved into intuitive clarity enters the mind's meditations.[43] The elevation of analysis and synthesis into complementary principles for clarifying ideas in the second and third rules of the *Discourse on Method* confirms the fundamentality of this attention-driven procedure for the Cartesian method. In effect, knowers must acquire the habit of proceeding like the precision craftsmen Descartes holds up as models: they must learn to belabor each part attentively, one at a time, before recombining the parts into a unified artifact that is, in the clarity of its composition from parts, fully transparent and intelligible to the mind.

It is therefore not simply wrong to claim, as Crary does, that classical knowledge strives for unity and coherence. The point to see is that this coherence is always manufactured. Descartes is ambivalent about the "constructive" role of attention in clarifying ideas.

---

43. The ninth rule distinguishes these functions as "*perspicacity* in the distinct intuition of particular things and *discernment* in the methodical deduction of one thing from another" (my emphasis). *PWD* I:33 (AT 10:400). They also correspond to different kinds of uses of "*attendo/animadverto*" in the Cartesian text.

At times he makes it seem as if it were enough for the mental eye to "stare fixedly" at an idea long enough for distinctness to emerge all by itself; at other times, as in the passage cited above, he portrays the directing of attention as a craft, akin to wielding a mental scalpel in the surgical clarification of perceptions (one of Descartes's terms for the mental eye is *acies mentis*, the "sharp edge" of the mind).[44] But even where Descartes downplays the mind's active contribution to the process, it is obvious that the certain knowledge produced by a method is no longer simply "theory" in the ancient sense of contemplation (*theoreîn*), by an "infallible metaphysical eye," of eternal truths of the cosmos that illuminate the eternal part of the soul. Rather than intuiting timeless forms directly and, as it were, passively, Cartesian mental vision actively directs its mental gaze to perform the precarious labor of analysis and synthesis. To be sure, the clear and distinct representations resulting from this mental labor lay claim to the metaphysical mantle of Platonic essences. Like the knowledge procured by the artificial tools of Bacon's *New Organon*, however, their unity and cohesion are of the second order; they are the result of an attentional procedure that first had to destruct the deceptive wholeness of ideas to then resurrect it from clearly distinguished parts.

Speaking more loosely, we might say that the cohesion of this type of knowledge bears more resemblance to a soap bubble than to a Platonic sphere. Depicting the kind of single-minded focus Descartes prized in precision artisans, the painting *Soap Bubbles* (1734) by Jean-Baptiste-Siméon Chardin (1699–1779) has repeatedly served as an allegory of the period's dominant mode of attention (figure 3).

Michael Fried saw the painting as an early emblem of "absorption," the deep attentiveness whose cultivation he viewed as a signature achievement of eighteenth-century French art.[45] For Crary, the window scene at the threshold of interior and exterior depicts the transformation of "formless liquid opacity into the transparent

---

44. As we shall see, eighteenth-century rationalists would openly embrace the "maker's knowledge" aspect latent in Descartes's portrayals of attention as a key to clear and distinct ideas—the notion that the mind has complete insight into such ideas because they are as good as self-constructed.

45. Fried, *Absorption and Theatricality*, 50.

Figure 3. Jean-Baptiste-Siméon Chardin's *Soap Bubbles* (1734) (Courtesy National Gallery of Art, Washington).

sphere of a soap bubble" as an "act of effortless mastery."[46] It took Natalie Phillips's focus on concepts of distraction to point out the obvious: this bubble looks like it is about to burst.[47] The painting evokes less an act of effortless mastery than a precarious balancing act. Even if the suggestive conversion of opacity into perspicuity succeeds by channeling the muddy liquid through a single point, the result is visibly not the perfect sphere in which ancient metaphysicians saw a picture of the timeless unity of the cosmos. The sphere's elongation and the pointy attachment to the blowpipe mark it, at its origin, as an ephemeral artifact. Perhaps it will burst; perhaps it will detach itself and drift off on its own for a while. We do not know, but we do know that something is about to happen, just as the sphere still trembles from the delicate distension that preceded it. Above all, the painting depicts attention as a process that unfolds in time and remains subject to the vagaries of time even at the moment of its consummation. As a practice, attention visibly relies on the combination of a bodily posture (one hand finding stability at the ledge, the other resting on top of it to steady the grip), a specific instrument (a straw cut for the purpose), and a mental absorption that directs these elements toward a single point or goal. No doubt it took some training to coordinate all these elements to successfully carry out the task. The onlooker seems as much fascinated by the spectacle as eager to learn the trick. If the painting does bear a reading as an allegory of attention, it portrays attention as a learned and learnable technique or skill that involves intense concentration as much as technical supports and a certain posture of the body.

Habits of Attention

Exploring the quasi-rhetorical structure of Descartes's rules for directing the mind, Thomas M. Carr has argued against the misunderstanding that the Cartesian method consists of "a fixed set of formulas, conveniently numbered steps, to be applied mechanically to a

---

46. Crary, *Techniques of the Observer*, 64.
47. Phillips, *Distraction*, 17.

problem. Commentators who complain that Descartes' four rules of method are banal and unexceptional miss the point; the precepts are less a series of procedures than an appreciation of the psychology of attention, reminders of how to purify and direct it."[48] But perhaps the term "reminder" is too timid and passive, suggesting that the Cartesian method merely instructs readers to heed a "psychology of attention" that is constant and given. The point of the method is not to describe the mind's attention but to guide and shape it. Like the spiritual manuals on which Descartes modeled his *Meditations*, the Cartesian writings on method are as much handbooks that guide readers in exercising a certain type of attentive behavior as they are epistemological treatises. Descartes himself famously acknowledges in a letter to letter to Marin Mersenne that his method consists "more in practice than in theory."[49] The crucial way in which his method differs from the spiritual practices on which he modeled the *Meditations* is that his meditator turns inward not to ready himself for divine illumination but to prepare for a cognitive reengagement with the world outside.[50] The imperatives of attentiveness that structure the Cartesian method emphasize that the camera obscura is not merely a neutral analogy for the process of cognition. It also institutes a specific kind of cognitive behavior. More than providing a descriptive theory, it models the shape of a knowledge practice. The commentator most attuned to this aspect of the Cartesian method was French philosopher Jean Laporte (1886–1948), who saw the cultivation of specific "habits of attention" as the ultimate objective of Descartes's epistemological and ethical program.[51] Emphasizing Descartes's references to the Aristotelean *héxis* tradition, which foregrounds the malleability of mental and corporeal states through training and habituation, Laporte argued that Descartes did not presuppose that mind and world were governed by a shared rational, lawful structure and was therefore not, in fact,

---

48. Carr, *Descartes and the Resilience*, 41. One does not have to agree with the psychologization of the Cartesian method to agree with the basic point.
49. *PWD* III:53 (AT 1, 349).
50. This point is emphasized in Mercer, "Methodology of the *Meditations*."
51. Laporte, *Le rationalisme de Descartes*, 34, see also 430.

a rationalist.⁵² I suggest turning Laporte's claim around: Descartes's concessions to the formative force of habituation in shaping the mind instead reveal the habitus behind the rationalist program. If Descartes often appears to be less conventionally "rationalist" than his philosophical successors, it is because the *pragmatic* presuppositions underlying the rationalist program are still more readily recognizable in this program's initial articulations, before the picture of mind and world it promoted hardened into an ontological axiom.

Admittedly, the phrase "habits of attention" has a dissonant ring. Does attention not usually suggest an intense and extraordinary focus that marks the very opposite of habit—a perceptual "state of exception," as Michael Hagner has characterized the defining feature of attentive states across historically variety?⁵³ The dissonance is instructive, and points to the peculiar structure of the perceptual routines behind Cartesian rationalism. By promoting habits of attention, the Cartesian method not only instructs a set of routines (habits) within a specified domain of cognitive activity (attention) but also—in doing so—advocates an altogether new attitude toward habit.

We see how this works by picking up where we left off in the *Meditations*: Descartes's claim, in the context of the meditation on the piece of wax, that what is usually thought of as sense perception should instead be understood as an inattentive form of mental inspection, so that the difference between the "confused" images of the senses and "clear and distinct" intellectual perception should be attributed not to different parts of the soul but to different ways of applying attention. In the sixth set of the *Objections and Replies* appended to the *Meditations*, Descartes clarifies this new view of perception by distinguishing three stages or levels of "sensory response." The first consists of the "immediate stimulation [*immediate afficitur*] of the bodily organs by external objects," which Descartes explains in a strictly mechanical manner, without any involvement of the mind. The second stage "comprises the immediate effects pro-

---

52. Laporte, *Le rationalisme de Descartes*, 269–77; see esp. 34, 429–30, for an overview of references to the formative role of "habit," "cultivation," "exercise," "training," and "practice" in the Cartesian oeuvre.
53. Hagner, "Aufmerksamkeit als Ausnahmezustand."

duced [*immediate resultat*] in the mind as a result of its being united with a bodily organ"—bare sensations of color, heat, pain, and so on triggered in the mind on account of mechanical affectations of the body. As underscored by the characterization of both these stages as "immediate," Descartes thinks of these initial stages as physiological—that is, as "natural," and therefore as beyond right or wrong, incapable of error.⁵⁴ Even if these stages give rise to a sensation of color, for example (which Descartes thinks ultimately reduces to colorless, geometrical microtextures of objects), the sensation is not wrong as such—as a mere sensation—so long as it is not taken to represent a real quality of external things. This kind of error can only occur in the third stage, which "includes all the judgments about things outside us which we have been accustomed to make from our earlier years" (such as the, in Descartes's view, erroneous judgment that objects are colored). Strictly speaking, sense perception is thus a misnomer for the third stage of perception, as Descartes points out yet again: even though it is "commonly assigned to the senses," this stage of perception in fact "depends solely on the intellect."⁵⁵ If the third stage comes to seem as natural and automatic as properly sensory responses—the mechanical affectations of the body and their immediate mental afterimages—it is only because these kinds of judgments occur "at great speed because of habit" and accordingly pass unnoticed.⁵⁶ The third stage, in other words, is not nature, but *second nature*—habits and routines that have become automatisms, composed of "preconceived opinions which we have become accustomed to accept from our earliest years."⁵⁷

To see the world for what it really is—or to share Descartes's new vision of the being of things—the automatized third level of

---

54. *PWD* II:296 (AT 7:438). One the same point in the main text of the meditations, see *PWD* II:26 (AT 7:37).
55. *PWD* II:295 (AT 7:437–38).
56. *PWD* II:295 (AT 7:438).
57. *PWD* II:296 (AT 7:439). The equation of habit and "second nature" becomes explicit in the passage of the Sixth Meditation, which the *Replies* elaborate: "There are . . . many other things which I may *appear to have been taught by nature*, but which in reality I acquired *not from nature but from a habit of making ill-considered judgements*; and it is therefore quite possible that these are false" (*PWD* II:56 [AT 7:82], my emphases).

perception must therefore be corrected through a fourth level of perception, which Descartes characterizes as the mature judgments of the intellect.[58] Based on reflection, these judgments then inform us (to use Descartes's examples) that a stick that appears bent when submerged in water is really straight or that colors we are accustomed to attribute to objects are a quality of sensations rather than of things. The critical point here—the point already previewed in the meditation on the piece of wax—is that the intellectual level of perception is not different in kind from a third level that is commonly, but mistakenly, identified as sensory: "the only difference is that when we now make a judgment for the first time because of some new observation [*animadversionem*], then we attribute it to the intellect; but when from our earliest years we have made judgments ... about the things which affect our senses, then, even though these judgments were made in exactly the same way as those we make now, we refer them to the senses."[59] What makes all the difference is that before arriving at mature perceptual judgments, we stop to pay the kind of attention elicited by new and unfamiliar things. The fourth level of perception is thus equivalent to the *deliberate* performance of the third stage, the mental inspection of sensory images, that usually happens habitually and automatically. By breaking the automatic chain that runs from affectations of the sense organs to immediate sensory images and *seemingly* immediate (but in fact only customary) judgments, proper attentiveness is the prerequisite for the intellect's mature judgments. The difference between "imperfect and confused" and "clear and distinct" perceptions is none other than that between habitual, rapid, and subconscious judgments that rely on an inner eye blinded by routines imbibed since early childhood—and mature judgments that follow the attentive—that is, gradual and deliberate—inspection of sensory images, as if they appeared before the mind for the first time.

---

58. In identifying the mature judgments of the understanding as a "fourth level," I am following Gary Hatfield's lucid account of sense perception in Descartes in Hatfield, "The Senses and the Fleshless Eye," here: 59.

59. *PWD* II:295 (AT 7:438). For the part in the Sixth Meditation on judgment and habit elaborated in this section of the *Replies*, see *PWD* II:56–57 (AT 7:81–83).

Descartes reframes the classical distinction between sense perception and intellectual perception, between *aisthesis* and *noesis*, as a distinction between two modes of performing mental judgments. To be precise, however, the specific difference does not lie in the act of judging *itself*—as Descartes points out, judgments occur in "exactly the same way" in both cases—but in the way the mind *inspects sensory images in the lead-up to the moment of judgment*. In perceptions we ascribe to the senses, this inspection occurs habitually—and that, for Descartes, means automatically, rapidly, and guided in advance by prejudices that are themselves rash and sloppy judgments that became ossified over time. Mature judgments of the intellect, by contrast, result from performing the same operations carefully and deliberately, with attention. In the final analysis, the traditional distinction between the senses and the intellect reduces to a distinction between habit and attention.

On closer inspection, however, this distinction is more unstable than it seems. Descartes appeals to attentiveness as the opposite and adversary of habit—as a perceptual state of exception that brings to awareness what habitually escapes notice. Yet the point of his meditations—which are themselves a practice in attentiveness—is to make a habit of breaking bad perceptual habits, to cultivate a habit that promises to expunge all habits. This peculiar doubling of habit as malady and antidote is reflected in two distinct contexts of usage of the Latin and early modern French verbs for "becoming accustomed to" or "acquiring the habit of" throughout the Cartesian oeuvre. *Consuesco, assuesco, s'accoustumer*, and their cognates refer *either* to the assimilation of suspect routines of perception from childhood onward *or* to the acquisition, through practice and training, of the new epistemic habits promoted by Descartes. To eradicate the "preconceived opinions which we have become accustomed [*assuevimus*] to accept from our earliest years," it is thus necessary to "acquire the habit [*assuescamus*] of intuiting the truth distinctly and clearly."[60] At times, both valences of habit are explicitly pitted against

---

60. The first quote is from *PWD* II:296 (AT 7:438–39), the second is from *PWD* I:33 (AT 10: 400). For habituation as a prerequisite of the method, compare:

each other, as in the following sentence from the *Replies*: "Protracted and repeated study is required to eradicate the lifelong habit [*totius vitae consuetudo*] of confusing things related to the intellect with corporeal things, and to replace it with the opposite habit [*contraria . . . consuetudine*] of distinguishing the two."[61]

Habits of attention are thus peculiar habits of the second order; meta-habits directed *against* habits. By promoting habitual attentiveness, the Cartesian method not only instills a set of cognitive routines but also—in doing so—advocates a revised attitude toward habit altogether. Like the defamiliarization techniques promoted by Bacon, the epistemic habits of the Cartesian method are geared toward *neutralizing* the detrimental habituality of first-order perception. The pathos of wiping the slate clean and beginning from new foundations that animates the Cartesian program depends on claiming that the two forms of habituation are categorically different from one another; that the counter-habit or *consuetudo contraria* instilled by the method is not just another habit—not merely *consuetudo*, a custom or tradition—but leads beyond the contingencies of habit altogether to the disembodied and context-independent space of reason. To de-

---

"We must . . . practise these easier tasks first, and above all methodically, so that . . . we may grow accustomed [*assuescamus*] . . . to penetrating always to the deeper truth of things" (*PWD* I, 36; AT 10: 405); "as I practised the method I felt my mind gradually become accustomed [*s'accoustumoit*] to conceiving its objects more clearly and distinctly (*PWD* I, 121; AT 6, 21); and "not many people are accustomed [*sunt assueti*] to clear and distinct perceptions" (*PWD* II, 348; AT 7:511). For habituation as a source of error to be eliminated by the new method, compare: "[false] judgements about things outside us which we have been accustomed [*consuevimus*] to make from our earliest years" (*PWD* II, 295; AT 7:437); "through habitual belief [*ob consuetudinem*] I thought I perceived clearly, although I did not in fact do so" (*PWD* II, 25; AT 7:35); and "we do not usually notice these circular motions when bodies are moving in the air, because we are accustomed [*sommes accoûtumez*] to conceiving of the air only as an empty space" (*PWD* I, 86; AT 11, 19). The list could be continued—the usage seems systematic, and the etymons rarely occur in any other context (although a significant variation in *The Passions of the Soul* will be discussed below).

61. *PWD* II:94 (AT 7:131). Similarly, a few pages later: "if he [the reader] attends carefully to what I have written he should be able to free himself from the preconceived opinions which may be eclipsing his natural light, and to accustom himself to believing [*credere assuescat*] in the primary notions, which are as evident and true as anything can be, in preference to opinions which are obscure and false, albeit fixed in the mind by long habit [*longo usu menti infixis*]" (*PWD* II, 97; AT 7:135).

fuse the habituality of second-order habits, Descartes therefore consistently frames the *re*habituation required by the method as the labor of forgetting—as a *dis*habituation, which requires practice and training only because it takes effort to unlearn bad habits and restore direct contact with the truth. Again, the parallels with Bacon's claim that the methodical disciplining of perception restores immediate contact with things, as in a second state of nature, are striking.[62]

The duality of habituation suggests that even the methodical break with mere habit—the reflexive, "critical" relationship toward mere custom and tradition so characteristic of the modern attitude—relies on cultivating a particular arsenal of routines. These routines form the antitraditionalist tradition of modernity that Descartes and Bacon undertook to establish. It is not necessary to couch this claim in the well-worn rhetoric of a great denouncement (which may have sounded fresher at a time when the mythology of reason in its recognizably Cartesian form still held greater sway). But shifting the perspective to recover the praxeological underpinnings of reason's break with tradition discloses how the new beginning that marks early modern thought must first be made in bodies—how, that is, modern and enlightened thought's break with traditions must take hold in the flesh. Descartes's reflections on attention then read less like the discussion of a technical problem in the philosophy of perception than like a micrological account of the reeducation of routines necessary to adopt a new psychophysical habitus. The meta-habit of attentiveness not only enforces the programmatic break with custom and tradition articulated in early modern philosophy. It also guarantees the absolute independence of the mind from the physical world that Descartes set out to demonstrate in his *Meditations* by acting as a kind of

---

62. See *PWD* I:218–20 (AT 8: 35–37), II:368 (AT 7:540). Habituation to the method is no more than a propaedeutic that falls away—cancels itself out—once direct contact with the truth is established. Descartes's "excuse" of the new habits as a mere propaedeutic may finally also explain one of the most salient departures of the *Meditations* from other early modern spiritual exercises: while the latter required constant, ceaseless practice, the Cartesian *Meditations* stage a once-in-a-lifetime cathartic exercise course that remains in force upon its successful completion, once the old habits are expunged and the seeds of the habit-free counter-habits of the method are firmly established in the practitioner's mind. On this latter point, see Mercer, "Methodology of the *Meditations*," 36–37.

circuit breaker: habitualized attentiveness interrupts the chain of mechanical compulsions that originates in first nature and threatens to extend into second nature—the mechanical automatisms of the mind. As I will detail in the following section, attention became the prerequisite of freedom in a defining new sense: the determination of the will by the rational mind rather than the mechanisms of habit or nature.

What are the habits of attention the Cartesian method instills? What cognitive practices do they support? And how precisely do they undergird the universalist claims of reason? Descartes's brief meditation on what can be known distinctly about material things previews the sequence of steps necessary to adopt his vision of things. The first step involves forgetting any semblance of similarity, instead conceiving of things solely in terms of quantifiable extension in three dimensions: "I distinctly imagine the extension of the quantity (or rather of the thing which is quantified) in length, breadth and depth."[63] The second step involves dividing the object under investigation into its spatiotemporal constituent parts: "I also enumerate various parts of the thing, and to these parts I assign various sizes, shapes, positions and local motions; and to the motions I assign various durations." The next step entails specifying the variables that pertain to these parts by focusing on them closely: "Not only are all these things very well known and transparent to me when regarded in this general way, but in addition there are countless particular features regarding shape, number, motion and so on, which I perceive when I give them my attention." To understand an object, one must learn to trace the schematic arrangements of parts in colorless three-dimensional space, then further direct the mind's focus to investigate the distinctive constitution of each part. The outcome of this procedure of conceiving material things as geometrical composites is the joy of an unexpected recognition: "The truth of these matters is so open and so much in harmony with my nature, that on first discovering them it seems that I am not so much learning something new as remembering what I knew before."[64] The procedure is complete when cognition becomes

---

63. *PWD* II:44 (AT 7:63).
64. *PWD* II:44 (AT 7:63–64).

anamnestic recognition—when the object is recognized as incarnating a set of quantifiable properties that, because the mind recognizes in them nothing but itself, are fully transparent.

Far from neutrally registering what is there, Cartesian habits of attention actively transcribe the world into intelligible properties so that it can be assimilated by the mind. This process effectively brings the world "home" to the mind, but at the cost of relinquishing all unguarded, seemingly immediate, yet indeed only habitual intercourse with the natural world. Anything that suggests the mind's natural familiarity or kinship with its environment must be suppressed, because the semblance of similarity between mental images and the external world—the inference from assumed resemblance to substantive correspondence—is at the root of the unexamined judgments made from mere habit. Analytical attention is therefore premised on a massive exercise of forgetting.[65] The loss incurred by attending to the world only in grayscale is outweighed by the "harmony with my nature" revealed when the world comes to be seen as geometry incarnate, manifesting nothing but eminently intelligible characteristics. The Cartesian tenet that the mind is different in substance from the physical world—that, as a thinking thing, it bears no resemblance whatsoever to extended things—paradoxically makes it possible to see the physical world as instantiating nothing but mind-like—that is, perfectly intelligible and "rational"—properties. In effect, the Cartesian method implements the same double move of distancing and approximation, of defamiliarization and refamiliarization, already encountered in Bacon, even if Descartes's rationalism offers a more elaborate philosophical justification for the procedure. The attentive habits promoted by the method excise the mind from its immediate environment by promising to bring the world much closer

---

65. In the chapter "Classifying" in *The Order of Things*, Michel Foucault seems to take the inherent "bias" of this mode of vision as an occasion to reject attention as an analytical category for explaining the novelty of seventeenth-century science: what goes on, he suggests, is much more active than merely paying attention to things themselves. I think the inverse is the case: attention, with its inbuilt connotations of foregrounding some things and backgrounding others, may be especially apt to describe the process of unseeing that founds this epistemic constellation. See Foucault, *The Order of Things*, 133.

than it was before. The method thus rests on a complex play of proximity and distance evident in Descartes's famous juxtaposition of naive and astronomical conceptions of the sun—an overdetermined example that simultaneously evokes the sun as metaphorical source of intelligibility and the challenges to perception posed by Copernican astronomy. The naive idea that the sun is small and not far away, "the idea that seems to have emanated from the sun itself from so close [or most directly, *quam proxime*] is the very one that least resembles the sun."[66] When the sun *seems* very close, it is in fact at its most distant. When we recognize through astronomical reasoning how distant it truly is—both in spatial terms and in its remoteness from naive perception—we approximate its true nature. The seemingly most proximate is the most remote, and the most remote is in fact the most proximate.

By forming the habit of focusing solely on spatiotemporal properties of extended things, one first "raises the walls"—to rephrase the idea with the camera obscura model—through which the external world is distanced as emphatically "outside" and radically different from mental interiority. Enacting the Cartesian method rests on perceiving the world as, or as if it were, its own shadow—a diminished internal image with muted colors, stripped of its power to overwhelm the mind. In this state, the world becomes susceptible to being scrutinized and decoded into entities that are as transparent to the mind as the geometrical shapes and mathematical truths it can intuit within the dark chamber when the pinhole is shut. This is the structure of the epistemic technique behind the Cartesian "mathematization of nature" and the corresponding limitation to mechanical explanations of the external world. Mechanical knowledge rests on attending to things in terms of intelligible composites of parts, which interact according to mechanical laws, like those of the clockworks or hydraulic machines that so fascinated Descartes. Knowing things becomes equivalent to identifying the

---

66. *PWD* II:27 (AT 7:39). Translation modified to follow Cress's translation. Cress's "so close" tries to preserve the ambivalence of spatial and epistemic distance; the standard translation "most directly" provided in brackets interprets it in epistemic terms.

part played by each cog in the machine until one has perfect insight into the blueprint the entity embodies.

Descartes considered the *Meditations* as an introduction to his physics, which has surprised some commentators because of the lack of scientific principles or axioms advanced by the text. What the text instead conveys are practices of attending to some features of the world (and ignoring others) to see it in a way that makes rational physics possible. If physics represents, according to Descartes's arboreal image of the sciences, the stem that rests on metaphysical first philosophy, then the epistemic habitus it conveys constitutes the root of the Cartesian tree of knowledge. This is the precise sense in which habits of attention constitute the foundation of Cartesian rationalism.

At this juncture it will be useful to recall that my focus on attention is not meant to psychologize Cartesian thought. My claim is not that Descartes ascribed a newly prominent role to an invariable mental faculty or that he was the first to discover a psychological fact about the human mind that had eluded previous thinkers. What I hope to show amounts almost to the contrary claim: that the Cartesian techniques for directing the mind's fleshless gaze critically shaped what came to be understood, from the eighteenth century onward, as the mental faculty of attention.[67] We accordingly gain a more promising perspective if we approach attention as a metaphysical rather than a psychological matter—so long as we probe metaphysics less for what it claims about a supernatural world below, behind, or above physical nature than for how it articulates distinctions that render the physical world intelligible in the first place, distinctions that are thus neither supernatural, nor physically determined, but "cultural."

Battles in the Brain over the Sovereignty of the Soul: Attention and the Will

The critical role of attention in ensuring the mind's freedom to act has recently become the subject of scholarly debate concerning the

---

67. The formulation "fleshless gaze" echoes the felicitous title of Gary Hatfield's "The Senses and the Fleshless Eye."

locus and nature of freedom in Descartes. Contrary to the long-prevailing view in Anglo-American scholarship, which locates freedom in the *doxastic* function of the will—its capacity to affirm, deny, or suspend the understanding's perceptions in acts of judgment—several commentators have recently argued that freedom should instead be located in the *attentional* function of the will. In this dissenting view, freedom lies in the will's power to shape the perceptual contents of the understanding by selectively focusing or withdrawing attention.[68] The rationale behind objections to the prevailing view stems from Descartes's consistent emphasis that judgments of the will are fully determined by the understanding, which Descartes construes in the *Meditations* as an essentially receptive faculty, in all relevant cases. When faced with clear and distinct perceptions, the will is compelled by the evidence before the mind to affirm them as true. The will is free (in the sense of indifferent) only in the face of confused and uncertain evidence, where it is imperative to neither affirm nor deny the matter at hand in order to avoid falling into error.[69] To avoid the apparent implication that the Cartesian agent lacks *self*-determination, proponents of "indirect attention voluntarism" contend that the will exercises its influence on judgments indirectly, by shaping the contents of the understanding through the will's attentional function, thereby actively determining the evidence that subsequently compels the mind's judgments.[70]

---

68. In the following, I offer a synoptic summary of common arguments advanced by scholars who ascribe "indirect attention voluntarism" to Descartes. My main reference point is Lex Newman's "Attention, Voluntarism, and Liberty"; I also take into account Youpa, "Descartes's Virtue Theory," and Ragland, "Is Descartes a Libertarian?" See also the overview in Johnson, "A Paradox of Attention." Many of the arguments advanced by supporters of "indirect attention voluntarism" in the recent debate were anticipated by Laporte, *Le rationalisme de Descartes*.

69. For Descartes's remarks on the will in the Fourth Meditation, see *PWD* II:40–41 (AT 7:57–59).

70. There are various accounts of how exactly indirect determination occurs. Newman emphasizes the ability to shift attention to consider reasons that then inform judgment. Youpa ("Descartes's Virtue Theory") and Johnson ("A Paradox of Attention") also focus on the ability to direct attention away from apparently clear perceptions to others in order to escape the former's deceptively compelling evidence. Laporte (*Le rationalisme de Descartes*) has a more expansive view of the attentional function, closer to the one I presented above, which includes all the ways

In this view, the Cartesian mind is autonomous to the degree that voluntary control over attention grants it independence from a receptive faculty that remains subject to external determination.[71] As Jean Laporte succinctly summarizes the assumption underlying this view, "we are free to the exact extent that we have control over our attention."[72]

The flipside of this correlation is that the loss of voluntary control over attention coincides with a loss of freedom. In the *Principles of Philosophy* (1644), published three years after the *Meditations*, Descartes offers two reasons "our mind is unable to keep its attention on things without some degree of difficulty and fatigue."[73] One

---

the will's direction of the mind's focus processes perceptual evidence through analysis, comparison, abstraction, and so on.

71. At stake in the context of this debate is not least the question of whether to understand Descartes as subscribing to "compatibilism" (the view that freedom is compatible with the will being determined by external causes) or "incompatibilism" (the view that causal determination is not compatible with freedom, which requires uncaused causation by the will). Locating freedom in a doxastic judgment determined by the mind's impressions suggests (although it does not necessitate) a compatibilist interpretation, whereas indirect attention voluntarism opens the possibility of an incompatibilist reading, according to which the will is undetermined in its attentional function and indirectly self-determining in its judgments. More pertinent for our purposes than the question of whether Descartes "subscribed to" compatibilism or incompatibilism is the question of how his focus on the mind's attentive capacity contributed to framing a specifically modern understanding of the compatibilism/incompatibilism dichotomy, in which the litmus test for any conception of free will becomes the question of how the immaterial mind's efficient causation interacts with the mechanical causation that governs the material world. This question would occupy, often to a breaking point, the eminent minds of modern philosophy.

72. "Nous sommes libres dans l'exacte mesure où nous disposons de notre attention" (Laporte, *Le rationalisme de Descartes*, 36). Laporte has provided the most extensive account of how attention, "that orientation of the mental gaze that presides over evidence" (cette orientation du regard mental qui préside à l'évidence, 42), serves as a prelude and condition of judgment in Descartes. At times Laporte goes as far as identifying attention with the will: "attention, the condition of evidence . . . and of that effort that results in representation . . . is nothing but another name for the will"; "l'attention, condition de l'évidence . . . et de cet effort qui aboutit à la représentation . . . n'est qu'un autre nom de la volonté" (470). Through prominent students like Paul Ricoeur, Laporte's account of attentional effort in Descartes as a condition and source of freedom influenced French postwar philosophy; see Johnson, "A Paradox of Attention," 80–82.

73. *PWD* I:220 (§73) (AT 8: 37).

is the (already familiar) force of bad habits acquired in childhood when the mind was still too preoccupied with the senses. But there is now another possible reason that does not easily respond to the Cartesian medicine of rehabituating the mind: the default of attention "may be due to the very nature that the mind has as a result of being joined to the body." This qualification helps to explain the curious juxtaposition of claims pronouncing the unrestricted freedom of attention (when considered as a function of the unrestricted will) and seemingly contrary claims acknowledging the feebleness and fragility of attention (when considered as a capacity of finite embodied minds). As pure volitions, acts of attention are absolutely within the mind's power. In souls united with bodies, however, such volitions must interact with (or at least ward off) the material brain to become effective—and can easily miscarry in the process. When trying to pay attention, in other words, the mind can will what it wills—but cannot always *do* what it wills.

Pressed by correspondents like Elisabeth of the Palatinate about the problem of mind-body interaction and the ethical dimensions of his new philosophy,[74] the later Descartes grew increasingly concerned about the tension between two sides of attention that would define discussions of the faculty in the following centuries. Shifts of attention can be internally directed by the will as well as externally triggered by the environment; the endogenous and exogenous demands on attention can also come into conflict with each other. Descartes began to reflect on such conflicts in earnest in his final philosophical treatise, *Passions of the Soul* (1649), which takes up Elisabeth's challenge to explain the affectations the mind suffers on account of its union with a body (and provide instructions for how to control them). The text reiterates that asserting control over attention is one of the ways in which the mind has indirect power over its perceptions and passions by insulating the mind against bodily stimuli: "The soul can prevent itself from hearing a slight noise or

---

74. Elisabeth opens the letter with a question that speaks of the difficulties of Descartes's conception: "Tell me please how the soul of a human being (it being only a thinking substance) can determine the bodily spirits and so bring about voluntary actions" (AT 3:661).

feeling a slight pain by attending very closely to some other thing."[75] If the stimuli hit the neural machinery with overwhelming force, however, they can wrest the mind's focus away from its intended object: the mind "cannot in the same way prevent itself from hearing thunder.... Likewise, it can easily overcome the lesser passions, but not the stronger and more violent ones."[76]

The battlefield of such struggles over the mind's focus is the pineal gland, the tiny organ in the middle of the brain through which, according to Descartes, the mind acts upon the body. When the mind chooses to attend to ideas that involve sensation or imagination (and that thus possess a neural correlate in the brain), this volition leans the gland in a specific direction to make it receptive to the relevant stimuli and keeps it arrested in this position as long as attention is sustained. Descartes's quasi-incarnation of the soul in the pineal gland thus literalizes the metaphor of "stretching toward" contained in Latin "attention" (*adtendere*; see figure 4).

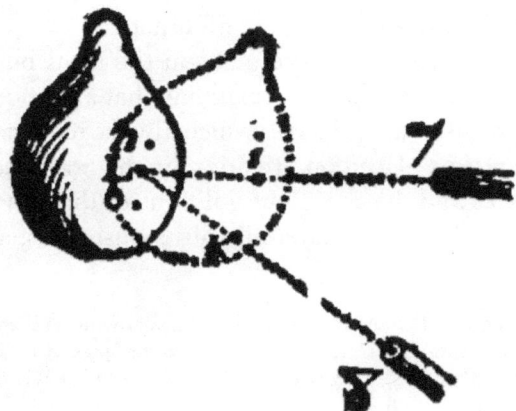

Figure 4. Schematic illustration of a leaning movement of the pineal gland from the *Treatise of Man* (Descartes, *L'homme*, 83).

---

75. *PWD* I:345 (§46).
76. *PWD* I:345 (§46).

80   Chapter 1

The same twitches of the gland commanded by the soul are also triggered, however, when an object affects the senses and impinges upon the neural apparatus from without. An illustration from Descartes, *Treatise of Man*, shows the pineal gland (h) tending toward impressions from the visual objects A-B-C, which eclipses the scent from flower D (see figure 5).[77]

Attentional conflicts arise when forceful agitations of the "animal spirits"—tiny material particles whose flow along nerve circuits conveys stimuli and controls the movements of the body machine—pull the gland in a direction different from the one intended by the mind: "The little gland in the middle of the brain can be pushed to one side by the soul and to the other side by the animal spirits . . . , and these two impulses often happen to be opposed, the stronger cancelling the effect of the weaker."[78] The gland in the brain where soul meets body thus finds itself torn between opposing forces that battle over its control. Struggles turn especially violent when the mind falls under the influence of passions that make certain things appear particularly desirable or undesirable—passions that "put blinders" on attention and attach the mind's focus excessively on the desired object at the expense of all others.[79]

Struggles over attention take place in the head but not in the mind. Descartes makes a point of claiming that attentional conflicts play out not within the soul itself, which always remains undivided, but between claims placed on attention by the body-machine's automatic reflexes and the conscious volitions of the mind, "between the force with which the [material] spirits push the gland so as to

---

77. For background on the caption to the figure showing a schematic profile of a human head, see Hatfield, "L'attention chez Descartes"; see also Lokhorst, "Descartes and the Pineal Gland"; Descartes, *The World and Other Writings*, 157–158.
78. *PWD* I:346 (AT 11:365).
79. The image is Laporte's: "Les passions ne sauraient porter atteinte à la volonté elle-même qui, comme telle, est toujours parfaite, mais elles gènent son exercice en mettant, pour ainsi dire, à l'attention des oeillères qui nous condamnent à l'ignorance" (The passions cannot undermine the will itself which, as such, is always perfect, but they hinder its exercise by putting, so to speak, blinders on attention that condemn us to ignorance) (Laporte, *Le rationalisme de Descartes*, 444). Youpa ("Descartes's Virtue Theory," 187) also observes that "a conflict between the will and the passions is . . . a struggle to govern an individual's attention."

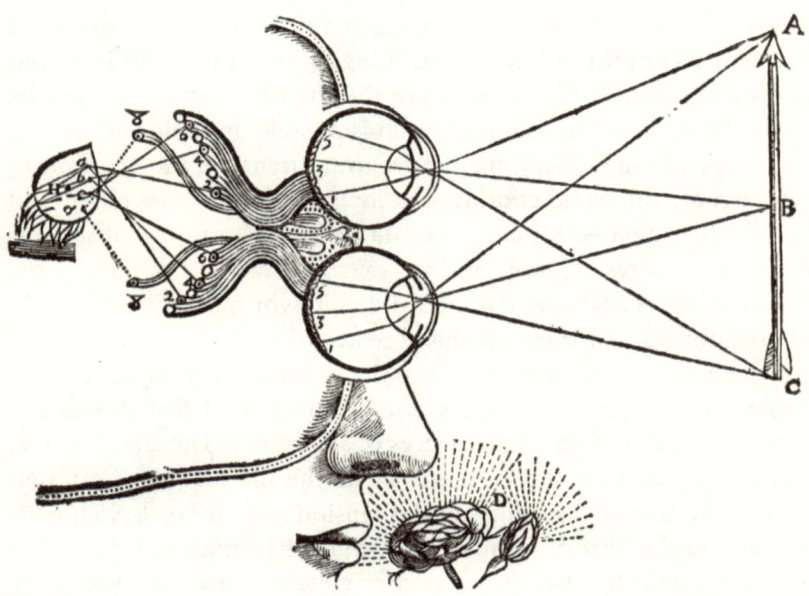

Figure 5. The neural machinery of attention and perception in Descartes (*L'homme*, 85). Visual object A-B-C creates an inverted image on the retina (5-3-1), which stimulates nerve fibers in tubes extending from the back of the eyes. By a quasi-hydraulic mechanism, "animal spirits" (tiny fluid particles) rush toward pores (6-4-2) opened by the stimulation of the nerves, creating a low-pressure pattern a-b-c on the pineal gland. This pattern of spirits flowing from the pineal gland, the seat of the common sense, constitutes the (unified and rectified) "material idea" of the external object, which causes a corresponding affectation (mental image) in a mind closely associated with the gland. The rush of animal spirits toward the pores opened by stimulations of the visual nerves makes the gland lean in their direction and facilitates the continuous flow of spirits toward them, drowning out olfactory sensations from flower D traveling through the nostrils. This is Descartes's neurological explanation of why "one cannot be very attentive to several things at the same time." (Transposed to the camera obscura model, the pineal gland corresponds to the mental canvas on which impressions of the external world are projected. The physical aspect of attention in Descartes is analogous to an adjustment of the mental canvas so that it receives certain impressions more readily and facilitates their uptake by the mind.)

cause the soul to desire something, and the force with which the soul, by its volition to avoid this thing, pushes the gland in a contrary direction."[80] The mind is not the site of the struggles, but its distinctness from the material brain is at stake in their outcome. If the will continues losing the battles over attention, the mechanism of the material world continues uninterrupted into the immaterial mind, corroding—*de facto* if not *de jure*—the ontological separation between *res cogitans* and *res extensa*. In *The Passions of the Soul* Descartes acknowledges the affects in which the mind becomes unfree not least to ward off this threat.

The rift between attention's "spiritual, voluntary" aspect and its "material, involuntary" aspect would come to define discourses, practices, and subjective experiences of attention in Descartes's wake, even up to present contexts. It will be the fate of post-Cartesian subjects to endure discharges of this tension in their heads. In the literature on the history attention, one thus often finds the claim that Descartes is the first to acknowledge or conceptualize the involuntary side of attention.[81] Things are not this straightforward. It is only the elevation of control over attention into the guardian of the mind's independence that accentuates whatever escapes this control as a distinct class. In the wake of Descartes, a range of phenomena whose only commonality is that they threaten the will's sovereignty over attention emerges as constituting "attention's involuntary side"—including attentional shifts caused by the amplitude of sensory stimuli, distractions of attention by the appeal of non-normative objects of desire, the dispersal of attention over so many things that none of them emerge into distinct focus, the "tunnel vision" effected by the passions, and so on. Does the Cartesian exaltation of voluntary attention therefore *produce* attention's involuntary side? This once refreshingly counter-intuitive claim would, in turn, imply a discursive idealism for which symbolic distinctions generate, without remainder, the reality that corresponds to them. Perhaps involuntary attention is neither a psychological or anthropological constant nor merely the effect of the text of culture inscribing itself in bodies. If discourses

---

80. *PWD* I:346.
81. See, for example, Waldenfels, *Phänomenologie der Aufmerksamkeit*, 20–21.

indeed produce their own pathologies, they do not do so simply in the way one encircles a space of normativity as if on a blank sheet of paper, simultaneously excluding and co-creating a non-normative side. The unintended side effects produced by administering medication may offer a more felicitous analogy. The attempt to produce a specific psychophysiological outcome through the addition of an extraneous substance brings about effects that are not simply reducible to the intended outcome or its immediate opposite. Marking the distinctions of culture in minds and bodies is possible only by producing tears in a fabric that is no neutral medium of inscription. And yet it is only through practices that impose structure on human minds and bodies that the limits of their malleability show up. These limits do not precede the imposition of structure as a stable subtext of nature but emerge as "natural"—as resisting and subverting normative symbolic formations—only in the very process of their shaping.

Training the Body

Descartes acknowledges that the mind cannot always win attentional struggles by mustering an overwhelming force of will. As in the example above, a mental effort to redirect attention can overcome slighter passions and weaker sensory stimuli. Yet when the agitations of the animal spirits grow more violent, the force exerted by the will is no match for the power with which the passions strike the mind. Conceding defeat in direct confrontations, however, is only the opening move of a strategy to win the war against the passions over the long run.[82] Once excited, oncoming passions overrun even the strongest mind's defenses. It is, however, possible to suppress their excitement in the first place by reprogramming, by means of habit (*par habitude*), the brain's reflex-like responses to stimuli that evoke passions and capture the mind's focus.[83]

The reference to habit may suggest that Descartes reverts to the prescriptions of the method to fortify and reinvigorate the mind's

---

82. *PWD* I:348 (§50) (AT 11, 368).
83. *PWD* I:348 (§50) (AT 11, 368–69).

attention through exercise. But the training program proposed here does not directly target attention itself; instead it targets the neural processes that thwart the mind's ability to control attention.[84] In the *Meditations*, the domain of habit was restricted to the mind's contribution to perception, an activity Descartes exposed as malleable—as susceptible to rehabituation—because its apparent automatisms were truly attributable not to nature but to fossilized habits that could be unlearned and reshaped. The habituation program proposed in the *Passions*, by contrast, marks a change of strategy—a concession, perhaps, that in order for the mental habits of attention to effectively take root, habituation must intervene at a deeper level, shaping bodily responses that were previously disregarded as mere nature.

The new training program targets precisely the first two sensory stages of perception outlined in the *Meditations* and the *Replies*: the neural mechanisms that convey stimuli in the brain and the immediate sensations triggered in the mind through cerebral movements. The first strategy to shield the mind from the passions involves rewiring the connections between physical stirrings of the pineal gland and the mental content evoked on their account—that is, "join[ing] them to others through habit."[85] Descartes's overdetermined example—overdetermined not least because the gland itself incarnates linguistic metaphors of mental functions—is the way language embodies meaning in letters and sounds. "By nature," physical manifestations of spoken or written words only trigger bare sensations of sounds or visual shapes (the way one hears an unfamiliar foreign language or sees a foreign writing system). On account of a profound rehabituation, however, they directly evoke the associated meaning in the mind.[86] The arbitrary union of physical characteristics and mental content in linguistic signs proves that it is possible, by force of habit, to shape how the little organ in the brain performs mind-body union, until physical affectations of the brain that used to spill over into passions of the soul are kept at bay. The main emphasis

---

84. *PWD* I:348 (AT 11, 368).
85. *PWD* I:348 (§50) (AT 11, 368–69).
86. *PWD* I:348 (§50) (AT 11, 369).

of the proposed training program, however, lies on interventions at the even earlier stage of nervous system responses to external stimuli. Again, in place of a detailed explanation Descartes provides an example, one that is equally suggestive. Hunting dogs, such as setters, undergo training that goes against their natural instincts: they are taught to freeze instead of chase upon encountering prey, and then to run toward the prey and retrieve it upon hearing gunfire, a stimulus from which they would naturally run. Dogs, as Descartes is quick to concede, do not experience passions in the strict sense because they lack the requisite souls; but they do exhibit the same stirrings of the animal spirits and the activations of kinetic energy that manifest as passions when a soul inhabits the machine. What the example of the hunting dog demonstrates is that it is possible to dissociate and reassign the natural linkages between neural mechanisms that convey external stimuli in the brain and mechanisms that coordinate the body-machine's responses to those stimuli.[87] By reprogramming responses to stimuli as one trains a dog's instinctive reflexes, it is possible to defuse and control the involuntary claims on attention that result from violent stirrings of the body. "Even those who have the weakest souls," Descartes writes, "could acquire absolute mastery over all their passions if we [*on*] employed sufficient ingenuity in training [*dresser*] and guiding them."[88]

This training program still benefits the mind and its freedom, but it marks a fundamental departure from all previous traditions of spiritual exercise, even more radical than their adaptation in the meditative exercises that precede the method. Rather than a mind or soul (understood to embrace sensitive as well as intellectual aspects) shaping *itself* through spiritual exercises, the mind here trains the body's neurophysiology the way one trains a dog. Training, in this case, is no longer reflexive but instrumental, with trainer and trainee divided between different parts of the person: one shouts

---

87. "It is ... useful to note that although the movements ... which represent certain objects to the soul are naturally joined to the movements which produce certain passions in it, yet through habit the former can be separated from the latter and joined to others which are very different" (*PWD* I:348 [§50] [AT 11: 369]).

88. *PWD* I:348 (§50) (AT 11: 370).

commands and wields carrot and stick, the other merely suffers the training.[89] (The relationship between moral expert instructor and apprentice referenced in the quote above is virtually already that between a person's mind and body.) The significance of individual acts of exercise changes as well. Whereas in spiritual exercises, every exercise marks progress toward the goal as an instantiation of the state to be achieved—just as attentive performances of perception are simultaneously the means and end of fortifying attention—there is no inherent relationship between exercise and outcome in the mind's conditioning of the body. The mind trains the body by whatever means are effective. In the precise sense of power *qua* the ability to achieve an effect, sovereignty over attention rests on an intrapersonal power relationship between mind and body. Conditioning the body—or rather, the aspects of perception Descartes *relegates* to the body on account of their intimate ties with external stimuli—is the pragmatic condition of possibility for attentional control. Only once this has been achieved can the mind effectively claim to be fully detached from a physical world emphatically outside and successfully perform the disciplined attention behind the new vision of the world.

Wonder and the Education of Attention

The claim that the mind's freedom depends on its control over the body raises a problem that will recur in various Enlightenment accounts of self-education and self-formation: How does the agency of rational control first come into being, if its constitution depends on carrying out an operation that presupposes its prior existence? How does the rational mind, in other words, pull itself up by its own bootstraps? The answer suggested in *Passions of the Soul* is that the reformation of attention can draw on, and begin with, a natural disposition toward wonder (*admiration*), defined as a "sudden surprise of the soul which brings it to consider with attention the

---

89. John Cottingham's lucid article "Philosophy and Self-Improvement" has sensitized me to the importance of these shifts.

objects that seem to it unusual or extraordinary."[90] As noted in the introduction, wonder occupies a unique place in Descartes's theory of the passions because it facilitates the transition from passive affectedness to active mental scrutiny. The neural response to novelty unleashes the animal spirits to automatically perform the work of representing objects impartially and distinctly. It thus models and jump-starts the active attention the mind must learn to initiate from within.[91] This transition from involuntary to voluntary attention also has an ontogenetic component: Although it is "good to be born with some inclination to wonder," eventually we "must attempt to free ourselves from this inclination as much as possible" and replace it with "that special state of reflection and attention which our will can always impose upon our understanding when we judge the matter before us to be worth serious consideration."[92] Achieving attentional control by converting what begins as an involuntary response into a deliberate activity is the pragmatic precondition for becoming a fully rational adult.[93]

As a *passion* that awakens the soul's *activity*, wonder assumes a role analogous to that of beauty in Platonic and Neoplatonic traditions, serving as a sensory appearance that leads the soul toward intellectual contemplation. It is easy to see that this characterization of wonder would be attractive to poets (see chapter 3). But wonder also played an outsized role in incorporating the attentive habitus of the "preternatural" sciences discussed above. The devices for educating scientific attention were philosophically formalized in Nicolas Malebranche's *The Search after Truth* (1674), where Malebranche systematically elaborated Cartesian motifs concerning attention. Among other aspects, Malebranche explicates the connection between fallibility of human attention and the compensatory need for philosophical method, produces a detailed account of attention's role in the clarification of ideas, and elaborates on the connection between

---

90. *PWD* I:353 (§70) (AT 11, 380).
91. Unlike all other passions, wonder also does not distort things as they appear through the lens of a particular desire but represents them as they are.
92. *PWD* I:355 (§76).
93. On the epistemic passion of wonder in this context, see Daston and Park, *Wonders*, 255–328.

voluntary control over attention and human freedom.[94] In what will prove to be a generalizable correlation, however, the higher the importance ascribed to attention in epistemic and ethical matters, the more vulnerable and susceptible attention becomes to distraction. Where Descartes had still thought that a mental effort would be capable of conquering the slighter sensations and passions, Malebranche tends to voice his exasperation: even "the buzzing of a fly, or some other slight noise . . . in spite of our resistance is capable of preventing us from thinking about the loftiest abstract truths."[95] Again Malebranche relies on wonder to come to the "aid" or "assistance" of an otherwise fragile attention:

> Nothing is more difficult than applying oneself for any length of time to something that fails to excite our wonder, since then the animal spirits are not so easily led into those parts of the brain necessary to represent it. It is easily said that we should be attentive; our attention is not forthcoming, or at least not for any length of time, however we may be convinced in the abstract (which in no way agitates the spirits) that the thing deserves our attention. We must trick our imagination in order to stir our spirits, and we must represent the subject we wish to think about in a novel way so that an impulse of wonder might be excited in us.[96]

The predilection of involuntary attention for the marvelous thus functions like a lure that makes the brain do the work required in the pursuit of scientific knowledge. Self-affectation with wonder is the carrot to the stick of the Cartesian disciplining of attention: tricking oneself into imagining things as marvelous makes the animal spirits flow in sync with the demands of the Cartesian method. Attention is here revealed as a psychophysical technology of the self

---

94. For these motifs, see Malebranche, *The Search after Truth*, 79–81, 212–16, 252–53, 410–19, 437–39. Malebranche explicitly identifies analysis (or attention to parts) as the source of mental clarity. As discussed in chapter 2, this identification would become central to German eighteenth-century philosophy.

95. Malebranche, *The Search after Truth*, 213.

96. Malebranche, *The Search after Truth*, 385–86. Translation of the beginning of the second sentence altered to convey the moment of futile self-command suggested in Malebranche's "On a beau dire que nous soyons attentifs, nous ne pouvons pas l'être (*sic*)" (Malebranche, *Recherche de la vérité*, 2:494). On wonder in Malebranche, see also Daston, *Kurze Geschichte*, 22.

that relies on harnessing and shaping the body to produce a properly focused mind.

In Conclusion: The Cartesian Subject

This chapter began with the observation that attention received a new direction in seventeenth-century science, toward a natural world that began to attract such attention in its newly prized curiosity and strangeness, but also revealed itself as increasingly curious and strange under the gaze of a sharply focused attention. In his effort to explicate the implicit logic governing the new mode of scientific inquiry, Bacon revealed in his *New Organon* that the reorientation of attention was premised on—and provided further evidence for—a fundamental incongruence between the inquiring mind and the world. A first characterization gleaned from Bacon's *New Organon* was that attention served as an *intermediary* between mind and world, a technique of methodical scrutiny capable of connecting the mind to a world that does not offer itself naturally to epistemic inquiry.

Compared with the worldly orientation of scientific attention, the Cartesian withdrawal into an interior space of meditation may look like a regression to an earlier model of spiritual exercise, one that promoted retracting attention from the world and gathering it into the ideal unity of a spiritual self directed toward transcendence. Empiricist enemies of Descartes from the eighteenth century onward would denounce Descartes along these lines as a thinker who philosophized with his eyes closed. To these critics Descartes was a philosophical dreamer or "spirit-seer" (as Kant denounced one-sided rationalism) who remained blind to the phenomena of the empirical world. This will have been a misunderstanding. In Descartes the withdrawal of attention from the world into an interior space instead serves to clarify the conditions under which experience can serve as the basis for the new "empirical" sciences in the first place. Blocking out the world and refocusing attention to the mind's own operations is a necessary step to separate out—and demonstrate the priority of—the mind's own contribution to perception and cognition, a contribution that otherwise remains shrouded in the apparent obviousness and immediacy of phenomena. Only an attention idling in abstraction from all given content reveals what properly and undoubtedly "belongs" to the mind alone, making it possible to establish an inventory of the mind's secure possessions. Descartes's redescription of "sensing" as a form of "attending" (*animadvertere, attendere*), in which the mind belongs fully to itself even when it appears to be absorbed in an object, is exemplary of Descartes's new conception of cognition and perception as processes that are conditioned by the mind's own operations. Ultimately the goal of the Cartesian meditative exercises is thus neither introspective, directed toward the mind's interiority, nor vertical, directed toward transcendence. Instead the goal is horizontal, directed toward an outside world that must now reveal itself in the light of the mind's self-controlled attention. With this shift Descartes explains how even a world devoid of inherent form and structure—a world without Aristotelean substantial forms that "in-form" the mind via the senses—can nevertheless be known, and can in fact be known with certainty for the first time (something that remained obscure in Bacon's belief that things would leap into place if collected in the right manner): it is under the condition that any reference to the external world is premised on a transparent self-reference. The condition for knowing a world that is of a categorically different ontological order than the mind—the mechanism through which attention can function as an intermediary between mind and world—is the subordination of all relations to the world to a self-relation.

Descartes acknowledges that attending to the world in this peculiarly self-aware manner takes some getting used to. Yet in a scheme that will become foundational to the claims of modern reason, he portrays the process of becoming accustomed to the new way of relating to the world as the recovery of a natural disposition. Here, a suspicious reading detects or posits a systematic repression in the Cartesian program. The principal symptom of this repression is the threat of involuntary attention, which emerges in direct proportion to the importance placed on the will's ability to remain in full possession of itself when directing the mind's focus. This emergent threat is upstream from the "classical" threats to the dominion of reason long identified in Enlightenment anthropology. That imagination produces images even against one's will, and the fact that the senses impinge upon the mind is not in itself a problem. Imagination and the senses become dangerous only inasmuch as they capture the mind's focus and thus undermine its self-governance. The mind's self-relation can serve as the principle of action and knowledge only as long as attention remains under voluntary control. The cost of fending off the threat posed by involuntary distractions of attention to secure the constitutive self-relation of the mind is a peculiar kind of training, of *dressage*, which relegates all interactions with the environment not premised on self-awareness—all interactions that occur "instinctively"—to the level of the body. Through this repression—identical to the intellectual-historical narrowing and transformation of the Scholastic *animus* to the Cartesian *mens*—the body emerges in its sharp opposition to a mind defined by self-awareness and self-consciousness. The technical term developed in the philosophy of the following century for an entity that acts and perceives through a constitutive self-relation is "subject." It is to this subject of attention—to attention's role in the formation of the subject—that we will turn our own attention in chapter 2.

2

SUBJECT BEFORE THE AUTONOMOUS SUBJECT

Disciplines of Attention in the German Eighteenth Century

The German word *Aufmerksamkeit* acquired its current meaning as the capacity for selectively focusing the mind during the early eighteenth century, a period when the German language was undergoing a series of rapid shifts. The word itself predates the eighteenth century but previously appeared predominantly in religious contexts, where it evoked the vigilance required in prayer and spiritual exercise.[1] This changed when Aufmerksamkeit became estab-

---

1. Typical collocations in these contexts include "Andacht und Aufmer(c)ksamkeit" (devotion and attentiveness) and "Wach(t)samkeit und Aufmer(c)samkeit" (wakefulness and attentiveness), which occur in seventeenth-century prayer booklets and Jesuit treatises on the Christian way of life and the proper conduct of spiritual exercises, often in connection with exhortations to empty the mind of material things; compare Saint-Jure, *Erkandtnuß und Liebe Deß Sohns GOttes*, 585; Du-Cambout de Pontchâteau, *Der Jesuiten Christenthumb*, 186; Arias, *Des unerschöpffter Schatzes*, 3:576. The early eighteenth-century French-German *Grand dictionaire royal* [sic] provides "Andacht, Aufmercksamkeit" as German equivalents of French *attention*, emphasizing the receptive connotation of an earlier sense of French *atten-*

lished as the loan translation of the Latin and French philosophical term *attentio(n)*, which in turn had acquired new significance with the spread of Cartesian philosophy and had similarly begun to shift from designating an attitude of expectant vigilance to designating the mind's deliberate focus on details in the service of clear and distinct knowledge.[2] Establishing *Aufmerksamkeit* as the standard German word for attention was largely the work of a single author, the philosopher Christian Wolff (1679–1754). While occasional claims in the literature that Wolff "introduced" the word into the German language are exaggerated, Wolff's preference for the term in textbooks such as his immensely influential *German Metaphysics* (1719) ensured that Aufmerksamkeit prevailed over other contenders like *Auffmerckung, Beachtung*, or *Achtsamkeit* as the loan translation of Latin *attentio* and its cognates.[3]

Wolff's formative influence on an emerging German philosophical terminology was not unique to attention; and especially in the

---

tion and the close association between *Aufmerksamkeit* and a state of devotional receptivity at the time (Pomey, *Le grand dictionaire royal*, 69).

2. In this transfer from religious contemplation to epistemic contexts, the early modern history of the word *Aufmerksamkeit* parallels the career of both Latin *observatio* and German *Beobachtung*, whose meanings similarly shifted around this time from religious observance to active observation, understood as a tool for the discovery and surveillance of inner and outer worlds. From vigilance and observance to observation and attention, both sets of terms trace a trajectory from spiritual exercises to practices of regulating perception. For the shift from observation and observance, see Daston and Lunbeck's introduction to their *Histories of Scientific Observation*, 1–10, and esp. Katharine Park's contribution to the volume, "Observation in the Margins," 15–44.

3. The first texts that began to reflect on attention in the vernacular, such as Christian Thomasius's 1691 *Einleitung zu der Vernunfft-Lehre* (Introduction to logic), still marked the absence of a German term by using the loanword *attention*, set off in Latin script against the Fraktur typeface of the German text. Five years later, in his 1696 textbook on ethics, Thomasius experiments with *Auffmerckung* and *Aufmercksamkeit* as possible German equivalents. In the same context, Reimarus preferred the term *Beachtung*; Mendelssohn preferred *Achtsamkeit* as late as the middle of the eighteenth century. For the (erroneous) claim that Wolff introduced the term *Aufmerksamkeit* into the German language, see, for instance, the editors' preface to Baisch, Degen, and Lüdtke, *Wie gebannt*, 9. See Wolff, *Vernünfftige Gedancken von Gott, der Welt und der Seele des Menschen, auch allen Dingen überhaupt* (hereafter cited by the common shorthand *German Metaphysics*), 149–51 (§§268–71).

case of attention, it was not merely terminological.[4] In a series of German and Latin textbooks published from the 1720s to the 1740s, Wolff aimed to establish secure foundations for all philosophical subdisciplines—and indeed, all fields of scholarship—by systematizing them along the model of mathematical demonstrations, thereby raising several fields of knowledge, including jurisprudence, sociology, and psychology, to the status of sciences for the first time. His comprehensive system effectively functioned as a one-man encyclopedia and common frame of reference for intellectual debates in Germany from around the 1720s up through Kant's time (with Kant famously developing his critical philosophy by grappling with the Wolffian approach he had previously embraced). The sweeping influence of Wolff's philosophy on the intellectual landscape of eighteenth-century Germany can be gauged by the fact that even opponents (such as Crusius) and dissenting successors (such as Baumgarten) were compelled to formulate their objections and revisions within the Wolffian framework, on the very intellectual terrain he had cleared.

In this chapter I take the first psychological account of attention in Wolff's *Psychologia empirica* (Empirical psychology; 1732) as a springboard for exploring the place of attention in German eighteenth-century thought and culture. The influence of Wolff's treatise on what came to be understood as attention in Germany and beyond can hardly by overestimated: roughly half of the entry on "attention" in Diderot and d'Alembert's *Encyclopédie*, for instance, is an unacknowledged paraphrase of Wolff's chapter on attention; and Wolff's doctrines continued to influence the late nineteenth-century psychologies of attention of, for instance, Wilhelm Wundt and William James.[5] The centerpiece of this chapter is therefore a close read-

---

4. Other German concepts that Wolf coined or defined philosophically include *Bewusstsein, Bedeutung, Verständnis, Vorstellung, an sich*, and such—terms that would form the matrix of German philosophical terminology and would also seep into ordinary language.

5. See Yvon and Formey, "Attention." A comparison of the encyclopedia entry with Wolff's chapter shows that at least 40 percent of the entry consists of unmarked translation and paraphrase from Wolff. James and Wundt quote Wolff prominently; see, for example, James, *The Principles of Psychology*, 1:409.

ing of Wolff's theory as a blueprint of the modern faculty of attention. Against the backdrop of Wolff's conception, I then briefly survey three strands of eighteenth-century thought to show how, in each one, attention came to define a new vision of the subject. In eighteenth-century pedagogy, reformers such as J. B. Basedow and J. H. Campe saw the improvement of attention as the bedrock of all further education. Read as the theoretical superstructure of emerging institutions for public education, this pedagogical discourse conceived of schools as sites for retraining minds to turn them into attentive subjects. In a philosophical anthropology pioneered by Johann Gottfried Herder, voluntary attention became the defining feature of human freedom and language in contrast with nonrational animals. In the moral philosophy of Wolff and the young Friedrich Schiller, finally, the capacity for attentive self-monitoring was considered a precondition of self-determined action. In critical dialogue with Foucault's account of discipline, I explore in this chapter what happens "before" the autonomous subject, in two senses: as the prehistory to Kant's ideal of individual autonomy and as its pragmatic prerequisite or foundation.

If Wolff's foundational psychology of attention has almost entirely been overlooked by historians of attention, this is in part owing to Wolff's switch from German to Latin in later works like the *Psychologia empirica*, ensuring an international readership in the eighteenth-century Republic of Letters but raising significant barriers to modern reception of the work.[6] In its own time, however, Wolff's psychology was pervasively influential: its architecture of the mind provided the framework in which the disciplines of psychology, anthropology, and aesthetics took shape in eighteenth-century Germany. Its influence even continued to be felt in late eighteenth-century works that departed from the Wolffian paradigm, such as Immanuel Kant's anthropology and Karl Philipp Moritz's journal on *Erfahrungsseelenkunde* (Empirical psychology; 1783–93).[7] The new

---

6. One important exception is Hatfield, "Attention in Early Scientific Psychology," 5–7. On the reception of the work, see Hinske, "Wolffs empirische Psychologie," 99. For the foundational importance of Wolff's work in the history of modern psychology, see Vidal, *Sciences of the Soul*, 89–95.

7. See Hinske, "Wolffs empirische Psychologie."

vision of the mind Wolff developed also radiated beyond German lands. His *Psychology empirica* was translated into French and, as noted above, prominently reflected in the *Encyclopedia*.⁸ It is necessary to recall the larger-than-life stature Wolff enjoyed for much of the eighteenth century because histories of German thought long diminished him to something of a dwarf on the shoulders of the giant Leibniz. (This is also why, in this chapter, I read Wolff without extensive references to Leibniz and instead reserve the discussion of Leibniz for the chapter 4, on Baumgarten, who revived certain Leibnizian motifs in opposition to Wolff.) The long-standing disparagement of Wolff as an unoriginal systematizer of Leibniz and philosophical pedant has only recently been challenged, mostly by scholars working outside of Germany.⁹ Undoubtedly, Wolff was not the innovator in metaphysics Leibniz was and, having once been a protégé and correspondent of Leibniz, he clearly adopted fundamental Leibnizian principles that defined his philosophical outlook. His meticulous writing style, which flies in the face of post-Romantic sensibilities, hardly helps his case. Yet the hostile affect that traditionally colors treatments of Wolff is perhaps also explained by the fact that Wolff's role as an innovator of German philosophical language is incompatible with the founding myth of the spontaneous self-generation of the German *Geist* in the final decades of the eighteenth century.

---

8. For Wolff's forgotten presence in the *Encyclopédie*, see Carboncini, "L'Encylopédie et Christian Wolff," and Schwaiger, "Wolff, Christian (Von)" (neither of which mentions his psychology of attention). The prominent presence of Wolff in the *Encyclopédie* was long eclipsed by Voltaire's later ambivalence toward Wolff and d'Alembert's hostility to Wolffian rationalism. Although Wolff's influence was most pronounced in German-speaking lands—by the middle of the century, Wolffians occupied prominent positions not only in most universities but also in state bureaucracies and Protestant as well as Catholic seminaries—it extended across eighteenth-century Europe. As a member of all major European learned societies, including the Royal Society and the Académie royal des sciences, Wolff was widely read in Italy, England, and the Netherlands; and students who had flocked to Marburg to study with Wolff were instrumental in spreading the new style of enlightened thinking to Eastern European countries and to Russia. Among the *philosophes*, Wolff's reputation was made by Voltaire's account of the former's expulsion from Halle after disputes with Pietists who objected to his favorable portrayal of Confucianism as a source of ethical perfection independent of divine revelation.

9. See the authors collected in Theis and Aichele, *Handbuch Christian Wolff*.

In trying to shed some light on the neglected prehistory of the German spirit, I will emphasize an aspect of Wolff's philosophy that has received little notice so far. A close reading of Wolff's philosophical psychology of attention shows that the alleged dogmatic metaphysician and one-sided rationalist was also a surprisingly pragmatic thinker, someone for whom discussions of cognitive faculties and metaphysical propositions were inseparable from precepts on the proper way to lead one's life. As my readings show, this pragmatism applies not only to Wolff's well-known claim that philosophy and science ultimately have an ethical end because knowledge of the good translates to a virtuous life. More important than such questions of explicit norms are the dietetic precepts on how to exercise the mind and control the body, which appear side-by-side with abstract metaphysical and metacognitive deductions. The effect of this writing is (what appears to be) a strange confusion of registers or genres, with passages that read like excerpts from an eighteenth-century self-help book on how to steady one's focus and avoid distraction interspersed with abstract claims about the nature of the mind and its cognitive faculties. Read from Kant backward, Wolff's remarks on attention look like a series of outrageous category mistakes between merely empirical or "anthropological" claims and quasi-transcendental claims. When reading from Wolff forward, however, we discover that his psychology of attention sheds light on some of the empirical and pragmatic conditions of the transcendental subject. Kant would banish such considerations to his anthropological writings, and they dropped out of the picture completely (or were, rather, pushed below the surface) in Idealist concepts of the self-generating spirit following Kant. As an outlook at the conclusion of this chapter suggests, however, the connection between the regulation of attention and the formation of the self would continue to haunt classical German philosophy.

Attention to Attention: Wolff's Concept of Psychology as a Science

Christian Wolff's pioneering science of the soul, elaborated in his complementary *Psychologia empirica* (Empirical psychology; 1732) and *Psychologia rationalis* (Rational psychology; 1734), hinges on the analogy between psychic and physical mechanics.[10] The analogy rests on the suggestive parallelism between Leibniz's explanation of changes in the mind as the expression of *vis repraesentativa* (a single "force" or power of representing) and the Newtonian concept of force (the principle that explains change in the motion of bodies). Just as physical mechanics can be explained by the laws of motion, the workings of mental phenomena can be described as the expression of a single force subject to determinate laws.[11] By conceptualizing the study of the soul as a "physics of the mind," Wolff gave to the term "psychology"—which previously designated metaphysical treatises on the nature and immortality of the soul—an influential new meaning: a science that aspired to a quantitative, observational, and lawlike explanation of mental phenomena.[12]

In prolegomena to his psychological works and to his philosophical system as a whole, Wolff justifies his new, scientific approach to understanding the mind by proposing that phenomena in the mind can be explained like physical ones in quantitative—mathematical—terms. Psychology, he suggests, should therefore have distinct "empirical" and "rational" parts just as physics had separate "experimental" and "dogmatic" branches at the time.[13] Like experimental physics,

---

10. This point is demonstrated compellingly in Blackwell, "Wolff's Doctrine of the Soul," 347. See a similar suggestion in Robert Richards's commentary to his translation of "Prolegomena to Empirical and Rational Psychology," 235n5.

11. The parallelism between the two senses of force (*vis*) is made explicit in the *Psychologia rationalis*: "Indeed, when the explanation [*ratio*] of corporeal phenomena is given from their structure, the explanation must also include the laws of motion; so likewise the laws of sensation, imagination, intellection, and appetition must be referred to when the explanation for those things which pertain to the soul is given from the force of representing the universe." See Wolff, *Psychologia rationalis*, 450 (§529); rendered in Richards's translation in "Prolegomena to Empirical and Rational Psychology," 235n5.

12. On Wolff's pioneering redefinition of the word "psychology" and his role as a founding figure of modern psychological science, see Vidal, *Sciences of the Soul*; Hinske, "Wolffs empirische Psychologie"; Rumore, "Empirical Psychology"; and Hatfield, "Attention in Early Scientific Psychology."

13. Wolff explicitly likens psychology to physics in *Psychologia empirica*, 3–4 (§§4–5), as well as in *Psychologia rationalis*, 7 (§4). He parallels the *quantifiability* of mental as well as physical phenomena at the heart of this comparison in his general introduction to his philosophical system in his *Philosophia rationalis, sive, Log-*

empirical psychology collects data through observation and experiment while formulating preliminary generalizations, regularities, and principles on this basis.[14] *Rational* psychology, in turn, proceeds like dogmatic physics in explicating the universal laws behind the findings of empirical psychology in the form of deductive demonstrations. The interaction between the two branches of psychology exemplifies what Wolff called the *connubium* (intermarriage) between experience and reason: empirical psychology provides the experiential foundation of rational deductions as well as a posteriori corroboration of the deductive conclusions reached by rational psychology. Rational psychology, in turn, articulates the findings of empirical psychology in the deductive form most adequate to the ideal of a science.[15] Historian of science Robert J. Richards summarizes: "Empirical psychology shows *that* something is true of the soul, and rational psychology explains *why* it is true."[16] Rational psychology is therefore superior with regard to the *form* of explanation, but empirical psychology takes priority with regard to its *content*: if the two come into conflict, Wolff emphasizes, rational psychology must yield because empirical psychology's closer contacts with facts of experience renders it more certain than the former, whose long demonstrations are liable to error.[17] At least according to its guiding ideal, Wolff's concept of how empirical and rational moments interact in psychological science is not too distant from the hypothetico-deductive model often advanced to describe the modern scientific

---

ica, 6–7 (§§13–14); translated by Blackwell as *Preliminary Discourse on Philosophy in General*, 8–9.

14. The bifurcation of psychology echoes the classical *historia/scientia* distinction but is not identical with it: As outlined in the *Preliminary Discourse*, Wolff emphasizes "mathematical" (quantitative) modes of explanation that cut across the traditional dichotomy between "historical" (factual) and "scientific" (certain philosophical) knowledge.

15. As Wolff explains, empirical psychology supplies principles (*principia suppeditat*) to rational psychology and serves to examine and confirm (*examinandies & confirmandis*) the results of its deductive reasoning, while rational psychology makes the teachings of empirical psychology more fully and correctly intelligible (*plenius ac rectius intelliguntur*). Wolff, *Psychologia empirica*, 3 (§§4–5); Wolff, *Psychologia rationalis*, 6 (§7).

16. See Richards's commentary in "Christian Wolff's Prolegomena," 238n14.

17. Wolff, *Psychologia empirica*, 34 (§5).

method: empirical investigation suggests hypotheses whose rational implications are elaborated and then, in turn, tested through observations and experiments. The risk of decontextualization notwithstanding, these resonances do suggest how little Wolff's project resembles the widespread caricature of a rationalistic attempt to derive explanations of mental phenomena from some a priori concept of the nature of the soul.

Critically for our purposes, attention reappears like a *mise en abyme* at all levels of the new psychological science. It is not merely a central subject of the new science but shapes Wolff's very conception of what psychological inquiry is and how it proceeds.

Attention is, first of all, Wolff's paradigmatic example of a mental phenomenon susceptible to quantitative treatment. In his *Preliminary Discourse on Philosophy in General* (the introduction to the Latin version of his philosophical system), Wolff explains that one can have quantitative or mathematical knowledge of all things that are finite and can therefore be measured by degrees (such as the temperature of air, or the velocity of a planet at a determinate place in its orbit). To demonstrate that things are no different in the psychic realm, Wolff invokes the finite human capacity for attention. It, too, exhibits definite degrees in different people: some people's attention is greater, others' is smaller; some people can sustain attention for longer, others for shorter periods of time. The notion that attention can be understood as a "limited reservoir," a definite psychic quantity, thus vouches for the transferability of a methodology based on measurement (of things like temperature) and calculation (of things like the speed of planetary movement) to the sphere of the mind.[18] The claim that attention can be quantified not only enables Wolff's scientific treatment of attention but also underpins his science of psychology as a whole.

At the methodological level, attention explains the mode of interaction between empirical and rational psychology. In psychological inquiry as Wolff conceives of it, this exchange plays out between the *receptive* and the *actively directed* poles of the psychological observer's attention. The receptive side of attention, its ability to simply take note of what is the case, defines what Wolff

---

18. For this avenue of argument, see Wolff, *Preliminary Discourse*, 8 (§13).

understands as the "experience" that makes one part of psychology "empirical": such experience is simply acquired by means of "attention directed to the conscious occurrences in the mind."[19] Facts established by introspective attention are quite certain because the conscious mind can count on its direct acquaintance with its own apperceptive acts in such self-observation. There is nothing in Wolff's conception of the mind that could block the mind's view as it watches itself apperceiving. And yet opacity can arise in this transparent self-relation due to what Wolff identifies as the mind's tendency to overlook what it does not *expect* to see. Left to its own devices, an indiscriminately receptive attention is therefore insufficient to the task of psychological observation. For a mind that does not know what to watch out for when watching itself, what occurs in it can remain hidden in plain sight.[20] It is precisely to compensate for this deficiency of human attention that *empirical* psychology must be complemented by a *rational* part: by inferring from findings established by simple introspection how the mind must be structured, it formulates hypotheses that give direction to empirical self-observation. In Wolff's words, rational psychology "increases our acumen for observing what occurs in the soul" because "truths deduced a priori warn us about what we ought to observe and what otherwise *escapes our notice*."[21] Knowledge about the mind can count as scientifically certain when empirical receptivity and rational prediction agree: "If something demonstrated of the soul *a priori* has not yet been recognized in empirical

---

19. Wolff, *Psychologia empirica*, 3 (§5); compare 2 (§2).

20. Attention is thus a *sine qua non* of psychological research but insufficient when left to observe on its own, without some direction from theory: "Attention, without which we cannot avert to what is in the soul, alone is insufficient for observation of such things" (Wolff, *Psychologia empirica*, §5; here and below quoted in Richards's translation). The tension within attention to which Wolff's conception as a two-pronged discipline responds is perhaps best illustrated by the semantic spectrum of Latinate *attentio(n)*. Whereas the French word emphasizes the expectant aspect of "waiting" (*attendre*) in a state of heightened anticipation, the word's Latin etymology foregrounds the active directedness of the mind's "stretching toward" (*ad-tendere*) some particular thing. Together, these word histories suggestively frame attention as a "waiting toward" something: one must already know what it is one is waiting for to find it when it comes.

21. Wolff, *Psychologia empirica*, 4 (§5), my emphasis.

psychology, our attention should be directed to our mind and focused upon that which ought to correspond to the *a priori* discovery, so that it becomes clear whether it agrees with the *a priori* discovery or not."[22] In other words, if the results of deductive reasoning suggest that something *should* be there, then empirical observers must recalibrate their attention to see if they can discover the facts hypothesized by rational psychology. In this regard, Wolff explains, the psychologist must proceed like an astronomer, "who derives theory from observations and corroborates theory through observations, and who, by the aid of theory, is led to observations that he otherwise might not make."[23] Theoretical models, then, suggest to astronomers that they point their telescopes to otherwise unremarkable and therefore structurally invisible corners of the night sky to see if the predicted phenomenon can be observed. If it can, the theoretical model is corroborated; if not, the model must be revised. Psychological attention—as a telescopic focus turned inward—explores inner worlds in an analogous way.

Finally, in Wolff's psychology, attention's role as a mediator between the "rational" and the "empirical" recurs at the level of content, where the faculties of attention and reflection serve as "intermediaries" (*intermedii*) between the lower (sensate) and the higher (intellectual) parts of the cognitive apparatus.[24] The "deliberately effected focus of attention" achieves "distance from the freedom and thrall of sensation" and thus renders the mind independent from sensations and from an environment with which sensations are contiguous.[25] Attention has thus more than a merely cognitive function. As an intermediary between the lower and the higher faculties of the mind, it establishes the boundary that separates the senses from the intellect and, by implication, the animal from the human, mere nature from the beginnings of culture. Attention is the fulcrum of the specifically human mind Wolff's philosophical psychology sets out to investigate.

---

22. Wolff, *Psychologia empirica*, 4 (§5).
23. Wolff, *Psychologia empirica*, 4 (§5).
24. Wolff, *Psychologia empirica*, 166 (§233).
25. Wellbery, *Lessing's Laocoon*, 19.

The perplexing recurrence of attention at every level of Wolff's new science of the soul reflects a structural feature of eighteenth-century psychology: "Psychology displayed a unique reflexivity, since it revealed the function and significance of attention through the practice of attention itself."[26] Psychology, that is, emerged when a scientific attention trained on external objects was then bent back onto the mind itself. This reflexive turn is not, to be sure, identical with the inward turn of the mind in the Cartesian meditations: the Cartesian suspension of external perception fortified the mind's attention in the service of a scientific investigation of the physical world. In eighteenth-century psychology, this scientific attention is turned back inside to investigate the mind—with the same defamiliarizing, analytic, and quantifying habitus that had proven so effective in the explanation of physical nature. As Wolff's elucidation of "reflection" as the "medium" of psychology makes clear, the conscious mind simply becomes new material for the same knowledge procedure previously applied to external nature. In psychology, the mind reflects on its own apperceptive activity in the same manner as it reflects on any object—by successively focusing attention on one aspect after another until the composite structure of the whole becomes distinct.[27]

And yet, redeploying the scientific gaze to the soul differs in one critical respect from analogous procedures in the physical sciences: from the beginning, psychology is also informed by therapeutic considerations—the desire to change or cure the soul that it begins to describe in scientific terms. Wolff himself emphasizes that the science of psychology borders on moral, social, and even theological considerations about what ought to be the case in the soul.[28] His psychology is thus exemplary (and perhaps paradigmatic) of the interfusion of the descriptive and the normative with which Foucault famously faulted the human sciences: it enforces the model of the

---

26. Vidal, *Sciences of the Soul*, 154.
27. Wolff, *Psychologia empirica*, §261. Scientific psychology à la Wolff thus becomes possible on the same grounds on which Kant denied psychology's possibility as a science: the claim that the temporal flux of consciousness is susceptible to being analyzed like the spatial simultaneity of external objects.
28. Wolff, *Psychologia empirica*, 6–8 (§§5–7).

soul it merely seems to describe.[29] Nowhere is this tension more striking than in Wolff's pioneering discussion of the faculty that made his new psychology possible.

The Anatomy of a New Mental Faculty

The section on attention in the *Psychologia empirica*'s chapter "On Attention and Reflection" begins and ends with a nearly identical claim: that we find it in our power to direct the mind's attention as we please. The observation that selective apperception depends on choice (*apperceptionis dependentia a nostro arbitrio*) provides the empirical evidence for positing a faculty of attention in the first place, as the mental capacity for effecting this conscious focus.[30] Yet the same dependence of mind's focus on choice (*attentionis directio pro arbitrio variabilis*) also represents the conclusion and culmination of Wolff's psychological investigation of attention—the point his chapter had to demonstrate in order to move on to "reflection," the capacity to direct attention successively to the parts of a compound perception.[31] What motivates the twenty pages of detailed scrutiny of the faculty, if the point to be demonstrated is already evident in the premise? The normative-descriptive double agenda of Wolff's psychological science suggests the answer: the point Wolff ultimately needs to prove is more pragmatic than theoretical, concerned with measures required to implement a cognitive ideal rather than a neutral description of facts. Effectively, the ostensibly empirical claim that the mind *has* apperception in its power amounts to a demand that the mind *have* apperception in its power. The difference between the premise and the conclusion of Wolff's chapter is that between a normative claim and its successful implementation: freedom of attention as a pragmatic accomplishment rather than a psychological fact.

---

29. Compare Foucault's classical archeology of the human sciences (so the subtitle) in *The Order of Things*. For the origins of psychology in particular, see the early studies in Foucault's *Madness and Civilization*.
30. Wolff, *Psychologia empirica*, 167 (§234).
31. Wolff, *Psychologia empirica*, 186–87 (§§256–57).

The second-person address prevalent in Wolff's supplementary remarks (or "scholia") in his chain of psychological deductions underscores the appellative quality of a psychology of attention that sometimes reads more like an eighteenth-century self-help book than a sober treatise on human psychology—or rather like an odd confusion of both. Consider the obstacles Wolff identifies as standing in the way of attentional control, vivid sense impressions and active imagination.[32] Wolff's otherwise brittle Neo-Latin prose becomes unusually vivid when dramatizing the struggles over the focus of attention within the psyche: When you find yourself in a garden, Wolff notes, trying to focus on a thought or mental image—such as a picture of Moses you saw in church the day before—it may happen that some sensory object, such as a nearby tree, catches your eye. Although you try to remain focused on the image, you can feel your attention abscond toward that tree (*attentionem ad ... illam deficere experiris*) with such force that it becomes nearly impossible to direct it back toward the patriarchal image (*nonnisi difficulter ... retrahi*), especially if you have not yet taken care to bring attention under your power (*in potestatem tuam redegisti*).[33] Conversely, an overactive imagination can steal the mind's focus away from present sensations you ought to be heeding. For example, when listening to someone giving a sermon, though the sounds still fall into your ears, you may, with your attention distracted, fail to hear to what the speaker has to say (*non audis ... etsi verba in aures incident*).[34] Attention's antagonists can even conspire to derail attention, as when sensory stimuli trigger associative flights and daydreaming that draw the mind away from its intended object.[35] These warnings about sensation and imagination may seem simply to reflect a rationalist's typical hostility toward the senses. In fact, however, they reveal the source of this hostility: sensation and imagination are not per se corrupt but pose a problem only *because* and *insofar as* they undermine the mind's capacity to direct its own focus. Wolff recommends a number of

---

32. Wolff, *Psychologia empirica*, 169–71 (§§238–41).
33. Wolff, *Psychologia empirica*, 170 (§238). The biblical imagery is evident.
34. Wolff, *Psychologia empirica*, 171 (§241n).
35. Wolff, *Psychologia empirica*, 172 (§242).

remedial measures to suppress external stimuli that lead the mind astray: close or divert your eyes when giving a speech; do scholarly work in the morning or at night to avoid being distracted by street noise or heat. Yet ultimately, he proposes, mastery over attention can only be achieved by modifying the mind itself to the point that one is able to sustain an unfazed focus even among the greatest external disturbances, "among greater and greater noise, or more and more intense agitations in the sense organs."[36] The positive qualities Wolff goes on to differentiate within the faculty of attention are therefore each correlated with exercises by which the respective attentional abilities can be achieved, as a diagrammatic overview of Wolff's treatment of attention demonstrates at a glance (see figure 6).

While Wolff's illustration of attentional struggles anticipates the rhetoric of self-help books, his taxonomy of positive powers or "degrees" (*gradūs*) of attention reads like an inventory of categories that continue to shape both the popular understanding of and psychological research on attention. The first (and most basic) degree explains attention by the greater or lesser ability to focus the mind by actively shielding it against distracting stimuli, such as vivid sense impressions.[37] This degree takes up Wolff's definition of attention in spatial terms—as the ability to focus selectively on one part of a total perception—and explains this ability through the active suppression (*obfuscatione*) of stimuli that interfere with the intended focus.[38] The second degree, defined as the ability to sustain attention for a longer or shorter period of time, introduces time as a further quantitative measure of attention.[39] It corresponds to what we now know as "attention span." The third degree of attention consists in the power to sustain one's focus on a larger or smaller number of simultaneous sensory stimuli,[40] what modern psychology would de-

---

36. Wolff, *Psychologia empirica*, 178 (§249).
37. Wolff, *Psychologia empirica*, 172 (§243).
38. Thus, pace Crary, the understanding of attention as active and selective "suspension" of perception was not first outlined in nineteenth-century psychology but already informed the first psychological treatise on attention. See Crary, *Suspensions of Perception*, esp. 21–22.
39. Wolff, *Psychologia empirica*, 173 (§244).
40. Wolff, *Psychologia empirica*, 174–75 (§245).

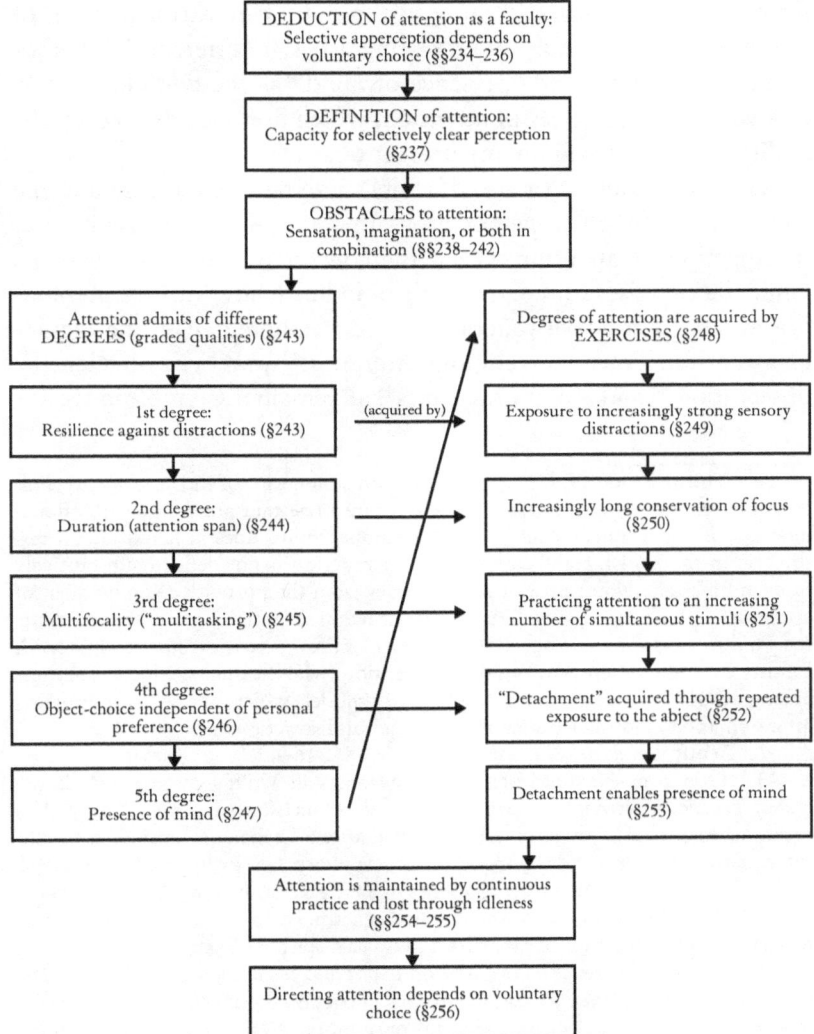

Figure 6. Structure of the section on attention in Wolff's *Psychologia empirica*. Each of the various graded qualities or "degrees" of attention is coordinated with an exercise by which it is acquired, increased, and maintained.

scribe as the "multifocal" attention required in various forms of "multitasking."[41] Finally, Wolff distinguishes "indifference" (or emotional detachment) and "presence of mind" as the two closely correlated supreme degrees of attention, which are both defined by the ability to focus at will on any present object.[42]

As the capstone of the new faculty's internal architecture and the culmination of Wolff's exercise program, the final two traits epitomize the function of attention within the concert of the mind's powers, while the exercises for acquiring them indicate how various premodern and early modern practices became sedimented in the faculty of attention. Traces of religious *exercitia*,[43] practices of scientific observation,[44] and Stoic virtue ethics[45] all remain discernible in Wolff's

---

41. The inclusion of this capacity in Wolff's blueprint of the modern psychology of attention suggests that it is futile to locate a resistant potential in attentional modes that undermine a single focus, as Natalie Philips does in her study on distraction in the British eighteenth century: distraction is not defined substantively or even functionally but as whatever diverges from the normative employment of attention—which can very well require focusing on several things at the same time; see Phillips, *Distraction*, esp. 4–9. Phillips identifies a tension in the eighteenth century between a "unifocal" model of attention (whose origin she locates in moralizing religious models) and a "multifocal" model, which allows de-moralizing attention and exploring the creative potential of distraction.

42. Wolff, *Psychologia empirica*, 175–76 (§§246–47).

43. Prominent examples of religious exercises in Wolff's context include the widely practiced *exercitia* of Ignatius of Loyola (which may be evoked by Wolff's name for his exercise program) and the meditational techniques promoted by Lutheran pastor Johann Arndt's popular devotional work *Von wahrem Christenthumb* (1605). They represent then-recent varieties of a long tradition of meditative practices rooted in early Christian asceticism and monasticism. For overviews of this tradition focusing on Ignatius, refer to Sluhovsky, "Loyola's Spiritual Exercises," and Marno, "Attention and Indifference." For more on Arndt and his influence, see Mücke, *The Practices of Enlightenment*, 1–26; for Arndt's impact on seventeenth-century writing practices, see Sonja Andersen's insightful dissertation, "The Everyday in Greiffenberg's Poetics."

44. See the beginning of chapter 1.

45. Pierre Hadot's work on Hellenistic spiritual exercises has emphasized the foundational importance of Stoic attention, or *prosoche*, the "continuous vigilance and presence of mind" required to live in tune with the cosmos; see Hadot, *Philosophy as a Way of Life*, 84–86, here: 84. While religious, spiritual, and scientific exercises thus inform Wolff's recommendations for how to shape the mind, his *conceptual* framework for explaining the formative effect of practice is thoroughly scholastic. The characterization of attentional capacities as *habitus* acquired through the fre-

exercise regime. As we shall see, however, his psychology of attention blends these into a new technique for insulating the mind that critically diverges from and sometimes inverts the traditions from which it draws. Given the significance of "indifference of attention" as the ultimate goal of Wolff's attentional exercises, it is worth quoting at length Wolff's instructions for attaining this attentional virtue:

> *If someone wishes to achieve an indifferent state of mind in order to be able to attach the same attention to any object whatsoever, he must apply his entire effort to attending eagerly not only to any object at hand but also to those of the inconspicuous kind, above all to those he judges unworthy of his attention and from which the mind is, as it were, repulsed* [retrahitur]. . . . Because this exercise consists in practical attention to indiscriminately any object that presents itself to us, it is necessary to make a conscious effort to bring utterly diverse objects before the eyes or before the mind, and to apply our entire effort to attaching the same attention to every single one among them for as long as we please. And because it is harder to preserve attention when things seem so abject [*abjecta*] to us that we deem them below our attention or recoil from them outright [*prorsus abhorreamus*], we must fastidiously strive toward keeping our attention fixed on objects of that kind for a long time: even if it is initially onerous to us, the feelings of disgust [*taedia*] must nevertheless be swallowed down [*devoranda sunt*] for a while, until we no longer find anything repugnant [*repugnantia*] in it.[46]

The orientation of attentional exercises toward a state of "indifference" co-opts a long-standing ideal of devotional attention: spiritual exercises like those of Ignatius of Loyola were designed to induce an attitude of detachment (*indifferentia*) toward created things—a freedom from personal desire and inclination that was prized by early Christian ascetics as *apatheia* and by mystics like Eckhart as *Gelassenheit*.[47] In the context of such religious practices, the pursuit of

---

quent repetition of pertinent acts evokes commonplaces of Suarezian scholasticism that ultimately trace back to Aristotelian *héxis*, which understands virtues as embodied dispositions acquired through the repeated practice of good actions (a principle also central to the Stoic tradition). See Wolff, *Psychologia empirica*, 339 (§428); Ritter, "Habitus"; Perler, "Suárez."

46. Wolff, *Psychologia empirica*, 183 (§252). Italics in original.

47. For this history, see Evans, "Sancta Indifferentia and Adiaphora"; Balthasar, *Glory of the Lord*, 21; Marno, "Attention and Indifference," 2014.

indifference required relinquishing worldly attachments in order to discern the divine will more clearly: "the soule in this indifferencie . . . willeth nothing, but leaves God to will what he pleaseth," as the seventeenth-century theologian and mystic Francis de Salle summarized this ideal. It becomes a state of "pure expectation [*une simple attente*], indifferent to all so that it shall please the Divine will to ordaine."[48] In the context of religious exercises, indifference of attention thus signals a state of dispassionate receptivity to divine guidance. Wolff repurposes the goal of spiritual exercise for an entirely different and, in some respects, contrary objective: what receives free rein once individual attachments have been cleared is no longer the divine but the individual will. The exercitant becomes *free from* all attachments only to become *free to reattach* their attention to whatever object they deliberately choose, regardless of idiosyncratic inclinations and preferences that prejudice the mind to pay attention to some things rather than others. With this redeployment or reoccupation of the traditional ideal, a practice of surrendering the individual will to the divine is effectively transformed into the former's apotheosis.

To achieve such indifference, Wolff's exercises are designed to gradually break attention's entanglement with things, until attention indeed becomes the pliable "tool" (*instrumentum*) of the will, as Wolff describes it.[49] In many ways this formalizes and expands techniques for domesticating the passions by controlling attention sketched out in the Cartesian playbook: exercising indifference means *exorcising* spontaneous attachments and aversions—modes of reactivity in which the mind responds to things immediately, before and without deliberate choice. The initial stages of such training consist in learning to focus on trivial and inconspicuous things that do not stand out as important or appealing and therefore exert no inherent pull, such that attention must be maintained by willpower alone. Wolff's language here echoes that of early modern naturalists, who had to defend their inordinate expenditures of at-

---

48. Sales, *A Treatise*, 168–69; discussed in Marno, "Attention and Indifference," 2014, 246.
49. Wolff, *Philosophia moralis*, 1:77 (§55).

tention on things as seemingly trivial as aphids and worms against attacks by moralists who deemed such things "below" (*infra*) or "unworthy" of (*indigna*) the serious attention of scholars.[50] For Wolff such microscopic attention is clearly no longer morally suspect but instead a precondition for acts that count as moral because they are guided by dispassionate examination of the good, rather than by a traditional consensus about what does and does not matter. Yet the strategy he prescribes to sustain such attention differs markedly from the practice of naturalists, who (as noted in chapter 1) tended to recondition their individual desire until even the smallest phenomena took on an aura of marvelousness that helped sustain their single-minded focus: acquiring indifference means *vanquishing* rather than rechanneling personal attachments.

The capstone exercise of Wolff's training program for attention therefore instructs exercitants to place themselves in situations where they must confront and overcome the strongest possible counterforce to voluntary control of attention: they must learn to focus on phenomena that do not merely lack inherent appeal but actively repulse the mind. In this endgame of attentional exercises, the mind must overcome overwhelming reflexes to "draw back" or "shrink back" from things (*retrahitur, abhorreamus*). In the final lines of Wolff's paragraph on indifference, the struggle over attentional control reaches a showdown that reveals what Wolff's concern with training attention is ultimately about. As its final antagonist, voluntary attention here faces the disgusting, which Kant famously characterized as an aesthetically irredeemable, extreme case of ugliness because its visceral impact cannot be defused by formally beautiful modes of representation. Kant explains the overpowering effect of disgusting objects through their ambivalent mode of appearance, "as if [the object] were imposing the enjoyment which we are nevertheless forcibly resisting."[51] In prescribing how to behave in the face of utterly revolting things, Wolff's again uncharacteristically vivid and carnal language happens to replicate this ambivalence all too literally. Disgust

---

50. For a detailed account, see Daston, "Attention and the Values of Nature," 103–5.

51. Kant, *Critique of the Power of Judgment*, 190 (§48).

is described as what must be "swallowed down [*devoranda*]," implying that it is so hard to swallow precisely because the thing we shrink from simultaneously summons voracious consumption.

In oscillating between extreme repulsion and unwanted attraction—a repulsion that is nearly insurmountable precisely because it is stained by an undercurrent of overwhelming attraction—disgust epitomizes the very obtrusiveness and, indeed, intrusiveness of things voluntary attention must overcome. It marks the paradigm case of a thing that is not simply and safely "outside" but threatens and beckons to encroach upon the self. Julia Kristeva would characterize such things that corrode the boundary between self and world (with a word that already appears in Wolff) as "abject," and trace the painfully joyous horrors they induce to the primal repression by which the self severs itself from the other.[52] In the imaginary of Wolff's time, the mind's demarcation against the pull and draw of things has a similarly fundamental and inviolable status because attraction and repulsion are the forces that govern bodies and subject them to each other in a physical world where things move only by being moved. For the mind to be of a truly different order—to be moved by its own "motives" alone, as Wolff's ideal of rational action demands—it must learn to suppress everything in which it (re)acts like a body. Indifference of attention marks the successful achievement of this repression. It signals that the mind has acquired immunity against the quasi-magnetic charges through which things exert a positive or negative traction on it—attractions and repulsions that amount to distractions because they draw the mind away from the course it ought to chart for itself. How effectively and pervasively this repression would be implemented can be measured not least by the various returns of magnetic, occult, and contagious forces that flow through people and things in the later eighteenth century; above all, Franz Mesmer's rather precisely named "animal magnetism."[53]

Staring down the abject is the final attentional exercise: Whoever has learned to remain unfazed even in the face of utter horror and

---

52. Kristeva, *Powers of Horror*, 1–31.
53. On the debates surrounding Mesmer in the context of eighteenth-century anthropology, see Steigerwald, "Die Normalisierung des Menschen," 19–32.

disgust has demonstrated perfect indifference against the alluring repugnance of things. Training attention seals the boundary between mind and world in order to regulate all intercourse across it. The final attentional virtue in Wolff's catalogue, "presence of mind" (*praesentia animi*), is then no more than the flipside of indifference of attention—the positive ability that results from the mind's effective insulation against things—and is therefore attained by the same exercises: "By the same diligence [*industria*] by which one acquires indifference of attention in the face of any object, one also acquires the power to continuously apply one's entire attention to any present object."[54] Wolff's "presence of mind" is thus a far cry from the "mindful presence" prized by contemporary meditation exercises designed to relieve and reinvigorate overstrained attentions—anything but the mind's "nonjudgmental" presence with things practiced in typical mindfulness regimens by savoring the flavors and textures of a raisin (and thus with the very act of ingestion Wolff's exercitants must symbolically learn to withstand).[55] It is perfected numbness as the ability to regulate presence, not to permit it; or to regulate it by permitting it only on one's own terms. It is the ability to attend to things of all kinds as if they presented themselves as objects, lined up on a tableau from which the mind can pick and choose at will because all things have equally been drained of their attractive and distractive powers. Surmounting the abject makes the object—this is perhaps the most succinct way to sum up Wolff's exercise regime.

The Tree of Knowledge and Its Subject

Achieving control over attention provides the mind with the power of "reflection," the successive direction of attention to the parts of a complex perception and, for Wolff, the basis of all higher thought.

---

54. Wolff, *Psychologia empirica*, 184 (§253).
55. See the "raisin meditation" in the best-selling Williams and Penman, *Mindfulness* (73–79), which includes step-by-step instructions on how to hold, see, touch, smell, place (in one's mouth), chew, and finally swallow a raisin.

The ability to freely "reflect" on its internal perceptions is what makes a mind fully human—what distinguishes what Leibniz called a mere animal "soul" (*âme*) from a "reflecting monad" or "spirit" (*ésprit*); a term Wolff translated as *Geist*.[56] At the threshold between the sections on attention and reflection in the *Psychologia empirica*, Wolff illustrates how one comes to know things through reflection by referring to a longstanding arboreal imaginary for the organization of knowledge. Imagine, he suggests, that your mind is confronted with a tree: Now that you have your attention under control, you "find it in your power to direct your attention to the leaves, from the leaves on to the twigs to which the leaves attach, from the twigs on to the branches from which the twigs spring forth, from the branches on to the trunk from which the branches proceed."[57] Against the direction of natural growth, the spotlight of attention glides down the tree from one component part to the next, until it becomes evident how the tree as a whole is composed—how the various parts successively singled out by attention (leaves, twig, branches, and so on) add up to a compound structure. In the final synopsis of parts Wolff calls *collatio* (collation or comparison), the tree emerges as "clear and distinct," recognized as a composite of clearly distinguished parts.[58] By analysis, the mind has so thoroughly penetrated the tree's structure that it can now, as it were, let the tree grow forth before the eye of the mind from its component parts, this time from the trunk up.

The real potential of this knowledge procedure lies in the fact that the division of the tree into its primary constituents is only the first step. As Wolff goes on to demonstrate, each of the constituent parts of the tree can in turn become subject to the same analytic procedure first applied to the tree as a whole: "Likewise, when you focus your attention on a leaf, you find it in your power to move your attention

---

56. Leibniz, *Monadologie*, 1998, 16–27 (esp. §§14, 19, 29–30); Wolff, *German Metaphysics*, 556 (§896).

57. Wolff, *Psychologia empirica*, 186 (§256). For a historical overview of arboreal imaginaries for the organization of knowledge, see Wankhammer, "Wurzel."

58. On *collatio*, see Wolff, *Psychologia empirica*, 189–90 (§259). This three-step process leading from attention (selectively clear perception) to reflection (the successive direction of attention to parts) and comparison (the synopsis of parts) would become canonical for the Wolffian school up through Meier and Eberhard.

to ... the extension of the leafstalk through the entire leaf along its length, thereafter on to the little branches that proceed from there along the leaf's breadth, further on to the veins that spread from the little branches everywhere, and finally on to the matter or the mass of tiny vessels visible between the veins."[59] As it turns out, the leaf itself exhibits a little "stem" in the form of the horizontal midrib, little "branches" (*ramuli,* "branchlets") or primary veins diverging vertically from it, and little "twigs"—that is, a network of secondary veins running throughout the leaf.[60] The leaf, although part of a tree, harbors another "little tree" inside of it, and thus perfectly illustrates the recursive nature of a knowledge procedure based on iterative analysis.[61] The knowledge of the tree thus illustrates the principle for constructing the tree of knowledge. In fact, Wolff's description of how to "reflect on" a tree could itself be drawn as a tree diagram of progressively fine distinctions branching off from each other until no more distinctions can be made and the unanalyzable remainder must be written off as "matter"—provisionally, to be sure, until a focus artificially enhanced by devices like microscopes can further distinguish the apparent lump of matter as a composite of "tiny vessels," as Wolff already knows.

The recurrence of the whole in the part in this knowledge procedure may seem to recall ancient ideas about the affinity of between macrocosm and microcosm. In Wolff's attentional rationalism, however, the basis of the analogy between part and whole is categorically different from that found in the cosmologies of similarity in ancient, medieval, or Renaissance thought. In Wolff's knowledge tree, the similarity of shapes is not the hieroglyph of a substantive affinity between part and whole to be deciphered by those who know how to read in the book of nature. It instead is a product of—and, in Wolff's example, is meant to demonstrate—the recursive structure of a knowledge procedure. Part and whole do not reflect

---

59. Wolff, *Psychologia empirica,* 186 (§256).

60. This structure becomes transparent through what Wolff calls the leaf's *perlustratio*—its thorough "examination" or "shining through"—as when a tree-like structure appears in a leaf when one holds it against the sun.

61. For the recursive analysis as a defining feature of epistemic attention in the early Enlightenment context, see Adler, "Bändigung des (Un)Möglichen."

each other here; they both reflect the structure of the mind's attention in the process of reflection. This is also what distinguishes Wolff's "indifferent" attention, despite all resonances, from the indifference of mind aimed at by the Stoics, for whom cultivating the good was tantamount to living in tune with an inherently rational cosmos.[62] In the view of the world that articulates itself here, the cosmos has ceased to be an echo chamber where things large and small resonate with one another. The objectivity of objects is instead a correlate of the subject; the objectivation of a cognitive procedure.

In the spotlight of attention, the mind not only recognizes its objects; it also recognizes itself, as the source of that light. The structure of this self-recognition is legible in Wolff's account of the genesis of self-consciousness.[63] For Wolff and his school, all consciousness arises from distinguishing acts: I do not distinguish things "in" consciousness but become conscious of what passes in the mind (on account of its connection with a sensing body) once I distinguish among these internal perceptions. *Self*-consciousness is no different: it, too, rests on a distinguishing act—namely, on the act of distinguishing the mind (as the distinguishing agent) from the things of which it is conscious (the things it distinguishes). Consciousness of self thus arises from the mind's recognition that conscious perception is its own activity. Controversies in the sparse secondary literature on this topic in Wolff revolve around the question whether consciousness and self-consciousness are coeval, as Udo Thiel has argued, or whether self-consciousness is derivative of object-consciousness for Wolff and his school, as Dieter Henrich has claimed. The priority can be constructed in both ways because Wolff understands self-consciousness as the recognition that first-order consciousness was "already" the mind's own doing, so that a reflexive relation to the self is latent in all consciousness of objects.[64]

---

62. For Stoic attention (*prosoche*) as an important component of spiritual exercises that aimed to establish "indifference to indifferent things," see Hadot, *Philosophy as a Way of Life*, 84–86, here: 86.

63. For the following, see Wolff's account in *German Metaphysics*, 454–57 (§§728–30), which is repeated at the opening of his Latin works on psychology.

64. See Thiel, *The Early Modern Subject*, 279–315; Henrich, "Die Anfänge der Theorie des Subjekts," 127–28. The first view points out that for Wolff even object-

The more interesting question for our purposes, however, is what allows the mind to recognize itself as the *agent* of apperception and, *on this basis*, as an entity distinct from the process of apperception in the first place. Wolff's preoccupation with controlling attention demonstrates that discretionary power over conscious perception is not a simple psychological fact. As his own warnings vividly recall, a mind captured by strong sense impressions or carried along by flights of the imagination is compelled to notice things despite itself; in such cases, its knowing co-presence with the things it perceives—its *con*-sciousness—seems closer to passive witnessing than to active distinguishing. Only retroactively, once I have truly made apperception my own by pruning attention, is it possible to discover that such agency was "already latent" in all conscious perception, and to consequently distinguish myself as the active power behind the entire process. The retroactive nature of self-consciousness's priority over apperception shines through in the terms by which Wolff recapitulates the genesis of self-consciousness in the *Psychologia rationalis* (1734), the last of his works to examine the nature of the soul:

> Indeed, when we turn attention to the fact that we are conscious of the things perceived, we are also conscious of ourselves. But then we perceive apperception—a certain action of the mind—and by means of it, distinguish ourselves as the perceiving subject [*tanquam subjectum percipiens*] from the objects that are perceived [*objectis, quae percipiun-*

---

consciousness always involves a reflexive relation to the subject of knowledge; the second emphasizes that Wolff thinks we are not always *aware* of this structurally reflexive relation. The two positions can be reconciled by noting that it takes a further distinguishing act to "mark" or "notice" the latent reflexivity of consciousness and so to become conscious of the difference between the mind and things. For a lucid summary, see Favaretti Camposampiero, "Anthropology," 47–49. For the broader context, see Wunderlich, "Die wolffianische Schulphilosophie"; Wunderlich, "Kant on Consciousness," 172–74. In a wonderfully overdetermined example, Wolff illustrates the latent reflexivity of object-consciousness by explaining how it is that I become conscious of a mirror. This happens when I distinguish the mirror from other things on the basis of details I can distinguish "within" it. As the example suggests, what I make out "within" the mirror is, however, nothing but my own reflection—distinctions I myself make. In distinguishing the object, I can therefore become aware of myself "within it." See Wolff, *German Metaphysics*, 454 (§§728–29).

tur], [thus] knowing for certain that the perceiving subject is something different from the thing perceived.[65]

However conventional this juxtaposition of perceiving subject and perceived object may seem today, it marks the absolute philosophical avant-garde in a text published in 1734, a decade before conceptual historians usually detect the first traces of this terminological contrast.[66] The same fact that led the mind to consciousness of itself—the discovery of conscious perception as its own "action"—now precipitates its self-recognition as "subject." That Wolff designates the self-conscious agent of apperception as *subiectum*, the traditional term for the substrate of predicates or the substance underlying properties, signals that he begins to understand self-consciousness as the fundamental ground of apperception despite its genetic derivation from object-consciousness. What allows self-consciousness to retroactively assume priority over the process of apperception as a whole is, however, the "active" character of all consciousness, which is only manifested (and de facto only established) by reining in attention and fully making it "my own." In this respect, surmounting the abject makes not only the object but also the subject, in the precise sense of the term that Wolff teases in this passage: the self-conscious agent of perception that knows itself as ground.

From this it becomes clear why the intractable side of attention first highlighted by Descartes has explosive potential for the foundation on which the philosophy of the subject will be built: the hybridity of attention as both active and passive threatens to subvert the

---

65. Wolff, *Psychologia rationalis*, 12 (§12).
66. The beginnings of the modern subject-object terminology are usually dated to German philosophical debates of the 1740s and the works of the first generation of Wolff's disciples and his Pietist detractors; specific sections of Alexander Baumgarten's *Metaphysica* (1743) and *Aesthetica* (1750) are often identified as the earliest systematic deployments of the subject-object opposition; see the introduction to chapter 4. The terms themselves are ancient but were previously used in senses different from and sometimes the reverse of the modern subject/object distinction; in Descartes, for instance, "objective reality" is a thing's reality *as* ("subjectively") *represented* in the mind. To be sure, Wolff's strikingly modern deployment of the contrast between the perceiving mind as "subject" and its objects remains tentative. The traditional ontological and logical meanings of *subiectum* (as substance of properties or subject of predication) prevail elsewhere in his oeuvre.

criterion that renders the subject into a substance categorically distinct from the *process* of apperception in the first place. Acknowledging the fluid spectrum of attentional phenomena between active and passive, voluntary and involuntary poles would rather suggest a view of the conscious self that (as we shall see in chapter 4 on Baumgarten) is still conceivable in Leibniz's framework: the self floating on a sea of unconscious perceptions, now skillfully parting the water, now washed over by a wave. The entwined discourses on attention and subjectivity in Wolff's wake would take a different direction and instead attempt to build on voluntary control over attention as if on solid ground, thereby producing involuntary attention as something to be both practically mastered and discursively repressed.

Discipline and Autonomy: Reading Wolff with Foucault

Zooming out from the micromechanics of philosophical reflection to the broader social and discursive history of the eighteenth century, the most influential account of what it meant to become a "subject" in the period remains Michel Foucault's *Discipline and Punish*.[67] Foucault's archaeology of techniques for shaping what he calls "docile" bodies in the context of an emerging disciplinary society lends itself to understanding the structure and context of Wolff's training of attention, because both accounts revolve around the same key term: "exercise." Foucault understands an exercise as a procedure designed in the context of modern mass institutions to train soldiers, correct prisoners, and educate students by "impos[ing] on the body tasks that are both repetitive and different, but always *graduated*."[68] Exercise in this historically specific sense is Foucault's analytical term for techniques calculated to adjust and correct the minutest operations of the body in a linear progression that charts normative and normalizing stages of individual development. Disciplinary techniques thus insti-

---

67. For the following, see Foucault's *Discipline and Punish*, esp. the chapter on "docile bodies," 135–69.
68. This is Foucault's definition of "exercise." *Discipline and Punish*, 161, emphasis mine.

tute what Foucault calls eighteenth-century "evolutive" time: a logic of gradual development that maps both the progressive formation of individuals and the historical progress of societies.[69]

Although designed to modify the mind rather than the body, Wolff's exercises conform strikingly to the structure of Foucault's disciplinary techniques: Whatever elements these exercises draw from premodern and early modern techniques are rearranged along a sequence of stages that build upon each other and must therefore be acquired in an orderly sequence. This is what qualifies Wolff's regimen as an exercise *program*: the repetitive "again and again" of habitus-formation is supplemented by the "more and more" of individual perfectibility and grafted upon a carefully curated logic of "one after another," the genetic logic of evolutive time. Wolff accordingly imagines each "degree" of attention as a point on a spectrum between extremes that mark the beginning and ideal endpoints of individual development, from the nearly complete absence of an ability to its perfect realization (from distractibility by the weakest stimuli to the ability to sustain attention in the face of any stimulus; from an extremely volatile to an arbitrarily long attention span; and so on).[70] This is why Wolff's exercises are always formulated in the comparative form: to acquire resilience against sensory stimuli, for instance, one must "frequently direct one's entire effort to keeping attention fixed on an object of one's choice, amid *greater and greater* noise, or *more and more* forceful agitations of objects in the sense organs"; to acquire a long attention span, it is necessary to "direct one's entire effort to sustaining attention *again and again*, for a *longer and longer* duration."[71] The various degrees of attention, in turn, build upon each other, so that the first stage (re-

---

69. Foucault, *Discipline and Punish*, 156–62.

70. Wolff's various "degrees" of attention are the same quantifiable, individually varying mental powers that informed his conception of psychology as a "physics" of the soul. Each of them constitutes a "degree" in the sense of a "quantity of a certain quality," measurable as gradation of a specific attentional capacity that is to be increased by exercise. Wolff, *Psychologia empirica*, 179 (§249).

71. Wolff, *Psychologia empirica*, 178 (§240), 180 (§250), my emphasis. Each *iteration* of the exercise leads to an (albeit imperceptibly small) *increase* of the attentional power that is exercised.

silence against sensory distractions) is both the easiest to acquire and a necessary condition for moving on to the next (sustaining attention for a longer period of time).

By the logic of gradual increase of individual powers, Wolff's exercises impose a norm that is both fine-grained and specific. Because each individual differs with regard to their powers of attention, Wolff notes, one must be careful to avoid overgeneralizing not only about "what is achieved in every case" but even about "what *ought* to be achieved."[72] Just as Foucault describes disciplinary power, Wolff's exercises reckon with measuring specific individuals not by the blanket application of an abstract norm but by what is possible for them in specific circumstances. At the same time, the measurement of such differences in terms of quantitative spectra ("degrees") makes it possible to accommodate infinitely many unique individuals within a single normative framework. *In nuce*, Wolff's psychology of attention already contains the radar charts used in modern personality tests, which allow plotting any individual's personality profile on a diagram by assigning a quantitative value to each personality trait. The qualities that make such personality profiles attractive to modern HR managers already distinguish Wolff's degrees of attention: they promise to account for individual difference by making any person quantitatively comparable to any other as well as to their own unique "development targets," which are always stated in the comparative form: toward higher, greater, stronger powers of attention.

As exercises of *self*-mastery and *self*-control, however, Wolff's exercises of attention do not resolve into Foucauldian discipline without remainder. At the heart of disciplinary training as Foucault describes it is a "constricting link between an increased aptitude and an increased domination," with the effect that docile bodies become *more obedient* as they become *more capable*.[73] This is Foucault's

---

72. Wolff, *Psychologia empirica*, 173 (§243), my emphasis.
73. Foucault, *Discipline and Punish*, 138. This is why disciplinary training is a form of *coercion*: its transformation of bodily potencies into socially useful aptitudes dissociates the increase in power resulting from the transformation from the body in which the social utility is implanted: "Discipline increases the forces of the body (in economic terms of utility) and diminishes these same forces (in political terms of

disciplinary reinterpretation of Marxian alienation: the more the body's forces are improved in conformity with externally imposed standards of utility, the less these forces "belong" to the exercising body. Disciplinary training thus "expropriates" bodies of their powers in the very act of increasing them. This inverse correlation does not hold—at least not prima facie—in the case of exercises that habituate the regulation of attention. The whole point of submitting attention to the will is to establish complete ownership over one's actions; to habituate a meta-capacity for performing all of one's actions "as" one's own, in accordance with reasons that are not determined by anyone or anything else. Disciplines of attention instill, in the first instance, an obedience to the *self*—however socially predetermined and suspicious such self-obedience may yet turn out to be from the perspective of critical social history. As quintessential techniques of *self*-governance—exercises whose surplus powers are, as it were, reinvested into regulating, transforming, and refashioning the self—practices of cultivating attention thus also display characteristics of what the late Foucault explored as "technologies of the self" or practices of "care of the self."[74] With these concepts, the later Foucault explored the reflexive aspect of subjectivation practices his earlier studies had neglected—how individuals partake in their own formation as subjects—albeit only by historically displacing this aspect to premodern spiritual exercises from which practices of attention derive, or late modern practices of aesthetic self-stylization that lie beyond their horizon.[75]

What are we to make of this oscillation of the discourse on attention between the machinery of normalizing discipline and the em-

---

obedience). In short, it dissociates power from the body ... it turns it into an 'aptitude', a 'capacity', which it seeks to increase" (138). Compare this with Foucault's contrast of modern discipline with monastic asceticism: "they were different from asceticism and from 'disciplines' of a monastic type, [which] ... had as their principal aim an increase of the *mastery of each individual over his own body*" (137).

74. Foucault, "Technologies of the Self"; Foucault, *Hermeneutics of the Subject*, esp. 1–24.

75. For the late Foucault's reinterpretation of subjective autonomy as quasi-aesthetic self-stylization, see Foucault, "What Is Critique?" and "What Is Enlightenment?" Foucault shares Pierre Hadot's thesis that epistemology displaced the praxeological focus of classical thought and monastic spiritual exercise.

powerment to individual self-determination? In *Discipline and Punish*, Foucault repeatedly confronts this type of question in the double index of references to Rome that were typical of the French eighteenth century (up to the Roman reenactments during the revolutionary period). Against traditional historiographies, Foucault points out that these references evoked Roman military discipline as much as the they did Roman Republic: the mechanisms of discipline perfected in the Roman legions as much as the ideal of representative self-government projected onto the Roman senate.[76] Of course, the two sides of the Roman reference do not carry equal weight for Foucault's understanding of subjectivation in the eighteenth century. The point of his paradoxical intervention is to reveal how one side of the reference overshadowed and masked the other; how a social formation that interpreted itself as resulting from the compact of autonomous individuals *in practice* functioned by the mass administration of disciplinary techniques. Methodologically, this pits an approach that analyzes practices and techniques of subjectivation against approaches that take the "superstructure" of legal and political ideas at its word and describe social power in terms of the unification of individual wills in representative self-government.

The ambiguity of practices of attention cuts through this supposed dichotomy between the reality of discipline and the illusion of individual autonomy. Practices of attention rather constitute the disciplinary techniques *behind* the politically axiomatic ideal of self-determination. Learning to control attention is supposed to ensure that the ideal of rational self-determination becomes a reality, that it becomes embodied or "ensouled" in individuals who must learn to "own" their actions. This requires an approach to studying practices of subjectivation that is less concerned with denouncing autonomy as a fantasy than with inquiring after the historical reality of this fantasy—the disciplinary substructure that implements this ideal in individual minds. Aporias of autonomy would then be revealed less by confronting the hard reality of disciplinary technique with the legal fiction of individual freedom than by exploring the techniques of the self necessary for enacting this fiction—the way

---

76. Foucault, *Discipline and Punish*, 146.

the battles over controlling attention so eloquently documented by Wolff habituate individuals to perform an ideal of self-determination premised on individual self-sufficiency. With this adjustment, the heuristic objective shifts from pointing out how disciplinary techniques contradict the "official" ideal of freedom to examining *what sort* of self-discipline supports *which specific* model of individual freedom—and what internal aporias plague each model. In representative readings, the following sections explore how Wolff's new faculty of attention came to articulate a new vision of the human subject in three fields of eighteenth-century German thought and culture: in pedagogical discourse and practice, in an emerging philosophical anthropology, and finally, in moral philosophy.

Pedagogy and the *Bildung* of Attention

The tension between discipline and autonomy pervades pedagogical discussions that accompany the emergence of public schools as paradoxical institutions for mass-administering individual maturity. As Michael Hagner has noted, the education of attention as a "bourgeois virtue" that promoted rational conduct and self-discipline was a central theme of eighteenth-century pedagogical theory and praxis.[77] In monastic education and in the confessional Latin schools of the early eighteenth century—forerunners and incubators of institutions for public education that soon multiplied across German lands—discussions of attention often still reflected the model of spiritual *exercitia* in their Catholic and protestant varieties: attentiveness was considered an important means and end in a student's moral education, cultivated by a spiritual teacher whose exercises would form an individual mind. A handbook on monastic education from 1740, for instance, recommends keeping a diligent record of one's attentional states to gradually extirpate the vice of distraction and implant the virtue of attention in its stead (see figure 7).[78]

---

77. Hagner, "Aufmerksamkeit als Ausnahmezustand," esp. 278–79; Hagner, "Toward a History," 672–74.

78. Neudecker, *Geistliche Lehr-Schuel*, 187–90.

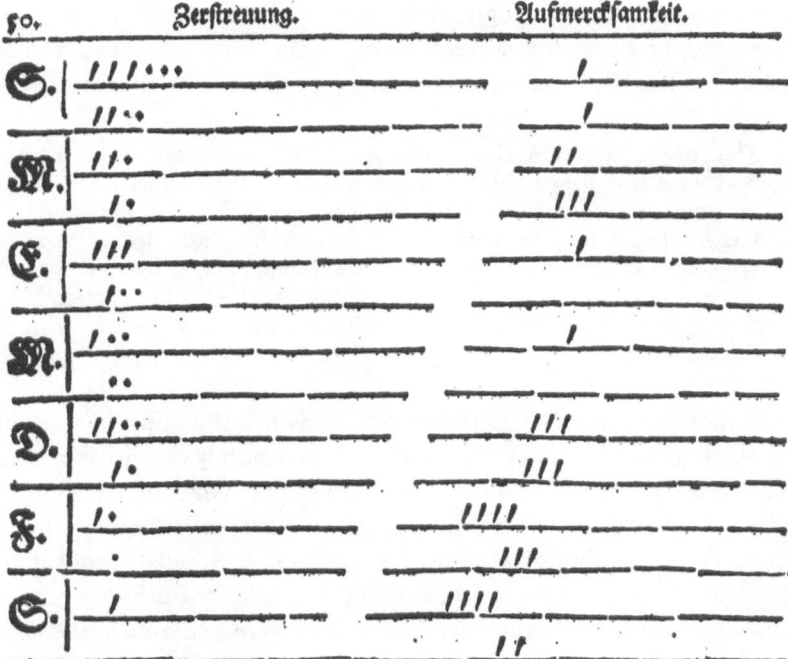

Figure 7. Sample record of a (strikingly successful) week of promoting attention over distraction printed in Franciscan provincial superior Sigismund Neudecker's *Geistliche Lehr-Schuel*. The letters on the left mark the days of the week and the columns titled *Zerstreuung* and *Aufmercksamkeit* provide space for marking instances of distraction and attention (with a full line for grave distraction and a dot for a minor lapse in attention). The decreasing length of lines in the "distraction" column (and vice versa) intentionally limits the space "because vices are supposed to diminish daily while the virtues increase" (187–90).

An aside by Alexander Baumgarten (1714–62) in a letter introducing the discipline of aesthetics he founded (and to which we will return in chapter 4) strikingly illustrates the entwinement of attention with learning and self-discipline at the time. Orphaned at a young age, Baumgarten, who spent his formative years at the Pietist educational reformer August Hermann Francke's Latin school and later taught there for several years, is speaking from experience when he insists on the elemental role on attention in education:

> The art of attention [*Kunst der Aufmerksamkeit*] takes the lead because it is indispensable for the improvement of all other cognitive faculties. Its necessity is instilled [*eingeschärft*] in us from earliest youth through frequent reminders: Focus on this! Consider why you are here! Pay attention! Take note! How would many a schoolmaster not be embarrassed [*betreten*] if one of his slaughter lambs [*Schlacht-Schafe*] responded: Well, how I am supposed to do it when I want to pay attention?[79]

Attention is the basal cognitive faculty on which the improvement of all further cognition depends, but it is not a purely cognitive matter. The series of imperatives in Baumgarten's note evoke the schoolmaster's call to attention as a primal scene of eighteenth-century education. The discipline of attention is externally induced, inculcated (*eingeschärft*) into future adults from the earliest youth, but also—and then—enforced reflexively: as Baumgarten explains in the sentence following this passage, paying the proper kind of attention requires repudiating (*sich entschlagen*—connotatively, by "beating out of one's mind") all those things to which one ought to pay no attention. Despite (or perhaps facilitated by) the ironic undertone, the confrontation of the schoolmaster and his "Schlacht-Schafe" (sheep to be slaughtered; to wit, students) stresses the disciplinary violence involved in educating one's attention or in educating oneself by learning to pay attention. Beyond its cognitive function, mastering the art of attention—learning how to direct inner and outer awareness, what to pay attention to and what to ignore, and how to perceive some things consciously and repudiate others from consciousness—is instrumental for the formation of mature subjects. Disciplines of attention instill a self-reflexive attitude by force that can then, however, become—quite literally in the scene

---

79. Baumgarten, "Philosophischer Briefe zweites Schreiben," 69–70. On Francke's pedagogy and its influence on Baumgarten, see Grote, *Emergence of Modern Aesthetic Theory*, 67–82.

recounted by Baumgarten—a tool for challenging hierarchies of power. As Baumgarten recounts, posing the question as to how attention actually works leaves the schoolmaster embarrassed and exposed (*betreten*).

In the second half of the eighteenth century, pedagogical treatises and manuals compiled by "philanthropic" educational reformers like Johann Bernhard Basedow (1724–90), Friedrich Gabriel Resewitz (1729–1806), and Joachim Heinrich Campe (1746–1818) all assign a foundational role to the education of attention in the gradual formation of the malleable human being.[80] Attention becomes a focus of pedagogical reflection because it is both the basic capacity that must be formed to strengthen the higher cognitive powers and the medium in which instruction takes place. In his *Elementarwerk* (Elementary book; 1774), for instance, J. B. Basedow, the founder of the philanthropic reform movement and an admirer of Rousseau, illustrated voluntary control over attention by voicing a teacher's warning to students that they can either choose to pay attention to what the instructor says or choose to divert their attention to things like flies buzzing around the room.[81] The accompanying copper plate engraving by Daniel Chodowiecki illustrates how attention can be diverted by such fluttering things (see figure 8).

The basal role these reformers ascribed to the education of attention is summarized in Campe's treatise "Über die früheste Bildung junger Kinderseelen" (On the earliest formation of young children's souls, 1785).[82] The section on attention essentially consists of a point-by-point application of the theory of attention elaborated by Wolff and his school to the art of molding young minds. For Campe as for Wolff, the training of attention marks the passage from an animal-like mind to a truly human mind and is accomplished by repeated exercise. To plant the seeds of rationality (*Verstandsfähigkeit*)

---

80. Compare Campe, "Ueber die früheste Bildung"; Basedow, *Das Basedowische Elementarwerk*; Resewitz, *Zur Verbesserung der öffentlichen Erziehung*. For context, see Ehrenspeck-Kolasa, " Aufmerksamkeit in der Pädagogik des 18. Jahrhunderts"; Scholz, "Aufmerksamkeit im Schulmännerdiskurs."
81. Basedow, *Das Basedowische Elementarwerk*, 174.
82. Campe, "Ueber die früheste Bildung," 260–69; for context, see Ehrenspeck-Kolasa, " Aufmerksamkeit in der Pädagogik des 18. Jahrhunderts," 31–32.

Figure 8. Attention and distraction in the schoolyard (from the appendix to Basedow's *Elementarwerk*). From left to right, the illuminated figures in the foreground illustrate each of the five senses: the rather tender senses of touch and taste are followed by the visibly more mature senses of hearing and vision, and finally, on the very right, the obtrusive sense of smell. The second boy from the right illustrates not a sense modality of attention but instead attention gone astray—so much so that he no longer hears the school bell's call to order: "The boy over there is directing his entire attention to the butterfly he wants to catch and doesn't seem to hear that the bell is ringing" (174).

in a young mind, the educator should direct the child attention's again and again to one and the same object while removing other objects from sight. In an elaborate illustration of how children should learn to pay attention to an apple, Campe explains that the educator should direct the child's attention to one "side" or aspect of the apple after another (first the color, then the skin, the stem, and so on) so as to instill an increasingly distinct notion of the apple in the child (*deutlichen und vollständigen Begriff einzuflößen*). After this visual dissection, he recommends performing the same procedure physically by cutting the apple up and putting it back together piece by piece while naming each of the parts, thus encouraging reflection on how the distinct parts relate to the whole. The same technique that Wolff illustrated by reference to the tree of knowledge Campe demonstrates with reference to its fruit.

The rift between individual empowerment and externally imposed discipline runs through these manuals themselves, as they oscillate between Rousseauian ideals of awakening a child's inner abilities and interventionist measures designed to actively implant these abilities in young minds. It also surfaces in discussions among the leading educational reformers: Campe, for instance, chides other theorists for their all-too-Rousseauian idea that education should only prevent aberrations of natural development, insisting instead that young souls must indeed be "made" to develop naturally by active intervention.[83] Campe may have in mind Resewitz, with whom he also sparred on other occasions. Resewitz had warned that attention should never be imposed by force or discipline, because these merely create "slavish attention" (*sklavische Aufmerksamkeit*) instead of free, inner motivation of the spirit (*freyen, inner Trieb des Geistes*).[84] In pedagogy, too, the nature and possibility of human freedom is at stake in the proper formation of attention.

For all the philanthropism animating the new reform pedagogy, the concrete measures proposed to increase attention in the classroom seem, at times, to be borrowed directly from the playbook of panoptic discipline. An anonymous review of Resewitz's *Gedanken, Vorschläge und Wünsche zur Verbesserung der öffentlichen Erziehung* (Thoughts, proposals, and aspirations for improving public education; 1778),[85]

---

83. Campe, "Ueber die früheste Bildung," 260–61.
84. Resewitz, *Zur Verbesserung der öffentlichen Erziehung*, 2:69.
85. Nicolai, "Gedanken, Vorschläge und Wünsche" (review). The review is of the second volume of Resewitz's multivolume enterprise.

for instance, chides the author for neglecting preventative measures for minimizing distraction, which the reviewer argues are much more important than the positive reinforcement of attention. The measures proposed by the reviewer reimagine the classroom as a miniature panopticon. First, it is necessary to immobilize students by restricting the movement of their always all-too-busy limbs (eyes, tongues, hands, feet), which only fire up the imagination.[86] Second, one must isolate and completely insulate students from one another so that all of their attention can be fixed in a single direction, toward the teacher: "As long as the boys can see, speak, and touch each other, no one will ever be able to achieve that . . . the majority remain quiet even *for an hour*, let alone pay attention *for several hours in a row*."[87] Finally, it is necessary to keep students' idle minds and limbs actively busy to preclude any distraction. It is not enough to give students something to see and hear; one must also regularly make them write to occupy their hands and prevent them from expending their surplus energy on defacing their desks.[88]

In such measures for educating the masses by separating and "singularizing" them as individuals, attention figures all at once as a resource to be controlled, a controlling device, and an educational outcome. Attention is the means by which instructors monitor the minds of students distributed before them and by which they ensure that students' attention remains focused on the teacher. The ultimate outcome of such disciplining measures, however, is a formation of attention that stays with students even after they have outgrown the classroom. The goal is to internalize the entire pedagogical setup so as to transform the single-minded attention students learned to pay to teachers into a device for self-monitoring, one that is as effective in suppressing distractions as the teacher's surveilling gaze on which they learned to hone their focus.

---

86. Nicolai, "Gedanken, Vorschläge und Wünsche," 2021.
87. Nicolai, "Gedanken, Vorschläge und Wünsche," 2022 (emphasis in original).
88. Nicolai, "Gedanken, Vorschläge und Wünsche," 2022–23.

Spinoza's Waking Vision

In a 1664 letter Spinoza recounted the following episode to his friend, the Dutch merchant Pieter Balling:

> One morning, as the sky was already growing light, I woke from a very deep dream to find that the images which had come to me in my dream remained before my eyes as vividly as if the things had been true—especially [the image] of a certain black, scabby Brazilian whom I had never seen before. For the most part this image disappeared when, to divert myself with something else, I fixed my eyes on a book or some other object. But as soon as I turned my eyes back away from such an object without fixing my eyes attentively on anything, the same image of the same Black man appeared to me with the same vividness, alternately, until it gradually disappeared from my visual field.[89]

Spinoza discusses his lingering dream image to assure his friend that omens Balling perceived before the death of his child occurred only in the imagination, not in reality. And while Spinoza grants that Balling's hallucinations may have had a premonitory quality because his friend's imagination sprang from the mind, he claims that his own dream-episode was caused by nothing but the stirrings of the body and was therefore without such significance. Spinoza's framing of the dream episode thus contends that there is nothing of importance to see here: it all happened only in the imagination, and only in the variety of the imagination stimulated by the whims of the body (just as, Spinoza goes on to suggest, fevers sometimes stir up a delirious madness in the mind). It does not take a reading committed to the "hermeneutics of suspicion" to sense something awry here.[90] As recent commentaries have pointed out, the lingering dream image of a Black man from the colonies at a time when the Dutch Republic was deeply involved in the transatlantic slave trade suggests that Spinoza's feverish imagination manifests problems simmering in the collective

---

89. Spinoza, *Collected Works*, 1:353. I thank Baeti (Bethelihem) Tebase for her thoughts on the role of imagination in the episode.

90. On this point, and on Spinoza's dream in the context of the repression of the fact of transatlantic slavery in an enlightenment philosophy teeming with metaphors contrasting enslavement and liberation, see Buck-Morss, *Hegel, Haiti*, 84.

imaginary, even without being fully conscious of it—or rather, in the twilight between dreaming and waking consciousness.[91] Depending on the motifs and merits imputed to Spinoza and his thought, the episode can then be read as the prescient "awakening" of an excommunicated Jew to the presence of the postcolonial at the moment of the modern subject's constitution, as Willi Goetschel has argued;[92] or as the symptomatic return in the philosopher's bad conscience of those materially oppressed and psychologically repressed in the emerging Enlightenment ideal of the free citizen.[93]

Yet the psychic dynamic so vividly dramatized in the episode cannot be explained solely as the workings of the imagination singled out by Spinoza (and most later commentators): it comes to a head in the imagination's interaction with attention.[94] Spinoza portrays the image as something that stubbornly imposes itself on his mind; something that "came to him" in his dreams and refuses to leave even after his waking. Only the purposeful direction of attention to some object or other dispels the unsolicited image, which then returns as soon as the focus of attention is relaxed again.[95] Although the book is a suggestive example of a focal object, it seems to matter less *what* the gaze is focused on than *that* it is focused; it is the very act of maintaining attention that keeps the image away. What at-

---

91. For the historical context and the extent of the Dutch Republic's (and Spinoza's immediate milieu's) involvement with the slave trade, see Feuer, "The Dream," 229–32; Goetschel, "Spinoza's Dream," 42–48; Taylor, "Nature," 40–43. Both Dutch and Latin versions of the letter identify the image as that of an African man (*Aethiops*) from the colonies. Spinoza, *Opera posthuma*, 471; Spinoza, *De nagelate schriften*, 526.

92. Goetschel, "Spinoza's Dream," here: 54.

93. Warren Montag and Susan Buck-Morss read the figure in terms of a (Freudian) "condensation" of those excluded even from Spinoza's radical-democratic vision of the multitude; Montag, *Bodies, Masses, Power*, 87–89; Buck-Morss, *Hegel, Haiti*, 84–85.

94. Focusing on the imagination, Klein, "Dreaming with Open Eyes" (157), mentions attention in the final paragraph but does not elaborate on its relationship with imagination.

95. The Dutch and Latin versions of the letter emphasize the presence of attention in the psychic drama, which the letter of the English translation preserves only in adverbial form: the image, Spinoza writes, reappears as soon as he looks at things "sine attentione" or "zonder met aandacht" (without attention). Spinoza, *Opera posthuma*, 471; Spinoza, *De nagelate schriften*, 526.

tention counteracts in propping up waking consciousness is unconstrained imagination—specifically, according to Spinoza's (rather dualistic) self-interpretation, an image caused by the body rather than the mind.[96] In fact, the persistent dream image suggests imagination's contrariness to the rational mind in the overdetermined manner Freud ascribed to dreams: imagination, which gives bodies (or imagistic extension) to things, bodies forth the specter of a Black man that, in its scabbiness, gives an image of diseased corporeality itself. Characterized as both Brazilian and African (*Aethiops*), the figure of the mangy Black man evokes the transatlantic slave whose geographic coordinates this double index recalls, whether as slave or maroon, a figure of unfreedom or rebellion. Imagination, as the capacity for giving to things a body, embodies its own unruliness in the imago of a Black man. It is both the image of a human figure and a figure that appears, in its abject corporeality, contrary to proper humanity, a haunting image of the inhuman within the human that only focusing attention can keep at bay.

Spinoza's dream anticipates how the ability to control attention would come to define the anthropological difference in eighteenth-century philosophy: the capacity to steady the mind's focus and thereby suppress the stirrings of the body establishes the rationality of the human *animal rationale*. At the same time, Spinoza's haunting image anticipates how attention would become entangled in a logic of racialization that effectively blamed the unfreedom inflicted on enslaved people on these people themselves, as their supposedly natural trait. In emerging racial hierarchies that repeated and legitimated the violence of racialized slavery, it was common to claim that "inferior" races were governed by mere "caprice" and, lacking the ability to direct attention, were unable to rule themselves.[97] In

---

96. It is tempting to "correct" Spinoza's insistence on the merely bodily origin of the image from the perspective of his own metaphysical monism, as scholars have done since Lewis Feuer's early commentaries on the episode. Yet a mind/body opposition with a rather Cartesian flavor indeed frames Spinoza's own explanation of the phenomenon, even if his mature metaphysics will hold that the two are aspects of the same underlying reality.

97. See Phillips, *Distraction*, 19–20. For the deplorable continuity of this racialized schema in German eighteenth-century thought, compare the writings of

becoming the prerequisite for human freedom, voluntary attention thus also came to mark hierarchies between the rational subject and its racialized others, who were excluded from proper humanity because they supposedly lacked the capacity for sustained attention.

Attention, Perfectibility, and the Anthropological Difference

As in other contexts, it was Wolff who gave systematic articulation to the idea—variously suggested by the likes of Descartes, Malebranche, Spinoza, and Leibniz—that voluntary control over attention distinguished rational humanity from other creatures, including from the creaturely side within the human being itself. In fact, Wolff's psychology of attention crystallizes an eighteenth-century "psycho-anthropology" of perfectibility that saw the mind as malleable and that singled out attention, the capacity on which higher thinking depends, as the principal medium for educating and improving the human being.[98] Wolff can therefore tell the story of individual anthropogenesis as the story of the progressive perfection of attention, spelling out with rare clarity what it meant for human beings to be "perfectible" in the early eighteenth century.[99] In the *Psychologia empirica* and in his late *Philosophia moralis* (1750), Wolff notes that human infants are incapable of paying attention to anything; their attentional faculty is still undefined but, by the same

---

J. K Lavater, for whom the more "animal-like" features of some humans (and some races) correlated with their inability to "mark" or observe features well (which is why the genius physiognomist—like Lavater himself, in his own estimation—also has the most beautiful features). It continues in Kant's writings on anthropology and physical geography, where some races are claimed to naturally lack the very capacity for self-directed activity that defines humanity in his critical philosophy; and in Hegel, who correlated the low level of culture in "savages" with their inability to pay attention. Lavater, *Physiognomische Fragmente*, 1775, 1:113–14; Lavater, *Physiognomische Fragmente*, 1778, 4:463; Kant, "Von den verschiedenen Racen"; Hegel, *Philosophie des Geistes*, 249–50.

98. For use of the term "psycho-anthropology" to describe the intersection of psychology and anthropology in the eighteenth century, see Vidal, *Sciences of the Soul*, 315.

99. For the following, see Wolff, *Psychologia empirica*, 177 (§248); Wolff, *Philosophia moralis*, 1:51–86, esp. 52 (§39), 78 (§55).

token, entirely definable. Eventually people "get used to" (*adsuescunt*) paying attention to some things through external stimulation by attractive objects and by imitating others.[100] The "mere progression of years" is, however, not sufficient to make this creature fully human. Left to its own devices and guided in its development by nothing but chance, attention remains weak or feeble—directed not *to* objects but *by* objects, to which it remains attached as long as whatever attraction drew attention to the object happens to last.[101] The critical turning point in human development (which corresponds to what Wolff sees as the hinge of attention in the architecture of the psyche) occurs when people take care to exercise their attention and gradually subject it to the individual will. Only deliberate training and exercise reverse the directionality of attention: from outer-directedness (by attractive objects) and other-directedness (by imitation) to self-directedness; from the determination of attention by inner and outer impulses to its submission under the free will (*libertas voluntandi*). The reversal of attention is the crucial event in the passage from infancy to maturity and, indeed, from nature to human culture.

That nothing less than the full realization of humanity is at stake here is underscored by the foils with which Wolff contrasts the mature human being—wild animals (*bruta*) and feral children ("those raised among the bears").[102] Animals lack intellect, perfectibility, and culture all at once *because* they lack attention: "Their actions all tend to self-preservation and defense, and to the propagation of

---

100. Wolff, *Psychologia empirica*, 177 (§248); compare Wolff, *Philosophia moralis*, 1:78 (§55).
101. The following two sentences encapsulate Wolff's characterization of "untrained" attention succinctly (if Wolff can ever be claimed to be succinct): "Attention left to itself [*sibi relicta*], in so far as it exists in man by means of a natural disposition, is . . . excited [*excitatur*] by . . . whatever causes offer themselves, and its use is not subject to free will [*nec libterati voluntatis subjacet*]. And therefore [such] attention is not directed to objects, but they draw attention to themselves [*in se trahunt*]; nor is it retained in the object which draws attention to itself longer than the cause of the attraction lasts, on which it alone depends" (*Philosophia moralis*, 1:52 [§39]).
102. Wolff, *Philosophia moralis*, 1:52 (§39), 77–78 (§55). Wolff gives a detailed account of reports on feral children and their induction into human civilization in *Psychologia rationalis*, 378–81 (§461).

the species, and are therefore limited within a very narrow circle [*ambitum*]; they only bring momentary attention to those things that are obvious to the senses."[103] Even pricked ears or startled gazes do not truly indicate attention in animals, however: "Indeed, they do not so much bring attention [to objects] as the objects themselves, while they strike the sensory organs, draw attention to themselves."[104] This, for Wolff, is what defines the animality of the animal as a foil for the humanity of the human: "Brutes" are confined to acting upon stimuli that trigger their instincts and to being startled by strong impressions that impose themselves on their sense organs. The lack of free attention arrests these "brutes" within a narrow sphere and precludes all development and culture. Feral children, who fascinate Wolff as they do other eighteenth-century thinkers because they evoke humanity's state of nature—the degree zero of perfectibility—are no better than animals in this regard: although "biologically" human, their attention remains as feeble and whimsical as that of beasts as long they err about in the woods. Only after foundlings are educated in matters of attention can one begin the work of humanization—including the acquisition of speech and higher thought.[105] For Wolff, the passage from animality to humanity is defined primarily not by language or reason but by the capacity to direct attention, as the prerequisite for both.

The ability to direct attention is the precondition for language use, yet to some extent the reverse holds true as well. As David Wellbery has shown in reading Wolff as an Enlightenment semiotician, attention precedes the institution of the (linguistic) sign in this paradigm because it establishes the distance from the flux of sensation

---

103. Wolff, *Philosophia moralis*, I:77 (§55), reading "momentaneam" for "monentaneam."

104. Wolff, *Philosophia moralis*, 1:78 (§55).

105. Wolff, *Philosophia moralis*, 1:52 (§39), 78 (§54). Learning to pay attention effects a transformation so profound that—like the Rotpeter of Kafka's "Bericht für eine Akademie"—such children remember nothing about their feral state after their induction into human society: because of their lacking attention, the experiences in their animal-like state were so fleeting that they could not be committed to memory (1:78 [§54]).

necessary to demarcate part of a perception and then mark it with a sign.[106] The sign, in this model, is essentially a name arbitrarily chosen for a distinct part of a compound perception "marked out" by attention in reflection (such as the various parts Wolff distinguishes in his sample reflection on a tree). Through comparison and abstraction, general notions of the intellect are formed by detaching such marks from individual perceptions and bundling them in notions that apply to all objects that share a set of characteristics.[107] Words, and human language in general, thus serve as placeholders, shortcuts, and condensations of perceptual marks (*Merkmale, notae*) singled out by selective attention. Yet in a dynamic that mirrors the interplay between empirical and rational psychology, directing attention in reflection in turn requires "guiding" or "directive" notions of the intellect signified by words: "For he who must bring sufficient attention to any object, must also know to what he should direct it. For that reason, certain guiding notions [*notionibus directricibus*]—and consequently, the intellect—exercise an influence on attention."[108] In reflecting on things, the attentive mind needs notions that guide its selective attention to the parts of an object that matter, "lest that which ought to be observed may escape it."[109] Words thus prime the attentive mind to register certain characteristics rather than others. In a circular movement that oscillates (like the hermeneutic circle) between selective attention to a part and a preconception of the whole, attention thus *depends* on signs that condense the labor of the human intellect as much as it *precedes* their institution. Because of this circularity, higher-order thinking is, as Wolff repeatedly claims, scarcely possible without human language.[110] Emphasizing this motif, Michael Forster has even made the case that Wolff (rather than Condillac or Hamann) is the source of

---

106. Wellbery, *Lessing's Laocoon*, 19–20. Campe follows the same sequence when recommending that educators should name each part of the apple to which they direct the child's attention.
107. Wolff, *Psychologia empirica*, 201 (§283).
108. Wolff, *Philosophia moralis*, 1:69 (§49).
109. Wolff, *Psychologia empirica*, 70 (§50).
110. Wolff, *Psychologia empirica*, 201–2 (§284), 248–49 (§342).

Herder's groundbreaking idea that thought depends essentially on language.[111]

In any case, it was Herder who conjoined all of these motifs into a comprehensive anthropology of language that, far beyond the eighteenth century, would shape negative-anthropological conceptions of the human as a being defined by its lack of positive essence. Herder's famous *Abhandlung über den Ursprung der Sprache* (Treatise on the origin of language; 1772) begins by arguing that all previous accounts of the origin of human language (a favorite topic of philosophical speculation in the eighteenth century) suffered from an inadequate understanding of the anthropological difference.[112] In a juxtaposition that clearly draws on Wolff, Herder argues that animals live in a sphere (*Sphäre, Wirkungskreis*) circumscribed by the instinctual fixation of attention to a limited set of stimuli in their environment, while "the whole remaining world is nothing for them."[113] This "enclosure" of attention is fundamental to Herder's understanding of animal life. Strictly speaking, instincts are for Herder not the *reason* but the *consequence* of animal attention's natural fixation to a small number of triggers: because of their unchallenged prominence in the perceptual field, these stimuli exert an irresistible force on animal behavior—a pull or tug of attention we then call instinct.[114] The strength or weakness of instinct is therefore inversely proportional to the range of things that can become possible objects of attention for a certain animal species: "The more

---

111. Forster, "Herder's Philosophy of Language," 323–41, esp. 333.

112. Herder's anthropological approach to human language is in dialogue with an emerging discipline of anthropology that combined philosophical and medical discourses to examine the human being, as echoed in the title of Ernst Platner's pioneering *Anthropologie für Aerzte und Weltweise* (1772). Synthesizing the state of anthropological knowledge in his *Erfahrungen und Untersuchungen über den Menschen* (1777), the Prussian anthropologist Karl Irwing, too, located the specific difference between humans and animals in the fact that anything can become an object of attention for the human mind—whereas the attention of animals only responds to a narrowly defined set of objects (2:210 [§147]). On the co-emergence of anthropology and aesthetics in the eighteenth century, see Borchers, *Die Erzeugung*, 60–135.

113. Herder, "On the Origin of Language," 79; Herder, "Über den Ursprung der Sprache," 713.

114. "When senses and representations are directed at a single point, what else can become of this but instinct?" (Herder, "On the Origin of Language," 79).

dispersed [*zerstreuter*] their attention is over several objects, . . . the larger and more diverse their sphere is, . . . the more we see their sensuousness distribute itself and weaken."[115]

For Herder, humans present the limit case of an animal with an attention so scattered and an instinct so blunted that it constitutes, by way of a qualitative leap, a new *kind* of being altogether, for whom *anything* can become the focus of perception or action.[116] It is this primordial openness of attention that gives rise to the specifically human capacity underlying thought and language, which Herder famously calls *Besonnenheit* or (appropriating Wolff's term) *Reflexion*: "The human being demonstrates reflection when the force of his soul operates so freely that in the whole ocean of sensations which floods the soul through all the senses it can, so to speak, separate off, stop, and pay attention to a single wave, and be conscious of its own attentiveness [*daß sie aufmerke*]."[117] This pivotal passage of the treatise should make it obvious that Herder recycles motifs from Wolff's philosophy of attention (even if they are articulated with incomparably more verve than Wolff's dry deductions)—from Wolff's understanding reflection as the direction of selective attention to part of a perception to his explaining self-consciousness by the reflexivity latent in any act of attention. What would grant this idea a long afterlife is the way Herder incorporates it into his own anthropology of language. Again not unlike Wolff, Herder goes on to claim that the signs of human language serve as markers (*Merkworte*) for *artificial fixations* of an inherently flexible human attention.[118] For a naturally distracted being, human language thus

---

115. Herder, "On the Origin of Language," 79; "Über den Ursprung der Sprache," 712.

116. The human is characterized by "dispersed desires, . . . divided attention, . . . more dully detecting senses" (Herder, "On the Origin of Language," 80; Herder, "Über den Ursprung der Sprache," 714).

117. Herder, "On the Origin of Language," 87; Herder, "Über den Ursprung der Sprache," 722. As we will see in chapter 4, Herder borrows from Leibniz the oceanic imagery for the flow of perceptions.

118. Herder's anthropological thesis was immensely influential. Among many others, it informed Jakob von Uexküll's theorization of the species-specific *Umwelt* of animals, conceived—in a terminology that betrays its provenance in the discourse on *Aufmerksamkeit*—as a *Merkwelt* (perceptual universe) organized by the

shapes the surrounding world in a way analogous to how stimuli shape animal environments: it imposes salience structures that determine what becomes significant to perception and action and what disappears into an unmarked "remaining world" that goes for "as good as nothing."

In and through Herder, the idea of selective attention as it emerged over the course of the eighteenth century would thus become foundational to a negative anthropology that understood the human as "the animal whose nature has not yet been fixed," as Nietzsche would famously formulate.[119] Herder's text reveals the genealogy and logic behind this influential conception of the human being. The nonfixity of human nature is, for him, derived from the openness of human attention, which is both the defining deficit of humans and their specific gift. An original scatteredness or distraction is the possibility condition of a flexible attention that can latch on to all possible kinds of features and can congeal in words, thereby establishing artificial environments maintained by language, which mediates access to reality for a being that lacks a natural environment. For Herder, language thus functions like a substitute for the stimulus-response loops given to animal perception. More clearly than in many later iterations of similar anthropological theses, which tend to emphasize either the original deprivation and neediness of the human *Mängelwesen* (deficient being) or its unique powers and freedoms,[120] the characteristic deficiency and the proficiency of human beings thus grows from a single root. Total distraction, in which *nothing* commands attention and the environment is dissolved into undifferentiated noise, coincides with the first moment of reflection, in which *anything* can be singled out as the focus of attention.

Herder's negative-anthropological rationale continues to influence the theoretical substructure of much scholarship in the humanities today. In its various post-Marxian and post-Nietzschean varieties, the idea that human beings are defined by their lack of

---

specific *Merkmalsträger* (marks) to which animal perception responds. See Uexküll, *Streifzüge*, 23–26.

119. Nietzsche, *Die Unschuld des Werdens*, 110. For Herder's influence on Nietzsche's thinking on language and anthropology, see Bertino, "'As with Bees'?"

120. See the typology in Blumenberg's "Anthropologische Annäherung," 406.

nature is the tacit assumption behind approaches that equate critique with "denaturalization"—with exposing, that is, the seemingly natural as being, in fact, socially (or culturally, historically, technologically) constructed and therefore changeable and malleable.[121] Indeed, the negative-anthropological conceit has offered an effective tool for debunking all human arrangements that claim to be necessary and inevitable as mere "second nature." Yet this cutting-edge tool of critique becomes rather blunt when it comes to confronting ailments that are caused—as is arguably the case with attention today—by the demand for infinite flexibility and malleability itself.[122] Where the tenet that there are no unalterable givens of nature itself takes on an air of inevitability, denaturalizing critique threatens not only to become useless but to reinforce the very status quo it claims to resist.

Historical reflection can perhaps prompt us to stop and reevaluate these assumptions. Wolff's training regimen suggested that the freedom of human attention from spontaneous reflexes and residual instincts assumed by negative anthropologies like Herder's must be actively *produced*. A mind that is, as in Herder's primal scene of language formation, so detached from things that it can freely choose where to place the focus of attention is the product of a specific and historically localizable regime of subjectivation. The absence of anthropological givens, in other words, is no simple anthropological datum. The human being as tabula rasa, as completely malleable creature free from instinct, had to be created by actively erasing modes of reactivity that entangle human body-minds with their environments. Perhaps a new model of critical scholarship will

---

121. For a recent analysis of this model of critique and its weaknesses, see Jaeggi, "Was Ist Ideologiekritik?," 281–83.

122. This conundrum is visible in Jonathan Crary's book-length essay *24/7: Late Capitalism and the Ends of Sleep*. Turning from earlier concerns with attention to the related problem of sleep, Crary begins by arguing that sleep, despite is semblance of naturalness, is deeply historical and malleable. This, however, precludes him from arguing what he seems to want to argue—namely, that sleep is a privileged site for analyzing the devastating effects of 24/7 temporality precisely because it highlights intrinsic limits to the malleability and flexibility of living beings. Crary's essay marks, but does not resolve, the constructivist critic's dilemma; see Crary, *24/7*, 11–17.

have to learn to reckon with the idiosyncratic inertias, the attractions and repulsions that link the mind with these environments, even if resistances to malleability only ever emerge in response to specific forms of life and do not preexist such forms as a transhistorical concept of human nature.

Moral Philosophy: Autocracy and Autonomy

The importance of attention for Wolff's moral philosophy can be gathered from the fact that his mature moral philosophy devotes thirty-six pages and twenty-four introductory paragraphs to the role of this particular faculty in morality.[123] The extensive section on attention in Wolff's final work repeats and elaborates much of what Wolff had to say about attention in his empirical psychology. However, the basic rationale for the importance of attention in moral philosophy can already be found in Wolff's German writings, where he portrays attention as the mind's trump card in the battle between reason and affect, between the will's determination by rational or sensitive desire.[124] In Wolff's ethics, actions count as moral if they conform to the human being's natural obligation to promote its own perfection. This happens when the will is moved solely by conscience, which Wolff understands as a form of syllogistic reasoning in which the major premise is provided by the notion that a possible action is of a certain type, and the minor premise (or "maxim") by the judgment that actions of this type do or do not promote overall perfection. What prevents the will from always being moved by moral reasons is the interference of powerful but confused images of the good that spring

---

123. Wolff, *Philosophia moralis*, 1:51–87 (§§39–63).
124. Wolff, *German Ethics*, 112 (§186); Wolff, *Philosophia moralis*, 1:84 (§61). The following is a condensed summary of main tenets of Wolff's moral philosophy based on the *German Metaphysics*, §§206–9, 414–16, 490–91, and the *German Ethics*, §§14–50, 90, 184–86. For a lucid overview of Wolff's concept of moral reasoning, see Grote, *Emergence of Modern Aesthetic Theory*, 24–28. Grote argues that Baumgarten's aesthetics emerged in part out of a Pietist concern with Wolff's overly intellectualist (and therefore potentially ineffectual) ethics. For the influence of Wolff's moral philosophy on Kant's conception of moral autonomy, see Klemme, "How Is Moral Obligation Possible?"

from senses, imagination, and affect and pull the will away from these rational motives, leading to a loss of self-control and enslavement by one's own passions: "Since we do not consider what we do when under the influence of affects ... and consequently do not control our actions ... the dominance of the senses ... constitutes the human being's slavery."[125] To regain mastery, it is necessary to cultivate a steadfast attention that shields the mind against distracting images and keeps it focused on the voice of reason and the laws of nature (which include the moral law, for Wolff). Those who want to achieve mastery over themselves must therefore "be able to sustain attention unperturbed."[126] Perfecting attention is a precondition for the rational self-rule that makes moral action possible. Because such "autocracy" marks the capacity for determining oneself in accordance with a rational law by excluding all influences of the senses on the will, Heiner Klemme has identified this concept as the "highest point" of Wolff's ethics and the direct predecessor of Kantian autonomy.[127]

None other than the young Friedrich Schiller demonstrates the vitality of this Cartesian-Wolffian motif in the late eighteenth century, at the threshold of the transcendental-idealist turn. In his first, rejected draft of a medical dissertation titled "Die Philosophie der Physiologie" (Philosophy of physiology; 1779), Schiller explains freedom of the spirit through the ability to direct attention. In a speculative synthesis of contemporaneous attempts by Albrecht von Haller (1708–77), Ernst Platner (1744–1818) and others to explain mind-body interaction through nerve activity, Schiller demonstrates that the will would be entirely determined by chains of mechanical causation that run from nerve stimuli to the "thinking organ," or brain, and finally to the understanding and the will—were it not for the mind's ability to actively influence material ideas in the brain by means of attention.[128]

---

125. Wolff, *German Metaphysics*, 298 (§491). Like Rousseau and Kant after him, Wolff identifies a free will moved by nonrational grounds with slavery to the passions. Wolff, *German Metaphysics*, 299 (§491); Wolff, *German Ethics*, 113 (§184).
126. Wolff, *German Ethics*, 112–13 (§186).
127. Klemme, "How Is Moral Obligation Possible?," 20–22.
128. Schiller, "Philosophie der Physiologie," 100–102. Schiller's rejected dissertation is not, as has sometimes been claimed, a highly visionary piece of Idealist

Essentially, Schiller's dissertation ventures a reformulation of Cartesian attention voluntarism on the basis of the latest neurophysiological knowledge. Attention thereby plays an intermediary role played by art in Schiller's later aesthetic anthropology. The will, Schiller argues, is neither free in choosing which impressions the mind receives from the brain nor in choosing whether to follow rational imperatives that compel one course of action or another in any given situation. Yet it *is* free in choosing how to *attend* to nerve stimuli by selectively amplifying or suppressing the material correlates of ideas in the brain. By way of directing attention, the mind can thus influence the motives behind its own actions and prove itself to be indirectly self-determining and free: "Attention thus has power over the strength of motives [*Beweggründe*], indeed, it is attention itself that creates these motives for itself. And now it becomes quite clear what freedom is. . . . All morality of human beings has its foundation in attention, i.e., in the active influence of the soul on the material ideas in the thinking organ."[129]

Ensuring the mind's independence from the brain and the physical nexus to which the brain is tethered through the nerves is not, Schiller emphasizes, a onetime event; it requires continuous practice. This is because the mind's influence on the brain by means of attention tends to solidify and calcify into automatic patterns such that acts initially performed out of freedom (*frei, moralisch*)—while actively paying attention—eventually become purely mechanical (*mechanisch*). Freedom can therefore be rendered permanent only by adopting a practice of self-monitoring that continuously controls and shapes the mind's impressions and decalcifies or "un-nerves" (*entnerven*) passions and fixed ideas by actively breaking engrained patterns of nerve activity.[130] At the conclusion of this chapter and

---

speculation but the summary of state-of-the-art anthropological-medical knowledge. It draws on Albrecht von Haller's recent research on irritability, Charles Bonnet's sensualist theory of attention, and Ernst Platner's identification of intermediary "nerve spirits" that are susceptible to stimulation by both the mind and the physical organs. Nevertheless, the early text does prefigure the later Schiller's aesthetic and dramatic concerns with mediating mind and body, senses and intellect, freedom and necessity, in intriguing ways.

129. Schiller, "Philosophie der Physiologie," 100–101.
130. Schiller, "Philosophie der Physiologie," 101.

of the section in this book that explores the origins of modern discourses on attention in rationalist philosophy, we find ourselves once again with Cartesian attention. From Descartes to Wolff and the young Schiller, attention served as the guarantor of rational self-determination.

In Conclusion: Attention and Autonomy from a Pragmatic Point of View

The scenes of attention considered in this chapter reveal striking isomorphisms between seemingly disparate fields. Technical problems in the emerging philosophy of consciousness began to resonate with questions in eighteenth-century social and cultural history and those in the broader history of knowledge. How does the subject arise as a unified and stable entity vis-à-vis the flux of perceptions? By what mode of perception is the surrounding world rendered so distant that it assumes the guise of inert objects? How did eighteenth-century pedagogical reformers envision and seek to implement the paradoxical Enlightenment ideal of mass education leading to individual maturity? What models of human action arose alongside the increasing individualization and dynamization of social life once traditional social roles no longer served as reliable guides of ethical conduct? How did an early anthropology understand the human species, if no longer simply as having been created in the image of the Creator? And how did emerging scientific articulations of the anthropological difference begin to define hierarchies between rational humanity and its "savage" others? Across this array of concerns, the faculty of attention that Christian Wolff placed at the juncture of the sensate and intellectual mind came to articulate a new vision of the human as a rational and autonomous creature. The successful incorporation of this new faculty into individual minds—the optimal submission of the mind's focus to voluntary control—became the practical prerequisite for realizing this ideal of autonomous subjectivity.

Although attention underlies the capacity for positive self-determination, it functions as a negative capacity before it assumes its assigned role in the concert of the mind's powers. This was most evident in Wolff, who identified "*in*difference of attention"—the capacity to not focus on things that *attract* attention and *distract* the mind—as the condition for "presence of mind," the ability to focus attention at will. A similar pattern emerged in Spinoza's letter, which highlighted the direct correlation between fixing the mind on an object and overcoming the fickleness of bodily imagination in any act of attention. In the models of self-determined action developed in the context of moral philosophy, the capacity to shield the mind against deceptive sensate images of the good preceded the ability to direct attention to rational motives. A somewhat different version of the same idea motivated Wolff's and Herder's anthropological reflections, where the idea that attention lacks a fixed goal—that the human mind is, in this sense, defined by an original "distraction"—characterizes the unique adaptability of the human species. Pedagogical discussions, finally, highlighted the discipline involved in learning to withdraw the mind's focus from unwanted stimuli, which already figured prominently in Wolff's attentional exercises. In debating how to form autonomous minds, pedagogical reformers agreed that overcoming distraction (or what appeared as such from the perspective of normative attention) required the gradual cultivation of young minds, although they disagreed about whether this cultivation merely reinforced a natural disposition toward attention, as the more Rousseauian among the reformers postulated, or required the active suppression of natural impulses. The emphasis on training and education was, moreover, not limited to pedagogy but permeated all the discourses on attention reviewed in this chapter. Whether exercises of attention were seen as a preparation for proper moral conduct, as a developmental process leading to individual maturity, or as part of the acculturation process distinguishing the human species, there was shared agreement that the capacity for voluntary attention had to be nurtured and acquired through deliberate cultivation. It was understood that one had to *learn to perform* the self-sufficiency of the mind necessary to direct attention from within.

If attention was indeed considered key to individual autonomy in the eighteenth century, it is all the more puzzling that it seems to have played such a marginal role in the work of the great philosopher of autonomy, Immanuel Kant. In the *Critique of Pure Reason*, the work that raised the mind's spontaneity into the starting point of a new philosophy, attention appears only once as a technical term. In the second version of the transcendental deduction, written in response to critics who had considered this section obscure in the book's first edition, Kant offers attention as an example of what it means that "inner sense is affected by ourselves." That such self-affectation of the inner sense is indeed possible should not cause his critics any difficulties, Kant insists; after all, "every act of *attention* can give us an example of this. In such acts the understanding always determines the inner sense, in accordance with the combination that it thinks, to the inner intuition that corresponds to the manifold in the synthesis of the understanding."[131] As Rodolphe Gasché has shown in a subtle reading of this passage, Kant's reference to attention offers anything but a marginal example: acts of attention instead appear to be Kant's paradigm for synthetic acts of the understanding that unify manifolds of intuition.[132] Such acts distinguish what Kant calls "empirical apperception" from transcendental or "pure apperception": whereas empirical apperception is a form of bare consciousness that is "dispersed [*zerstreut*] and without relation to the identity of the subject,"[133] in pure apperception I recognize myself as the author of the synthetic unity of intuitions and thereby grasp them as *mine*. Because this recognition depends on the understanding attending to its *own* contribution to the synthetic unity of intuitions in abstraction from their content, awareness of the transcendental unity of apperception—the self-awareness that defines this unity—is itself achieved by an act of attention that involves a form of abstraction. The "I think" that "must be able to accompany all my representations," as Kant defines the transcendental unity of apperception at

---

131. Kant, *Critique of Pure Reason*, 259 (note to §24), AA (=*Akademieausgabe*) 3: B156–57n. Highlight in the original.

132. Gasché, "On Seeing Away." Gasché goes so far as to suggest the *identity* of acts of attention with synthetic acts of the understanding (9–10). While it is not possible here to assess his reading by returning to the detail of Kant's text, it is notable that his account parallels—apparently unwittingly—Wolff's explanation of the emergence of self-consciousness by second-order acts of attention to the attention that accompanies first-order consciousness.

133. Kant, *Critique of Pure Reason*, 247 (§16), AA 3: B133.

the outset of the deduction, relies on the act-character of attention.[134] Following this reading, attention is only absent from the first *Critique* because it is so ubiquitous, presupposed throughout Kant's analysis of transcendental consciousness.

Further evidence for the infrastructural role of attention in Kant's understanding of the mind can be found in his *Anthropology from a Pragmatic Point of View*, which presents attention and abstraction as elemental operations of consciousness. Kant learned from Alexander Baumgarten's empirical psychology (see chapter 4) that acts of attending and abstracting—of focusing on and disregarding mental content—constitute closely related aspects of the same operation: highlighting one thing in consciousness requires actively pulling attention from others or (in Kant's language) "abstracting" from them.[135] Teasing out attention's implication with the ability to "abstract from" distraction, Gasché draws the post-structuralist lesson that the mind's dispersion structurally precedes the unity of consciousness achieved in attention and concludes that distraction and abstraction, as seemingly secondary terms, are, in fact, constitutive of the mind's attention, into which the original dispersion of consciousness continues to be inscribed.[136]

Reading Kant as an inheritor of the practices and discourses on attention discussed in this chapter suggests a different, or differently accentuated, lesson. What negotiates between attention and distraction in practice—what brings this opposition into relief in the first place—is the array of techniques devised to control the mind's focus. Attention and distraction do not merely depend *structurally* on each other, the way the privileged term of an opposition always depends on its counter-term; they also depend on each other *pragmatically*, as

---

134. Kant, 246 (§16), AA 3: B131.
135. In fact, Kant seems temporarily to have forgotten Baumgarten's insight about the co-implication of attention and abstraction when he introduces the two early in the anthropology as if they were merely opposite mental acts; see Kant, *Anthropology*, 19–20 (§3), AA 5:131–32. As Gasché's reading confirms, however, Kant himself does not uphold this separation in later examples and instead portrays attention and abstraction as co-dependent faculties. For more on Baumgarten's empirical psychology, on which the structure of much of Kant's anthropology is based, see chapter 4.
136. Gasché, "On Seeing Away," 25–26.

two sides of a normatively structured practice. As Kant himself notes in the *Anthropology*, the ability to draw the mind away from unwanted stimuli depends on implanting in the mind a certain power, a "strength of mind [*Gemüthsstärke*] that can only be acquired through practice."[137] This irreducibly pragmatic mental strength does not lend itself to transcendental analysis and yet is presupposed in the spontaneity of the understanding that makes this analysis possible. Perhaps this is why Kant assumes this capacity as a *fait accompli* in the first *Critique*'s transcendental deduction while relegating the discussion of the measures by which it is attained and perfected to an anthropology explored "from a pragmatic point of view." As already indicated by Wolff's identification of self-consciousness as the "subject" of perception, the ability to collect the mind out of its distraction must be incorporated before I can recognize all my representations as acts that are emphatically "mine." The disciplining of attention, then, can be considered the *Vorschule*—the propaedeutic or elementary education—of the transcendental subject.[138]

There is one more seemingly peripheral yet profoundly illuminating reference to attention in Kant's critical philosophy, in the third of his three *Critiques*. In discussing the subjective purposiveness of representations of the beautiful—their suitability for maintaining the subject's powers suspended in a state of pleasant animation—Kant alludes to another manner whereby the mind can sustain an intense focus: "We linger over the consideration of the beautiful because this consideration strengthens and reproduces itself, which is analogous to (yet not identical with) the way in which we linger when a charm in the representation of the object repeatedly attracts attention, where the mind is passive."[139] An attention stimulated by sensory charms offers itself as the best analogy for this sustained concentration because in both instances no effort is required to keep the mind focused. Yet this remains a mere analogy between states that are, as Kant insists, not at all identical because

---

137. Kant, *Anthropology*, 20 (§3), AA 5: 132.
138. To be sure, techniques of attention are the pragmatic precondition of only the most basic operations of the mind. For a performance-theoretical account of the poetic prehistory of Kant's categories, see Morrow, "Schematism."
139. Kant, *Critique of the Power of Judgment*, 107 (§12); AA 5:223.

the mind is actively engaged when lingering over a beautiful representation. This unique form of focus is active, but it does not require mental effort in the way acts of attention usually do; it is effortless, but not at the price of the mind's passivity and heteronomy. What defines this sort of attentiveness, then, is that it is in a double sense *not imposed*: it is imposed *neither* by the subject (because it takes no mental effort to sustain it) *nor* by the object (there is no material charm that compels a passive mind). The contemplation of the beautiful, rather, marks a state in which the mind actively yields to how it feels itself affected in contemplating a representation. In some respect this effortless absorption is close to what Kant called "empirical apperception" in the first *Critique*—a state in which consciousness is fully immersed in the manifold contents of perception, incapable of (or relieved from) imposing synthetic unity on the play of intuitions. Yet again, however, the analogy only goes so far: the free play of the faculties in aesthetic contemplation marks not the absence or loss of self but its unexpected discovery—a consciousness that finds itself, or its capacity for synthetic unity, reflected in the unforced play of intuitions.[140]

The kind of attention toward which Kant gestures in third *Critique* transcends the usual oppositions between voluntary and involuntary, between attention and distraction, just as Kant's third *Critique* ventures beyond freedom and nature and the faculties—reason and the understanding—associated with them in his architectonic. In this, the third *Critique* examines a faculty for judging of which Kant remarks in the *Anthropology*—as he does of the faculty for abstracting—that it can never be taught by rules, only exercised or practiced.[141] This is true for judgment in general, but all the more so for the aesthetic reflective judgment Kant identifies with "taste," which can only be cultivated and refined, not defined by rules. It, too, requires an education—though perhaps an education

---

140. Expressed in terms of Kant's transcendental faculty psychology: the understanding finds what the imagination synthesizes on its own accord suitable to effortless unification, even though no determinate concept is available to guide imagination in its combination of the manifold of intuition.

141. "The power of judgment ... cannot be instructed, but only exercised [or practiced, *geübt*]." Kant, *Anthropology*, 91 (§42), AA VII:199.

different from the one that underlies the attentive subject of the first *Critique*. In evoking another possible focus of the mind, Kant echoes in terms of his transcendental aesthetics what was taking shape in the eighteenth century as the idea of an aesthetic education of the subject—an education that promised another formation of the self based on another formation of attention. The genesis of this other model of *Aufmerksamkeit* is the subject of chapters 3 and 4.

3

POETICS
Wonder and the Poetics of Attention

Poetry as Education of Attentiveness in B. H. Brockes and J. J. Breitinger

Hamburg, in the 1720s. Barthold Heinrich Brockes, a poet and city official who had just made a name for himself with a collection of poetry celebrating the marvels of nature, takes a stroll with his eldest daughter on the outskirts of the city, and a swarm of winged grasshoppers catches their eyes.[1] With the dazzling profusion of insects fluttering against the sun, it is impossible for Brockes and his daughter to make out any distinct contours.[2] According to the poeticized ac-

---

1. Brockes, *Irdisches Vergnügen in Gott*, 1724, 2:303–5. "Ilschen," the name of the speaker's oldest daughter in the poem, is also the name of Brockes's oldest daughter. The gendering of the speaker seems appropriate given the autobiographical flavor of the poem (as well as the symbolic gendering of the forms of attention contrasted in the poem).
2. "A small blue host of grasshoppers drew/Through their mobile, constantly shifting appearance/Our eyes almost entirely to themselves" (Ein kleines blaues Heer von Grase=Pferdchen zog/Durch den beweglichen beständig regen Schein/Die

count (or invention) of the outing Brockes published in the sequel to his first book, his daughter begins to chase after the insects, catches one of them, and hands it to her father. What follows evokes a very different kind of attention than the one that sends children running after fluttering insects. As the insect lies before the speaker's eyes immobilized and removed from its teeming context, he directs the focus of attention from one part of the creature to the next to see how the whole figure is composed: First, he notes, we find a round head with bulbous insect eyes; next, several feet attached to the front of the body; then an elongated body with several indentations—and so on.[3] Described in such precise detail, the grasshopper again appears strange and marvelous, but it is a marvelousness of the second order—not the initial allure of a fluttering swarm but the amazing order of delicately arranged parts one can discover when submitting the insect to a kind of visual vivisection (it remains open, in the poem, whether the insect is alive or dead). Far from an expression of spontaneous curiosity, the gaze modeled by the bureaucrat-poet enacts a precise protocol: isolate the entity from context; render it immobile; turn attention to one part after another until the parts and their composition appear clearly before the mind. Whether the events described in the poem "actually" happened or Brockes invented them seems almost secondary compared with the precision with which the poem outlines the new procedure for establishing what counts as "really" real.

In this chapter, I read Barthold Heinrich Brockes (1680–1747) and the poetic theorist Johann Jakob Breitinger (1701–76) as representatives of a poetics of the marvelous (*das Wunderbare*) that

---

Augen fast auf sich allein) (Brockes, *Irdisches Vergnügen in Gott*, 1724, 2:303). The German *fast allein auf sich ziehen* can also be read as suggesting that this capturing of attention occurs "automatically," without an effort of the will.

3. "The strange figure,/The round clear head which seems nothing but eyes,/Many a leg that almost seems to merge with the head,/The thin, long body, which here and there/[Is] quite delicately notched" (Die seltsame Figur,/Den runden klaren Kopf, der nichts als Auge scheint,/So manchen Fuß, der sich fast mit dem Kopf vereint,/Den dünnen langen Leib, der hier und dar/Sehr zierlich eingekerbt) (Brockes, *Irdisches Vergnügen in Gott*, 1724, 2:304).

highlighted the power of the rare, strange, and extraordinary to captivate an audience. According to the theory of the passions we encountered in Descartes, wonder at strange objects sparks active attention and, in this way, models the transition from passivity to activity that distinguishes a mature human mind. The poetry of the marvelous thus offered itself as a solution to the problem of involuntary attention that plagued the rational subject: poetry appealed to a passive side of the mind unmoved by the rational will and harnessed the charms of strange objects to jolt the mind into action. I argue that it was in this context that poetry acquired a function that would define literary language in modernity: The goal of marvelous poetry was no longer to imitate nature (*imitatio*) or convey moral precepts (*prodesse*) but to enable readers to reflect for themselves by estranging habitual modes of perception. In their poetics of defamiliarization avant la lettre, both Breitinger and Brockes hit upon a dialectic of attention and habit that would become formative for modern reflection on perception and its problems. Both initially saw poetry as a tool for rejuvenating attention, capable of breaking a habitual blindness to the beautiful complexity of the world. In their poetic theory and practice, however, Breitinger and Brockes eventually discover the idea that *all* perception may rely on a contingent pattern of habituated attention, such that we may ever only see things as they are "for us" rather than as they are "in themselves." Their experiments in poetics thus also catalyze problems in epistemology and representation that would motivate Kant's "Copernican" turn to the subject as one possible solution.

The scholarship on Brockes, author of one of the first literary best-sellers in the German language, has long emphasized the importance of perception, and the sense of vision in particular, for the poetics of his nine-volume *Irdisches Vergnügen in Gott* (Earthly delight in God; 1721–48).[4] In a foundational study, August Langen saw an "apotheosis of vision" at work in Brockes's texts; more re-

---

4. Brockes's volumes of poetry went through forty-two editions and reissues during in his lifetime alone, and reached a larger audience than any other literary author in the first half of the German eighteenth century (Welle, *Der irdische Blick durch das Fernrohr*, 61).

cently, Martina Wagner-Egelhaaf characterized Brockes's poetry as a "school of seeing."[5] What is at stake in Brockes is, however, not vision as such but—to appropriate John Berger's felicitous term—a historically specific *way of seeing*.[6] The characteristic innovation of Brockes's poetry has sometimes been located in his expansion of the subject matter of poetry to include trivial and mundane phenomena, especially the kind of phenomena also studied by contemporary natural sciences.[7] Yet Brockes's descriptions of such particulars as the anatomy of a moth, the corona of the sun as seen through a telescope, or the reproductive organs of a pumpkin plant do not simply expand the range of the poetically visible but instead model a new form of visibility altogether.[8] The same applies to Brockes's prominent endorsement of physicotheology, a theological movement popular in the eighteenth century that attempted to prove the workings of divine providence on the basis of an apparent "design" of nature that could be discovered by means of the emerging natural sciences.[9] Rather than advancing theological proofs, Brockes's poems produce physicotheological evidence in the sense of rhetorical *evidentia*—that is, in staging, experimenting with, and propagating a particular type of epistemic vision. His poetry is thus positioned quite literally as a "school" that instructs readers in a way of seeing that Brockes dubbed an "art of

---

5. Langen, *Anschauungsformen*, 18; Wagner-Egelhaaf, "Gott und die Welt," 186.

6. Berger (*Ways of Seeing*, 7–112) is concerned with ideologies of seeing that are embodied in images such as early modern oil painting, which he links to the rise of the commodity form.

7. Preisendanz, "Naturwissenschaft," 474.

8. As a "popularizer" of the natural-scientific worldview, Brockes has recently attracted renewed interest in a recent "poetics of knowledge." As I will try to show, the connection to the natural sciences consists less of a direct borrowing of scientific content than of formal techniques of perception and description. For recent work on Brockes from the perspective of poetics of knowledge, see Borgards, *Poetik des Schmerzes*, and Rössler, "Weltgebäude/Mögliche Welt."

9. On the tradition of physicotheology in Brockes's context, see, for instance, Zelle, "Das Erhabene," 228–33; Steinmann, *Absehen–Wissen–Glauben*, 27–150. As several commentators have pointed out, however, the alleged physicotheologian is strangely uninterested in providing any arguments or proofs; Wagner-Egelhaaf, "Gott und die Welt," 184; Thums, *Aufmerksamkeit*, 34.

attention."[10] Brockes's best-selling poetry functioned as a medium for seeding the new attentive gaze among an early eighteenth-century general readership, reaching well beyond the lecture halls and scientific societies where the epistemology of attention was formulated as an explicit epistemic program.

In conjunction with Brockes, I read Breitinger's *Critische Dichtkunst* (Critical poetics; 1740) as a theoretical engagement with the poetry of the marvelous that was in vogue in the early eighteenth century.[11] Much of the literature on Breitinger's *Critische Dichtkunst*—the mature formulation of the poetological endeavors of the Swiss critics Breitinger and Johann Jakob Bodmer—is concerned with positioning the work within a history of the emancipation of the poetic imagination in the eighteenth century. Disagreements arise over whether Breitinger had "already" developed a productive, subjective, or autonomous concept of the imagination and thus anticipated the genius movement and Romantic irrationalisms or whether he is "still" committed to rationalist principles and a corresponding depreciation of the freedoms of the imagination.[12] This focus on the productive imagination, especially when coupled with the rationalism/irrationalism schema, has sometimes obscured rather than illuminated the specific set of assumptions that informed Breitinger's poetics, even those concerning his concept of the imagination itself. In the broadest sense, Bodmer and Breitinger understood imagination as the mind's capacity

---

10. Brockes (*Irdisches Vergnügen in Gott*, 1724, 6:302) already characterized his own technique as a "Schule des Gesichts" (school of vision). For the designation of attention as an art, see the poem "Mittel gegen die Unachtsamkeit" (Measures against inattention) discussed below.

11. On Breitigner in the context of a transnational poetics of the marvelous (*merveilleux, meraviglioso, das Wunderbare*) in the late seventeenth and early eighteenth centuries, see Gess, *Staunen*, 38–55.

12. I follow Gabriele Dürbeck's overview of the secondary literature on Breitinger and Bodmer on the question of imagination; see Dürbeck, *Einbildungskraft und Aufklärung*, 266–67. Assessments of Bodmer and Breitinger's merits usually coincide with the position authors take in the famous *Literaturstreit* of the Zürich critics with Gottsched. For a representative exchange, see Hans Peter Herrmann's book-length study *Naturnachahmung und Einbildungskraft*, with its emphasis on Bodmer and Breitinger's modernity against Gottsched's backwardness; and see Bruck et al.'s extensive and scathing review of the book, "Der Mimesisbegriff Gottscheds," which stylizes Gottsched as the real innovator in early Enlightenment poetics.

for imagistic representation—as the mind's internal "wax tablet" that receives, stores, and retrieves mental images.[13] Above all, the Swiss critics' focus on imagination grounds a poetics of internal representation, for which poetry unfolds as a series of images on the canvas of the mind. In a close reading of the opening chapters of *Critische Dichtkunst*, I argue that the early eighteenth-century discourse on attention I traced in chapters 1–2 provides the matrix for several of Breitinger's most distinctive poetological concepts: his central notion of "poetic painting" (*Poetische Mahlerey*), his legitimation of poetic license through a theory of "the new" (*das Neue*) and "the marvelous" (*das Wunderbare*), and the "immanent deconstruction" of the principle of nature imitation in Breitinger's conceit of "imitating possible nature" (*Nachahmung der Natur in dem Möglichen*).[14] Rereading *Critische Dichtkunst* in this new context makes it possible to observe an event of some consequence: how a discourse on attention, concerned with a nonmimetic moment in *perception*, catalyzed a nonmimetic concept of *poetic representation*.[15]

Brockes is one of the authors most frequently cited in Breitinger's *Critische Dichtkunst*, eclipsed only by Breitinger's countryman Albrecht von Haller, whose descriptive poetry pursued a similar poetological program. Yet the point of collocating Breitinger and Brockes is not to trace lines of influence or provide additional historical details about early eighteenth-century literature. Instead, it is to outline a discursive event to which the oeuvres of both authors attest in their own ways: the short-circuiting of philosophical epistemology—the epistemology of attention—and rhetorical poetics. These two traditions—epistemology and rhetoric—had long evolved in isolation from each other but intersected in a poetry that

---

13. In their early works, Bodmer and Breitinger repeatedly use the Lockean wax tablet as an analogy for the imagination; see Herrmann's *Naturnachahmung und Einbildungskraft*, 185–87. Herrmann's study remains perhaps the most lucid account of late seventeenth- and early eighteenth-century poetics in German lands.

14. For the formulation "immanent deconstruction," see Menninghaus, "Klopstocks Poetik der schnellen Bewegung," 291.

15. David Wellbery has convincingly situated German literary theory and aesthetics in the eighteenth century (especially from 1740 to about 1780, beginning with Breitinger) in the context of the representational paradigm; see Wellbery, *Lessing's Laocoon*, 1–8, 203–27.

set out to comprehend the world and in a poetics that undertook to explain poetry in epistemological terms.

The juncture at which the two traditions merged was *evidentia*, the classical rhetorical technique for "making-appear before the eye of the mind," which became the master trope of representational poetics in the early eighteenth century. *Evidentia* provided the joint at which rhetorical poetics was eventually transformed into a discourse on aesthetics.[16] What has not been sufficiently noted is that the prominence of *evidentia* in eighteenth-century poetics and aesthetics is itself a consequence of the poetic adaptation of attention discourse. The two aspects of *evidentia* conceptualized in the rhetorical tradition—*enargeia*, or detailed description, and *energeia*, the affective force of poetic visualization—conveniently mapped onto the two sides of attention as an active and passive, voluntary and involuntary faculty.[17] According to the poetic interpretation of the wonder/attention matrix, the affective force associated with *evidentia* captivated readers by eliciting involuntary attention. Detailed description, in turn, mimicked the successive attention to parts that brings clarity to representations. Through its charms, poetry was thus seen as capable of imposing states of attentiveness that could teach audiences to see things with the precision the new type of enlightened knowledge demanded. For early eighteenth-century figures like Breitinger and Brockes, poetry was above all an institution for the education of attention.

Because my focus is on reconstructing the outlines of a discursive event, my readings are necessarily selective and cannot do jus-

---

16. This process has been the focus of a series of insightful essays by Rüdiger Campe. See especially his essays "Bella Evidentia" and "Effekt der Form." For context, see also his essays "Shapes and Figures," and "'Improbable Probability."

17. The *enargeia/energeia* dichotomy has become established as a scholarly shorthand for two aspects conceptualized in the context of the rhetorical *evidentia* tradition: *detailed description*, and the vivid and forceful *presencing effect* achieved through such description. The two-sidedness of the multifaceted *evidentia* tradition is not necessarily negotiated in these terms in the tradition, but both elements are already present in Quintilian's and Aristotle's descriptions of language's capacity to "place things before the (inner) eye" (Quintilian, *Institutio Oratoria* 8.61–8.71; see also Aristotle's *Rhetoric* 3.11.1). For an overview of the *enargeia/energeia* distinction in this context, see Müller, "Evidentia und Medialität," 61–62.

tice to all, or even most, aspects of Breitinger's and Brockes's complex but still understudied oeuvres. Especially in the case of Breitinger's *Critische Dichtkunst*, this means that I am less concerned with reconstructing authorial intentions in order to disambiguate and smooth over the considerable contradictions and paradoxes that riddle the text. I instead approach such contradictions as indices of subtle discursive shifts and breaks resulting from Breitinger's amalgamation of rhetorical poetics and philosophical truth-discourse. The following notes trace the effects of this encounter on poetics as well as philosophy. They excavate how Wolff's concept of attention informed Brockes's and Breitinger's conception of poetry, and how the poetic transformation of attention then recoiled on philosophical epistemology, forcing a reckoning with the latent poetics of representational knowledge. Marking the fault lines of an epistemic break, Breitinger's poetics and (to a lesser degree) Brockes's poetry render legible the genesis and stakes of the idea that literary language does not reflect preexisting orders but defamiliarizes the schemata in which empirical reality is given—schemata that define what does or does not become salient in things.

Dialectics of Habit and Attention in Brockes

Many of the more than 1,500 poems from Brockes's *Irdisches Vergnügen in Gott* are variations on a basic pattern.[18] In a typical "observational" poem, speakers are placed in a situation—often in nature or in a garden—where they encounter an object of interest. Sometimes after an initial moment of confusion or feeling overwhelmed,[19] they compose themselves and begin to observe what

---

18. In addition to descriptive "observational" poems, the *Irdisches Vergnügen in Gott* also includes brief sententious poems of a few lines and more reflective/didactic poems, especially "Neujahrsgedichte." Georg Guntermann has gone to the trouble of counting all of Brockes's poems and arrived at the number 1,540 poems on 5,098 pages (Guntermann, *Barthold Heinrich Brockes' "Irdisches Vergnügen in Gott,"* 339).

19. Carsten Zelle ("Das Erhabene," 228) has elaborated on the dialectic of the speaker's initial confusion/nausea/terror and the recuperation of his bearings

is in front of them "with an attentive gaze" (*mit aufmercksamen Blick*) or "more attentively than usual" (*aufmerksamer, als sonst*).[20] In Brockes's poems, *Aufmerksamkeit* or *Achtsamkeit* marks the beginning of a state of perceptual exception that enables the pleasant discovery of splendor and order (*Schmuck und Ordnung*) in things that initially seem to lack both, such as a worm, a moth, a vegetable, or a fallow field. The discovery of such amazing splendor then leads, in a third and final stage, to an invocation of the glory of God as the origin of the order revealed by the attentive gaze.[21]

The meat of Brockes's poems lies in their middle parts, the scenes of attentive observation, which are often wedged between rather formulaic beginnings and endings. One of the striking features of Brockes's poetry is that in these scenes, his speakers often reflect not only on the splendor and order of observed objects but also on the perceptual techniques through which these objects can be made to appear *as* marvelous; so much so that the reflections can sometimes take over the poem and eclipse the object under observation.[22] A number of poems are staged exclusively on this meta-level and thus have no topic other than the technique of perception itself. As the titles of these poems suggest, they are essentially meta-reflections on attention: "Aufmercksamkeit" (Attention), "Unselige Unaufmercksamkeit" (Deplorable inattention), "Sinn=reiche Bestraffung der Unachtsamkeit" (Evocative punishment of inattention), "Unglückselige Folgen der Unachtsamkeit" (Miserable consequences of inattention), and—with a title that could well serve as the heading

---

that follows (typical of many Brockes poems), which he sees as marking the beginning of an aesthetics of the sublime.

20. Brockes, *Irdisches Vergnügen in Gott*, 1740, 6:301, 7:660. These two examples stand in for many similar formulations in Brockes's poems. The spelling of "Aufmer(c)ksam(keit)" seems to change randomly between versions with a "k" and "ck." The masculine pronoun seems warranted, given the proximity of speaker figures to the author Brockes and the gendering of "proper" attentiveness as male.

21. Wolfgang Preisendanz arrived at a broadly similar schema in "Naturwissenschaft," 481.

22. This has also been emphasized in Wagner-Egelhaaf, "Gott und die Welt," 186–87, 191–92 (with several examples).

of Brockes's entire poetry collection—"Die Kunst vernünftig sehen zu lernen" (The art of learning to see rationally).[23]

Here I focus primarily on one such meta-poetological reflection, the poem "Mittel gegen die Unachtsamkeit" (Measures against inattention). Reproduced below in the original German, the poem begins with an *ex negativo* definition of the properly attentive way of seeing:

Daß man an so vielem Guten sich so selten nur vergnügt,
kommt, daß der Gewohnheit Stärke die Aufmerksamkeit besiegt.
Doch es schadet zum Vergnügen die Gewohnheit nicht allein;
Nein, auch dieß, daß die Gedanken mehrentheils zerstreuet seyn,
Der Beschäfftigungen Vielheit, und der Vorwürf. Es verhindern
Auch die Trägheit des Gemüths, nebst der Unempfindlichkeit,
Andrer Irrenden Exempel, Stolz und Unzufriedenheit,
Den Genuß des vielen Guten. Diese Feinde muß man mindern,
Und sie zu bekämpfen suchen, eh wir zur Aufmerksamkeit,
Als dem Schlüssel zum Vergnügen und zum Dank, gelangen können.
Wann nun dieses sonder Mühe, ja fast sonder Kampf und Streit,
Nicht erhalten werden kann,
Und sie wirklich eine Kunst, eine solche Kunst zu nennen,
Welche nicht so leicht zu lernen; ach! So fange man doch an,
Sich mit Sorgfalt zu bemühn,
Die sich stets zerstreunden Blicke, den nicht minder flüchtgen Geist,
Zu bezähmen, und sie beyde fest auf einen Punkt zu ziehn,
Weil, auf solche Art zu sehen, eigentlich nur sehen heißt.
Beyder concentrierte Kräfte werden dann zuerst erblicken,
Wie die Werke der Natur sich Bewunderns=würdig schmücken
Dadurch muß und wird Bewunderung in der regen Seel' entstehen.
Man wird tausend Ding' entdecken, die man nie vorher gesehn.[24]

---

23. For these poems, see Brockes, *Irdisches Vergnügen in Gott*, 6:365, 6:429–30, 4:123, 8:567–68, 6:300–304. As Jörg Kreienbrock ("'Merk's! Merk's!,'" 253–54) has shown, attention is not *always* visual attention for Brockes but can include modes of auditory attention as well. The great majority of Brockes's attention poems, however, do focus on visual attention in accordance with his own hierarchy of the senses, which values the visual sense as the most important one, with hearing in a distant second place.

24. Eight lines celebrating the creator follow. Brockes, *Irdisches Vergnügen in Gott*, 1746, 8:572–73.

[That we so rarely delight in so many good things
Is because the force of habit prevails over attention.
Yet it is not habit alone that injures such delight;
No, 'tis also this: that our thoughts are for the most parts distracted,
[Along with] the multitude of occupations and of objects. Moreover
The mind's inertia, along with lack of sensitivity,
The erroneous examples of others, pride and discontentment
Also hinder this delight. We must weaken these enemies
And seek to combat them before we can achieve attentiveness,
As the key to delight and gratitude.
If it is impossible to sustain [or attain] this without effort, nay
almost without strife and struggle
And if it [attention] is indeed to be called an art, such an art
that is not easy to learn; alas! Let us begin
To exert ourselves with care
To tame the constantly distracted glances, the no less volatile mind,
and to contract them both firmly into a single point,
Because only seeing in this manner ought to truly be called "seeing."
The concentrated powers of both will then first behold
How the works of nature are marvelously adorned.
In this way, wonder must arise in the alert soul
One will discover a thousand things never before seen.]

The poem might not count as one of Brockes's masterpieces, but it does spell out with unusual clarity the psychological mechanism that underlies his descriptive poetics. The attention Brockes models in poetic descriptions collects the mind from its thoughtless dispersion and draws attention to habitually overlooked details. In this fresh presentation, even seemingly trivial things reveal themselves as worthy of wonder or admiration (*bewunderns=würdig*), which fills the soul with the appropriate affect of wonder (*Bewunderung*).[25] The resulting pleasure of discovery (*tausend Ding' entdecken*) is

---

25. "Bewunderung" translates the Latin/French term *admiratio(n)* (wonder, admiration, amazement). The double valence of (subjective) amazement and admiration (of something) points to the combination of affect-theoretical and theological motifs in Brockes: ultimately, one's awe for nature's works extends to awe for the creator of these works.

identical to the titular "delight" (*Vergnügen*), to which attention is thus the key (*Schlüssel*).

Attention may unlock the pleasures of seeing in this way, but these are pleasures hard won. The poem's most salient formal feature is the truncation of two lines, both of which deal with difficulties of attaining and sustaining the proper kind of attentiveness. While Brockes often uses relatively free madrigal verses that give many of his poems a rather proselike quality, this poem features a strict trochaic octameter with a clear caesura after the first four feet (the meter may be familiar from Poe's "The Raven"). In the curtailed lines on the exertions of attention, the caesura seems to perform the active interruption of the unregulated stream of experience that the initial lines decry as "habit" and "inertia of the mind." It takes considerable effort, indeed internal strife and struggle to domesticate (*bezähmen*) the tendencies of the inner and outer gaze to flee into distractions—which is why, in a typical invitation to imitate the kind of gaze demonstrated in the poem, the speaker recommends, after an interjected "ach" at the center of the poem, that readers should begin practicing themselves in the art of attention right away.

Brockes's conception of poetic technique assumes that wonder results from the artificial interruption of perception's more detrimental habits; the effect not of presenting something unfamiliar but of a defamiliarizing gaze that reveals the familiar *as* strange. For Brockes, poetic descriptions instruct readers to truly *see* what they see.[26] Their target is not physiological vision but the act of "noticing" what falls into the eyes, as highlighted by the suggestive stress on the usually unstressed *merk* syllable of *Aufmerksamkeit*.[27]

---

26. This recurring point in his poems on attention—"Aufmercksamkeit," "Unselige Unaufmercksamkeit," and "Die Kunst, vernünftig sehen zu lernen"—often is conveyed by seemingly paradoxical formulations such as "Man sieht nicht, was man sieht" (One does not see what one sees) or "daß wir, auch mit offnen Augen, nicht sehen, was wir sehen" (that, even with eyes open, we do not see what we see). Compare Brockes, *Irdisches Vergnügen in Gott*, 6:366, here: 6:430, and see 6:302.

27. In "Mittel gegen die Unachtsamkeit," the stress on *Aufmérksamkeit* could (especially in the first occurrence) also be interpreted as a deviation from Brockes's usually highly regular meter that preserves the natural stress. Yet whether the meter is interpreted as overriding the natural stress, or the natural stress as overriding the

164   Chapter 3

Brockes's poetics of detailed description thus imagines perception as an activity of the soul, equivalent in the topology of the mind traced by the camera obscura with the internal observer's inspection of mental images.[28] The underlying model of perception assumes that we always take note, even when we do not consciously notice that we do so. As Brockes says of the soul in a free translation of a poetic reflection on the senses by Charles-Claude Genest, "its secret reflecting . . . accompanies the senses at all times."[29] Perception guided by poetic language dishabituates this activity and brings to awareness what usually passes by the mind "like a rapidly flowing stream" (*als wie ein schneller Strom*), as Brockes puts it in another one of his attentional poems.[30] To accomplish this and perform perception consciously, it is necessary to stop and focus.

---

meter, both instances of the word mark centers of rhythmic tension in the poem. (The unusual stress seems less ambiguous in poems such as "Iris Persica" and "Betrachtung des Mondscheins"; Brockes, *Irdisches Vergnügen in Gott*, 1747, 3:588, 1:50.)

28. In the remarkable "Die Werckstatt der Seelen" (Workshop of the soul), Brockes directly addresses the camera obscura model: holding a skull in his hand, the speaker is inspired to engage, not in a *memento mori*, but in reflections about the "duncke[l] Kammer" (dark chamber) of the skull as the seat of the soul, which he imagines in terms reminiscent of both a peep box (*Guckkasten*) and a theatrical stage on which a train of representations passes by: "Ich stelle denn den Kopff der Menschen, als einen kleinen Schauplatz mir,/Worauf der Schmuck der schönen Welt verkleinert uns sich zeigt, für" (I thus envision the human head as a small stage/on which the splendor of the beautiful world shows itself to us in miniature form). In the same poem, he reflects (as in the poem "Rothe Glas-Scheibe" discussed later in this chapter) on the problem of the blind spot in a way Crary and Foucault deemed structurally impossible within the classical episteme: "Der Geist so wohl, als unser Auge, kan alles, nur sich selbst nicht sehn" (The mind, just like our eye, can see everything except for itself). As a consequence, the speaker resolves to become "Schauplatz, Spieler, Schauer zugleich" (at once stage, actor, and audience) and to "kehr das Fern=Glas auf mich selbst. Auf mit dem Vorhang! Alles frey!" (turn the telescope upon myself. Raise the curtain! On with the show!) (Brockes, *Irdisches Vergnügen in Gott*, 1739, 5:401–12).

29. "Die Seel ist allemal dabey,/Wenn, daß sie gegenwärtig sey,/Sie selber gleich nicht glaubt. Ihr heimlichs Ueberlegen . . . Begleitet allemahl die Sinnen" (The soul is always there,/Even when it does not believe/To be present. Its secret reflecting . . . accompanies the senses at all times). We only forget that this is so "durch Gewohnheit und durch Zeit" (due to habit and time) (Brockes, *Irdisches Vergnügen in Gott*, 1747, 3:473).

30. See the poem "Unselige Unaufmercksamkeit," Brockes, *Irdisches Vergnügen in Gott*, 1740, 6:430. Compare Leibniz's and Baumgarten's aquatic metaphors for unconscious and preconscious perceptions, as discussed in chapter 4.

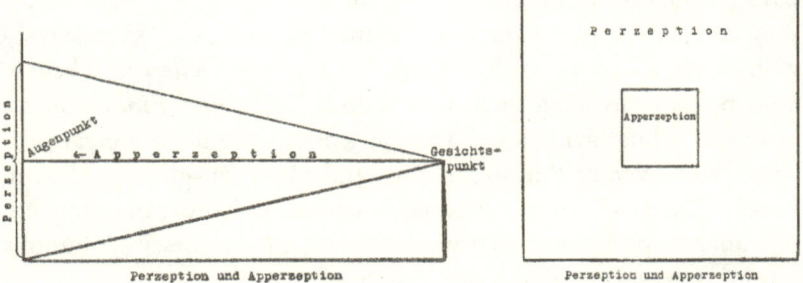

Figure 9. Two diagrams from Langen, *Anschauungsformen in der deutschen Dichtung*, 7–8. The first, illustrating what he terms "Rahmenschau" (framed vision), relies on Leibniz's distinction between perception and apperception to illustrate how attention was thought to function in the early eighteenth century. The second diagram suggests the potentially recursive quality of the epistemology of attention we also encountered in Wolff: what is framed as a partial selection can again be divided into smaller focal parts; attention can go into deeper and deeper detail.

Paying the right kind of attention requires both temporal deceleration (focusing on one detail at a time) and spatial narrowing (focusing on a small fraction of the perceptual field). In a classical study on rationalist poetics, August Langen illustrates this narrowing of perception in two diagrams that suggests what it means for Brockes to focus the mind into a single point (*auf einen Punkt zu ziehn*) (see figure 9).[31]

Because attentive processing must pass the expanse of things through the bottleneck of a single point of heightened consciousness, though, Brockes's poetic descriptions face the same problem as the philosophical epistemology of attention—how to avoid the fragmentation of perceptual objects into a series of disconnected details. Mirroring what Wolff calls "reflection" and "comparison,"

---

31. Langen, *Anschauungsformen*, 7–8. In the much-discussed "Bewährtes Mittel für die Augen," Brockes reinforces this narrowing of vision by holding one hand before one eye in the form of a telescope to create "tunnel vision" (Brockes, *Irdisches Vergnügen in Gott*, 1748, 7:660).

parallel poems on attentive seeing therefore insist that it is necessary to follow up the stage of detailed noticing by "successively going over all parts" of an object (*nach allen Theilen durchzugehen*) before "drawing them into a unity" (*zu einer Einheit sie zu ziehn*) in a final synopsis.[32] This, at least, is the poetological program. However, as Barbara Thums and Hans Drügh have shown, Brockes's excessively detailed poems often fall short of achieving this unity in practice (which was, after all, already Lessing's famous objection to this model of descriptive poetry).[33]

The mission of Brockes's poetry—to refresh the mind's capacity to notice things—presumes that even habitual perception is an ossified form of the mind's attending to things. Habit is already a (diminished) form of attention. Conversely, his poetry calls on readers to make conscious attention a habit. In the poem "Die Kunst vernünftig sehen zu lernen" (The art of learning to see rationally), for instance, he directly invites the reader to become accustomed to (*dich nur . . . gewöhnen*) an attentive way of seeing, and to teach this art to children by having them practice detailed sketching.[34] The defining struggle between attention and habit thus ultimately unfolds between two conflicting "habits of attention": one blunted by repetition and blindly following the "erroneous examples" of others, the other—the art of attention Brockes propagates—a habituation of the mind to constant attentiveness. The dialectical continuity between habit and attention is the reason why there can be a struggle on shared terrain. If the blindness of the senses to the pleasures of creation were simply a fault of human nature—a mark, say, of original sin—it could be mourned but hardly corrected and improved. Brockes's poetry, in short, aims to instill in the reader the

---

32. "Sinn=reiche Bestrafung der Unachtsamkeit" (Brockes, *Irdisches Vergnügen in Gott*, 1753, 4:123). "Bewährtes Mittel für die Augen" (Brockes, *Irdisches Vergnügen in Gott*, 1748, 7:660).
33. See Thums, *Aufmerksamkeit*, 35–42. Channeling Lessing through de Man, Heinz Drügh suggests that Brockes's attempts to describe reality produce a dense verbiage that *blocks* rather than grants access to the extratextual world—with the paradoxical effect that such texts become particularly self-enclosed and self-reflexive. See Drügh, *Ästhetik der Beschreibung*, 32–134.
34. Brockes, *Irdisches Vergnügen in Gott*, 1740, 6:304.

second-order habits of attention that defined the post-Cartesian subject. This is the primary lesson Brockes's poetry conveys—far more important than any explicit or moral teachings, and more significant even than its physicotheological motivation. If Brockes's poetry is, as is often said, didactic, this is because it teaches and promulgates a certain type of attentive gaze. Poetry, for and through his work, becomes a medium for the retraining of perception.

Breitinger's Poetics of the Inner Eye

To explain the mental operations involved in the production and reception of poetry, the introductory chapter of Breitinger's *Critische Dichtkunst* performs a detailed exegesis of the Horatian *ut pictura poesis* analogy based on the different modes of signification employed by poetry and painting. As a verbal art, Breitinger offers, poetry works with arbitrary signs understood, with eighteenth-century semiotics, as conventional but perfectly reliable conduits for mental content. By means of arbitrary signs, poetry "paints" its images directly into the audience's minds ("[die Poesie] kan . . . dadurch ihre Bilder unmittelbar in das Gehirn anderer Menschen schildern").[35] The art of painting, by contrast, works with natural (or iconic) signs that affect the mind indirectly, through afterimages perceptible to the mental eye once the visual shapes of material paintings have passed through the physical sense organs. For Breitinger, the essential "painting" therefore does not happen on external canvases but on the internal canvas of the mind. What matters are the mental images painters evoke *by means of* material painting ("welche der Mahler *vermittelst der Farben durch das Auge in dem Gemüthe* erwecket").[36] Because actual painting can affect the mental canvas only through the detour of the physical eyes, whereas poetry conveys images directly into the minds of readers, poetry is,

---

35. Breitinger, *Critische Dichtkunst*, 1:20. For a lucid discussion of Enlightenment semiotics and its connection with the aesthetics of representation, see Wellbery, *Lessing's Laocoon*, esp. 17–24.
36. Breitinger, *Critische Dichtkunst*, 1:20. Emphasis mine.

according to Breitinger's startling conclusion, better in many respects at "painting" than the art properly so called.

Directness of representation is not the only, and not the most important, advantage of poetry over painting. Ultimately, poetry is superior because it can instruct the eye of the mind in how to *inspect* internal images: "Poetic paintings . . . give instructions on how to observe [*anschauen*] things piece by piece with reason and reflection."[37] This seemingly innocuous claim marks a momentous meeting of rhetorical poetics with the new epistemology of attention. Breitinger interprets the detailed description that is characteristic of rhetorical *evidentia* as modeling to the pupils of the audience the kind of gradual inspection of visual manifolds, feature by feature, that the epistemology of attention identified as the basis of enlightened knowledge. His observing inner eye thus effectively merges the rhetorical *evidentia* topos (vivid visualization "before the eye of the mind") with the internal observer presupposed by the epistemology of the camera obscura.[38] In Breitinger's adaptation, detailed description thus becomes a means of guiding the attentive inspection of images imprinted on the wax tablet, screen, or canvas of the mind. It is accordingly the discourse on attention (*Aufmercksamkeit*) and its associated terminology (*Zerstreuung, sammeln, merckwürdig, Absonderliche,* and so on) that organizes his account of poetry's unfolding in the space between the mental canvas and an attentively observing inner eye:

> By contrast, the poetic painter gathers the eye of the mind out of its distraction [*Zerstreuung*], leads it without haste from one remarkable [*merckwürdigen*] feature to the next, and compels it to make at each par-

---

37. "Gemählde der Poesie . . . geben Anweisung, wie man die Sachen von Stücke zu Stücke mit Vernunft und Ueberlegung anschauen soll" (Breitinger, *Critische Dichtkunst,* 1:28).

38. The merging of an Aristotelean rhetorical topos ("putting-before-the-eyes") with the discourse of representational philosophy ("clear representation of objects") is apparent in Breitinger's first citation of the *evidentia* topos as part of his definition of poetic painting: "dem Auge der Seelen die Gegenstände in solch einer Klarheit vorstellen, als ob sie gegenwärtig vor uns stühnden" (to present objects to the eye of the soul with such clarity as if they were presently standing before us) (Breitinger, *Critische Dichtkunst,* 1:12–13).

ticular feature the specific observation that serves to further his purpose. Because this artificial [*künstliche*] painter performs his painting in the imagination of the reader with every word as with a new brushstroke, and continuously adds one notion to the other, he leaves the reader no freedom to leisurely wander about with a volatile and uncertain eye of the mind, or to get lost in the confusion [*Vermischung*] of the manifold. Instead, the poet directs the reader's attention to particular details [*das Absonderliche*], whose artificial connection he demonstrates to the reader in accordance with their order, while also slipping in short but useful lessons at times, through which light and clarity must necessarily arise in the notion.[39]

Such references to attention in *Critische Dichtkunst* do more than vaguely suggest that poetry captivates the minds of an audience: they specifically evoke Christian Wolff's influential concept of attention, which would have been familiar to Breitinger's educated readership. As we have seen, for Wolff the perceptual labor of attention in cognition involves two levels or stages. Attention proper (*Aufmercksamkeit*) focuses on one feature of a compound representation at the expense of all others in order to increase the clarity of that feature; and reflection (*Überdencken*) strings these attentive acts together into a sequence until all relevant features, as well their interconnection, can be surveyed by the mind. Breitinger follows Wolff—but only to a point. Poetic descriptions guide the mental eye from one mark (or "remarkable feature") to the next. In this way, poetry, too, concentrates the mind's attention on features isolated from a compound perception (*das Absonderliche*) and demonstrates the interconnection (*Verknüpfung*) of distinctive parts.[40] In one decisive aspect, however, Breitinger's poetic attentiveness differs from Wolff's cognitive program. Poetry, to be sure, does bring some light

---

39. Breitinger, *Critische Dichtkunst*, 1:22–23. All translations from Breitinger's *Critische Dichtkunst* are mine and reflect the gendering of the original.

40. Similar to the term *merckwürdig*, the word *absonderlich* should be understood in two parallel senses: literally, as what the mind has "sundered from" (*abgesondert*) from a compound representation; and figuratively, as what stands out as "strange" (*sonderbar*). The duality of the term suggests the hybrid nature of attention as a voluntary and involuntary activity. This hybridity, and the transition from being *affected* by poetry to paying active attention to its subject matter, figures prominently in Breitinger's theory of the new and the marvelous, which I will discuss in the following section.

and clarity into the mind's notions by foregrounding distinctive features of things. But it does not, as philosophical cognition must, strive toward a complete inventory of these things' essential features. The goal of poetry, in other words, is not clarity and distinctness—perceptions in which all relevant distinguishing features are clearly recognized—but patterns of selective perception that move and please. In Breitinger's words, a philosopher "must . . . carefully detect and collect . . . all features and marks [*Merckmahle*] of a thing, . . . whereas the poetic painter, who . . . wants to move the mind, must only select [*auslesen*] and connect the smallest and most particular features."[41]

With the telos of philosophical apperception suspended, attention is released from the task of cataloging essential features and can come into view for its own activity—that is, for its constitutive selectivity or one-sidedness in distinguishing and combining marks and features. Affirming this selectivity has the effect of highlighting the divergence between images and their inspection by the inner eye. Breitinger's account of poetic painting pivots on this "freedom" of the mental eye vis-à-vis images. The argument for the inferiority of painting already presupposes this freedom as the potential to go astray: because the mental eye is free to take note of this or that feature of a representation (or let features go unnoticed altogether), it can get lost in the manifold pictorial material conveyed by paintings. Poetry compensates for this deficiency by collecting the reader's focus and guiding perception. That it can and must do so, however, again presupposes that images, in general, leave open how they are to be inspected by the inner eye.

Even in philosophy, the idea that the features discerned in a representation could perfectly map onto all essential characteristics of the thing being represented had been relegated to the level of a regulative ideal rather than an actually attainable goal.[42] Neverthe-

---

41. Breitinger, *Critische Dichtkunst*, 1:48.
42. Countering Descartes, Leibniz claimed that even clear and distinct perceptions do not exhaustively capture the "real essences" of things but merely provide "nominal essences," sufficient marks for explicitly distinguishing things from others; see Leibniz's foundational "Meditations on Knowledge, Truth, and Ideas," 23–24. On the importance of Leibniz's adjustment of Cartesian epistemology for

less, the ideal of completeness continued to give philosophical apperception its teleological orientation to strive for an inventory of features that was as exhaustive and explicit as possible. In the philosophical context, the inevitable difference between the world and its apperception was no more than a mark of a finite mind's relative imperfection. In Breitinger's poetics, however—certainly less by programmatic intention than as a consequence of cross-wiring poetic description and philosophical apperception—the activity of the inner eye renounces its alliance with the pre-given structure of things and begins to take on a life of its own. Drawing the consequences from these reflections on poetic attention, the introductory chapter concludes by emphasizing that poetic representation does more than simply *reflect* objects as they are already in given nature:

> Nature and the skillfully imitating painter offer their already fabricated [*schon verfertigten*] and completed works to be viewed at once, but have to leave it to the ability of the spectator what impression they make on his mind.... [By contrast,] the poetic painter also has the effect of his paintings in his power, and controls this effect at will.... Therefore, one can justifiably say that his skillful imitation can not only reach, but exceed, the beauty and force of its original; for the effect of a good poetic description is necessary and certain... whereas the beauty and art of a painting, or of an original in nature, often remain hidden to the coarser senses.[43]

Breitinger's shift of perspective announces itself in his peculiar use of the term "impression [*Eindruck*]," which conflicts with its usually passive connotations. According to the passage, impressions are "made" by the spectator's attentional capabilities rather than by external things or their painterly depictions. This constructive aspect of apperception was, to be sure, foundational for philosophical cognition as well; it was, in fact, the implicit basis for the epistemic certainty of clear and distinct representations. In this paradigm, the mind has complete insight into such representations precisely because they are, in the clarity of their composition, as good as self-constructed—internally "reassembled" from parts that a sharply

---

the development of aesthetics in the eighteenth century, see Adler, *Die Prägnanz des Dunklen*, 1–11, 38–40.

43. Breitinger, *Critische Dichtkunst*, 1:27–28.

focused attention had discerned within compound representations. Breitinger's formulation also echoes the maker's knowledge principle at the core of this paradigm, as he views works of painting as having the disadvantage of being "already fabricated and complete." Poetry, by contrast, demonstrates the process of manufacturing its works right before the eye of the mind and is therefore more closely aligned with the operations essential to philosophical cognition. In the case of philosophical apperception, however, the constructive moment remains contained as *re*construction—as a sufficiently accurate mental reconstitution of things as they are in themselves (or as God had made them). Because poetry is not bound by such reconstruction, it is free to "construct imitations" that surpass originals in nature. The paradoxical implications audible in such a formulation mark the irritation of traditional conceptions of poetics as well as metaphysics that lurks in Breitinger's poetic adaptation of philosophical cognition. With the *impression* made by things having become dependent on the *activity* of attention, a systematic gap opens up between things and their perception. It is within this gap, in the interstices between mind and world, that Breitinger develops his theory of poetic representation. The key terms of this theory are "the new" (*das Neue*) and "the marvelous" (*das Wunderbare*).

The New and the Marvelous: Poetic Representation as Defamiliarization

Breitinger's reflections on the new begin by evoking a prelapsarian state in which *no* gap would exist between things in nature and the impressions they make on the mind. If that were the case, he reasons, poetry could be "imitation of nature" in the sense of a simple *re*-presentation of natural objects. Successful representations would make impressions commensurate with those made by things themselves, and poetry would borrow all its power to affect the mind from the originals it represents. However: "This would indeed happen if numbing habit [*betäubende Gewohnheit*] did not, on the side of humans, block all access to and influence these effects have on the mind. The force of this habit [*Macht dieser Gewohnheit*] is so strong that it ... sinks us into an inattentive stupor; to the point where neither the beautiful, nor the great, nor the instructive, nor the moving can touch us in the least if they daily hover before our eyes and we become all too familiar with them."[44]

Breitinger's opening comparison between poetry and painting had already shown that things and their impressions diverge. Evoking the force of habit, Breitinger now provides an explanation for this discrepancy. As Brockes also complained, repeated exposure to the same thing anaesthetizes the mind and (to read Breitinger with Blake) "clogs up the doors of perception." We still see "all too familiar things," to be sure, but we no longer *see* what we see: impressions continue to enter the dark chamber of the mind, but their inspection has fossilized into worn-out patterns that no longer excite the inner eye and, as a result, drain overly familiar representations of their ability to move and please. The source of the pleasure evoked by poetic representations consequently lies in the new and unfamiliar. Novelty—the new, unusual, strange, and extraordinary—reactivates the attentiveness required for things to make forceful impressions by inducing wonder (*mit einer angenehmen Bewunderung überraschen*).[45] Confronted with new and unusual material, the perceiving inner eye is reawakened from its phlegmatic slumber and set in motion.[46] For Breitinger, poetic beauty is accordingly equivalent to "what ... pleasantly charms the eye of the soul

---

44. Breitinger, *Critische Dichtkunst*, 1:107–8.
45. Breitinger, *Critische Dichtkunst*, 1:109–10, quote at 110.
46. Breitinger's conception of poetic imitations as stimulants of attention invokes anthropological reflections from the poetics of Jean-Baptiste Dubos (from whom Breitinger also borrows in other contexts, including in his comparison of the signs employed by poetry and painting and his conception of the marvelous in poetry). In Dubos's sensualist poetics, however, poetry's stimulation of attention serves the different function of legitimizing the arts as an antidote to the potentially destructive human drive for distraction: fictional representations provide a harmless outlet for the mind's incessant need to occupy itself and thus defuse the power of the passions. Broadly speaking, Dubos follows Aristotle in ascribing a cathartic function to the arts, while Breitinger aligns with the Neoplatonist tradition by identifying poetry's occupation of the mind with sensory images as a steppingstone toward intellectual knowledge (as detailed below). For the relevant sections in Dubos, see his *Critical Reflections*, 5–35, 196–201, 321–31 (an eighteenth-century translation of his *Réflexions critiques sur la poesie et sur la peinture*).

through the luster of wondrous [*verwundersamen*] novelty and fills the mind with sweet unrest."⁴⁷ In a defamiliarization theory avant la lettre, he explains poetic pleasure through the movement of an inner eye aroused from its habitual stasis. The emotive force of poetry rests above all on the sweet unrest of a mind that avidly scans new and unfamiliar material.⁴⁸

Breitinger's understanding of the nexus of wonder and defamiliarization so closely resembles Brockes's because both draw on a historical network of knowledge concerning wonder and attention that, like the paradigm of clear and distinct knowledge, finds its locus classicus in Descartes (although in his doctrine of the passions rather than in his theoretical philosophy). As I discussed in chapter 1, Descartes defined wonder, in words still echoed by Breitinger, as the "sudden surprise of the soul which brings it to consider with attention the objects that seem to it unusual or extraordinary."⁴⁹ In the early eighteenth century, the transition from passivity to active attention facilitated by wonder became the centerpiece of a new type of descriptive poetry, in the German context most prominently represented by Brockes, that sought to reveal the "marvels" of nature. Breitinger again interprets the epistemological precept in terms of rhetorical *evidentia* and its two sides—the detailed description of *enargeia* and the power to move associated with *energeia*, which mirror the voluntary and involuntary, the active and passive aspects of attention. Because the affective force of poetic visualization has the power to elicit attention to details without requiring a strenuous effort on the part of the audience, poetry is capable of inducing the attentiveness necessary to attain clear and distinct knowledge. Inheriting the role ascribed to beauty in Platonic and Neoplatonic metaphysics, poetic marvelousness thus functions as a sensory repre-

---

47. Breitinger, *Critische Dichtkunst*, 1:296.
48. Despite anticipatory echoes, Breitinger's combined theory of poetic novelty and beauty is not a theory of "free play": As the opening chapter makes clear, the inner eye's activity is not free to roam on its own but guided by the descriptions of the poet, in whose traces readers perform their observations.
49. Descartes, *The Philosophical Writings*, 1:353 (§70). Descartes's reflections on wonder acknowledge the involuntary side of attention, but only as a gateway to active and voluntary attention.

sentation that awakens the mind to its own intellectual activity—
which means, for Breitinger, to its ability to pay careful attention.

Breitinger's account of how wonder and marvelousness arise in
poetic representations, however, immediately complicates this new
version of the old idea that poetry serves as a handmaiden of philosophical knowledge. The distinctive shift in the discourse on wonder and attention around the turn of the eighteenth century pointed
out by Lorraine Daston also helps to illuminate the context and the
trajectory of Breitinger's theory of poetic representation. While the
wonder produced by unusual and extraordinary objects was initially
seen as a psychological crutch to assist the mind in observing particulars with the sustained attention required by the new scientific
method, by the early eighteenth century the sequence had switched.
Proper attentiveness was newly seen as capable of revealing the marvelousness of even seemingly ordinary things. Wonder was considered a reward of, rather than an incentive for, disciplined attention.[50]
Just as in Brockes's poetry, wonder as both "subjective" amazement
and "objective" marvelousness of nature was reconceived as the effect of a specific mode of perception.

As indicated by several comparisons of poets with scientists
conducting observations and experiments,[51] Breitinger's burgeoning theory of poetic representation relies on this relocation of wonder to the eye of the beholder. Novelty, Breitinger clarifies, lies less
in a particular set of marvelous objects than in the way any object
is perceived or represented.[52] Poetry is thus not the representation
of the extraordinary but an extraordinary mode of representation
(*Art der Vorstellung*).[53] This conceit of "extraordinary modes of

---

50. Daston, *Kurze Geschichte*, 15–35; see also Daston and Park, *Wonders*, 215–328.
51. See, for instance, Breitinger's comparisons of marvelous poetic representations with Réaumur's microscopic observations of insects or the work of astronomers (*Critische Dichtkunst*, 1:110, 112, 120). On the central importance of wonder for Breitinger's poetics, see Gess, *Staunen*, 45–53.
52. Breitinger, *Critische Dichtkunst*, 1:123–25.
53. Breitinger, *Critische Dichtkunst*, 1:295, 300. Breitinger uses *Vorstellung* (in a
manner analogous to the English term "representation") indiscriminately for representation in the mind and artistic (re)presentation. A concept of *Darstellung* was not
yet available.

representation" provides the *Critische Dichtkunst* with the language for effects of representation that cannot be explained by reference to the represented object. Throughout the work, Breitinger struggles to articulate a place for this contribution of what we now tend to call "form" in representing a given "content." Sometimes he draws on the classical imagery for rhetorical ornament and explains the effect of modes of representation as the outward draping of truth in new and unusual clothing, makeup, or sugarcoating, implying that the inner core of the represented content remains essentially unchanged by its outward costumes.[54] At other times, however, especially when giving a more technical account of the process in terms of the representational paradigm, Breitinger understands the formal contribution as a *transformation* or *deformation* of things modeled on the distortion of mental images under the influence of the passions (which make things appear "in a wholly different size, figure, and shape [*Gestalt*] than they [really] have").[55] The distortion of things seen through the "eyes of the passions"[56] thus becomes a general model for the way rhetorical devices "deform" representations.[57] In Breitinger's representational poetics, the purpose of such devices is not the embellishment of language but the deformation of mental images to make things appear in a new, strange, or extraordinary shape. *Evidentia* effectively becomes the paradigmatic trope of poetry, the master trope in terms of which all other figures and tropes are reformulated—as so many techniques of (dis)figuring things on the mental canvas before the eye of the mind.

Breitinger's concept of poetic estrangement anticipates (and helps to inaugurate) the cognitivist as well as the vitalist strains of modern

---

54. Breitinger, *Critische Dichtkunst*, 1:6, 53–56, 115, 132, 292, 299, 346, etc.
55. Breitinger, *Critische Dichtkunst*, 1:309.
56. The distortion results from the fact "daß die Leidenschaften alles mit eigenen und gantz andern Augen anschauen" (that the passions behold everything with peculiar and completely different eyes) (Breitiner, *Critische Dichtkunst*, 1:308).
57. This parallels the genealogy of the term "sensate" for a type of representation in Baumgarten's aesthetics. In Wolff, *sensitivus* had designated a desire accompanied by a confused or distorted representation of the good; Baumgarten generalizes this epithet to denote all "confused" representations below the level of clear and distinct ones. See Baumgarten, *Meditationes*, 8–9 (§iii); also Heinz Paetzold's introduction to the same text, xi; and Campe, "Effekt der Form," 127–36.

theories of poetic defamiliarization, paradigmatically articulated in Bertolt Brecht's *Verfremdung* and Viktor Shklovsky's *ostranenie*. In portraying perceptual estrangement as a propaedeutic to active attention, Breitinger prefigures the connection between cognitive distancing and critical thinking central to Brecht's understanding of defamiliarization. Because Breitinger explains poetry's power to move in similarly cognitive terms—as the animation and rejuvenation of perceptual powers—he also, however, ascribes to estrangement the revitalizing function for the "life" of the mind that would become central to Shklovsky's approach.[58] Poetry stimulates people to think for themselves, yet the same cognitive activation also sets the mind's powers in passionate motion and rekindles their vitality. The two sides of attention model the two strands of poetic defamiliarization theory.

Breitinger's own interpretation of his defamiliarization theory avant la lettre oscillates between two poles: Either the renewal of perception through unusual representation *renews the possibility of (correct) perception* (and merely facilitates recognition of a preexisting truth through the detour of a defamiliarizing poetic representation). Or it reveals *new possibilities of perception* (suggesting that what seemed like distortions were in fact different modes of perceiving). Both interpretations are explored side by side in the *Critische Dichtkunst*, without ultimately resolving the tension between them. The characterization of poetic artifice as a "semblance of novelty" (*Schein der Neuheit*) condenses both moments in a single phrase.[59] According to the first interpretation, defamiliarization is only temporary and therefore restorative. Poetry represents things in a new light—in the alluring luster (*Schein, Glantz*) of strangeness that spurs the inner eye into action and boosts the natural light of truth otherwise dimmed by the force of habit.[60] The novelty of representation,

---

58. On the vitalist objective of Shklovsky's formalist defamiliarization theory, see Gess, *Staunen*, 109–15, which also suggests similarities to Breitinger.

59. Breitinger, *Critische Dichtkunst*, 1:110, 295, etc.

60. This type of light imagery (light of truth, light of nature, light as clarity of representations, poetic representation "in a new light") suffuses *Critische Dichtkunst*; see, for instance, 1:112, 131, 231, etc. Breitinger's nonterminological use of *Schein* anticipates the word's career as a defining concept for aesthetic truth-content beginning around 1800.

however, also remains *Schein* in the sense of mere semblance, as the strange representation ultimately does nothing but restore an inherent recognizability that was temporarily obscured. The other interpretation comes into play when Breitinger distinguishes between the new and the marvelous. The terms are sometimes used interchangeably, with the marvelous merely implying a greater degree of divergence from the ordinary. When a distinction is made, however, it marks the point where the difference of *degree* that separates original truth from its "novel" representation turns into a difference of *kind*; the point where the connection to ordinary truth is stretched so thin that it breaks down—or rather, where it *seems* to break down: "The wonder that arises in us through the feeling of novelty grows and intensifies in accordance with the degree of divergence [from the course of things]. When this divergence proceeds to a point where a representation seems to contradict [*entgegen zu stehen scheinet*] the usual order of things, it loses the name of the new, and obtains the name of the marvelous instead."[61]

If this contradiction is to remain merely apparent—if marvelous representations are to continue to convey a form of truth—then this truth must be of a kind that can no longer be recovered by "subtracting" the temporary semblance of novelty. In the qualitative leap from a gradual to a categorical deviation, the factor of refraction separating the original light of truth from the *Schein* of its poetic presentation becomes indeterminable. Such inextricable entanglement between mode of representation and represented content finally finds expression in the paradoxical image of truth's concealment behind a completely unfamiliar and yet transparent disguise: "The marvelous, by contrast, casts off the semblance of truth and possibility, and assumes a nondeceptive semblance of falsehood and contradiction; it disguises truth in an entirely strange but transparent mask [*gantz fremde aber durchsichtige Maßke*]."[62] The imagery of clothing has transformed into one of masking and disguise: the artificial addition no longer enhances the truth's natural features but completely obscures them. At the same time, however, the mask is supposed to remain entirely

---

61. Breitinger, *Critische Dichtkunst*, 1:129.
62. Breitinger, *Critische Dichtkunst*, 1:130.

transparent and to reveal truth. The coincidence of total defamiliarization and transparency suggests that the disguise itself generates its own kind of transparency here: one can no longer distinguish what is visible "on the mask" from what is visible "through the mask." According to Breitinger's second interpretation of poetic defamiliarization, truth is no longer what remains after subtracting artificial additions, but the function of a specific mode of representation. A similar suspicion and similar theoretical quandaries also surface occasionally in Brockes's poems.

Brockes and the Contingencies of Perception

The term best suited for bringing into focus how Brockes interprets the effects of his "art" of perception is the German *Perspektiv*. In Brockes's time, the term had a wider spectrum of meaning than it does today, including not only "perspectives" in the sense familiar to modern German and English speakers but also optical instruments of vision such as telescopes or spyglasses. In Brockes's oeuvre the neuter noun *Perspektiv* regularly appears both in the sense of an optical instrument and in the sense of a perspectival gaze running from a specific point of view toward a single focal point, what Lange distinguished as *Gesichtspunkt* and *Augpunkt*. Philosophically, the term is interesting because it has become the shibboleth of a kind of epistemological relativism. That knowledge is "perspectival" suggests that it is marred by a limited standpoint and reflects only a one-sided, necessarily incomplete picture of the whole. Similarly, *Perspektiv*s in the sense of optical instruments are associated with the historical moment when, as Joseph Vogl argued with regard to Galileo's telescope, knowledge became media-dependent.[63] In Brockes's poetry, however, *Perspektiv*s in either sense do not yet carry these connotations—and often, in fact, instead take on a significance opposed to the partiality we tend to ascribe to the term. Take, for instance, the poem "Gedancken über ein Perspecktiv" (Thoughts on perspective),[64] which

---

63. Vogl, "Medien-Werden."
64. Brockes, *Irdisches Vergnügen in Gott*, 1753, 4:287.

has the observer gaze down a shaded alley to notice "daß alles sich zuletzt in ein klein Pünctchen zieht" (that everything contracts toward a single point in accordance with the laws of central perspective).[65] This observation, notably, does not lead the speaker to reflect on the perspectival conditions of seeing and understanding in today's sense—that is, the one-sidedness, partiality, and distortions of a gaze that is bound to a limited standpoint. On the contrary, the speaker reverses the lines of sight and instead finds "daß alles sich *aus* einem Pünctchen zieht" (that everything flows from a single focal point).[66] For Brockes, even the perspectival condition of the gaze thus turns into evidence of a world focused around a divine center. The same equation of perspectival gaze and cosmic harmony is on display in the frontispiece of the eighth volume of Brockes's *Irdisches Vergnügen in Gott* (see figure 10).

Similarly, Brockes's famous eulogies on *Perspektiv*s, now in the sense of optical instruments, describe the visual defamiliarization effects of such devices in great detail but consistently interpret them as amplifications of the natural gaze—as an extension of the visual field rather than its essential alteration. Telescopes, the speaker of one poem assures, generate *more* but not an essentially *different* kind of visibility.[67] There, are, however, moments in Brockes's poetry when this neutralization of the distortion effects of artificial techniques of seeing threatens to break down. One particularly striking example, from the fourth volume of the *Irdisches Vergügen*, is the poem titled "Rothe Glas-Scheibe" (Red glass pane), in which the speaker's eye is supplemented not with a microscope or telescope but, as the title suggests, with a piece of colored glass. It begins in the characteristically guileless style of much of Brockes's poetry, only to take a quick turn to the terrifying:

---

65. Brockes, *Irdisches Vergnügen in Gott*, 1753, 4:287.
66. Brockes, *Irdisches Vergnügen in Gott*, 1753, 4:287, my emphasis.
67. See, for instance, the poem "Die dritte Offenbarung" in Brockes, *Irdisches Vergnügen in Gott*, 1748, 9:438–39.

Figure 10. Beyond the conspicuously inconspicuous foreground composed of pastoral motifs, the actual subject matter of the engraving is the conelike shape of the perspectival gaze itself. Like the encasement of a spyglass, the carefully arranged hedges of the French garden limit peripheral vision and conduct the gaze toward the vanishing point, their edges marking vanishing lines that converge just below the main entrance to the building. All elements in the middle ground of the engraving—but above all the water spout—mark the outlines of perspectival vision and are, in this sense, central perspective incarnate. The façade of the mansion at whose entrance the perspective converges appears like the natural telos of the gaze—which seems to look back at the observer. The pediment of the building in the center of the engraving features an oculus, a circular window suspended in a triangle like the eye of providence, overseeing the garden landscape from above. The epigram praises the beauty of art entwined (*verschwistert*) with nature, and underscores the harmony of art, nature, and divinity suggested in the engraving.

Als ich jüngst mich dergestalt an der schönen Welt vergnügte,
Und, zu meiner Augen=Lust, ein Gott schuldigs Dancken fügte;
Sah' ich dieser Landschaft Pracht, durch ein rothes Scheibgen Glas,
Mit Erstaunen, mit Vergnügen, aber halb mit Schrecken an.
Alles Grüne war dahin, roth war alles Laub und Graß[68]

[As I recently delighted in the beautiful world,
And, to the pleasure of my eyes, added due gratitude to God,
I viewed the splendor of the landscape through a small red pane of glass,
With amazement, with delight, but also with a touch of terror.
All the green was gone; red was every leaf and blade of grass]

Viewing the color-inverted landscape, the amazement and pleasure Brockes's speakers typically feel when experimenting with different modes of vision is now mixed with terror. In the red glass pane, the eye is supplemented with a prosthesis that does not expand or contract but *colors* the field of vision. As a device whose effects cannot be neutralized in the way Brockes domesticates the distortion effects of telescopes and microscopes, the tinted glass raises serious questions:

Ist das Grüne denn nicht grün? sind die Blumen denn nicht bunt?
Kan ein Umstand, der so klein,
Auszurichten fähig seyn,
Daß der gantze Kreiß der Welt anders scheinet, anders wird?
Denn wer weiß, ob unser Auge sich bishero nicht geirrt.[69]

[Is green not green then? are flowers not colorful after all?
Can a circumstance so small
Be capable of effecting
The whole circle of the world to seem different, become different?
For who knows whether our eye has not erred until now.]

As if to emphasize the speaker's perplexity at the little glass pane's outsized effect, the trochaic octameter is split into separate tetrameters in

---

68. Brockes, *Irdisches Vergnügen in Gott*, 1739, 5:171. The image of the tinted glass is not without precedent in the skeptical literature—Montaigne, for instance, uses similar imagery—but appears recontextualized as one of many artificial supplements of vision Brockes explores in his poetry; compare Montaigne, *Essais*, 2:428.

69. Brockes, *Irdisches Vergnügen in Gott*, 1739, 5:172.

the respective lines. The asyndetic juxtaposition of mutually exclusive alternatives on the axis of selection—"anders scheinenen" and "anders werden," or (only) *seeming* and (actually) *becoming* different—mirrors the speaker's main dilemma. In contrast to modifications of quantity, which are by necessity comparable by a common standard, modifications of quality lead to irreducibly different *kinds* of perception. It is not least for this reason that contemporaneous philosophy from Locke to Wolff sought to establish an observer-independent reality in quantitatively determinable primary qualities (such as extension and motion) while demoting *qualia* like taste, smell, and color perception to the level of observer-dependent secondary qualities. Things, as Wolff explains in his metaphysics, can differ in size without changing their essence—just as geometric shapes like triangles retain their properties when increased or diminished in magnitude.[70] The gaze through the red glass pane and the unobstructed gaze, by contrast, are categorically different modes of vision irreducible to a common standard or measure. As in the case of Breitinger's "seemingly marvelous" representations, the semblance of change can therefore no longer be reduced to the uncolored gaze by a quasi-quantitative operation—which means, in turn, that the eye's own nature provides only one possibility of seeing among others, and therefore a potentially fallible one at that.

Indeed, the artificial modification of the gaze threatens to recoil on the naked eye: "Hätten wir ein rothes Häutchen in den Augen überkommen,/Hätte ja für uns die Welt andre Farben angenommen" (If a red membrane had covered our eyes,/The world would have taken on different colors for us),[71] the speaker speculates. Faced with other possibilities of seeing, Brockes hits upon the thought that the supposedly natural gaze might be not only *artificial*—this is something he already presupposes—but *biased* by this artificiality. The suspicion arises that it may be one art of seeing among others that merely shows the kind of world that corresponds to its gaze. Half a century before Kant's *Critiques* and Heinrich von Kleist's letter to Wilhelmine von Zenge, Brockes articulates the suspicion that we might only ever be dealing with phenomena, with things (and

---

70. Wolff, *German Metaphysics*, 31 (§66).
71. Brockes, *Irdisches Vergnügen in Gott*, 1739, 5:172.

Brockes's phrase here anticipates the terminology of German Idealism) as they are "für uns" (for us)—although they may reveal themselves differently to a different kind of gaze.[72]

Brockes's speaker goes on to explore this epistemological dilemma in terms of contemporaneous speculations about the plurality of worlds. These astronomical speculations provide the poem with a language for conceiving of categorically different possibilities that, as multiple different totalities or "worlds," cannot easily be subordinated to a single overarching whole:

> Und wer weiß, ob in den Cörpern, welche wir Planeten nennen,
> Nicht dergleichen den Geschöpfen zugeordnet werden können,
> Daß denselben alle Vorwürff' anders, als sie würcklich, scheinen,
> Und, durch ein gefärbtes Auge, sie, von Cörpern, bald vermeinen,
> Daß sie roth, dort, daß sie blau, da sie doch von allem nichts,
> Und nur bloß ein falsches Blendwerk eines irrenden Gesichts.
> Dieser Zweifel quälte mich, und ich konnte mich nicht fassen[73]

> [And who knows whether among the bodies we call planets
> There are not those sorts assigned to creatures
> That to them all objects appear different than they really [are]
> And that they believe of bodies, through a colored eye,
> That some [are] red, others, blue, when they [are] really nothing of anything,
> Just false phantasmagorias of erroneous vision.
> This doubt tormented me, and I could not find my bearings]

Ostensibly a speculation about the perceptual apparatus of extraterrestrials, these lines in fact negotiate the contingency of *human* perception. What troubles the speaker is, after all, the thought that "we" could be such creatures to whom objects always appear different than they really are. The subsequent lines try to make the glass pane less terrifying and save the neutrality of perception by arguing that the human eye can, thanks to divine providence, perceive a variety colors, whereas the glass tinges everything in a mo-

---

72. Brockes's formulation hits the mark of what Friedrich Kittler describes as the genealogy of Kant's transcendental philosophy and German Idealism from optical media; see Kittler, *Optische Medien*, 114–19.

73. Brockes, *Irdisches Vergnügen in Gott*, 1739, 5:172.

notonous red.⁷⁴ But this time the speaker himself seems less than convinced by his own explanation. His thoughts therefore continue to digress into extraterrestrial regions:

> Aber, ob in andern Welten, oder anderen Planeten,
> Die bey uns begrünte Felder sich nicht etwan würcklich röthen
> Oder blau, wie ein Sapphir, oder gelb, wie Gold, vielleicht,
> Oder sonst gefärbet sind, kann man nicht mit Recht verneinen⁷⁵
>
> [But whether in other worlds, or other planets,
> fields that are green here do not perhaps actually turn red,
> Or blue like a sapphire, or perhaps yellow like gold,
> Or have some other color, one cannot deny with certainty]

Revealingly, the formulations that entertain the possibility of different color perceptions on other planets leave open whether this happens, as before, because of the different perceptual apparatus of extraterrestrials—or "in fact," in things themselves. It is precisely the undecidability between the two options that troubles the speaker. The closing lines of the poem try to provide a final justification for why it is impossible to rightfully deny the fact that the world can always *be* as well as *seem* possible in another way as well:

> Weil des Schöpfers Wunder=Werck' in der bildenden Natur,
> In derselben Form und Farben Mannigfaltigkeit nicht nur,
> Sondern in der Aenderung unerschöpflich sind und scheinen.⁷⁶
>
> [Because the Creator's marvels in formative nature are and seem
> Inexhaustible not only in their forms and colors,
> But also in their alteration]

The final line of the German text coordinates the two options previously kept separate, seeming and being different, and traces both to the common denominator of the creator's inexhaustible capacity for *Änderung* or alteration. This is perhaps a less idiosyncratic solution

---

74. This point is emphasized in Stadler, *Der technisierte Blick*, 74n37. Stadler's footnote provides the only, albeit brief, discussion of the poem I found in the secondary literature.
75. Brockes, *Irdisches Vergnügen in Gott*, 1739, 5:173.
76. Brockes, *Irdisches Vergnügen in Gott*, 1739, 5:173.

to the problem than it may seem. The problem of contingency that confronts Brockes in this poem—the suspicion that things do not exist by necessity but could also always be and be perceived otherwise—is, if we take Hans Blumenberg's word for it, above all a legacy of monotheistic religions and their idea of a universe contingent upon an *act* of creation in contrast to the eternal, self-sustaining cosmos associated with classical antiquity.[77] But solving the problem of epistemological uncertainty by referring it to a divine power for arbitrary creation is more convincing as a genealogy of the problem than as a viable solution. A *Schöpfer* (or creator) with an *unerschöpflich* (or inexhaustible) power of creating ever-different entities and semblances hardly seems fit to play the role of a reliable anchor for the order of things.

The pluralization of the world not only multiplies the possibilities of seeing but also creates something that lies beyond all these possibilities. The fact that upsets Brockes is, after all, not the artificial changeability of perspectives itself—this remains a source of viewing pleasure as always—but the prospect that none of these perspectives may capture the world as it is "in itself." This idea, however, becomes undeniable once no form of observation can claim validity as the single correct one and once multiple different perspectives can no longer by reduced to a common denominator. In this way, the many possibilities of seeing not only exclude each other but also preclude the possibility of ever completely understanding things as they are. They thus produce a systematic excess that all attempts of understanding must presuppose without ever being able to retrieve it into comprehensibility. The entanglement of *being* and *semblance* at the conclusion of Brockes's poem marks the breakdown of the mechanism of containment that kept artifice and art within the bounds of the natural order. Of course, the event of this breakdown is not localizable to this particular poem. By the next poem in the collection, Brockes will have recovered from the shock and will delight in the marvelous harmony of nature as ever before. But what this poem can show is the basic structure of a discursive event in the

---

77. Blumenberg therefore sees contingency as a genuinely monotheistic concept. See, for instance, his early "Das Verhältnis von Natur und Technik."

making. That Brockes's reflection on the contingencies of perception is not an isolated incident but tracks a broader discursive problem is indicated by an analogous dilemma in Breitinger's poetics. Breitinger, too, explores the problem with reference to the plurality of worlds, though he resorts to Leibniz's possible worlds instead of the astronomical worlds visited by Brockes's poetic speculations.

Possibilities of Poetic Representation: Imitating "Possible Nature"

Breitinger's adaptation of the discourse on attention for poetics subtly transformed the subservient role played by attention in Wolff's gnoseology. By granting greater leeway to attention's selective and constructive aspects, it carved out a space for reflecting on the independent contribution of modes of representation to the presented content. These may still seem like rather technical matters, limited to the history of poetics in a narrow sense. But the importance of such technical matters for the broader history of reflection on knowledge becomes evident in the chapter on the principle of the imitation of nature. As a long-standing principle that ties poetics to classical metaphysics by relegating art to the derivative order of an imitation, reflection, or copy of nature, nature-imitation compels Breitinger to confront the metaphysical implications of the license he grants to poetic artifice. Commentators who gauged the intellectual-historical significance of Breitinger's poetics beyond its contribution to the *Literaturstreit* have in fact tended to focus on this principle, especially on Breitinger's extension of imitating nature to the realm of Leibniz's possible worlds. Hans Blumenberg attributes to Breitinger's conceit of imitating possible worlds a pivotal role in the modern abandonment of the principle of imitation of nature, a process that, for Blumenberg, encapsulates modernity's epochal reversal of the ontological priority of the order of nature over human production.[78] Ernst

---

78. See the pertinent works of Hans Blumenberg, especially the early essays "Nachahmung der Natur" (references to Breitinger at 42–45) and "Das Verhältnis von Natur und Technik."

Cassirer locates Breitinger's innovation in the appropriation of Leibniz's logical idealism for artistic creation, which transferred the prerogative of logic over determinate existence onto the aesthetic powers of the artist.[79] Closer inspection of the chapter titled "Nachahmung der Natur" (Imitation of nature) shows that these epochal implications of *Critische Dichtkunst* also hinge on a changed understanding of how attention mediates between mind and world.

We have already seen that the hierarchical distinction between original and copy, between natural model and artificial imitation, begins to erode in Breitinger's reflections on the force of poetic representations. Breitinger's stunningly paradoxical attempt to fend off the challenges his conceptions pose to the priority of nature leaves the imitation relation intact while expanding the realm of what may count as a natural model. Even distortions of the given world, he claims, continue to reflect nature in the broadest sense. This is the logic behind his idea that poetry represents not actual nature but possible nature; that it shows things not as they are but, he asserts invoking Leibniz, as they could be in other possible worlds: "Imitation of nature in the realm of possibility is the intrinsic and principal work of poetry."[80]

Surprisingly, Breitinger seems to think that the conceit of "imitating possible nature" is suited to *deflect* the hubris of poiesis and poetics vis-à-vis the order of nature. Responding to contemporary interpretations of what it means to imitate nature, according to which poetry can improve upon nature by combining (like the legendary Zeuxis in his portrait of Helen) the best features of various models into a new picture that exceeds the beauty of any single original, Breitinger rejects such "proud expressions"[81] and argues that what others take to

---

79. See Cassirer, *Freiheit und Form*, 109–11.
80. Breitinger, *Critische Dichtkunst*, 1:57 (see also 1:60). The characterization of poetic fictions as "stories from possible worlds" has antecedents in Leibniz, Wolff, and Gottsched. Breitinger is the first to elaborate it into a full-fledged theory.
81. "Nur kann ich nicht ungeantet lassen, daß die stoltzen Ausdrücke ... der Ehre des Schöpfers der Natur höchstnachtheilig und verkleinerlich seyn, wenn sie under andern sagen, der Poet sey vermögend die Natur zu verbessern" (Only this I cannot leave unchallenged, that these proud expressions are ... most disadvantageous and detrimental to the glory of the Creator of Nature, if they claim, among

be an improvement of nature should properly be called an "imitation of possible nature."[82] This defense strategy is hardly convincing, especially once it becomes clear what imitating possible nature entails. It is not bound to an idealization of nature that exceeds the actual for the exemplary (as Zeuxis did); it instead allows for the representation of any possible entity so long as that entity remains consistent with formal logic (that is, free from internal contradiction). It thus effectively grants to poets a license to deviate from given nature that would make Zeuxis's apologists blush. "Imitation" of a nature synonymous with formal possibility prescribes and obliges very little and can hardly seems to function as a check on the hubris of poetic production, as Breitinger claims it does.

Breitinger's insistence on the imitation of nature may be internally inconsistent, but it would be wrong to attribute these inconsistencies to a lack of philosophical rigor, as some commentators have done.[83] On the contrary, it is instead the excessive literalism of his adaptation of Wolffian motifs that lays bare how the concept of nature prevalent in eighteenth-century metaphysics had already changed in ways that complicated its role in classical metaphysics. The classical principle of the imitation of nature prescribed that the productions of human art reflect a cosmos of unchanging essences. "Imitating possible nature" is an entirely consistent reoccupation of this topology with the concept of essence Wolff articulated in the wake of Leibniz, which defines "essence" as the inner possibility of a thing,[84] or the principle behind an internally noncontradictory set of essential

---

other things, that the poet is capable of improving Nature) (Breitinger, *Critische Dichtkunst*, 1:267).

82. "Wenn man diese Reden im rechten Lichte betrachtet, so wollen sie nichts mehrers sagen, als, der Poet könne vermöge seiner Kunst nicht alleine würckliche Dinge, sondern auch mögliche, die zwar nicht sind, aber dennoch seyn könnten, geschickt vorstellen" (If one considers such statements in the proper light, they essentially suggest nothing more than that the poet, by virtue of his art, can not only represent actual things but also possible ones, which do not exist but could exist potentially) (Breitinger, *Critische Dichtkunst*, 1:268).

83. See Herrmann, *Naturnachahmung und Einbildungskraft*, 248–49; Finken, *Die Wahrheit der Literatur*, 63.

84. "Das Wesen eines Dinges [ist] seine Möglichkeit" (The essence of a thing is [its] possibility) (Wolff, *German Metaphysics*, 19 [§35], see also §§16, 34–44).

properties. Geometric shapes like triangles exemplify these essences because their possibility or impossibility becomes immediately evident in the act of constructing them before the mental eye.[85] Yet for Wolff the same equation of essence with logical possibility applies to any entity in the world—even such a seemingly nongeometrical one as a "wooden plate," whose evident logical possibility he contrasts with the inherently self-contradictory "wooden iron."[86] Immediately evident to the mind before any empirical investigation, such knowledge has the advantage that it holds true independently of all existence, across all possible worlds (notwithstanding what we might consider the thorough empiricity of "wooden plates"). The disadvantage is that one still has to determine in which possible world one happens to find oneself—or, with regard to the cognition of any particular entity, which "possible" essence the thing in question happens to embody. While knowledge of essences (that is, insight into the compossibility of essential of properties) is thus absolutely certain, the specter of uncertainty returns in the question as to which of the infinitely many possible essences conceivable by the mind is at hand in the case of any actual thing.

At this juncture between the actual and the possible, the question of attention asserts itself again. For Wolff, attention and its deriva-

---

85. Wolff, *German Metaphysics*, 19–23 (§§34–44). Wolff demonstrates that we can construct a polygon with three angles in our minds line by line without running into a contradiction. The essence of a triangle ("polygon with three angles") thus consists in its possibility—that is, its constructability without contradiction. Other, nonessential properties of the triangle (such as an angle sum of 180 degrees) are demonstrably derived from the instruction to draw a polygon with three angles. By contrast, we would find ourselves unable to construct a polygon with only two angles without running into a contradiction, as it is impossible (in Euclidean geometry) to draw a figure with only two angles that also encloses a plane. The essence of a thing is thus equivalent to the principle of how a thing can be constructed without contradiction before the eye of the mind—an entity's specific logical-geometrical construction design.

86. Wolff, *German Metaphysics*, 7–8 (§12). The example is telling not least because it shows that things we might consider as prototypically "material," such as iron and wood, are matters of formal logic for Wolff (the Greek term *hýlē* [wood] is, after all, the grandfather of the word "matter"). The order of logic and the order of being are coextensive in his metaphysics; at its most fundamental level, the universe is logic incarnate.

tive operations, such as reflection and abstraction, are crucial to coordinating the order of possible mental constructs with the order of actually existing entities. Attention's focused gaze *analyzes* manifolds of sensation into basic elements and *selects* what to include as an essential property and what to ignore as accidental.[87] By converting actual entities into sets of properties whose inner possibility is transparent to the mind, methodical attention thus apprises the mind of the "essences" that individual things are supposed to incarnate. Selective focus on isolated properties, in other words, identifies the constituent elements of things to allow for an internal reconstruction that provides immediate insight into how things are logically composed. It is obvious that attention's mediation between empirical manifolds and possible essences is structurally identical with the attentive inspection of impressions that guided Breitinger's opening comparison of poetry and painting. At stake in both cases is perception understood as the activity of converting given manifolds into mental constructs. To put it in terms of the camera obscura metaphor, attention processes impressions in such a way that they can be mapped upon the possible construction designs the mind can draw up when the pinhole is shut.

When spelling out what poets do in imitating possible nature, Breitinger consequently relies on the same terminology of attention that served to distinguish poetry from painting. Poetic imitations of possible entities are formed by abstracting features from various objects and recombining them into new logically possible entities.

---

87. According to Wolff (*Philosophia prima*, 122–123, §§147–148) essences contain accidental properties (modes) that are determined only when the possible essence becomes actual. Wolff's essences thus correspond to what Leibniz calls "nominal essences" (rather than "real essences"). Nominal essences are "internally" possible; that is, their essential properties include no contradictions. Real essences, by contrast, are "possible in the context of a world." Insight into their possibility would thus require knowing that they do not contradict any other entity in this world. Such insight is open only to the divine eye that surveys all entities in a possible world in one stroke. The shortcoming of Wolff's essence concept—that it pertains, in effect, to nominal essences only, and thus remains stuck on the level of abstract universals—is, according to Alexander Aichele, the entry point for Baumgarten's critique of Wolff, and a systematic motivation for Baumgarten's aesthetics. See Aichele, "Wahrheit-Gewißheit-Wirklichkeit"; Aichele, "Allzuständigkeit oder Beschränkung?"

Like attention in philosophical cognition, what we might call poetic attention—Breitinger proposes the neologism *abstractio imaginationis*[88]—transforms the actual into the possible; that is, transforms given manifolds into mental constructs.[89] Yet the goal of the poetic conjunction of actuality and possibility is no longer that of bringing the two into congruence. In its analytic as well as synthetic capacity, poetic attention is released from the cognitive task of matching actual things to the possible essences they incarnate (essences that Breitinger's reflections on habit had already begun to debunk as habitualized patterns of perception). In a poetic context, attention is free to select and disregard this or that aspect of a thing, and free to rearrange such fragments of "world" into all kinds of possible entities, including those that find no correspondence in the actual world. Poetic attention, in other words, does not scan the world for what possible essences it does embody but for what essences it could possibly been seen as embodying.

Actual works of poetry come about through the linguistic reexternalization of such processes of creative perception—through the figuration, that is, of entities gathered and assembled in the poet's mind. With the domain of the possible unchained from the actual through alternative modes of attention, poets become masters of the possible, as unconstrained by any given version of reality as the maker of worlds in Leibniz's and Wolff's metaphysics. Breitinger's poet thus effectively occupies the place reserved for the creator-God in these metaphysical systems: "Any well-invented poem should therefore be considered as nothing other than a story from a different possible world: And in this respect the poet alone deserves the name ποιητοῦ, of a creator, because he . . . creates, as it were, things that do not exist for the senses; that is, he transfers

---

88. In the Wolffian school, attention and abstraction are closely associated; abstraction is conceived as selectively attending to some features rather than others (making it possible to "detach" select marks from the original representation). Like reflection, abstraction is thus understood as a type of attention. Breitinger, *Critische Dichtkunst*, 1:286.

89. Breitinger, *Critische Dichtkunst*, 1:286, etc.

them from the state of possibility into the state of actuality, and thus imparts to them the semblance and the name of the actual."[90]

Breitinger is, of course, not the first to compare the poet with a god, but he articulates the *alter deus* motif on new philosophical ground in a way that makes the analogy newly metaphysically potent. For him, poets resemble the creator-God in their free disposal over the realm of possibility and in their ability to turn select possibility into actuality. The difference between the two figures is that, in the creative poet's mind, things do not dwell as possibilities *before* their actualization in creation but *after* given reality is, as it were, dissolved back into possibility. Breitinger's continued language of imitation notwithstanding, the given order of nature that was meant to delimit what is possible and permissible in art seems to have been replaced by the limitless field of the logically possible, as the playing field of the creative artist.

Critische Dichtkunst is thus extraordinarily instructive about the emergence of a nonmimetic concept of poetic presentation (*Darstellung*) from a constructive moment inherent in the paradigm of representation (*Vorstellung*). As Blumenberg and Cassirer suggest, the *Critische Dichtkunst* may also help us to understand an emerging sensibility for creative production (*Herstellung*) in the eighteenth century, which began to see humans as creative beings and human production (both within and outside the fine arts) as eccentric to a given order of nature. My analysis allows us to spell out the basic mechanism that constitutes this place before determinate existence: the claim to an external vantage point relied on the disposal over an interiority in which the limits of the outside world have been liquefied into possibility ("negated," as the German idealists will say), and from where the creative subject can then externalize, like a second creator, new entities constructed within.

---

90. Breitinger, *Critische Dichtkunst*, 1:60; also 136, 426. Gottsched also suggests at one point that one could understand fictional plots like those of novels as "Historie aus einer andern Welt" (history from a different world); see Gottsched, *Versuch einer critischen Dichtkunst*, 204. Both Gottsched and Breitinger pick up on a similar formulation in Wolff, *Deutsche Metaphysik*, 349–50 (§571) and earlier suggestions by Leibniz.

And yet we will not fully grasp the structural function of "imitating possible nature" in the *Critische Dichtkunst* by abstractly opposing the possible to the actual, as Blumenberg's and Cassirer's readings tend to do. In the context of poetics, the "imitation of possible nature" is, after all, not supposed to recommend narratives (such as the closing parable of Leibniz's *Theodicy*) that actually report what transpires in other metaphysically possible worlds. The point of poetic digressions into possible worlds is instead to reimagine *this* world in the range of other possible modes of its representation. The "imitation of possible nature" conceit is thus best understood as articulating in ontological terms what Breitinger's reflections on defamiliarization had discussed in terms of representational technique: how to disrupt habits of perception through the use of estranging modes of representation. This also complicates teleological narratives that place Breitinger within a progression from (premodern) mimesis to (modern) poiesis, as Blumenberg does. Breitinger's introduction of heterocosmic possibility into poetry ultimately serves to authorize poetic *constructs* that *reveal* the world in a fresh light (to draw on Breitinger's own imagery for the effect of poetic representation). This is neither reflective mimesis nor constructive poiesis, but a vision of poetry as the art of rejuvenating attention through fictions that disclose other ways of seeing.

Although "imitating possible worlds" ultimately concerns representational technique more than ontology, there are, to be sure, repercussions for ontology as well. If different modes of representation yield different possible worlds, it may become difficult to determine what the world "really" is independently of any form of perception or representation. This is the same problem Brockes encountered while experimentally observing the world through a red pane of glass. In the *Critische Dichtkunst* this difficulty announces itself in a systematic confusion between *models* and *modes* of representation. Later chapters continue to elaborate on the various ways poets should modify things for a forceful effect. Some of these chapters, such as "Von der Verwandlung des Würcklichen ins Mögliche" (On the transformation of the actual into the possible) focus on altering models of representation; other chapters, such as "Von der Kunst gemeinen Dingen das Ansehen der Neuheit beyzulegen"

(On the art of giving ordinary things the appearance of novelty) and "Von etlichen absonderlichen Mitteln die schlechte Materie aufzustützen" (On several special means of propping up bad material), focus on altering modes of representation.[91] Yet the recipes prescribed across these sections, as well as the terminology used—creating new, strange, or marvelous representations by deforming things or combining select aspects of things into new entities—make strategies for altering originals increasingly indistinguishable from those for altering their representations. We already encountered the reason for this indistinguishability in the effect captured by the completely strange but transparent mask. As seen in the initial comparison between poetry and painting, Breitinger's poetics is based on the structural dissociation of modes of perception and representation from pre-given reality: how the inner eye attends to things, in short, is not prescribed by images themselves. This very dissociation, however, tends to fuse representation and reality in a novel way, because reality is therefore no longer given independently of a particular form of representation. Niklas Luhmann has described this problem as the contingency effect of second-order observation: observing other observations reveals that access to reality is based on schemata that could also be chosen differently and is therefore contingent.[92] Breitinger's *Critische Dichtkunst* edges toward this insight. Poetry's possible worlds are thus not located in other metaphysical universes: they traverse this world, as so many possibilities of perceiving and representing it.

In Conclusion: The Poetics of Attention

The fact that Breitinger and Brockes modeled their respective renovations of poetry and poetics on the rationalist concept of attention justifies characterizing their work as *poetics* of attention. In

---

91. Breitinger, *Critische Dichtkunst*, 1:262–347, 377–420; esp. 270–72, 295–300, 307–10, 384–91.
92. See Luhmann, *Beobachtungen der Moderne*, 98–101. On the connection between second-order observation, artificiality, and art in modern societies, see Luhmann, *Die Kunst der Gesellschaft*, 104, 148–53.

short-circuiting poetics and philosophy, however, both also hit upon the poetics of *attention*: that is, the poietic moment inherent in a model of apperception that Wolff and his school already understood in (re)constructive rather than mimetic terms. In the case of philosophical and scientific cognition, the poetics internal to attention remained latent because of the stipulation that there was, at least in principle, *one* correct way of selecting (and discarding) features. Distractions from the proper form of attention were, of course, possible; but only as relative imperfections that, as such, merely confirmed attention proper. The right kind of attention successfully "winnowed the wheat from the chaff" and discarded only those features that did not constitute essential properties of an epistemic object in the first place.[93] Faith in the mind's capacity to focus on the essential marks of things made it possible to contain attention's defining selectivity and partiality as a temporary moment in the reconstruction of epistemic objects. Capable of disassembling and reassembling nature at its inherent joints, the internal reconstruction of objects could seamlessly take the place of mimetic accounts of perception and cognition. Breitinger's transfer of this concept of attention to the field of poetics destabilized classical models of cognition and poetic imitation. By exploring the selectivity of attention for its capacity to produce representations that move and please, even if—or rather, precisely because—they "distort" and "deform" ordinary schemata, Breitinger created a space to reflect on the various possibilities of selective perception as something other than a failure of the mind to measure up to its object. The question of what is foregrounded and backgrounded in perception—the basic problem of attention—thus began to take shape as an epistemic problem in its own right.

Breitinger and, to a lesser extent, Brockes seized on attention as a nonmimetic element in cognition to carve out a place for artifice in poetic representation. Yet their reflections on attention as an active mediator between mind and world also signaled profound consequences for the classical paradigm of enlightened knowledge in the seventeenth and eighteenth centuries. The epochal ideal of a purified perception that would register clearly and distinctly what the

---

93. Daston and Galison, *Objectivity*, 240.

power of tradition had clouded in the mist of prejudice did not simply ignore the technical mediation of knowledge. Indeed, that instruments and artificial techniques must come to the aid of an all too fallible human perception was a key premise behind promoting the focused exercise of attention and other sensing instruments. As we saw in Brockes's poetry, though, the function ascribed to such techniques and technologies was purely ancillary and compensatory. Breitinger's and Brockes's reflections on the distortion effects of artificial techniques—in the processes of both identifying constituent elements of epistemic objects and of reassembling them in the mind—hit upon the thought that various techniques of mediating knowledge might contribute to the understanding of a world they were only enlisted to reflect. By exploring how representations are *made*, the *Critische Dichtkunst* not only harnesses the representational paradigm of knowledge to renovate poetics but also exposes the latent poetics of representational knowledge.

In addition to reflecting and promoting developments in the history of knowledge, Breitinger's poetics also shed light on a largely forgotten chapter in the history of attention as mental faculty. Recent research on the cultural history of attention has largely followed Crary's *Suspensions of Perception* in tracing modern culture's concern with selective attention to the fragmentation of perception in late nineteenth-century industrial modernity. Rereading Breitinger and Brockes in terms of the poetics of attention suggests that the fragmentation of perception was preceded by another, less noisy but no less incisive type of perceptual disintegration. It confirms the finding in chapter 1 that the effortless coherence Crary ascribes to classical models of perception was already the product of an assemblage—of a reintegration of attentional fragments into a unified picture. Selectivity was thus already the basis of concepts of attention in the eighteenth century, even if the official role assigned to the faculty contained and defused this selectivity within a concept of cognition as seamless reconstruction. As Breitinger's case illustrates, the selectivity and variability of attention catalyzed the emergence of emphatically "creative" conceptions of art, replacing imitation of nature with novelty and originality as new guiding principles of artistic production.

Breitinger's example would catch on. Alexander Baumgarten's aesthetics also begins, as Baumgarten writes in an early project sketch, with assessing perception's reliance on an "art of attention"; he, too, would articulate central problems of his new science of sensate cognition in terms borrowed from Wolff's concept of attention. The difference between Baumgarten and Breitinger—the difference that would turn Baumgarten into the founder of a new philosophical discipline—is that Baumgarten would go on to challenge the traditional topology between the active eye of the mind and passive sensory impressions more systematically than Breitinger does. Baumgarten would fold, as it were, the inner eye back into the mental canvas. Sensory cognition and its representation would therefore become a topic of philosophical import in their own right—the *explanandum* of the new discipline of aesthetics.

4

AESTHETICS
ATTENDING TO THE MARGINS

Baumgarten's Unredeemed Foundation of Aesthetics

In chapter 1, I traced the early modern discourse on attention to Descartes's famous contemplation of a piece of wax in his *Meditations on First Philosophy*. A seemingly minor detail from this episode is worth recalling at the outset of this chapter, because it illuminates in a single flash why Alexander G. Baumgarten (1714–62) would call for a new philosophy of sense perception he named "aesthetics." Distinctly understanding the nature of the wax, Descartes concluded in the Second Meditation, is achieved through methodical attention to its constituent elements. This insight followed an earlier, frustrated attempt to know the piece of wax by means of the five Aristotelean senses, beginning with the senses of taste and smell. In an unguarded moment of relaxed attention and almost poetic reverie, the Cartesian meditator notices that the wax "has been taken quite recently from the honeycomb; it has not yet lost all the honey flavor. It retains some of the scent of the flowers from which it was collected."[1] For a fleeting moment, a whiff of flowering meadow and teeming beehive seeps into the meditation chamber. What the meditator senses in the aromatic piece of wax is not merely its sweetness, but a sweetness that lingers from the wax's origin in a honeycomb; not just the floral quality of its fragrance, but this fragrance as a token of the flowers from which the honey was collected. For an instant, the wider expanse of the world enters the space of the Cartesian meditations—only to be immediately shut out again: brought closer to the fire, the wax loses its scent and taste, changes its color and shape, demonstrating to the meditator's doubting mind that sensory qualities, in their ephemerality, cannot convey what sort of thing the wax truly is.

As objects before the mind become increasingly distinct over the course of the Cartesian meditations, so does the meditator's sense of self, until the thinking ego finally comes to see itself as a substance categorically different from the entire world of bodies. By contrast, Descartes's initial reverie gives a fleeting sense of another mode of perception in which self and world appear as contiguous as things are with one another: one must imagine the Cartesian meditator sampling the piece of wax with their tongue and raising it to their nose to take in its scent. Via the aromatic piece of wax, the meditator's mind is mediately "in touch with" the honey and the pollen that the honeycomb retains. Rather than distancing the corporeal world by un-seeing (un-tasting, un-smelling) sensory qualities and focusing intently on a few distinctly understood features,[2] the mind attending to the taste and scent of the wax finds itself at the endpoint of an associative chain that runs from the piece of wax to the honeycomb and the honey, to the bees and the pollen, and so on, potentially ad infinitum. The self's distinctness unravels just as the thing before the mind dissolves into a complex web of relations.

Descartes's reverie strikingly prefigures the argument Baumgarten would later advance in favor of his new philosophy of sense

---

1. Descartes, *Meditations*, 20 (AT 10: 28).
2. That is, by "pay[ing] enough attention to all the things that I perfectly understand, and separate them off from the rest, which I apprehend more confusedly" (Descartes, *Meditations*, 42).

perception. Having learned the Cartesian lesson that even apparently passive sense perception rests on a manner of the mind's attending to things—even though, by Descartes's verdict, a sloppy, "imperfect" one—Baumgarten wagers that something important is lost in the transition to distinct perception. This loss warrants taking a second look at the kind of perception Descartes and his rationalist successors denounced as "confused." In contrast with much of the later aesthetic tradition that took its name from Baumgarten's new philosophy, Baumgarten himself did not locate this surplus of sense perception in its phenomenal richness or in its alleged intuitive grasp of an *individuum ineffabile*. What drew Baumgarten to sense perception was instead its sensitivity to traces of an entity's embeddedness in a relational context. In sense perception as Baumgarten (re-)imagines it, one can learn to discern things—such as the Cartesian piece of wax—as nodal points of a wider nexus, individuated by manifold relations to adjacent things. While such traces of a thing's embeddedness in various contexts can be sensed in "confused" modes of perception, they vanish with the narrowing of attention to distinctly understood properties.

In his own meditations on poetry, Baumgarten therefore introduced a new type of mental clarity to rival and complement the "clarity and distinctness" canonized by Descartes as the epoch's ideal of knowledge. What Baumgarten named "extensive clarity" has long been recognized as the nucleus of his aesthetic project, as it developed from the *Meditationes philosophicae de nonnullis ad poema pertinentibus* (Philosophical meditations on some matters concerning the poem; 1735) to the pioneering presentation of the new discipline in his *Metaphysica* (Metaphysics; 1739) and his mature, unfinished *Aesthetica* (Aesthetics; 1750/60).[3] What scholarly accounts have overlooked is that Baumgarten's new type of perceptual

---

3. The concept of "extensive clarity" or "extensive clarification" is central to standard accounts of Baumgarten's aesthetics, beginning with Bäumler, *Das Irrationalitätsproblem*, 198–231, and continuing in a long tradition, including: Cassirer, *Die Philosophie der Aufklärung*, 363–64; Schweizer, *Ästhetik als Philosophie*, 78–79; Solms, *Disciplina aesthetica*, 40–44; Mirbach's introduction to Baumgarten, *Aesthetica/Ästhetik*, 1:xl–xliii; Beiser, *Diotima's Children*, 127–33; Guyer, *History of Modern Aesthetics*, 1:323–25; and Buchenau, *The Founding of Aesthetics*, 121–30.

clarity hinged on a new understanding of the dynamics of attention. In this chapter I recover what Baumgarten called the "art of attention" (*ars attendendi*) as a linchpin of his aesthetic thought. As I will show, Baumgarten's defense of sense perception pivoted on an economy of "narrowing" or "widening" the mind's focus, which he explored as the constraint conditioning all finite cognition. Against the Cartesian restriction of experience to what narrowly focused attention can pin down as a distinct object vis-à-vis the mind, Baumgarten rehabilitated modes of attention in which the boundary between self and world is less rigidly drawn, including daydreaming, peripheral awareness, and chains of association—the very states of mind Wolff's concept of attention aimed to suppress. These "extensive" forms of attention open the mind to what the "intensive" attention of distinct cognition was supposed to keep at bay: the self's exposure to the world through the passive or passionate side of the mind, the senses, and an imagination that tends to overshoot the boundaries of the self. Art was central to this rehabilitation of alternative forms of attention because it proved to Baumgarten that subrational states of mind were not merely privative inattention or distraction but were capable of their own kind of "perfection." Conversely, cultivating such modes of attentiveness became, with Baumgarten, the primary function of art in his new aesthetic sense.

As should be clear from this brief sketch, the Baumgarten I present in this chapter looks rather different from the portraits of the thinker circulating in current scholarship. He certainly bears little resemblance to the dogmatic rationalist depicted by historians of philosophy who continue to take their cues from Kant's polemical self-definition against the Leibniz-Wolff tradition.[4] Yet neither does he fit neatly into the categories developed in more recent controversies about Baumgarten's new science of aesthetics. Some 275 years after the publication of the first volume of the *Aesthetica* in 1750, there is little consensus in the scholarship on what exactly

---

4. This framing continues to be widespread in philosophy departments, where Baumgarten tends to receive attention mostly as a precursor to Kant. See, for example, most essays collected in Fugate and Hymers, *Baumgarten and Kant on Metaphysics*.

Baumgarten wanted to propose with his "science of sensate cognition," as he defines aesthetics in the opening paragraph of his main work.[5] Indeed, it is only after all this time that the question is being asked again, as the weakening of teleological narratives has made it possible to recognize, in Baumgarten's project, potentials that went unrealized in more canonical aesthetic theories, from Lessing to Moritz and Kant, which absorbed and displaced Baumgarten's inaugural vision of aesthetics. And so the verdict is still out—or has been reopened—as to whether Baumgarten's aesthetics furnished a theory of sense perception in general (*aisthesis*) or articulated a new conception of art;[6] whether it heralded, in Ernst Cassirer's formulation, the "emancipation" of the senses from the dictates of reason, or instead, in the terms of Terry Eagleton's pointed rejoinder, their "colonization";[7] finally, whether it marked the beginning of an "ideological" suppression of the rhetorical and semiotic conditions of meaning or was instead perhaps an early attempt to reflect on these conditions.[8]

The portrait of Baumgarten I sketch in this chapter stands askance to these binary framings, but it also indicates what makes such divergent readings possible. What Baumgarten examined in the pragmatics of attention are the problems condensed in the figure of the subject: how finite human mindedness conditions all knowledge and action. Baumgarten consequently codified the subject/object terminology for modern philosophy in the very sections of the *Metaphysica* and the *Aesthetica* that explore the dynamics of intensive

---

5. Baumgarten, *Aesthetica/Ästhetik*, 1:11 (§1).
6. Wolfgang Welsch and Martin Seel have cited Baumgarten as an authority for their attempts to conceive aesthetics as a theory of *aisthesis* beyond the confines of beautiful art. Ursula Franke has argued against this view. See Welsch, *Ästhetisches Denken*, 9–40; Seel, *Ästhetik des Erscheinens*, 15–17; Franke, "Sinnliche Erkenntnis."
7. Cassirer, *Die Philosophie der Aufklärung*, 370; Eagleton, *Ideology of the Aesthetic*, 15.
8. The identification of aesthetics with the suppression of rhetorical technique lies at the heart of Paul de Man's *Aesthetic Ideology* and subsequent media-theoretical critiques of aesthetics. Rüdiger Campe has suggested in a series of essays that Baumgarten's aesthetics is on the edge between transfiguring (rhetorical and technical) *effect* into (metaphysical) *form*, or revealing *form* to be a mere technical *effect*; e.g., Campe, "Effekt der Form," 2014. Frauke Berndt recently argued for the centrality of media theory for Baumgarten's aesthetics; see Berndt, *Facing Poetry*, 8–15.

versus extensive clarification and attention.⁹ Even though he helped to establish the subject as a focal problem of modern thought, he refused (or failed) to turn it into *the* central problem of philosophy in the manner of Kant's transcendental-idealist turn. In the tension between Leibniz's monadology and modern subject philosophy, Baumgarten explored the subject in a way that continues to invite opposing readings—as a rational and embodied creature, as a figure of discipline and liberation, as new metaphysical ground, or as the modern dissolution of substance metaphysics.

Given this emphasis on the subject, a fourth controversy in the scholarship does have a more direct bearing on my reading: the question as to whether Baumgarten's aesthetics protested against a one-sidedly rationalist understanding of the human being in the name of a holistic conception of the *felix aestheticus* (happy aesthete)—or instead promoted a form of repressive subjectivation.¹⁰ In recent scholarship, these opposing views are marked by Gabriel Trop's redemptive interpretation of Baumgarten's aesthetic exercises as the model for a poetic form of life and Christoph Menke's claim that these exercises unwittingly spell out the logic of power opera-

---

9. The sections "Empirical Psychology" in the *Metaphysica* and "Aesthetic Truth" in the *Aesthetica* are the first instances of a consistent use of the subject/object opposition in the sense later adopted and disseminated by Kant. On Baumgarten as the originator of subject/object terminology in modern philosophy, see Beck, *Early German Philosophy*; Hacking, "Let's Not Talk About Objectivity," 21 (quoting Beck); also Menke, *Kraft*, 33; Schweizer's commentary on *Zur Grundlegung der Ästhetik*, 89n53; and Gawlick and Kreimendahl in their notes on the German edition of the *Metaphysica*, 554–55. At the very least, Baumgarten contributed decisively to establishing this terminology in German philosophy after 1750; see the detailed account in Ritter, "Subjekt/Objekt; subjektiv/objektiv."

10. The fourth controversy can be understood to focus the three previous ones in relation to Heidegger's claim that aesthetics extends the modern "metaphysics of the subject" to the domain of art (and the contrary view that the aesthetic subject is the *other* of the modern subject). Interpretations highlighting "rationality," "disciplinary subjectivity," and "suppression of rhetorical techne" can then be lined up as confirming Heidegger's diagnosis. These can be opposed to interpretations that see in Baumgarten's aesthetics a "protest against rationality," understand the aesthetic subject as a "whole human being," and emphasize the self-aware rhetoricity of his aesthetics. (The "aisthesis versus art" debate is less easily assimilated to this schema.) For a background on these debates, see Christoph Menke's excellent overview in "Subjektivität."

tive in what Foucault described as an emerging disciplinary society.[11] For all their divergence, however, Trop and Menke tend to approach the problem from the same side—the side of the isolated subject—while assuming in good Kantian fashion that the entire nonsubjective sphere depends on this subject's (either poetically molded or socially disciplined) powers. This focus on the constitutive role of the subject has eclipsed the monadological basis of Baumgarten's conception of subjectivity. With Leibniz (or a certain reading of Leibniz), Baumgarten considered the self within relations to its environment and understood the self's *separateness* as a gradual and never complete process of *separation*. His aesthetics marks neither the discipline of the subject nor its apotheosis as a poetic creator of its own life, but an exploration of the subject in tension with what Baumgarten called the *nexus rerum*—an interconnection of entities in the world that exceeds and encompasses the self. The version of Baumgarten that will emerge from this chapter is therefore no mere precursor of Kant. Instead he belongs to a lineage leading from Leibniz via Baumgarten to Herder, Goethe, and Humboldt, thinkers who explored art and aesthetics as privileged modes by which the subject accesses the complex nexus of things—as in Humboldt's famous *Zusammenhang* (interconnection) of all things, which would inspire modern ecological thought.[12]

In highlighting the problem of attention in this chapter, I portray, as much as possible, the contours of Baumgarten's overall thought in a single detail.[13] This approach is justified, and to a degree

---

11. See Trop, *Poetry as a Way of Life*, 25–49; Trop, "Aesthetic Askesis"; Menke, *Kraft*, 11–45; Menke, "Die Disziplin der Ästhetik." As even the titles suggest, both interpretations build on Foucault in different ways by understanding aesthetic exercise either as technology of the self or as a technique of disciplinary power (see chapter 2).

12. For the later development of this tradition in Herder and Humboldt, see Nassar, *Romantic Empiricism*. For Baumgarten's concept of *nexus rerum* and its appropriation by Goethe, see Ross Shields's lucid "Zusammenhang (Nexus)."

13. In the wake of an initial phase of scholarship that sought to reconstruct the main intentions of Baumgarten's new discipline, more recent studies on Baumgarten have tended to argue for understanding Baumgarten's aesthetics on the whole through what they highlight as a single aspect of his project—seeing his aesthetics, for instance, as a response to early eighteenth-century debates about the foundation of morality (Simon Grote, *Emergence of Modern Aesthetic Theory*); as literary theory

necessitated, by Baumgarten's style of writing, which reflects his assumption that understanding any one thing requires grasping that thing's connections to others. Baumgarten's writing performs this theorem by spinning a dense web of internal references in which each proposition is explicated by its cross-relations. In reading Baumgarten, understanding any single proposition therefore requires branching out to other parts of his thought. I take a similar approach to the question of historicism, which has divided recent studies on Baumgarten by Simon Grote, Stephanie Buchenau, Gabriel Trop, and Frauke Berndt.[14] Rather than insisting on either historical specificity or contemporary import, I suggest that the most "historical" part of Baumgarten's aesthetics—namely, its seemingly dated revival of Leibnizian metaphysics—offers the freshest impulses for contemporary thought. His critical adaptation of Leibniz's monadology enables Baumgarten to understand perception not merely as a matter of individual experience but as a comprehensive dynamic of individuation by which the self emerges from and remains linked with the context from which it emerges. And so it is that when Baumgarten speaks the idiom of "rationalist" metaphysics, he will suddenly seem to speak the language of ecology, of the ecological self, and of other possible ecologies of attention. To be sure, a healthy dose of speculative intellectual history is necessary here, but one that draws on and is no more ambitious—in fact, is far more timid—than the rigorously speculative element inherent in Baumgarten's own philosophical aesthetics.

---

avant la lettre (Frauke Berndt, *Facing Poetry*); or even as the unwitting ideology of an emerging disciplinary society (Christoph Menke, *Kraft*). The initial phase includes Bäumler, *Das Irrationalitätsproblem*; Cassirer, *Die Philosophie der Aufklärung*; Schweizer, *Ästhetik als Philosophie*; Paetzold, *Ästhetik des deutschen Idealismus*; and Franke, *Kunst als Erkenntnis*.

14. Some recent studies—including those by Buchenau (*The Founding of Aesthetics*) and Grote (*Emergence of Modern Aesthetic Theory*)—insist on locating Baumgarten within local developments in eighteenth-century moral philosophy and logic. Others—such as those by Trop (*Poetry as a Way of Life*) and Berndt (*Facing Poetry*)—play up the topicality of Baumgarten's aesthetics for contemporary theoretical discourse. Trop's afterword to Berndt's *Facing Poetry* calls for a "reanimation" of Baumgarten's thought (218). I agree, but such a reanimation can be successful only if Baumgarten is not turned into a sock puppet. The animating force must draw from the work itself, or whatever is brought to life will be a zombie.

A final note is in order to explain why this chapter on attention and the emergence of aesthetics focuses on Baumgarten rather than his collaborator and popularizer, Georg Friedrich Meier (1717–77). To anyone broadly familiar with the material, this may seem like an odd choice: Meier is much more direct about the importance of attention for the new discipline and explicitly states many of the claims that must be teased out slowly from Baumgarten's dense philosophical prose.[15] It therefore comes as no surprise that extant studies of attention and wonder turn to Meier as a proxy for Baumgarten to discuss the role of attention in what is often portrayed as their shared project.[16] The problem with this approach is that Meier is prone to avoiding and downplaying conflicts, such as the critical trade-off Baumgarten posits between intensive and extensive clarity (and between concomitant modes of attention).[17] Especially in recent studies of *Frühaufklärung* in Germany, emphasizing Meier's vision has contributed to situating the problem of *Aufmerksamkeit* within a discourse on the "whole human being" (*ganzen Menschen*) and a dietetics of moderation that balances out extremes. This view does have some grounds in Meier but has limited application to Baumgarten, whose rather austere intellectual precision undermines all half-measures of moderation.[18] If Baumgarten is after harmonization, it

---

15. For instance, in the first two volumes of his *Anfangsgründe der schönen Wissenschaften*, which were based on Baumgarten's ideas although published before the *Aesthetica*, Meier spells out that attention is the foundation of the sensate cognitive faculty whose refinement is the telos of aesthetics, and that its various subfaculties are nothing other than species of attention and abstraction. He explicitly identifies attention as the source of all varieties of mental clarity, correlates these different kinds of clarity with different kinds of attention, and insists that the fine arts altogether can be understood as vehicles for cultivating and refining attention. See Meier, *Anfangsgründe aller schönen Wissenschaften*, 2:48 (§283), 50 (§284), 81 (§294), 151 (§331).

16. See Thums, *Aufmerksamkeit*, 137–56; Gess, *Staunen*, 38–46.

17. While Meier retains Baumgarten's notion of extensive clarity and its definition, the concept loses its origin in a trade-off between different ways of cultivating the anthropologically limited resource of attention; instead, intensive and extensive clarity become relative perfections of attention between which there are empirical conflicts but no systematic connection.

18. For this focus, see Thums, *Aufmerksamkeit*; and the essays collected in Steigerwald and Watzke, *Reiz, Imagination, Aufmerksamkeit*, especially the introduction and the contribution by Carsten Zelle, "Erfahrung, Ästhetik und mittleres Maß."

is not the harmony of moderation but a harmony *in extremis*—in the same way that the Pietist-educated Baumgarten sought the reconciliation of faith and reason by venturing that the most uncompromising form of philosophy would coincide with whatever was more than dogmatic in faith. Despite the heavy lifting necessary to uncover the coherence of the problem of attention in Baumgarten's own writings, it is more illuminating to stay with Baumgarten while occasionally referring to Meier's works for confirmation or contrast.

A Science of the Art of Attention: On the Genesis of Baumgarten's Aesthetics

Two documents from the formative phase of Baumgarten's aesthetics demonstrate how the scientific, psychological, and poetic discourses on attention discussed in chapters 1–3 coalesced in Baumgarten's new discipline. The first is a companion letter to his aesthetic project published in a philosophical journal. The second is Baumgarten's early dissertation on poetics, which anticipates in germinal form many of his later ideas.

In 1741, having just been appointed full professor at Frankfurt an der Oder, Baumgarten initiated a philosophical weekly aimed at spreading *Weltweisheit*, the new secular philosophy taught in German universities, to a nonacademic audience. Composed of fictional letters penned by Baumgarten himself, the *Philosophische Brieffe von Aletheophilus* (Philosophical letters of Aletheophilus) met with little success and had to be abandoned within the first year; still, the weekly survived long enough to produce a document of some importance for understanding the genealogy of Baumgarten's aesthetics.[19] In the second of his fictional philosophical letters, Baumgarten introduces his readership to a new branch of philosophy concerned with directing the faculties of sensate cognition in the same way logic provides rules for the proper use of the understanding. Baumgarten calls this new discipline of philosophy *Ästhetik*. Writing as "Aletheophilus," he pre-

---

19. See the editors' introductions to Baumgarten, *Metaphysica/Metaphysik*, xxv, and Baumgarten, *Zur Grundlegung der Ästhetik*, xv.

sents an anonymous manuscript containing an encyclopedic ground plan that deviates from conventional divisions of philosophy in claiming that the organon of philosophy (its methodological toolset) is not, as philosophers had hitherto assumed, exhausted by logic. The mind, Baumgarten argues, has sensate cognitive faculties—designated as "lower" in the Wolffian tradition—that are irreducible to the intellectual or "higher" faculties of distinct cognition.[20] The remaining "lower" part of the philosophical organon, whose space the new ground plan creates by restricting the domain of logic, is occupied by the new science of aesthetics.

As the letter explains, this new science of sensate cognition "begins with the art of attention [*Kunst der Aufmerksamkeit*]" because the latter is "indispensable for the improvement of all other powers of cognition."[21] The art of attention comes first in aesthetics both as the new science's initial subdivision and as its fundamental problem. In Wolff's empirical psychology, attention was foundational only for the higher powers of cognition, which depended on attention because focusing the mind at will was necessary to transition from "passive" sensate perception to "active" intellectual cognition. For Baumgarten, by contrast, a form of attending to things—a faculty of noticing (and un-noticing, as Baumgarten describes attention's flipside of "abstraction")—already underlies the indistinct perceptions of the senses.[22] This seemingly small adjustment in fact marks a major reimagination of sense perception. It was a widespread tenet of eighteenth-century thought, shared from Wolff to Rousseau and Kant, that "the senses do not judge," and that error in cognition only creeps in with the understanding's judgment of sense data.[23]

---

20. Baumgarten, "Philosophischer Briefe zweites Schreiben," 69.
21. Baumgarten, "Philosophischer Briefe zweites Schreiben," 69. For a discussion of a passage from this letter, see the section on pedagogy in chapter 2.
22. Baumgarten, "Philosophischer Briefe zweites Schreiben," 70.
23. Compare Kant, *Kritik der Reinen Vernunft*, 405 (A293/B350); Rousseau, *Émile*, 133. Baumgarten holds a version of this idea but locates unimpeachable percepts one level "deeper," in the confused reflection of the world in the obscure "ground" of the soul (*Metaphysica/Metaphysik*, §§544, 546). Even the "relief" of more or less clear elements in any sensation results from the conscious mind fashioning perceptions from this obscure ground. As Meier would put it, the soul produces clear perceptions and images of the world from this ground "in the manner

Baumgarten's placement of attention at the foundation of the sensate faculty complicates this dichotomy. Patterns of attention, he suggests, subtly shape what becomes "clear" or salient in sense perception even before the judgments of the understanding intervene. This base-level "filtering" of experience, Baumgarten warns, is impervious to logical correction, because it occurs at the level of perceptual routines that determine what comes to appear obvious in the first place (Baumgarten follows up with examples of people who erroneously think they know something from immediate experience). To begin the examination of cognition with logic is therefore to put the cart before the horse: the organon of logic is useful for forming distinct notions, judgments, and inferences on the basis of empirical data "once they are already given" (*wenn sie schon gegeben sind*).[24] Yet it says nothing about how such apparent "givenness" is fashioned by the elusive workings of attention in the first place. This is the domain Baumgarten claims for his new organon of the lower faculties.

Baumgarten's emphasis on the pitfalls of the initial data-gathering stage in the formation of knowledge strikingly echoes the claims of seventeenth-century pioneers of the natural sciences, who faulted scholasticism for focusing on rules for higher-order reasoning while neglecting the basic observation of nature that ought to inform such reasoning. The remainder of Baumgarten's letter places his aesthetics precisely in this genealogy: he describes "aesthetic empiricism," the second subdivision of the proposed science following and building on the "art of attention," as a meta-theory guiding the proper conduct of practical "observations [and] experiments." This would include the discussion of such "weapons of the senses" as "magnifying glasses and telescopes, artificial ears and mouthpieces," as well

---

of a creation" (*durch eine Art der Schöpfung*); Meier, *Lehre von den Gemüthsbewegungen*, 85 (§51).

24. Baumgarten, "Philosophischer Briefe zweites Schreiben," 70. At stake is still an understanding of the workings of attention: "die Logik sagt: gib acht auf das zu Empfindende, und hüte dich für dem Erschleichungs-Fehler. Wie aber soll beides in besondern Fällen geschehen?" (logic says: pay attention of what is to be senses and beware of the error of subreption. But how can both be done in particular cases?) (71).

as various measuring devices.²⁵ Among the works of other early experimental scientists, Baumgarten references Bacon's *New Organon* as the original call for the reform of Aristotle's logic or organic philosophy.²⁶ Baumgarten's new organon of the lower faculties thus emerged from the same concern with regulating the interface between mind and world that catapulted the problem of attention into the center of the early natural sciences.

The literature on the emergence of Baumgarten's aesthetics commonly identifies three previously independent traditions that converge in his new discipline: the metaphysics of beauty (beauty as sensate cognition of perfection), practical rules for the arts (notably the rhetoric and poetics of Renaissance humanism), and rationalist faculty psychology (in the manner of Wolff).²⁷ The disciplines of attention developed in the wake of Bacon's call for a new natural philosophy should be added as a fourth strand. In fact, the practical conception of the senses Baumgarten inherited from Baconian science, which saw sensory observation as simultaneously fundamental and malleable—susceptible to "improvement" or "perfection"—is not merely one more tradition that coalesces in his aesthetics but the space within which its different strands can be woven into a common thread.²⁸ Only under the premise that sense perception already shapes

---

25. Baumgarten, "Philosophischer Briefe zweites Schreiben," 71–72.
26. Baumgarten, "Philosophischer Briefe zweites Schreiben," 71–72. The enumeration of works listed by Baumgarten adds up to a (roughly) reverse chronological genealogy of Baumgarten's own approach: At the beginning are Bacon's *Novum Organon* (1620) and his *De Augmentis Scientiarum* (1623); next, Malebranche's *De la recherche de la vérité* (1674) and Boyle's "On the Unsuccessfulness of Experiments" (1661), which were roughly contemporaneous; and Musschenbroek's *Tentamina experimentorum naturalium* . . . , which appeared close to Baumgarten's own time (1731).
27. Mirbach, for instance, speaks of a "Verklammerung von Erkenntnistheorie, einer . . . metaphysisch fundierten Schönheitslehre und einer Kunsttheorie" (integration of epistemology, a . . . metaphysically grounded theory of beauty, and a theory of art) in the introduction to her translation of Baumgarten's *Aesthetica/Ästhetik*, 1:xxvii. For the same claim, see Paetzold's introduction to Baumgarten's *Meditationes*, xlvii, and similar passages in Schweizer's introduction to Baumgarten, *Zur Grundlegung der Ästhetik*, viii–ix.
28. This should not be confused with the claim that Baumgarten introduced an "empiricist" element into an otherwise "rationalist" tradition, as Baumgarten warns when commenting on what it takes to improve sense perception: "Initially, it appears

its object does beauty *qua* perception of perfection become a question of art and technique with an internal poetics. Only in this case can rhetoric and poetics provide a vocabulary for describing both perceptual processes and techniques of representation, with the lower faculties appearing as foundational rather than inferior. This is the precise sense in which Baumgarten's aesthetics has, as Frauke Berndt and other recent interpreters of Baumgarten have claimed, a "medial" a priori:[29] not quite in the modern media-theoretical sense that all meaning depends on or is generated by signs and material media systems but in its exploration of what *mediates between* mind and world. The problem of attention thus constitutes a fundamental condition for the emergence of aesthetics as a philosophical discipline.

Wonder and the Knowledge of Poetry in Baumgarten's *Meditationes*

Whereas Baumgarten's philosophical letter indicates how his new science of aesthetics incorporated rationalist psychology and responded to problems of attention in the emerging natural sciences, his 1735 dissertation *Meditationes philosophicae de nonnullis ad poema pertinentibus* (Philosophical meditations on some matters concerning the poem) indicates his debt to the poetics of the marvelous. It is in this early dissertation that Baumgarten first defines poetic representations as those that are "extensively clearer" than others—richer and more variegated—so that comparatively "more is represented" in them.[30]

---

as if there is not much more to say here than: Open your eyes and see! Open your ears and listen, etc. Anyone who investigates the nature of these sensations somehow deeper, however, will arrive at a completely different judgment" (Baumgarten, "Philosophischer Briefe zweites Schreiben," 70).

29. For Berndt's claim that the defining ambiguity of Baumgarten's project lies in his combination, or deliberate "confusion," of epistemology and media theory, see Berndt, *Facing Poetry*, esp. 8–15. (Like much of recent German media theory, Berndt uses "medial" in the sense of "relating to media," understood broadly as the material conditions of meaning and communication.)

30. Baumgarten, *Meditationes*, 16 (§xvi). I have consulted Aschenbrenner and Holther's English translation of Baumgarten's doctoral dissertation as *Reflections on Poetry*, but translations from Baumgarten's Latin are mine, as the existing

Baumgarten would only fully work out the logic of such "extensive" clarification in contrast with its "intensive" counterpart in his 1739 textbook on metaphysics, where we will pick up the thread again.[31] Yet already in this early work, he probes the idea that extensive clarity correlates with a mode of attentiveness different from the one that makes perceptions increasingly distinct.

Baumgarten arrives at this other form of attention by rehearsing a dispute between Descartes and Christian Thomasius (1655–1728) about the nature of wonder. Quoting Descartes's definition of wonder as the mind reacting with attention to things that seem extraordinary, Baumgarten's treatise imports the discursive complex surrounding the new, the unusual, and the marvelous as attractors of involuntary attention we saw in Breitinger and Brockes.[32] Yet he immediately cites objections to this conception of wonder by unnamed critics—almost certainly Thomasius and his school—who insisted that wonder resulted from ignorance rather than from the soul's reaction to the rare and strange. In this opposing view, wonder was no passion of the soul (as Descartes had claimed) but a mere epistemic defect.[33]

---

translation is not always reliable. Although I will speak of "extensive clarity" (as is common in the scholarship), Baumgarten consistently phrases the concept in the comparative form of "extensively *greater* clarity" to emphasize that clarity is not an inherent quality of representations but the result of *attending to* perceptions (and thus clarifying them) in one way or another.

31. For a contrasting reading that prioritizes the discussion of extensive clarity in the *Meditationes*, see Berndt, *Facing Poetry*, 55–75. Berndt gives priority to the earlier reflections on poetry because she understands extensive clarity to be modeled on the structure of literary discourse, whereas I highlight Leibnizian motifs elaborated in the *Metaphysica*.

32. Baumgarten, *Meditationes*, 36–37 (§xliii); compare Descartes, *Philosophical Writings*, I:353 (§70), AT 11, 380.

33. In his *Liber de remedio amoris irrationalis* (1706) Thomasius had objected to the Cartesian account of wonder on precisely the grounds to which Baumgarten feels obliged to respond. Thomasius had claimed that Descartes's mono-causal explanation of wonder by rarity overlooked ignorance as a more important second source. For Thomasius, wonder amounts to ignorant people gaping at rare things they do not understand (while they remain ignorant of their ignorance of most everyday things, and never stop to wonder, for instance, at the nature of fire). See Thomasius, *Liber de remedio amoris irratationalis, et praevia necessaria notitia sui, sive praxis philosophiae moralis*, chap. IV, 88–96, §§15–51, previously published in German as *Von der*

Baumgarten's own position emerges in his rejoinder to this Thomasian objection: Wonder is no mere daughter of ignorance, he insists, because "in the extraordinary, something relatively inconceivable is rather implicitly said [*implicite dici*]."[34] Some cognitive content is indeed conveyed in marvelous representations, albeit only implicitly, so that it easily looks like ignorance to those who equate knowledge with what can be stated explicitly. What can be (and perhaps can *only* be) conveyed in extraordinary and marvelous representations is the "relatively inconceivable [*inconceptibile relativum*]," which is Baumgarten's technical term for something that can be clearly and distinctly conceived *in principle* but exceeds a given understanding's capacity for distinct comprehension.[35] In the view Baumgarten is beginning to develop, marvelous representations therefore do not convey irrational content, or some categorical other of reason. Poetry is less than fully rational and yet more adept than philosophy at expressing certain "hyper-rational" truths that contain so much objective rationality that a finite mind cannot comprehend them in adequately rational form. This is where poetry excels, what marks the relative advantage of its "perfect sensate discourse" over the formally rational discourse of philosophy. For Baumgarten, the poetic affect of wonder results not from ignorance but from the strange recognition that something relatively inconceivable shines through in poetic representations even though we cannot say exactly how we know what we know.

This implies that Baumgarten understands the attention induced by wonder in a way that diverges from *both* the Cartesian and the Thomasian definitions. Wonder is neither Thomasius's gaping of the ignorant at things they do not understand, nor, as Descartes and the poetics of the marvelous had assumed, a propaedeutic for the mind's deliberately focused attention. It instead thrives on a form of

---

Artzney wider die unvernünftige Liebe und der zuvorher nöthigen Erkäntniß Sein Selbst, chap. 4, 114–26, §§15–51 (see the bibliography for the early eighteenth-century titles in full). Baumgarten's Latin phrasing reflects Thomasius's in *Liber de remedio . . .* , chap. IV, 8, §20.

34. Baumgarten, *Meditationes*, 36 (§xliii). The extant English translation unfortunately misconstrues this sentence.

35. Baumgarten, *Metaphysica/Metaphysik*, 334–35 (§633).

attentiveness that registers aspects and nuances that might escape a more narrowly focused attention. The attention distinctive of poetry does not lead from confusion to distinctness—this would defeat the purpose in the case of the "relatively inconceivable" (by definition, indistinct) content conveyed in poetry—but fuels a different sort of mental clarity: "We generally pay marked attention to those things which have anything of the wonderful in them. Provided they are confusedly represented, those things to which we pay such attention are represented in an extensively clearer way than those to which we do not."[36] In adapting the poetic discourse on wonder, Baumgarten first probes a kind of attention by which things are not noticed *more distinctly* but *more* is noticed *indistinctly*. This requires imagining a kind of attention that achieves the opposite of what had defined attention in the Enlightenment paradigm: one that does not disentangle but rather increases the perceptual "confusion." By registering a multitude of perceptual details in their entanglement, such attention enfolds more cognitive content in a single perception than a finite mind could grasp in distinct form. Although this argument remains germinal in the early dissertation, Baumgarten sets out to recuperate the attention evoked by wonder as the source of a perceptual clarity that is more than a defect or a transitional stage in the acquisition of distinct knowledge.

Whose attention, though, is at stake here? The poet's, the audience's, or even the one that is objectively "encoded" in poetic representations themselves? In principle, all three. Although Baumgarten highlights different aspects of this continuum between poet, poem, and audience in different contexts, the attention involved in poetic production and reception, as well as those attentional patterns programmed into the work itself, are commensurate because they all concern the relative salience of parts of compound "representations." This versatile key term of Baumgarten's poetics allows him to switch effortlessly between the internal "representations" composed in the mind of the poet, those designated by linguistic signs, and those activated in the minds of the audience. To simplify things

---

36. Baumgarten, *Meditationes*, 36–37 (§xlv); translation is based on and modifies *Reflections on Poetry*, 52–54 (§45).

somewhat, we can understand the chiaroscuro of attentional highlights and shadows as patterns of noticeability that structure the salience of representations conveyed in the poetic communication from poet to audience via signs.[37]

Baumgarten's *Meditationes* conclude with his call for a new discipline of "aesthetics" that would expand the meta-poetics of his dissertation into a general science of sensate cognition.[38] He began to take up this task four years later in the first edition of his *Metaphysica* (1739). The *Metaphysica* elaborated Baumgarten's early intuitions regarding extensive clarity as an "implicit" form of knowing that relies on a yet untheorized mode of attention. It thus laid the conceptual foundation of Baumgarten aesthetics—but it did so on top of an epistemological ground plan devised by Leibniz, which we must briefly recall before returning to Baumgarten's elaboration of his new science.

Marks (Leibniz I)

Between Descartes's *Meditations on First Philosophy* (1641) and Baumgarten's *Meditationes* on matters of poetry (1735) lies Leibniz's "Meditations on Knowledge, Truth, and Ideas" (1683), a brief essay that laid the groundwork for much epistemological or (as it was known at the time) "gnoseological" reflection in German thought up to Kant. Leibniz's new theory of knowledge emerges as a response to

---

37. This remains a simplification because, for one thing, Baumgarten and Meier sometimes speak of attention when discussing an audience's general receptivity to a work, in which case attention serves the "phatic" function of keeping the channel of poetic communication open rather than the salience structure internal to the message conveyed. Although all three dimensions are in principle commensurate, Baumgarten notes that they can often diverge in practice and therefore prioritizes the representations the poet "intended" to convey as an ideal object of poetological analysis; *Meditationes*, 12 (schol. to §xiii). A further complication arises from the fact Baumgarten begins to emphasize that the material side of signs becomes important in the communication of confused ideas but that it matters less in conveying distinct ideas that can be dissolved into explicit marks. This point has recently been highlighted by Berndt, *Facing Poetry*, 49–54.

38. Baumgarten, *Meditationes*, 84–86 (§§cxv–cxvi).

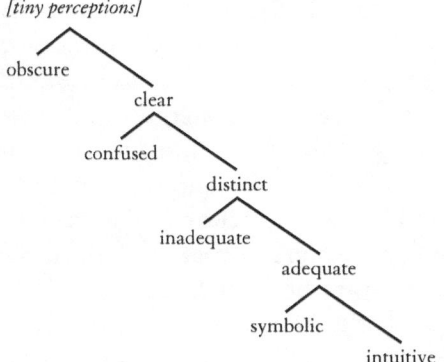

Figure 11. Leibniz's schema for the classification of knowledge.

his objection against Descartes's and Locke's equation of perceptions with conscious or potentially conscious mental states. Opposing this view, Leibniz famously claimed that there is in the mind at any moment an infinite number of "tiny" perceptions—*petites perceptions*—of which the mind has no conscious awareness. (We will return to these perceptions later.) For Leibniz, conscious perceptions emerge gradually from this opaque pool of tiny perceptions by distinguishing a small number among them, thereby "raising" them into the clarity of consciousness, like figures from the background pane of a relief. Because this emergence into conscious awareness rests solely on one's capacity to notice distinctions, Leibniz's classification of knowledge hinges on a single operation, that of distinguishing "marks" or "notes" (*notae*) by which things can be recognized (see figure 11).[39]

Emerging from the level zero of "obscure" notions that are too vague to afford recognition, "clear" notions—the kind of notions gained from the sense perception—contain sufficient marks for recognizing a thing and distinguishing it from others across changing contexts. They are *merely* clear when the differential marks are themselves not explicitly understood but implicitly "sensed" (that is, registered but not consciously differentiated by the mind). Knowers by

---

39. For the following, see Leibniz, "Meditations on Knowledge, Truth, and Ideas." For helpful overviews of Leibniz's essay, see Adler, *Die Prägnanz des Dunklen*, 4–8; Beiser, *Diotima's Children*, 37–39.

sense can effectively differentiate but are not aware of the criteria by which they do so. They cannot define their notions, or, in Leibniz's words, "cannot enumerate one by one [*separatim*] marks [*notas*] sufficient for differentiating a thing from others."[40] Because the differential marks are not disentangled but "fused together" (*con-fusa*) at this level, such merely clear notions count as "clear and confused." They become "clear and distinct," or clear in the second order, when the marks themselves are analyzed—that is, clarified reflexively, so that one is consciously aware of enough distinguishing marks to know explicitly how to identify something as a certain kind of thing.

Perhaps an example familiar to modern travelers can bring these technical distinctions closer to intuition. I have a "clear" notion of my checked bag if I can confidently pick it out from other bags on the airport baggage carousel; if I cannot, my notion is "obscure." My notion is clear but "confused" if I recognize my bag when I see it but am unable to describe my bag to an airline representative in sufficient detail for them to identify the bag based solely on this description. My notion becomes clear and "distinct" once I am able to list a sufficient number of characteristics. As this example implies, clear and distinct notions can be communicated to others, whereas confused notions are tied to first-person sense experience. Notice, however, that someone with good drawing skills might be able to convey their confused notion to the representative through a well-drawn sketch, even if they are unable to communicate the bag's identifying features in explicit terms. And indeed, Leibniz's early essay already exemplifies the workings of clear and confused knowledge by the judgments of painters who recognize the quality of a work even if they are not able to explain their reasons.[41] Confused knowing may not be based on explicit criteria like distinct knowledge, yet it is based on a kind of expertise that can be refined by practice. Those who make and judge artworks might not explicitly *know what* it is they are doing (this is art's famous *je ne sais quoi*), yet they still implicitly *know how* to do things well (they possess a kind of *savoir faire*). Despite this suggestive comment on the

---

40. Leibniz, "Meditations on Knowledge, Truth, and Ideas," 24.
41. Leibniz, "Meditations on Knowledge, Truth, and Ideas," 24.

affinity of confused perception and art, indistinct knowledge remains essentially deficient in Leibniz's classification, a necessary but intermediate step in the progression from obscure to increasingly distinct knowledge.

Orders tend to pile up in Leibniz, and the second level of clear and distinct notions is not the final one; after all, the marks used to distinguish a thing are *merely* clear in clear and distinct notions, not yet themselves distinctly understood down to their minutest differentiations. A notion that explicitly contains *all* distinctions that mark an individual thing—one so precise that it would unfailingly distinguish my unique bag from all other versions of the same mass-produced model—would not only be clear and distinct but "adequate." The transition from clear and distinct to adequate notions thus functions like a placeholder for the orders of analysis necessary to make a notion distinct all the way down the smallest differentiating marks. Because such a complete analysis tends toward infinity, adequate knowledge is practically unattainable for finite human minds. Knowledge, finally, counts as "intuitive" if it is possible to survey all marks contained in a notion immediately, in a single stroke, without the help of mediating signs. Perfectly adequate and intuitive knowledge is the privilege of the epistemic vision of an omniscient being. By contrast, finite human minds, even where they attain clear and distinct knowledge, must make do with "inadequate" notions that are also "symbolic" to some degree, mediated by symbols like words that serve as placeholders for marks that are not immediately present to the mind's inner vision.[42]

Although Leibniz's taxonomy may suggest static "tiers" of knowledge, it is better understood—and was certainly understood by

---

42. The recursive structure of Leibniz's classification is evident even when reformulating his schema in the following way: In "obscure" notions, I register no marks (but may have a vague sense of them); in "clear and confused" notions, I register marks sufficient to recognize a thing (but am not consciously aware of these marks, which therefore remain obscure *as* marks); in "clear and distinct" notions, I register sufficient marks of the marks necessary to recognize a thing (which marks therefore become clear, so that I can enumerate them); in "adequate" notions, I register all marks of all marks that distinguish a thing, down to the minutest distinctions; in "intuitive" notions, I register all marks of all marks, and so on, immediately and all at once.

Baumgarten—as tracing a dynamic process of clarification by which perceptions gradually gain relief.[43] As the sculptural metaphors by which Leibniz describes this process of apperception suggest, the mind gradually "chisels" distinct notions from the background noise of perception by making and marking distinctions.[44] The power behind this gradual clarification of perception is attention, the capacity to take note of marks, which drives the dynamic apprehension of increasingly distinct notions. Wolff's translation of attention as *Aufmerksamkeit* perfectly captures his Leibnizian understanding of attention as a "remarking-capacity" that gives contour to perception. At the most fundamental level, the *phenomenal clarity* of perceptions in the conscious mind results from this basic *capacity to register marks*, as Baumgarten later formulates the "law of attention" (*lex attentionis*) in his *Metaphysica*: "That of which I perceive *more and less obscure marks* than I do of other things, I perceive *more clearly* than these."[45] The mind thus constructs phenomenally clear perceptions out of the distinctions it "marks" among its representations. In a finite mind, this power is limited; it can only ever hold a small number of marks at a time, so that taking note of some marks or features necessarily comes at the expense of ignoring others. These, in broad strokes, are the Leibnizian assumptions against the background of which Baumgarten will rethink the dynamics of perception in his *Metaphysica*.

---

43. As indicated by Leibniz's consistent emphasis on thresholds at which the marks contained in notions become "sufficient" for one mode of recognition or another, cognitions develop gradually and "tip over" into distinct levels only when a critical mass of marks turns a difference of degree into a qualitative one. This gradualism results from applying his metaphysical principle of continuity to the workings of cognition.

44. Compare Leibniz's recurring analogy between the process of apperception and a sculptor's carving the latent shape of Hercules from a block of marble—in, for instance, "Preface to the New Essays," 294, and "Meditations on Knowledge, Truth, and Ideas," 27.

45. Baumgarten, *Metaphysica/Metaphysik*, 331 (§627); emphasis mine.

Extensive and Intensive Clarity in the *Metaphysica*

Baumgarten modifies Leibniz's progressive schema by inserting a lateral branch that maps how clear notions can be perfected at their own level, without advancing to distinctness. While the "philosophical letter" made a case for examining sense perception as an important but preliminary stage of *all* cognition, this side branch formalizes Baumgarten's claim in the *Meditationes* that poetry (and now the arts in general) models the inherent perfection of cognition at the sensate level.[46] The introductory section on the lower cognitive faculty in Baumgarten's *Metaphysica* thus culminates in the claim that there are two independent ways of augmenting the clarity of perceptions:

> Suppose that there are two clear thoughts of three marks each, but such that the marks that are clear in the one thought are obscure in the other: the first will be clearer (§528). Therefore, clarity of perception is increased by the clarity of the marks due to distinctness, adequacy, etc. Suppose that there are two clear thoughts of equally clear marks, where one thought contains three marks and the other contains six: the later will be clearer (§528). Therefore, clarity is increased by a multitude of marks (§162). Greater clarity due to the clarity of marks can be called INTENSIVELY GREATER CLARITY, while greater clarity on account of the multitude of marks can be called EXTENSIVELY GREATER CLARITY. An extensively clearer PERCEPTION is LIVELY.[47]

The overall clarity of perceptions can be increased not only by further clarifying a few distinguishing marks (until a perception eventually graduates to distinctness) but also, and apparently paradoxically, by increasing their confusion; that is, by multiplying the number

---

46. The burgeoning distinction between aesthetics as a science concerned, on the one hand, with the sensate element in *all* cognition and, on the other, with the internal perfection of sensate cognition as modeled in *art* marks the beginning of a distinction between a "wider" and a "narrower" sense of aesthetics that is reflected in, for instance, Kant's respective usage in the first and third *Critiques*. For a lucid overview of this distinction in Baumgarten, see Peres, "Die Doppelfunktion der Ästhetik."

47. Baumgarten, *Metaphysics*, 204 (§531); Baumgarten, *Metaphysica/Metaphysik*, 280 (§531). The parenthetical paragraph numbers in the quote represent Baumgarten's own cross-references to arguments found in other sections of his text.

of indistinctly registered marks. In simpler terms, we might say that perceptions become clearer not only by sharpening but also by broadening them, such that things are not perceived more distinctly but more is perceived indistinctly. There are now two different paths for increasing perceptual clarity. The first, "intensive clarity," leads down the levels of Leibniz's schema ("to distinctness, adequacy, etc.") by isolating and sharply demarcating a small but sufficient number of distinguishing marks. The second branches off into the variegated vividness of "extensive clarity" by binding a larger number of marks, even if the individual marks themselves may not be as clear as the marks that make notions distinct—or rather, *cannot* be equally clear. Increasing one type of clarity necessarily comes at the expense of the other. The constraint requiring this trade-off is easily missed because it is rests on a premise that is unstated—or rather, only stated in a remark on the finitude of attention that precedes and frames the contrast between the two kinds of clarity:

> I AM ATTENTIVE to that which I perceive more clearly than other things. I ABSTRACT away that which I perceive more obscurely than other things. Therefore, I have a faculty of being attentive and one of abstracting (§216), but both of these are finite (§354) and hence they are only in a certain degree and not the supreme degree (§248). The more that is taken away from a finite quantity, the less is left over. Therefore, the more I am attentive to one thing, the less I am able to be attentive to others. Therefore, a stronger perception that greatly occupies [my] attention obscures a weaker perception, or causes [me] to abstract from a weaker perception (§528, 515).[48]

---

48. Baumgarten, *Metaphysica/Metaphysik*, 280 (§529). In a register characteristic of the dense prose of the *Metaphysica*, Baumgarten speaks in the mode of a thetic definition here: to represent something more clearly than others *is what it means* to pay attention to something (and vice versa for abstraction). It is therefore unlikely that Baumgarten wants to suggest a sequence of mental acts in which the act of clear representation precedes and attracts a secondary attentive act, as Rüdiger Campe seems to read the passage in "Baumgartens Ästhetik," 151. What stands out in perception as relatively clearer than other things is, by definition, what I am attentive to—regardless of whether this is because my attention is attracted by the inherent strength of the perception or whether an effort to focus "adds strength" to an otherwise weaker perception. At the level of sensate attention, in other words, voluntary and involuntary attention are indistinct, so that in the final two sentences

In the first instance, Baumgarten's framing of attention and abstraction as complementary poles of any act of focusing the mind merely restates the premise behind the discourse on attention since Descartes's *Regulae*: A finite mind can achieve a maximum of perceptual clarity only by concentrating all of its limited discerning power into a single point (and withdrawing it from everything else).[49] Yet by positivizing the flipside of attention as an active unseeing or "abstracting away," Baumgarten highlights the obscurity incurred by this strategy of creating clarity in the mind—the shadows produced by the spotlight of attention. Bringing any one thing or feature into clear focus comes at the cost of blurring others into the background or "discarding them in thought" (*in Gedanken wegwerfen*), as Baumgarten glosses *abstrahere*.[50] Consistent with this shift in emphasis, Baumgarten's explanation of focusing the mind does not state the *direct* correlation between focusing attention and increasing clarity but the *inverse* correlation between focusing attention and the ability to notice what lies in the periphery: "the more I am attentive to one thing, the less I am able to be attentive to others." The opposite is also implied: the less my attention is absorbed by one thing (alone), the more I will be able to notice about others. In a finite mind, there is a necessary trade-off between achieving a maximum of distinctness in a narrow section or a maximum of contextual awareness at a lower degree of distinctness.

Baumgarten can illustrate the act of *attending* to something by the state of having one's attention *occupied*.

49. See chapter 1. In his *Psychologia rationalis*, Wolff had boiled this down to the following lawlike correlation, which anticipates the trade-off between intensive and extensive clarity: "The greater the attention we direct to something visible, the smaller the part at which it is directed" (*Psychologia rationalis*, 288 [§360]). Gary Hatfield reformulates Wolff's law in proto-Baumgartian terms: "an inverse relation between the intensity of attention and the extent of the cognitive material that can be brought under it" (Hatfield, "Attention in Early Scientific Psychology," 5).

50. Baumgarten offers an instructive series of possible German glosses of the Latin term: "das lasse ich aus der Acht, das werfe ich in Gedanken weg, das verdunkle ich mir, das entziehe ich meinen Gedanken"; *Metaphysica/Metaphysik*, 280 (§529). All these glosses underscore the active quality of abstraction. Focusing attention entails active suppression, forgetting, or "un-noticing" of parts of the perceptual field.

Because of this trade-off between unifocal attention and peripheral awareness, intensive and extensive clarity are not merely *different* but *competing* ways of augmenting the overall clarity of a perception. In Baumgarten the "economic" constraint expressed in the entwinement of attention and abstraction assumes a quasi-transcendental function as the condition under which a finite mind can know anything at all, the horizon of all humanly possible cognition. Rüdiger Campe has suggested that the respective precedence of either the attention-pole or the abstraction-pole defines the relationship between the lower and higher cognitive faculties, between the senses and the intellect, and—by topological association—between *scientia* and *ars*, metaphysics and *technē*.[51] According to this interpretation, the mind can prioritize either "increasing attention (in the domain of the senses)" or the abstractive faculty's "fight against distraction (in the domain of the understanding)."[52] Campe's vital insight into the foundational quality of the interplay between attention and distraction must, however, be qualified. The difference between the senses and the intellect cannot be defined by prioritizing either attention or abstraction, because *both* intensive and extensive clarification represent rivaling strategies for increasing the mind's *attention*. As Baumgarten's discussion of the twin faculties in the *Metaphysica* and elsewhere makes clear, focused attention correlates with heightened abstraction at the sensate as well as the intellectual level, so that the mere emphasis on one or the other pole can hardly explain the difference between the two.[53] The real trade-off is between two conflicting strategies for maximizing attention *under the overarching constraint* that narrowing attention always increases abstraction in a finite mind. What secures the independence

---

51. Campe, "Baumgartens Ästhetik," esp. 150–56. Baumgarten's equation of the "liveliness" of extensive clarity with "persuasion" and of the "dryness" of intensive clarity with "conviction" more than implies the association. His two kinds of clarity are indicative of rhetoric and rational discourse as two ways in which the clarity of mental evidence can be produced.

52. "Aufmerksamkeitssteigerung (im Bereich der Sinnlichkeit) und Kampf gegen die Zerstreuung (im Bereich des Verstandes)" (Campe, "Baumgartens Ästhetik," 152).

53. Compare the discussion of sensate attention and abstraction in Baumgarten, "Philosophischer Briefe zweites Schreiben," 69–70.

of sense perception is Baumgarten's wager that beyond the narrowing of the mind's focus into a single point—which had traditionally been equated with attention tout court—a different way of attending to things is also possible and also leads to an increase in overall clarity of the mind (even if its light is more diffuse). Aesthetics becomes necessary not least to explore what becomes possible in and through this other mode of attention.

That *in*tensive as well as *ex*tensive clarity result from different forms of attention is already suggested by etymology, whose importance for Baumgarten's practice of coining and transferring terms between spheres Frauke Berndt has recently emphasized.[54] The tension of the mind suggested by *in-tensio* is so close to the mental "stretching toward" implied in the etymology of *ad-tensio* that the idea of an intensity of attention suggests something close to a redoubling of the attentional effort. (In an Augustinian and scholastic terminology still echoed in Husserl, the terms *intentio* and *attentio* were often interchangeable.)[55] By contrast, the idea of increasing attention by *ex*tending the mind—by loosening the directed focus that defines intensive attention—signals a rupture with the established imaginary of what constitutes attention. At the threshold of the part of the section on "empirical psychology" that explicates the higher cognitive faculty, Baumgarten makes this bifurcation of attention terminologically explicit by distinguishing between the extension of attention ("ATTENTIONIS EXTENSIO"), defined like extensive clarity by the capacity to notice "more" (*plura*), and the intensity of attention ("ATTENTIONIS INTENSIO"), defined by the ability to increase the clarity of already clear marks.[56] While both intensive and extensive attention have a place in the lower and

---

54. Berndt, *Facing Poetry*, 21–27. On Baumgarten's practice of coining new terms and its importance for conceptual history, see also Schwaiger, *Alexander Gottlieb Baumgarten*, 32–34. Berndt's characterization of Baumgarten's thought as a "philosophy of style" in which "argument retreats into the background" to give way to "the surface of discourse" (*Facing Poetry*, 26, 35) seems less convincing. It seems to me that Baumgarten draws on etymology to condense rational argument into suggestive terms, not to displace it.

55. Neumann, "Aufmerksamkeit."

56. Schwaiger, *Alexander Gottlieb Baumgarten*, 332 (§628); Baumgarten, *Metaphysics*, 229 (§628). Translation altered, as Fugate and Hymers misleadingly

the higher part of the cognitive faculty, each kind of attention defines the *perfection* of one level: extensive breadth defines the perfection of sense perceptions, whereas intensive depth defines the perfection or unmixed "purity" of the intellect.[57]

At stake is thus not only "where" attention is located in Baumgarten's architecture of the mind—the question foregrounded by the sparse literature on attention in Baumgarten[58]—but more importantly, as Campe suggests, what configuration of the dynamic between attention and abstraction is paradigmatic for sensate or

---

translate "EXTENSIO" as "span," which suggests temporal duration (a quality Baumgarten instead discusses under the term *protensio*) rather than breadth of focus.

57. Intensively focused perceptions can be "merely" clear, just as distinct perceptions can be made more extensive (for instance, when they are embellished by lively examples and thus contribute to what Baumgarten calls "the beauty of the intellect"). In each case, however, the distinctive perfection lies in the opposing quality (in extensiveness in the case of merely clear perceptions and intensiveness in the case of distinct ones). In case of conflict, intellectual perceptions must prioritize intensity, which marks the intellect's defining "purity" (Baumgarten, *Metaphysica/Metaphysik*, 336 [§637]; Baumgarten, *Metaphysics*, 231 [§637]).

58. Most commentators claim that Baumgarten "relocates" attention to the lower cognitive faculty, while some suggests its proper place remains the traditional one in Wolffian psychology, at the hinge between the lower and the higher cognitive faculty (for the first view, see Asmuth, "Strenge Aufmerksamkeit," 5; Braunschweiger, *Aufmerksamkeit in der Psychologie*, 24; for the other view, see the suggestions in Solms, *Disciplina aesthetica*, 36–37; Paetzold, *Ästhetik des deutschen Idealismus*, 16; and Makkreel, "Baumgarten and Kant," 97). The first view points out that Baumgarten speaks of the dynamic of attention as it manifests itself in all the lower faculties, whereas the second view can claim that Baumgarten speaks of an actual "faculty" of attention (rather than activities of attending and abstracting) only in the context of higher cognition. A closer look at the paragraph (§625) where attention and abstraction are first designated as "faculties" shows that Baumgarten refers back to the same basic capacities that, he points out, already express themselves in the various operations of the lower cognitive faculty. In the end, attention is not "contained" in either part of the cognitive faculty, because different uses of attention (as the capacity for clarifying perceptions) *define* what counts as the lower faculty (by definition, the part of the mind that deals with merely clear perceptions) and the higher faculty (by definition, the part that deals with distinct perceptions). One insight Baumgarten retrieved from Leibniz, after it threatened to be lost in Wolffian philosophers' increasingly sclerotic systems, was a dynamic view of the mind whose different parts must not be understood as static "tiers," or categorically different faculties in the Kantian vein, but as gradually differentiated functions that transition into each other as varying expressions of the single power of representing (*vis representativa*).

intellectual perception, respectively. The shortest formula is that sensate attention strives to *reduce abstraction* and the form of attention generative of the intellect strives to *reduce distraction*. It is legible in the paragraph that characterizes the kind of attention constitutive of distinct cognition, where Baumgarten explains how abstraction's active inhibition of peripheral awareness promotes the mind's focus:

> If [my] attention to a certain object [*ad certum obiectum*] diminishes while I am being attentive to many associated and heterogeneous perceptions, I AM DISTRACTED.... When a distracted mind abstracts away from many heterogeneous perceptions, so that attention to a certain object [*ad certum obiectum*] is increased, this is the COLLECTION OF ONE'S MIND. And hence the collection of one's mind, as well as abstraction, are impediments to distraction (§221).... Hence, the collection of one's mind will promote attention, as will abstraction.... Attention will promote abstraction, and hence also the collection of one's mind (§529).[59]

Importantly, this paragraph does not outline a strategy for increasing the overall amount of attention and clarity of perceptions, only the attention directed, as Baumgarten consistently qualifies, *to a certain object*. When it comes to object-oriented attention, the same side-glances that enrich extensive clarity count as no more than attention wasted, and thus as mere "distraction." In fact, what Baumgarten describes as distraction in this context comes very close to the wide attention at the heart of extensive clarity, as its characterization in terms of a multiplicity (*plura*) or variety (*heterogenea*) suggests—a kind of attention (*attendere*) nonetheless, but one so wide that it includes additional marks tangled up or associated with the central perception.[60] From the perspective of the intellect, which must form distinct notions by singling out intensively clear marks, what counts as the virtue of the lower cognitive faculty appears as

---

59. Baumgarten, *Metaphysica/Metaphysik*, 336 (§638); Baumgarten, *Metaphysics*, 232 (§638). Second sentence of the translation modified.

60. It is very close but not identical, because extensive clarity must have its own kind of unity, as we shall see. The variety of extensive clarity is a virtue only when it is combined with the unity that defines beauty.

a defect that must be fought by withdrawing the mind from its dispersion into various things, concentrating it into itself, and refocusing the collected powers of the mind on one thing only.[61] In explaining how to pay attention in such a way that things become pinpointed as "certain objects" of the mind, Baumgarten's directives of attention in the context of the higher cognitive faculty spell out, with his characteristic concision, the structure of the mental routine underlying the post-Cartesian paradigm of attention.

Reading Baumgarten's terse philosophical prose, it is easy to overlook how provocative his counter-ideal of "extensive clarity" is by contrast: in effect, it revokes the very epistemic imperative that founded the classical paradigm of knowledge. As I discussed in chapter 1, that paradigm was founded on the assumption that a world exceeding the mind's capacity for distinct comprehension can only be known if one concentrates all of the mind's attention on one point at a time. Attention was called upon to handle overly complex perceptions by resolving them into their elements—in practice, by training the mind to focus on one detail after another rather than trying to take in the swarming confusion of simultaneously occurring perceptions all at once. Extensive clarity demands the very

---

61. In the same context Meier makes the connection between extensive attention and distraction explicitly (albeit somewhat grudgingly) clear: "One must accordingly admit, however, that the extension of attention is always combined in a necessary manner with some amount of distraction. . . . Whoever therefore wants to acquire an extensive attention must accept the distraction of the mind, and admit that individual representations do not become as clear as they could." (Man muß demnach allerdings zugestehen, daß die Ausdehnung der Aufmerksamkeit, jerderzeit mit einiger Zerstreuung, auf eine nothwendige Art verbunden sey . . . Wer also eine weite Aufmerksamkeit erlangen will, der muß sich die Zerstreuung des Gemüths gefallen lassen, und also zugeben, daß die einzeln Vorstellungen nicht so klar werden, als sie seyn könnten.) The justification for this necessary evil is as close as Meier comes to spelling out the trade-off between the different kinds of attention, which for him, too, is defined by the capacity-limitation of a finite mind: "True, if we possessed infinite attention, we would not have to worry about this evil. Yet our powers have limits, and all their perfections are shot through with imperfections." ("Ja, wenn wir eine unendliche Aufmerksamkeit hätten, so würden wir dieses Uebel nicht zu besorgen haben. Allein unsere Kräfte haben Grenzen, und alle ihre Vollkommenheiten sind mit lauter Unvolllkommenheiten durchflochten") (Meier, *Anfangsgründe aller schönen Wissenschaften*, 1976, 2:64 [§290]).

thing the imperative of analytical attention proscribes: taking in as much of that swarming confusion as one can.

Heightening peripheral awareness to notice less salient details in this way produces what Baumgarten calls "complex perceptions," which he defines as perceptions that "in addition to the marks to which I pay the most attention also contain others that are less clear."[62] Complex perceptions convey a "confusion" or entanglement of marks that the narrow attention of perceptual analysis must unravel.[63] And yet, according to Baumgarten's provocation, this other way of tending to perceptions also augments clarity rather than plunging the mind into obscurity. What hitherto counted as the very opposite of attention—as mere inattention or a privative lack of focus—is attention in a different form. After Baumgarten, attention can no longer be measured on a single quantitative scale as a matter of "more" or "less" but allows for different *qualities*, even if the Leibnizian calculus of differential marks (fewer very clear marks versus more less-clear ones) makes it possible to express these competing qualities in terms of a common denominator.[64] The senses and the intellect, as gradually differentiated expressions of the mind's constitutive power of representing, are defined by these different ways of paying attention. Baumgarten's much-discussed "revaluation of the senses" wagers another way of paying attention

---

62. Baumgarten, *Metaphysica/Metaphysik*, 280 (§530); Baumgarten, *Metaphysics*, 204 (§530) (translation modified). Baumgarten glosses "complexa" in German as *gehäuft* (piled up, accumulated), evoking the multiplicity and heterogeneity (*plura*) central to his definitions of extensively clearer perception. The importance of complex perceptions that contain a fringe of "adherent" marks along with the more salient ones has been largely missed by scholarship on Baumgarten; I will return to them later in the context of aesthetic exercises.

63. In the suggestion—implicit throughout Baumgarten's rehabilitation of "confused" perception—that the entanglement of elements leads to qualities irreducible to these elements considered separately, Baumgarten anticipates a key idea of modern complexity theory.

64. At least in principle, the overall clarity of perceptions can be determined by "adding up" the clarity-values of all marks contained in a perception. The sum total of differential marks detected even in more muddled extensively perceptions can thus be higher than the total of those detected in intensively clearer, explicitly differentiated ones. Baumgarten sometimes performed such calculations in lectures on aesthetics, as recorded in a student transcript.

and thus other ideals of knowledge and selfhood than those established by cultivating what now turns out to have been only the intensive variety of attention. It is thus unsurprising that the distinction between "intensive" and "extensive" attention preserves a terminological echo of the Cartesian distinction between the intensive quality of thinking substance (*res cogitans*) and the extended world of bodies (*res extensa*) first established by the training of attention.

Attention as Gender Performance

Filing Baumgarten's modification of perceptual clarity under the internal development of a "Wolffian school," as much of the scholarship that takes seriously this sort of technical problem in Baumgarten does, underestimates the degree to which Baumgarten's finely spun web of conceptual distinctions concerns historical forms of life that are as material as they are ethereal. The question of how we pay attention is in this regard not merely an epistemological problem, even if it is predominantly negotiated in this register in Baumgarten's philosophical psychology. As Baumgarten notes in the paragraph following his remarks on how to battle distraction and fortify unifocal attention, the ability to reliably form clear and distinct notions is a prerequisite for the "use of the understanding," an "acquired skill" (*habitus acquisitus*) whose successful incorporation defines the mature person as "naturally of age" (*naturaliter maiorennis*)—the juridical term Kant would adopt to describe the individual condition for *Mündigkeit* (maturity) in his essay on Enlightenment.[65] In general, entanglements between Baumgarten's philosophical investigations of the soul and historical routines of "performing a soul" are more evident in his readers, like Georg Friedrich Meier, who spun Baumgarten's empirical psychology and lectures on aesthetics into the widely read *Anfangsgründe der schönen Wissenschaften* (Foundations of the beautiful sciences); or Kant, who lectured on Baumgarten for decades and used the em-

---

65. Baumgarten, *Metaphysica/Metaphysik*, 336 (§639), my translations.

pirical psychology of the *Metaphysica* as a blueprint for his anthropology.⁶⁶

That performances of attention imply performances of the self is especially evident in Meier's and Kant's consistent gendering of Baumgarten's technical distinction between intensive and extensive clarity. Both Meier and Kant code the less strained and more lively extensive attention as feminine and juxtapose it with an intensive attention, the kind of attention that makes the mature subject, which is the prerogative of men. Meier, for instance, points out how *das Frauenzimmer* (antiquated for "woman") develops an unusually extensive attention by learning to notice many details in polite society, which is certainly charming and represents a kind of attentional virtue but is ultimately also trivial and leads to annoying chattiness ("She'll harp on to you about everything, including what shoe buckles the young men wore").⁶⁷ Kant, always more to the point, distills this gendering to its basic logic. Recording Kant's lectures on Baumgarten's empirical psychology, Kant's student Herder jots down elliptical notes that are best reproduced in the original: "Frau[en]z[immer] extens.[iven] schön[en] V[er]st[an]d: der Man intens.[iven]" (Women [or woman] extensive beautiful understanding: man an intensive one).⁶⁸ But this is apparently not merely a simple fact of life, as Kant's additional comment to the men in his audience suggests: "Frauenz[immer] V[er]st[an]d also nicht tief machen woll[en], sondern schöner . . . bey Män[n]ern ist die Schönheit Neb[en]sache: die Tiefe d[ie] H[au]ptsache" (Women therefore not (to) want make their understanding deeper, but more beautiful . . . with men, beauty is a mere accessory: depth is the main thing). The ellipses in Herder's notes make it impossible to decide whether Kant thinks he knows what women want or prescribes what women

---

66. Hinske, "Wolffs empirische Psychologie."
67. Meier, *Anfangsgründe aller schönen Wissenschaften*, 1976, 2:60 (§289). Compare also remarks in the section on exercises of attention, where Meier claims that the attention of women and children typically remains weak, even if it is vivid, because of the triviality of the things they focus on (71, §292).
68. See the online transcription of manuscript XXV.46a3 at "Herder's Notes from Kant's Metaphysics Lectures," https://users.manchester.edu/FacStaff/SSNaragon/Kant/HerderNotesComplete/MP/Texts/Text-EP531.htm.

ought to want. While it remains ambiguous whether the claim is normative or descriptive, its performative implication is clear: at stake is an understanding that can be *made* deeper or not—Baumgarten's *habitus acquisitus*—and not the transcendentalized faculty of Kant's critical philosophy. The reminder that depth of understanding has priority for men, whereas beauty—that feminine side of the understanding—is of secondary importance, reminds his male audience how they ought to form and perform their minds.

The gendering of Baumgarten's opposition of intensive and extensive attention not only indicates one field of routinized performance by which men and women are made in the eighteenth century; it also confirms once more the extent to which the rising ideal of the self-reliant and purpose-oriented subject is the creature of a sharpened, "intensified," and masculinely gendered attention. As a pragmatic precondition for the use of the understanding that defines the person capable of enlightenment, *Aufmerksamkeit* is the prerequisite not only of *Aufklärung* in the original epistemological sense (the clarification of notions toward clarity and distinctness) but also of cultivating an "enlightened" subjectivity. At the same time, this again raises—this time in a gendered register—the question that has divided interpretations of Baumgarten's attempt to give a philosophical account of reason's others: Does his project articulate an internal protest against the one-sidedness of a certain kind of rationality, or does it represent the fury of a rationalism run amok in including, as excluded, even what is different from it? Is it a first deconstruction of "Western metaphysics" or does it universalize its claims by subsuming all aspects of the human being? Is Baumgarten's insistence on an alternative mode of developing one's mind a protest against the dominant model of gendered subjectivity that makes space for other modes of selfhood, or does it not rather stabilize this ideal by giving the lower effeminate part of the mind its due only to keep it in its place, as Adam needed an Eve to fully become himself?[69]

---

69. Echoes of this gendering will be loud and clear in Schiller, and in a general gendered metaphorology that contrasts the "femininity" of beauty with masculine reason.

In lieu of making a premature choice among such alternatives, we should note that the gendering is not contained in Baumgarten's own text. In what is (by his own admission) a bone-dry examination of the pragmatic conditions that make one kind of mindedness or the other, his empirical psychology renders legible one mechanism by which selves are made—a mechanism that, in its twofold nature, has now forfeited its air of necessity. In a sense reminiscent of (though also oblique to) Paul de Man's emblematic juxtaposition of the critical philosopher Kant with his reader Schiller, who metaphorized, psychologized, and similarly gendered the critical philosopher's examination of the aporetic structure of aesthetic judgment, Baumgarten would here play the role de Man assigns to Kant (and vice versa): that of a sober examiner of a transcendental pragmatics of cognition in all its conflictual ambiguity, which Kant's lectures then turn into a naturalized (and in this sense, "ideological") dichotomy.[70]

Matter and Form: Extensive Clarity in the *Aesthetica*

Although Baumgarten rarely mentions attention or even the concept of extensive clarity in the *Aesthetica*, both are foundational for his mature aesthetic theory. In fact, it is their foundational character that explains why they recede from sight in Baumgarten's most comprehensive elaboration of the discipline. The *Metaphysica* develops the conceptual infrastructure on which the theoretical edifice of the *Aesthetica* is then erected. Just as a ground plan determines all parts of a building without occupying a determinate place within it, the juxtaposition of intensive and extensive clarity is presupposed throughout Baumgarten's explicit aesthetic theorems. As several commentators have noted,[71] the most obvious way in which the concept carries over into the *Aesthetica* is in the quality of *ubertas*, the richness or

---

70. De Man, "Kant and Schiller." For the gendering of this juxtaposition, see the introduction to Spivak, *An Aesthetic Education*, esp. 31–34.
71. Guyer, *History of Modern Aesthetics*, 1:332–33; Dagmar Mirbach's introduction to Baumgarten, *Aesthetica/Ästhetik*, 1:xl–xliv.

abundance of representations that constitutes one of the six "perfections" of sensate cognition whose detailed discussion constitutes the extant part of Baumgarten's aesthetics.[72] Extensive clarity cannot, however, be limited to just one of these perfections; instead it pervades all six aspects, which converge in the "perfection of sensate cognition as such," as Baumgarten defines beauty at the outset of the work.[73]

The pivotal importance of the trade-off between the two kinds of clarity is particularly evident in the section focused on aesthetic truth (esp. §§555–65), which is suffused with imagery that contrasts the "formal" perfection of the logical pursuit of truth with the "material plenitude" of its aesthetic counterpart. This juxtaposition rests on a prior distinction between "subjective" and "objective" truth that seems all too familiar yet is in fact first introduced by Baumgarten into the philosophical terminology in this context.[74] In Baumgarten, the pair of terms distinguishes between the "objective" determination of things in accordance with the principles of reason (he also calls this "metaphysical" truth) and the way objective truth is rendered present in a certain mind *qua* "subject," which can happen in either a *logical* or an *aesthetic* form of apprehension. Baumgarten then elaborates this contrast on the basis of an extended

---

72. For the canon of perfections, see Baumgarten, *Aesthetica/Ästhetik*, 1:24–25 (§22). As the first of aesthetic perfections, *ubertas* is the "primary concern" (*prima cura*) of aesthetic thought (Baumgarten, *Aesthetica/Ästhetik*, 1:92 [§115]). The second volume breaks off before the discussion of the final perfection, the "life" of aesthetic cognition (see below). Baumgarten's canon of six epistemic "perfections" is not limited to his aesthetics but reappears in similar form in his theoretical and moral philosophy. Focusing only on the *Aesthetica*, recent scholarship has tended to interpret these categories in rhetorical terms as a direct adaptation of the Ciceronian "canon of style" (Berndt, *Facing Poetry*, 43–44; Buchenau, *The Founding of Aesthetics*, 117), whereas others have pointed out that Baumgarten's list is indebted to Wolffian and Thomasian philosophers such as Baumgarten's teacher in Jena, Johann Liborius Zimmermann (1702-34); see the detailed overview in Nannini, "Six Faces of Beauty." Perhaps it is not necessary to decide which of the two genealogies is correct: the dual genealogy may simply indicate Baumgarten's assimilation of one to the other—his rationalist rhetoric and his rhetorical rationalism.

73. Baumgarten, *Aesthetica/Ästhetik*, 1:21 (§14).

74. Baumgarten, *Aesthetica/Ästhetik*, 1:402-3 (§§423-24). Baumgarten's apologetic use of the terms and his offering of synonyms and explanations demonstrate that he is aware of his terminological innovation.

background metaphor borrowed from Leibniz that portrays the formation of clear and eventually distinct representations from the noise of tiny perceptions as the chiseling of a determinate shape from a block of marble.[75] The following passage, one of the most famous in Baumgarten's work, contains this imagery in condensed form: "Whatever logical truth contains in terms of formal perfection could only be accomplished by a great loss of material perfection. For what is abstraction, if not a loss [*iactura*]? By the same token, you would not be able to make out of an irregularly shaped piece of marble a marble globe without losing at least as much material as the greater value of roundness demands."[76] The loss of abstraction required to achieve the formal perfection of logic is then contrasted with an aesthetic approach, which savors material perfection instead: "The aesthetic horizon delights in most determinate individuals as its forest, its chaos, its material, from which it carves out [*exsculpat*] aesthetic truth ... in such a way that as little materially perfect truth is lost as possible."[77]

This juxtaposition is foundational for hylomorphic contrasts in aesthetics thought, marking the first instance in a long tradition that would see aesthetic art, in contrast to or as a corrective of reason, as especially attentive to the "material" side of things. For Kant, the aesthetic unity of the manifold will appear as if it were not imposed by the forms of the understanding but emerged uncoerced from the content of intuition. Schiller would later objectivize this uncoerced unity as "freedom in appearance" and find in it the model of a new

---

75. Leibniz had introduced the image for apperception according to which the process of clarifying ideas is analogous to a sculptor's carving the shape of Hercules from a block of marble (and thus, analogous to a craft). Baumgarten draws on the same imagery, with the difference that his analogy drops the "veins" that, according to Leibniz, harbor the shape of Hercules in latent form. In a metaphorological reading, this weakens the sense in which what can be "brought to light" in the craft of perception exists before the act of perception. For Leibniz's use of the image, see, for instance, his "Preface to the New Essays," 294, and "Meditations on Knowledge, Truth, and Ideas," 27.

76. Baumgarten, *Aesthetica/Ästhetik*, 1:538 (§560). My (admittedly not so perfectly rounded) translation. In the absence of an English translation, all translations from the *Aesthetica* are my own.

77. Baumgarten, *Aesthetica/Ästhetik*, 1:542–43 (§564).

harmony in the human being in which the formal or intellectual side no longer oppresses its material side. The motif itself will resonate far beyond Baumgarten's immediate successors and define even reflections on art and literature that reject the label of aesthetics, such as Heidegger's claim that artworks are distinguished from equipment by a special sensitivity to a quasi-material "earthly" moment that resists integration into a "world" of intelligibility.[78]

No doubt it would be wrong to read these later conceptions directly back into Baumgarten's text. If this is so, however, it becomes even more important to specify what the "material" perfection of aesthetic truth amounts to in Baumgarten's own terms. Baumgarten's explication of the passage makes it clear that the contrast between formal and material perfection is effectively identical to the trade-off between intensive and extensive clarity. Logical and aesthetic truth results, for him, from different modes of apperceiving a given segment of world. What figures as "formal" truth, Baumgarten suggests, is achieved by a rigorous narrowing of attention that desensitizes the mind to differences that no longer register as making a difference in the formation of distinct notions of the understanding. The intensive attention behind the logical approach operates with an aperture that blurs large regions of the perceptual field into the background, or, to use Baumgarten's more incisive imagery, amputates them from perception (*amputare per abstractionem*).[79] In the formation of clear and distinct notions, innumerable differentiating marks (*notas differentiarum . . . innumeras*), all those that are not necessary to identify a thing as a member of a certain class (*ea, quibus non opus est ad distinguendum*), fall out of the picture like excess stone in cutting a perfectly regular globe from an irregular block of marble.[80] This is how the general concepts of the sciences are "born from" (*enatis*) individuals and how they achieve their own kind of perfection.[81] The

---
78. Compare Kant, *Kritik der Urteilskraft*, esp. 66–70 (§9, B27–32); Schiller, *Über die ästhetische Erziehung*, 51–97 (letter 13–23) and the letter to Körner from Feb. 8, 1793; Heidegger, "Der Ursprung des Kunstwerkes," esp. 27–44; de Man, *The Resistance to Theory*, 8–12.
79. Baumgarten, *Aesthetica/Ästhetik*, 1:542 (§561).
80. Baumgarten, *Aesthetica/Ästhetik*, 1:536–37 (§559).
81. Baumgarten, *Aesthetica/Ästhetik*, 1:536 (§560).

more relaxed aesthetic mode of apprehension, by contrast, is wide enough to pick up details that a more strained attention might blind out, yet alert enough not to let them slip into immediate oblivion.[82] It thus carves out its beautiful shapes with as little loss of material complexity as possible—that is, by registering differential marks from which logical truth had to abstract.[83]

Of course, aesthetic *and* logical truth both constitute conflicting *forms* of representation, which—as forms—prioritize either the formal or the material aspect of truth, its distinctness or its breadth. Material truth can, in other words, only be apprehended in the subject in a certain form, always mediated by one art of attention or another. It can never be grasped all in one stroke, as material truth is in the divine mind, which does not have to apprehend and does not pay attention.[84] Even extensive attention therefore cannot take in the complexity of things wholesale but must filter and select (although its lower threshold allows it to filter differently and allows perceptions habitually blocked out to enter in the formation of notions). Immediately after the passage quoted above, Baumgarten emphasizes that the aesthetic attention, too, must be selective, and lose "material truth" in the process, even if it "delights" in its chaos: the beautiful form (*pulcra forma*) resulting from the labor of aesthetic attention is a "brief but elegantly rich round shape" (*brevis, sed eleganter plena, rotunditas*) polished from the excess marble—not unlike the perfectly regular sphere of logical truth.[85]

Baumgarten's juxtaposition of logic (philosophy) and aesthetics (art) radiates beyond the section on aesthetic truth where he discusses it. This is demonstrated by the recurrence of all six categories of perfection that structure the *Aesthetica* within the section on aesthetic truth.[86] In contrasting logical and aesthetic perfections of

---

82. Baumgarten, *Aesthetica/Ästhetik*, 2:602–5 (§§614–16).
83. Baumgarten, *Aesthetica/Ästhetik*, 1:542–43 (this is a paraphrase of §564).
84. In God, there is no sensate cognition; he therefore does not pay attention (Baumgarten, *Metaphysica/Metaphysik*, 466 [§870]).
85. Baumgarten, *Aesthetica/Ästhetik*, 1:542 (§565). See also Dagmar Mirbach's introduction, lxii–lxv.
86. In §556 Baumgarten lists ten perfections of "aestheticological truth" (an umbrella term for the two ways truth is apprehended in the subject); the first six

truth, Baumgarten goes over all six categories and characterizes the respective aesthetic varieties by greater material plenitude. Material plenitude—what the *Metaphysica* had discussed as extensive clarity and explained by extensive attention—is thus not merely one component element of Baumgarten's aesthetic theory but defines the specificity of the aesthetic in general. To be sure, this does not mean that the six perfections of Baumgarten's aesthetic theory simply reduce to the notion of extensive clarity; it only suggests that Baumgarten relies on the contrast between "extensive" and "intensive" clarity, between formal precision and material richness, to differentiate between the logical and aesthetic varieties of *each* of the six perfections of discourse. The point is not to simplify the various dimensions of Baumgarten's aesthetics (for instance, the "ethical" dimension discussed below in the section on "aesthetic life") to an epistemological one ("extensive clarity"), but to show that all of these dimensions, including the ethical one, rely on material richness of representations. The aesthetic thus remains defined by its opposition to "abstraction" in his peculiar sense, as the active suppression of peripheral features effected by narrowly focused attention.

Yet if abstraction is *iactura*, a loss, a throwing-overboard: What it is that is thrown out in the process? What warrants retaining the "material" of truth against its "formal" attenuation in the logical approach? What do extensively clear or, in Baumgarten's new ter-

---

items characterize truth's formal perfection, the final four its material perfection. The four *material* perfections in fact echo the first four *formal* perfections in a material register, as the "content-side" of the same categories ("certainty" and "life," the remaining two formal perfections, have no counterpart in material truth, presumably because they concern the subject-side alone). Baumgarten's hylomorphic matrix may lead one to expect that the first six perfections distinguish logical truth and the remaining four the aesthetic one. Contrary to the received view in the scholarship, this is not the case: when discussing *aesthetic* truth, Baumgarten goes over all six *formal* categories of perfection, just as he does when he discusses the logical approach. (After characterizing their logical varieties in §559, Baumgarten discusses them at least twice in respect to aesthetic truth in §561 and §565; because he does not number them there, the continuity of categories is easily lost.) The distinctive quality of aesthetic truth lies in the fact that it implements the *formal* categories in such a way that the four *material* perfections are prioritized. (By contrast, Schweizer and Mirbach seem to directly correlate aesthetic truth with the "material" categories of perfection; see the introductions to 1:lx; and *Theoretische Ästhetik*, xiv.)

minology, "aesthetic" perceptions register that intensive or logical ones, *in* seeing more distinctly, necessarily fail to see?

Indeterminacy or Determinacy of the Aesthetic?

Answering this question must begin by noting what this loss *does not* entail for Baumgarten. With the long shadow of Kant's *Critique of the Power of Judgment* looming over modern aesthetic thought, it is easy to misinterpret the greater "material" perfection of aesthetic perception as a surplus of "indeterminacy." According to an influential narrative, the development of modern aesthetics can be understood as an almost linear progression toward indeterminacy as the defining feature of aesthetic experience. Aesthetics, it is said, began with the aporetic rationalist formula of the artwork's *je ne sais quoi*, came into its own with Kant's authoritative explanation of such "not-knowing" through the free play of faculties unconstrained by a determinate concept, and reached maturity when indeterminacy was raised into the hallmark of the aesthetic (for instance, in twentieth-century reception aesthetics). As "radical indeterminacy," the idea finally emerged as a pivotal thought-figure of post-structuralist theory (which is avowedly anti-aesthetic but arguably informed by key motifs of Romantic aesthetic theory).[87] Following Schiller's famous characterization of the aesthetic condition as a state of "zero" determination or pure determinability, much post-Kantian aesthetics identified the specific kind of freedom afforded by the aesthetic with its indeterminacy.[88] As freedom from

---

87. Whether post-structuralist theorizing followed an aesthetic logic (and was indebted to the aesthetics of German Romanticism in particular) despite its overt criticisms of the aesthetic tradition was (sometimes polemically) debated in the context of modernism/postmodernism discussions in Germany and France. The claim of upstanding postwar defenders of reason like Habermas that post-structuralism "aestheticized philosophical discourse" thus clashed with post-structuralist attacks on "aesthetic ideology." Christoph Menke's *Souveränität der Kunst* (1991) offers a nonpolemical account of the "aesthetic" logic of post-structuralist theory that is centered around the concept of indeterminacy.

88. See the twentieth and twenty-first letters of Schiller's *Über die ästhetische Erziehung*, 81–87, here: 85.

the kind of determinations imposed by theoretical or practical concepts, such indeterminacy became increasingly appealing as the supposed rationality of these concepts came under the suspicion of masking hidden forms of violence.

Given the weight and the unbroken appeal of this narrative, it is no wonder that Baumgarten's pioneering aesthetics has also been interpreted in its light. Petra Bahr, for instance, understands Baumgarten's protest against abstraction as a protest against the "loss of *indeterminacy*" that is incurred when the understanding determines perceptual manifolds.[89] The problem is that all such attempts to insert Baumgarten into a narrative focused on the indeterminacy of the aesthetic collide head-on with the letter of Baumgarten's text: from his early *Meditationes* to the mature *Aesthetica*, Baumgarten never wavers in his claim that aesthetic perception is especially attuned to individual things and their specific determinations. As indicated in the passage above, it is not *indeterminacy* but *determinacy* that is "lost" in logical abstraction but retained, as far as possible, in aesthetic modes of perception.[90]

Is this just an odd archaism, better swept under the rug when it comes to probing what Baumgarten may mean to contemporary thought? Perhaps the contrary is the case: perhaps an untapped po-

---

89. Bahr, *Darstellung des Undarstellbaren*, 91–98, here: 92, my translation and emphasis. For the same line of interpretation, see Niehle, *Die Poetik der Fülle*, 69–70. Trop considers "indeterminacy" understood as the "incapacity of sensory cognition to analyze the complexity of the object" as the hallmark of Baumgarten's concept of beauty. Interpreting Baumgarten's aesthetics as literary theory avant la lettre, Berndt claims in similar terms that "Baumgarten's theory of literature depends on [the] conceptually undefinable abundance of marks in poetic passages"; see Trop, *Poetry as a Way of Life*, 27; Berndt, *Facing Poetry*, 58, compare 180.

90. Baumgarten, *Meditationes*, 16–18 (§§xviii–xx); Baumgarten, *Aesthetica/Ästhetik*, 2007, 1:536–39 (§§559, 561, etc.). For a similar insistence that "die Poetizität der einzelnen Begriffe liegt aber nicht in ihrer Verworrenheit und *Unbestimmtheit*, sondern ganz im Gegenteil in ihrer umfassenden *Bestimmtheit*," see Buchenau, "Die Sprache der Sinnlichkeit," 162–63, here: 163; Buchenau, *The Founding of Aesthetics*, 126–28; Paetzold also notes that "Baumgarten entwickelt eine Theorie ästhetischer Bestimmtheit"; see Paetzold, *Ästhetik des deutschen Idealismus*, 18. Compare also Gabriel, who begins to sketch out how aesthetic richness eventually came to be interpreted as indeterminacy in "Baumgartens Begriff der 'perceptio praegnans,'" 69–70.

tential of Baumgarten's aesthetics lies precisely in his seemingly out-of-place insistence on the relative determinacy of aesthetic experience. Kant's detailed analysis of the form of aesthetic judgment notwithstanding, what connects Baumgarten's rationalist predecessors to his Kantian heirs is a structurally *negative* definition of the cognitive content of aesthetic experience as the *in*distinct or *in*determinate other of rational knowledge. As indicated, for instance, by Christoph Menke's contemporary aesthetics of negativity in its various guises, this otherness of aesthetic experience to rational determination has since been reinterpreted beyond Kant's philosophy of consciousness—semiotically, as the breakdown of signification; praxeologically, as the radical otherness of aesthetic force to teleological practice. Typically, however, such reinterpretations continue to operate within a Kantian schema that opposes the rational imposition of determinate form through concepts onto an intuitive material that remains unstructured and blind without such determination.[91]

---

91. In Menke's reformulation of Kant's aesthetic judgment as aesthetic semiosis in *Die Souveränität der Kunst* (1991), the indeterminacy of the concept becomes the inability to univocally select signifying differences from the background material in which all signs must be encoded—the inability to determine, in other words, which features of the manifold material of an aesthetic object count or do not count as signs. Aesthetic experience thus enables an encounter with the surplus of materiality on which signification depends but which is itself devoid of significance. Menke's more recent focus on an aesthetic anthropology in works like *Kraft* (2008) recast the difference between rational determination and its material underside as that between socially normative practice and a pre-subjective play of forces on which all social practice is grafted. According to this model, the curated eruption of pre-subjective force through art makes it possible to experience freedom aesthetically as freedom from social discipline, thus founding an anthropology that understands the "human being" in its specific difference from the social "subject." Like the nonsignifying background material of Menke's earlier aesthetics, however, the definition of force as pre-subjective, non-normative, and asocial continues to define the aesthetic-anthropological difference in abstractly negative terms as the flipside, underside, or breakdown of rational determination. This condensed summary certainly does not do justice to the finer points of Menke's thought, which perhaps offers the most ambitious and compelling contemporary aesthetic theory in the German context. Precisely because of its sophistication, however, it epitomizes the stubborn persistence of Kant's hylomorphic schema and its privative definition of the aesthetic (Menke, *Kraft*, 7–88, here: 62; Menke, *Die Souveränität der Kunst*, esp. 19–91). On Menke's view of Baumgarten's role in the genealogy of aesthetics, see the section "Ground of the Soul" below.

How does Baumgarten define the specificity of the aesthetic if not through conceptual indeterminacy—and through a "bare materiality" or "pure phenomenality" that surfaces when conceptual determination is aesthetically suspended? His answer rests on a set of entwined epistemological and metaphysical assumptions that begin to converge in his characterization of the sensate faculty as *analogon rationis*, the analogue of reason.[92] Baumgarten adopted the term from the animal psychology of the time, where it described the capacity of nonhuman animals to orient themselves in the world by making connections and registering patterns among representations even without rational insight into the nature of such connections— that is, without understanding the reason *why* one thing follows from another.[93] Baumgarten's *analogon rationis* has sometimes been criticized as aporetic, because it seems to portray the senses through a mere analogy to what they are not; namely, reason.[94] When contrasted with the Kantian understanding of the sensate mind as pure receptivity that supplies raw material to the intellect, however, Baumgarten's parallelization of sense perception and reason can be said to accomplish the opposite: it expresses Baumgarten's view that the sensate part of the mind performs, in its *own* way, the *same* function that also defines reason for Baumgarten—that of representing the *nexus rerum* or interconnection of things that constitutes the given world.[95] Reason and its sensate analogue are the respective capacities for disclosing the nexus of things in a distinct or an indistinct manner.

Against this background, a dimension of Baumgarten's aesthetics comes into relief that a merely *epistemological* characterization

---

92. For illuminating discussions of this central term of Baumgarten's aesthetics, see Franke, *Baumgartens Erfindung der Ästhetik*, 17–21; Aichele, "Ding und Begriff," 122; Guyer, "18th Century German Aesthetics."

93. Franke, "Analogon rationis"; see also Solms, *Disciplina aesthetica*, 42–43. Like many of Baumgarten's other key concepts, the term is prefigured in Leibniz; see *Monadology*, 19 (§26).

94. Schweizer, *Ästhetik als Philosophie*, 26; Solms, *Disciplina aesthetica*, 43n151.

95. For Baumgarten's parallelization of reason and its sensate analogue as two ways of disclosing the *nexus rerum*, see his *Metaphysica/Metaphysik*, 338–39 (§640).

of extensive clarity by the multiplicity of marks and a merely *rhetorical-affective* one by the liveliness of rich perceptions equally miss. Through their abundance of intertwined marks, extensively clear perceptions serve the purpose of conveying more about the interconnection of things than the rational faculty can make explicit through distinct representations. In narratives that equate the rise of aesthetics with increased emphasis on subjective indeterminacy, this ontological foundation of Baumgarten's aesthetics has often been disregarded or regarded as an embarrassing liability—an awkward rationalist relic in the otherwise progressive framework of Baumgarten's thought. A relic it may be, but it is much more central to Baumgarten's vision of his discipline than has previously been recognized. To understand the coherence of this vision, we must turn once again to Leibniz—this time to the metaphysical side of his theory of perception.

All Things Conspire (Leibniz II)

The fundamental level of Leibniz's cosmology is constituted by a divinely instituted network of metaphysical points or monads. About these metaphysical points, Leibniz makes two equally famous but seemingly conflicting claims. Monads are, on the one hand, perfectly self-enclosed: without "windows" that would admit outside influence, a monad's perceptions are self-produced internal states, propelled by nothing but the monad's own appetites or strivings for new sets of perceptions.[96] On the other hand, each monad's perceptions are perfectly attuned to and "express" all the others, so that each monad also functions as a "perpetual living mirror of the universe."[97] Because the perceptual programs of all monads are perfectly accommodated to each other, perceptions are thus entirely internal and entirely external at the same time; a mirror, likewise, shows everything but itself. Yet if *each* element in the network at the same time reflects the *entire* network, how are monads individuated

---

96. Leibniz, *Leibniz's Monadology*, 15–17 (§§7–15).
97. Leibniz, *Leibniz's Monadology*, 25 (§56).

at all? What keeps this universe from collapsing into a single metaphysical point—say, a Spinozian substance and its modes?

Leibniz's response accounts for the originality of his metaphysical vision: Monads are individuated by their unique selection of perceptions that stand out as clear from the diffuse ground of tiny perceptions, in which all monads share: "It is not in the object, but in the modification of the knowledge of the object, that monads are limited. They all go confusedly to infinity, to the whole, but they are limited and distinguished by the degrees of their distinct perceptions."[98] Monads *distinguish themselves* from others *by distinguishing* in their perceptions. They all share in the same set of tiny perceptions—Leibniz quotes Hippocrates, "súmpnoia pánta"[99] (all things "conspire," all things "breathe together")—and they share in them to a greater extent if they distinguish less sharply among them. Inversely, the degree to which a monad possesses a distinct identity correlates with the distinctness of its clear perceptions. This is why the highest level of "reflecting" monads that are (like human minds) capable of distinct perceptions have a more heightened sense of self than animal souls, which in turn have a more defined self than bare monads existing in the unconscious numbness of a dreamless sleep, ignorant of themselves and others, and of themselves as different from others.[100] Monads thus do not so much *have* a point of view or perspective on the world; they *are* this perspective, as the collection of the network into a singular node whose "position" corresponds to those relations that are accentuated more clearly than others. Leibniz's explanation of the monad's distinctness as its gradual differentiation *of* and *from* the nonself thus offers a dy-

---

98. Leibniz, *Leibniz's Monadology*, 26 (§60).
99. Leibniz, *Leibniz's Monadology*, 26 (§61).
100. Leibniz, *Leibniz's Monadology*, 18–19 (§§24–30); "Principles of Nature and Grace," 208–9 (§5). (Even bare monads must, to the degree that they inhabit a unique position in the cosmic concert, possess a unique profile of unconscious states that reflects occurrences in their proximity relatively more pronouncedly than distant ones.) When, in vertigo, sleep, or death, higher "reflecting" monads lose their ability to distinguish things, they also forfeit their conscious selves. Death is thus like a ceaseless vertigo—the end not of existence but of the ability to make out anything in the dizzying swarm of perceptions that constitute the monad.

namic account of the monad's individuation rather than presupposing the self-thinking ego as an already accomplished fact.

At the phenomenal level of bodies, which supervenes on the world of monads, Leibniz's argument for the all-encompassing interconnection of things is perhaps more intuitive. Assuming that the universe is a plenum, "each body is affected not only by those which touch it, and in some way feels the effect of everything that happens to them, but also by means of them it is affected by those which touch the former ones.... From this it follows that this communication extends indefinitely."[101] By touching the bodies in its immediate surroundings, each body is mediately—via bodies adjacent to those bodies, and so on—in contact with the entire material universe. Bodies function as each other's media, transmitting motions from one to the next, although the ripple effect decreases with distance such that only close surroundings are clearly perceived.

To the single perceiving monad, the interconnection of things of which it is part shows up as no more than noise. Leibniz likes to explain the background murmur of tiny perceptions through which the monad confusedly senses the expanse of the universe in analogy with the noise of the sea.[102] Like the combined noise of countless waves washing into each other, the incessant stream of tiny perceptions that grounds consciousness perception without ever rising to consciousness is indistinguishable in its parts; it is impossible to tell where one wave begins and the other one ends. One can hear the noise but not make out determinate sounds. Or if one does listen in and, at times, pick out distinct waves, it is because the waves gush forth forcefully enough to become distinguishable from the background before they fade again into the general murmur. At the seashore, Leibniz suggests, one can thus "hear" what usually escapes awareness: "At every moment there is an infinity of perceptions in us ... that is, changes in the soul itself, which we do not consciously perceive [*appercevons*], because these impressions are either too small or too numerous, or too homogeneous, in the sense that they

---

101. Leibniz, *Leibniz's Monadology*, 26 (§61), my emphases.
102. See, for instance, Leibniz, *Philosophical Essays*, 65, 81, 211, 295.

have nothing sufficiently distinct in themselves."[103] If the unconscious quality of tiny perceptions follows from their indistinctness, the reverse holds as well. Conscious perceptions arise from the background noise by being distinguished, so that they are gradually raised into consciousness like figures from the background pane of a relief. Only a fraction of tiny perceptions can ever become conscious; the ground of perception is never resolvable into its figure. Only in the depthless vision of the divine mind do figure and ground collapse. A finite mind, by contrast, possesses a particular viewpoint defined by the perspectival limitations of its body: "The soul . . . represents the whole universe by representing this body, which belongs to it in a particular way."[104] Leibniz thus develops a metaphysics of the situated perceiver in which the position of the sensing body in the interconnection of things defines the mind's outlook on the world—not by causing it or because bodies are the corporeal "seat" of the soul but because bodies "embody" each monad's per-

---

103. Leibniz, "Preface to the New Essays," 295. The example is sometimes read as an illustration *by instance*, as if the roar of the sea were a particular *case* of a conscious perception arising out of unconscious tiny perceptions (the infinity of water droplets or waves battering the rock). The sea noise would then be a regular conscious perception composed of infinitely many unconscious ones, and the relation between the two would indeed seem to be one of wholes and parts. There are, however, abundant indications in Leibniz's text that the image is intended as an example *by analogy*: it is usually introduced by comparative particles ("like," "just as," "almost like") to mark the analogy's limits. The sounds of innumerable waves are thus *like* the infinity of tiny perceptions; and the effect of all tiny perceptions together is *like* the noise of the sea—although the combination of tiny perceptions is, in contrast to actually hearing the sea, not normally clearly and consciously perceived. This is precisely what makes the roar of the sea such a useful example: in it, indeterminate *noise* is perceivable as a determinate *sound*; the background noise of perception becomes perceptible "as such." For the quoted comparative particles, see Leibniz, *Philosophical Essays*, 81, 211, 65.

104. Leibniz, *Leibniz's Monadology*, 27 (§62). That the monad's set of clear perceptions should depend on its embodiment has puzzled commentators, so much so that some assumed Leibniz made a category mistake; see Lloyd Strickland's commentary on §62, 129. Others have avoided the problem by translating it away: in Hartmut Hecht's Reclam translation, the monad reflects the universe "according to the universe's order" rather than "according to their [the monads'] body' (*Monadologie*, 1998, 47). The reason for this confusion is the complicated question of mind-body relationship in Leibniz. For a complex account that troubles the standard account of mind-body parallelism in Leibniz, see Adams, *Leibniz*, 217–307.

spectival limitations, its unique zone of perceptual clarity. Bodies are the monad's finitude incarnate.[105]

Although Baumgarten is rightly recognized as the most Leibnizian philosopher in Wolff's school, his philosophy does not so much return to Leibniz as critically appropriate and transform the monadological vision as a whole. This is evident, for instance, in the way Baumgarten reaccentuates and remotivates the two central motifs of the monadology, the monad's windowlessness and its quality as a universal mirror. For Leibniz (and even more so for his modern readers), the monad's windowlessness has a certain explanatory priority: At the deepest level, each monad unfolds a perceptual program driven by its own internal strivings. Only under the added hypothesis that the perceptual programs implanted in each monad by the creator are perfectly accommodated to each another (their "preestablished harmony") do each monad's perceptions also reflect all others. In Baumgarten, the order of explanation is notably reversed: his reformulation of the monadology in the *Metaphysica* sets out from the universal nexus of substances in any world, from which he infers that monads are "active mirrors of their universe" and "concentrations of their own worlds."[106] By contrast, the monad's "windowlessness" is not merely absent from Baumgarten's monadological reflections; he even asserts that interconnected substances do indeed exert influence on one another.[107] He does stick to Leibniz's terminology that such influence is only "ideal," but sees this

---

105. On this point, see Deleuze, *The Fold*, 86: "It is *because* every monad possesses a clear zone that it must have a body, this zone constituting a relation with the body.... It is because we have a clear zone that we must have a body charged with traveling through it or exploring it, from birth to death."

106. Baumgarten, *Metaphysica/Metaphysik*, §400. This follows from Baumgarten's distinctive understanding of the principle of sufficient reason and its supplementation by the principle of consequence (*principium rationati*), which Baumgarten considered to be one of his major achievements in metaphysics. Baumgarten believes he can prove not only that nothing is without ground but also that nothing is without consequence; and because all things are necessarily "connected on both sides (with regard to what precedes and what follows after)," they must be understood as "grounded" (*rationatum*) in one another, thus forming a nexus. See Baumgarten, *Metaphysica/Metaphysik*, 58–65 (§§14–24), here: §24.

107. On this point, see the editor's introduction to Baumgarten, *Metaphysica/Metaphysik*, lix.

condition met when "the suffering of a substance that is influenced by another is at the same time the action of the very substance that suffers."[108] Because every monad in the universal nexus is ground and consequence of every other, it is indirectly also the ground of the action it suffers from another monad.[109] Monads, in other words, are so enmeshed with the nexus of things that their acting and being acted upon cannot ultimately be disentangled.

At the deepest level, events in the world do not fit neatly into the categories of actions or passions, where one thing acts upon another thing that is entirely distinct from it. In the densely interconnected world of Baumgarten's metaphysics, all action is reciprocal *interaction*; the action of one is always also the action of the other, and the suffering of the one therefore also its own action. The "ideality" of influence between monads means that influence cannot be conceived as a one-way street, as "flowing from" one substance to the other. Effectively, Baumgarten thus assimilates the monad's windowlessness to its mirror-like quality. For Baumgarten, monads can count as "windowless"—as admitting no *external* influence—only because they are so enmeshed in the web of things that *no influence is truly external*. We can perhaps picture this metaphysical theorem by analogy to how movement proliferates through a spider web: It is futile to ask whether it flows from one node to the other or vice versa. Each node instead becomes the site of a (more or less proximate) event in which the whole nexus acts in and through the monad.

The monadology pervades Baumgarten's aesthetics not least because it defines what it means for Baumgarten to represent, and to represent in the sensate and intellectual manners contrasted in the *Aesthetica*. In a profound sense, representation for Baumgarten is not only representation *of* the world but representations *out of* the world, and it is the former as a consequence of the latter. In a detailed analysis of Baumgarten's concept of sense perception, Fred

---

108. Baumgarten, *Metaphysica/Metaphysik*, 212.
109. Baumgarten, *Metaphysica/Metaphysik*, §400, §463. He goes on to note that "the sufferings of the monads of any given world, which they suffer from other mundane monads, are, *to this extent*, ideal" (my emphasis).

Beiser has emphasized this synecdochic quality, according to which sensations are "also a fact about the world ... because they are the effect of all nature acting upon me, and because they are what nature becomes in and through me."[110] That the mind as representing power is contiguous with the world it represents underlies Baumgarten's rationale for why sensate perceptions in their "aesthetic" perfection surpass distinct representation with regard to objective content: they represent *more* of the world because in them, the perceiving subject is *more part* of the world, less distinct than it becomes after selectively lifting a small number of perceptions into distinctness.

This dynamic notably resurfaces in the metaphysical function Baumgarten ascribes to art, which is indicated by two distinct roles the term "nexus" plays in his aesthetics. The word designates not only the interconnection of things in the world (as presented in the mind through the *analogon rationis*) but also the interconnection of representations that constitute the poem or artwork as a miniature world.[111] As Ursula Franke noted early on, this implies that the microcosm of the artwork presents the perfection and harmony of the greater universe in sensible form.[112] Baumgarten thus forges a link between art and the representation of the absolute that would haunt Idealist and Romantic aesthetics. Yet this relationship between artwork and world is not merely one of *analogy* but also (and first and foremost) one of *contiguity*: the nexus of the artwork reflects the complexity of the whole because it draws on representations that are, as perfected sensate representations, less rigidly filtered and more "in touch" with the wider nexus of things than others. In a terminology with more cachet in contemporary discussion, we might say that the nexus of the artworks is drawn from

---

110. Beiser, *Diotima's Children*, 138–43, here: 141. Beiser goes on to note that the "net effect" of Baumgarten's view is "to question the Cartesian dualism between consciousness and world. Baumgarten refuses to see representation as a conscious state that somehow mysteriously represents or corresponds to an extended being in the world outside it."
111. Baumgarten, *Meditationes*, vi, x, lxv, esp. lxviii.
112. Franke, "Sinnliche Erkenntnis," 92–93; Franke, *Baumgartens Erfindung der Ästhetik*, 61–64; Franke, *Kunst als Erkenntnis*.

representations that "resonate" or "vibrate" with the wider nexus of things.[113] Artworks thus function simultaneously as iconic and indexical ciphers of the whole (to put it in Peirce's taxonomy of signs): they crystallize features that resemble the perfection of the whole (like an iconic sign) because they are (like an indexical sign) contiguous with it; that is, made of the same stuff.[114]

Much of what follows is simply an attempt to take the monadological foundation of Baumgarten's aesthetics more seriously than previous commentators, who have tended to read him as taking a "step away" from Leibniz toward a more subjectivist and aestheticist understanding of harmony and perfection. I do this by highlighting two key terms that crystallize the respective "objective" and the "subjective" axes of the monadological presence in Baumgarten's aesthetics. First, I elaborate on the importance of the *nexus rerum* to explain *what* it is that aesthetic perceptions disclose. Second, I focus on Baumgarten's concept of the *fundus animae*, the subconscious "ground of the soul," to explore the monadological substrate of Baumgarten's understanding of the aesthetic subject and its exercises of attention.

Nexus rerum: Baumgarten's Aesthetics of Connectivity

Although now mostly forgotten, *nexus* was a key term not only for Baumgarten but for the entire period of philosophical reflection in the period between Leibniz and German Idealism. The assumption that things exist within a general nexus was, in the first instance, a corollary of the principle of sufficient reason, which posited that things must be understood as grounded in one another if they are to be understood at all.[115] Drawing heavily on Baumgarten, Zedler's

---

113. In preferring sonic over visual imagery, Leibniz's *petites perceptions* anticipate elements of modern resonance theory as developed, for instance, in Rosa, *Resonanz*. For the concept of "vibration," see Bennett, *Vibrant Matter*.

114. This duality points back to the two ways the sensible world relates to the absolute in Plato: as likeness and reflection (*mímēsis*) and as participation (*méthexis*).

115. For this quasi-epistemological motivation of the principle of sufficient reason (or "ground") in Baumgarten, see Fugate, "Alexander Baumgarten."

encyclopedia explains that the concept highlights complex interdependencies between seemingly distant things, such as the earth and the sun, rainfall and vegetation growth, the temperature of the atmosphere and the conditions for human life.[116] Yet the assumption of a general nexus drew attention not only to connections between different orders but also to different orders of connection. The concept's reception has tended to reduce such thinking of connectivity to the distinct problems of "causal determinism" and "natural teleology," but nexus-thinking was in fact concerned with interactions between things (*Wechselwirkungen*) of various sorts. Baumgarten, for instance, includes interactions described by efficient and final causality as well as semiotic and aesthetic relations, and even those that hold between moral action and its incentives and reasons. In practice, the concept fostered a manner of thinking that gives priority to connections over the things they connect. Baumgarten therefore regularly emphasizes that a finite human mind can never exhaustively know any single thing in the world because knowing one thing exhaustively would amount to knowing the entire world in which it participates and whose interrelations (or "correlations") determine it *as* what it is.[117]

When Baumgarten maintains that aesthetic perception is concerned with individuals and singulars rather than generals or universals,[118] he sounds, in some ways, much like modern and postmodern aesthetic theorists. Yet he does not mean that aesthetics is especially attentive to what is incommensurable, irreducible, or nonidentical, and in this way (as the cluster of negative particles suggests)

---

116. Zedler defines "Zusammenhang der Dinge" (nexus of things) as a "reciprocal relationship of things with one another . . . e.g., the sun and the earth . . . rain and plant growth . . . air and the warmth in it . . . and why we can live in this warm air" (Zedler, "Zusammenhang der Dinge," 567). I thank Ross Shields for pointing me to this entry.

117. For a particularly emphatic formulation of this common motif, see Baumgarten, *Gedanken vom vernünftigen Beyfall*, 23 (§7): "Each and every thing is in a universal nexus with all others. Whoever therefore wants to think anything completely distinctly must also think all its relations completely distinctly. This includes all its correlates, or those things with which it stands in a relation; otherwise its nexus, and thus the thing itself, would not be represented completely distinctly."

118. Baumgarten, *Aesthetica/Ästhetik*, 1:417–19 (§§440–441).

resists something about "thought" or "rationality" that is deemed oppressive. While Baumgarten insists that contingent singulars, rather than timeless universals, contain the greatest metaphysical truth, he does so based on the idea that such singulars are marked by the intersection of the highest number of connections or reasons. Following a brand of rationalism that aligns "rationality" with "relationality," the abundance of connections within these singulars corresponds to a higher degree of objective reason or metaphysical truth.[119] For Baumgarten, singular beings and events are "contingent" in the sense that they have their reasons for being (and for being determined thus and not otherwise) not in themselves, but in another, and therefore do not exist by necessity.[120] Strictly speaking, contingent singulars have their reasons for being (or are "contingent upon") *all* others. As part of a world—of a "nexus of interdependent singulars"—they are individuated by their immediate and mediate relations to other things that participate in this nexus.[121]

What the orientation of aesthetic perception toward the singular and the individual implies for Baumgarten is thus not a privileging of things considered in their radical disarticulation from everything else but, on the contrary, an openness for registering the manifold entanglements of things. As Hegel would after him, Baumgarten therefore understands the "concrete" and the "abstract" in ways that invert some of their common connotations: the concrete is not the isolated, self-contained, materially bounded entity, but instead what is literally "grown together," a thing in its in embeddedness and determination by its context. The abstract, in turn, is necessarily isolated from the interconnectivity of things, disconnected from the rest and circumscribed by clearly definable boundaries.[122] The "concrete" relations

---

119. Baumgarten, *Aesthetica/Ästhetik*, 1:418–19 (§441); Baumgarten, *Metaphysica/Metaphysik*, 108–11 (§§148–154).
120. This follows from Leibniz's and Baumgarten's ontological understanding of the principle of sufficient reason and excludes the divine singular, which has its reason for being in itself and is by definition a necessary being.
121. Baumgarten, *Metaphysica/Metaphysik*, 198–99 (§357): "a world admits of no islands." see also Baumgarten, *Metaphysics*, §400.
122. The idea is that correlates cannot be thought without the relation; therefore, thinking one thing entails thinking those it is related to—that is, mediately,

of things are lost in abstraction precisely because abstraction works by isolation. Aesthetic truth then ultimately functions as a kind of sensorium for interconnections ignored by systems of abstraction. The trouble with such systems is not that they do not respect the individuality of things, but that they are, in a way, never systematic enough: the relations they register necessarily fall short of the wealth of actual interrelations that determine any one thing in its singularity.

To be sure, Baumgarten's sensibility for the interdependence and the interconnectedness of things seems to stand or fall with his rational theism. In Baumgarten's (as in Leibniz's) metaphysics, the mutual determination of contingent things is metaphysically explained as the coordination of independent substances by the necessary being who ensures that all things are perfectly attuned to one another. Yet what Adorno remarks about Hegel's absolute idealism—that "precisely the construction of the absolute subject," by drawing everything into an immanence that gives equal weight to all beings, "does justice to an objectivity indissoluble in subjectivity"[123]—might also be said of Baumgarten's nexus-thinking: the theistic premise of the mutual accommodation of substances allows him to register an immanent interdependence of things that tends to press beyond the premise that allowed its articulation. Baumgarten's *theological* sensibility for the all-connectedness of things, in other words, prefigures what we might today see as an *ecological* sensibility for complex interconnections even between seemingly disparate entities.

In the final analysis, Baumgarten's aesthetics of determinacy can thus be understood as an aesthetics of connectivity. His basic intuition is that human minds register more connections among things than they can distinctly grasp. Expressed in more technical terms, they notice more differential marks than can register in the selective formation of distinct notions of the understanding. While

---

the entire universe. "Understanding one thing fully" would consequently entail knowing the entire universe.

123. "One consequence of the unrestrained expansion of the subject to absolute spirit in Hegel is that, as moments inherent in this spirit, not only the subject but also the object are presented as substantial and making the full demands of their own beings ... precisely the construction of the absolute subject in Hegel that does justice to an objectivity indissoluble in subjectivity" (Adorno, *Hegel*, 5–6).

Baumgarten allows that sense perception is indistinct, its perfection—aesthetic perception in a narrow sense—is precisely not defined by this *in*distinctness from the perspective of the intellect but by its positive capacity to register "material truth" or the (by Kantian standards oxymoronic) "material determination" of things. Although this surplus of perceptions cannot be communicated explicitly through distinct notions, it is transmissible to others through the figuration of perceptual marks in linguistic, visual, or tonal signs that follow the logic of examples—signs that embody a specific bundle of marks that is not separable from this particular embodiment.[124] Baumgarten's insistence on the determinacy of aesthetic things—both of things as perceived in the aesthetic mode and things made to convey such perceptions—contains the promise of an aesthetics defined not by the freedom *from* the intellect's determination but by the *freedom to attend* to another kind of determination: one we would have to understand with Baumgarten as the mutual determination of things through each other.

In its more Baumgartian moments, Kant's third *Critique* still has an inkling of this other possible aesthetics. There are suggestions in Kant's aesthetics that the independence of the imagination from the understanding in the free play of the faculties is not merely freedom from determination by concepts but a freedom to synthesize manifolds of intuition in ways that seem not to be merely imposed on them.[125] In this reading of the third *Critique*—or in the Baumgartian subtext of the third *Critique* that allows such a reading—the

---

124. Baumgarten, *Meditationes*, 20–25 (§21–22); Allerkamp and Mirbach, "Unter produktiver Spannung," 23–24.

125. Compare especially Kant's framing of the third *Critique* in the two introductions, which emphasize that nature must be sufficiently ordered for moral actions to attain objective reality in the sensible world, and that no coherent understanding of nature is possible unless we assume that nature is inherently organized (given that the laws contributed by the understanding leave too much unspecified about the empirical laws of nature). Compare also §42 on natural beauty, where Kant famously considers interpreting natural beauty as a "trace" or "sign" (*Wink*) that its products and our faculties may be united in some deeper ground, as well as Kant's repeated suggestions in notes that beauty indicates the mind's "fit" with the world. In effect, Kant worries about how to patch the rift he created by his own Copernican turn. For a reading that emphasizes such moments in Kant (and Schiller), see Welsch, "Schiller Revisited."

experience of natural beauty in particular hints at an inherent organization of things within a system of nature that the second part of the *Critique* then addresses through the heuristic device of natural teleology. Kant's concept of aesthetic ideas, which is formulated in terms largely borrowed from Baumgarten, similarly suggests that intuitive content can be internally structured without the intervention of determining concepts. Yet in the end, aesthetic ideas remain negatively defined as rich intuitive content that provides a lot to think about—provides a lot of "food for thought"—but remains cognitively blind without the conceptual determination of intuitive content required for all possible cognition.[126] What Baumgarten's *Meditationes* probed as the "relatively inconceivable" in poetry—an implicit figuration of knowledge that conveys what a finite mind cannot distinctly conceive—reverts to mere ignorance again.

Idealist aesthetics following Kant would pursue traces of this other kind of aesthetic determinacy only by making all determination dependent on the self-determining activity of an absolute subject (even where this subject tends to merge, as in Schelling's objective idealism, with nature itself). And yet an undercurrent of Baumgarten's aesthetics of connectivity would continue to surface throughout the German aesthetic tradition. Refracted through Kant's third *Critique*, different versions of the idea that art registers forms of interconnection not imposed by the subject have proliferated through aesthetic thought, including where these connections were thought of negatively in terms of dissonance and fragmentation. Even an aesthetic theory that appears under the banner of negativity, like Adorno's, would offer a paradoxical definition of the language character of art as "determinacy [*Bestimmtheit*] of the indeterminate," one that gives voice to "selfhood not first excised by identificatory thought from the interdependence of entities."[127] Usually understood as a mere metaphor, the "monadological" character

---

126. For Baumgartian terms such as "related representations" (*Nebenvorstellungen*) in Kant's presentation of aesthetic ideas, see Kant, *Critique of the Power of Judgment*, 191–95 (§48), AA 5: 311; for the "blindness" (or noncognitive character) of aesthetic ideas, see also the first note to §57, 218, AA 5: 342,

127. Adorno, *Aesthetic Theory*, 124, 112. Modernist experiences of "epiphany" as described in the *Chandos Letter*, in which an infinitely complex connectivity

of works of art often invoked by Adorno and others would instead indicate the long afterlife of Baumgarten's metaphysics of connectivity in German aesthetics.

Aesthetic Exercises of Attention

Baumgarten's reflections on the aesthetic subject are concentrated in the *Aesthetica*'s sections on aesthetic exercises, which describe the gradual formation of the *felix aestheticus*, the "happy aesthete" exemplified in the figure of the artist. Recent scholarship has increasingly highlighted the systematic importance of exercise for a field that deals, in the *analogon rationis*, with abilities that can only be perfected by training and practice rather than by following explicit methods or rules.[128] Views on what the subject formed through aesthetic exercise signifies, however, could not be more contrary. Christoph Menke finds in Baumgarten's exercise regime the blueprint of what Foucault described as "disciplinary" power, a mode of power that no longer governs bodies through the direct exertion of force but by shaping them in accordance with imperatives of social utility.[129] At the other end of the spectrum, Gabriel Trop reads Baumgarten's aesthetic exercises as a modern, aestheticized version of "spiritual exercises"—practices of self-cultivation and self-modification that Pierre Hadot explored as the forgotten kernel of ancient philosophy.[130]

To shed light on this controversy, we must begin by analyzing the micro-logic of attentional routines discussed in Baumgarten's exercise regime. Aesthetic exercises are, as Rüdiger Campe has noted, first and foremost exercises of attention and abstraction, the two basic faculties of the sensate cognitive faculty, and should therefore be analyzed as such.[131] When Baumgarten recycles Wolffian phrases

---

of things is momentarily revealed once the usual concepts and schemata are cleared out of the way, also belong in this lineage.
  128. For a good overview, see Frey, "Zur ästhetischen Übung."
  129. See Menke, *Kraft*, 11–45; Menke, "Die Disziplin der Ästhetik."
  130. See Trop, *Poetry as a Way of Life*, 25–49; Trop, "Aesthetic Askesis."
  131. Quoting Baumgarten's definition of aesthetic exercise, Campe states that "attention and abstraction were the paradigm of what becomes a skill and art

in defining aesthetic exercises as the gradual acquisition of a "habitus" of beautiful thinking "through the frequent repetition of similar actions," it may initially seem as if he merely extends Wolff's exercise regime of attention to the aesthetic sphere.[132] A more detailed look at Baumgarten's exercises regime, however, reveals it to be in many respects the precise inverse of Wolff's.

Baumgarten's exercises aim at establishing mental harmony by having the mind mull over a single item or "theme" again and again.[133] In sharp contrast to the attentional indifference trained by Wolff's exercises, for Baumgarten the choice of object depends on idiosyncratic preference, what someone happens to feel especially attracted to. Baumgarten's designation of the focus of aesthetic exercise as a "theme" identifies the *focal object of aesthetic exercises* with the *unity in which the components of an aesthetic manifold (such as a poem) converge*.[134] What Baumgarten describes as the focal theme of aesthetic exercises bears more than just metaphorical resemblance to the concept of "focus" he defines in his metaphysics: the determining ground of the unity-in-multiplicity that constitutes a thing's "perfection."[135] At stake in the "theme" of aesthetic

---

through repetition focused on a theme. All aesthetic exercise . . . was also always and primarily that of *attentio* and *abstractio*" ("Baumgartens Ästhetik," 168, my translation). Both Campe and Frey also explore the rhetorical origins of Baumgarten's exercises. Although Frey does not discuss it in these terms, her overview suggests that what the aesthete exercises and molds are indeed unconscious habits of noticing.

132. Baumgarten, *Aesthetica/Ästhetik*, 1:38–39 (§47).
133. Baumgarten, *Aesthetica/Ästhetik*, 1:38–39 (§47).
134. Baumgarten, *Meditationes*, 54–55 (§§lxvi–lxvii).
135. Baumgarten, *Metaphysica/Metaphysik*, 88–89 (§94); Baumgarten glosses Latin *focus* as "Brennpunct" (focal point). Meier uses the same metaphor (and nearly the same phrasing!) to explain how the many elements of an artwork and the collected powers of an attending mind converge in a single and thus brightly lit focal point. Compare Meier's characterization of *beauty*: "Just as infinitely many light rays fall onto a concave mirror and are refracted and bent toward each other in such a way that they converge into a single point, thus causing penetrating brilliance of that point, so too must the various things, the manifold in a beauty, be the sufficient grounds of a purpose." The same image applied to *attention*: "Just as scattered rays of light are brought together into a single point by a concave mirror, so too do we, through attention, direct our cognitive power to a single point, to a single representation" (*Anfangsgründe aller schönen Wissenschaften*, 1:40–41 (§24), 2:50 (§284), my translation). (Meier, however, substitutes the concept of purpose for Baumgarten's

exercises is the unity-in-multiplicity that defines perfection and its phenomenal appearance as beauty; not only on the subjective side—as the harmony of the aesthetic exercitant's powers—but also on the objective side—as the convergence of manifold heterogeneous perceptions in a unifying element. Aesthetic exercises thus explain how there arise in the mind of an artist complex perceptions that can reconcile the "wideness" (*extensio*) of extensive attention with the "conciseness" (*brevitas*) Baumgarten also ascribes to "concise, yet elegantly rich" aesthetic form. In continuously training what Baumgarten's lectures call the "powers of attention" (*Attentionskräfte*) on a given item, the focal notion gradually accumulates more and more associated perceptions.[136] Despite their dispersion, these perceptions remain unified by their convergence in a single theme. Like a convex mirror (and as one might picture a monad), the focal theme thus gathers its surrounding world into a small yet dense sphere.[137] In honing my focus on a theme, I do not so much focus *on* the world as train my attention on a medium that focuses the world *to me*. (This is the kind of "focus" Descartes anticipated when his meditation over a piece of wax gave way, for a moment, to unguarded reverie.)

In contrast to the unity-in-multiplicity of distinct perfection, mulling over a focal perception in such a way that it gradually increases in complexity unseals forms of coherence that draw from the manifold ramifications between things in the general nexus.[138] To be sure, the unity of these heterogeneous perceptions is not simply the one

---

thema to describe the ground of unity in beauty. As Beiser has shown, this is the source of Kant's (mis-)understanding that unity in rationalist aesthetics always implies the notion of a purpose.)

136. In the lectures, Baumgarten uses the term *Attentionskraefte* (powers of attention) to describe the faculties of the mind involved in aesthetic exercises; see Poppe, "Alexander Gottlieb Baumgarten," 114 (§78).

137. This is the image Baumgarten uses in the *Aesthetica* to characterize the brevity of aesthetic form.

138. To achieve distinct perfection, the mind bundles its powers to pulverize intricate perceptions into their constituent elements in order to then, through an analytic-synthetic procedure, reconstitute a second-order unity from clearly distinguished parts. As we have seen in previous chapters, this technique substitutes the mind's own unity, its collection into itself (Baumgarten's *collectio animi*), for the deceptive unities of things found in naive perception.

found in naive perception. This is why it initially takes aesthetic exercises, the honing of a skill or technique (*habitus*), to form such intricate perceptions in the mind. As Gabriel Trop has shown in a detailed analysis of the structure of Baumgarten's exercises, however, the various stages of Baumgarten's regime for training this technique (natural disposition, aesthetic exercise, and aesthetic doctrine) build toward the "event" of inspiration, the moment in which the exercising self surpasses itself in a felicitous loss of self-control—or as a result of the paradoxical ability to lose control of oneself in a felicitous way.[139] As the telos of the Baumgarten's exercise regime, "inspiration" (*impetus aestheticus*) plays the same paradigmatic role for the aesthetic subject that "indifference" (*indifferentia attentionis*) played for the rational subject of Wolff's exercises. As we saw in chapter 2, the goal of Wolff's exercises was to steel attention against all stimuli by training the mind to focus at will on any entity whatsoever, including inherently repugnant ones, to make the mind's determination of itself independent from contingent environments. Baumgarten's exercises of attention, by contrast, prepare the mind to become deliberately receptive to what lies beyond the self. As Baumgarten repeatedly emphasizes, their goal therefore lies beyond the reach of what can be forced through exercises altogether and depends as much on the training of the mind as on *chairos*, the confluence of the right moment and opportune circumstances.[140]

Aesthetic exercises therefore do not simply orient the powers of the mind toward a different end (that of "beautiful thinking"). They imply a different performance of these powers altogether. Baumgarten's training regimen aims not to produce a subject in full possession of its own faculties but instead to cultivate a state of preparedness for a moment of deliberate "dis-possession," in which the subject becomes receptive to something beyond itself. Trop is thus right to reject Menke's reading of Baumgarten's aesthetic subject as a Foucauldian subject of discipline and control: Menke's account of aesthetic

---

139. Trop, *Poetry as a Way of Life*, 39–49; Trop, "Aesthetic Askesis," esp. 68–70. The latter shows especially clearly how natural disposition, aesthetic exercise, and aesthetic doctrine lead up to the moment of inspiration as event.

140. For instance, Poppe, "Alexander Gottlieb Baumgarten," 116 (§81).

exercises as the incorporation of predictable and socially useful aptitudes misses (or dismisses) the point that these exercises prepare for a moment of inspiration. And yet Trop's own account tends to portray aesthetic inspiration as a mere catalyst for the creative act of generating "coherence in a world saturated with contingency."[141] He therefore has little to say about what it is the subject becomes receptive *to* in such moments. Baumgarten's detailed answer to this question crystallizes in his concept of the "ground of the soul."

Ground of the Soul

The term "ground of the soul" (*Grund der Seele*) itself circulated in the Baumgarten's Pietistic context in Halle and has roots in medieval mysticism.[142] Baumgarten, however, gave it a nonmystical (or rather, rationally mystical) reinterpretation as the myriad of "obscure" perceptions in the mind that lie below the threshold of consciousness.[143] In moments of inspiration, the waking mind becomes

---

141. Trop, "Aesthetic Askesis," 65. The moment of active imposition of coherence by the subject is somewhat toned down in the account Trop gives in *Poetry as a Way of Life*, 34–35.

142. The Pietistic context of the term is emphasized by Schwaiger, *Alexander Gottlieb Baumgarten*, 103 (esp. note 289). Grote seems to pay no attention to the concept, even though it would support his thesis of a Pietistic origin of Baumgarten's aesthetics. The concept's mystical roots are discussed in Largier, "Plasticity of the Soul," 536–44.

143. According to Baumgarten's topology of the soul, these subconscious perceptions make up the soul's "realm of darkness" ("REGNUM TENEBRARUM"), which is situated below a "realm of light" ("REGNUM LUCIS") comprising all clear or conscious perceptions (Baumgarten, *Metaphysica/Metaphysik*, §511, §514, §518). How thoroughly Baumgarten transforms an "Enlightenment" topology that traditionally prioritized the light of clear and distinct perceptions over darkness, obscurity, and confusion is evident in a new metaphorology operative in Baumgarten's text that codes the deep stratum of the soul as *hot* (like the fervor of passion) rather than cold; as *lively* (and "wet") rather than dry, like the abstract intellect; and—as suggested by the overdetermined connotations of (germinal) seed and pregnant womb contained in the term *perceptio praegnans* (see below)—as *fertile* rather than sterile. (For the opposition to "sterility" and "dryness," see §515, §531, etc.; for the "fecundity" of obscure perceptions, see Meier's description and Baumgarten's gloss of *praegnans* as both *körnig* and *trächtig*—a kind of hermaphroditical fountain of fertility [Meier, *Anfangsgründe aller schönen Wissenschaften*, 3:271 (§126)].

unusually receptive to this obscure ground. In the *Aesthetica* Baumgarten describes inspiration as a state of heightened excitation of the soul's powers in which "almost the entire ground of the soul [*fundus animae*] rises a little higher and breathes something greater [*maius aliquid spiret*] and readily supplies things that seemed forgotten, never experienced [*non experti*], or which seemed to us and yet more to others impossible to foresee."[144] In such a state of mind, obscure perceptions usually confined to the unconscious ground of the soul surge above the threshold of clear perception: memories surface that seemed long forgotten, things that seemed to have escaped experience altogether register in the conscious mind, and one suddenly even seems to have foreknowledge of things that are yet to come. Given the extraordinary expansion of consciousness in such states, Baumgarten grants that it is easy to misattribute them to divine influence, as the ancients did. What the ancients lacked, he emphasizes, was the new philosophical psychology's awareness of unconscious perceptions, which explains the mechanism behind inspired knowledge without any recourse to supernatural forces.[145]

These small remarks have major implications, because they demonstrate Baumgarten's full-fledged monadological understanding of the unconscious perceptions in the ground of the soul. Not only did Baumgarten, like Wolff and others, accept obscure perceptions as an anthropological fact and a limitation on human knowledge.[146] As his reference to the ground of the soul as the source of an extraordinary cognitive power implies, he assumed with Leibniz that

---

"Hotness" is suggested by their description of affects in terms of "fervor/Glut" [for instance, in Poppe, "Alexander Gottlieb Baumgarten," 79]; "wetness" is suggested by the etymology of "confusa" as flowing into each other and Leibniz's streaming imagery of tiny perceptions.) The new metaphorology is oblique to the light/darkness hierarchy because the privileged terms—life, warmth, fertility—all attach to an obscure underside of the soul that Baumgarten's predecessors had defined negatively by its privative lack of light. For a detailed discussion of this point, see Adler, *Die Prägnanz des Dunklen*, 16–17.

144. Baumgarten, *Aesthetica/Ästhetik*, 1:64–65 (§80).
145. Baumgarten, *Aesthetica/Ästhetik*, 1:65 (§80); Poppe, "Alexander Gottlieb Baumgarten," x.
146. For a summary of Wolff's view on this matter, see Adler, *Die Prägnanz des Dunklen*, 25–26.

unconscious perceptions reflect the soul's inchoate cognizance of itself and of its context, together with the infinite contexts this first context enfolds (Leibniz's doctrine of "confused omniscience"). The groundswell of the soul in a state of inspiration brings some of this buried awareness "to light"—to the light of conscious or clear perception. In this way they become a source of seemingly impossible knowledge, granting even the uncanny ability to foresee the seemingly unforeseeable. Leibniz had assumed that an infinitely capacious mind could read the future out of the present state of each monad's tiny perceptions. A mind that dips into its own unconscious ground in a state of inspiration shares a fraction of this power to detect in its complex present state traces of things that are yet to come. It does not receive a gift of divine prophecy, as the ancients believed, but simply becomes more acutely aware of what already registers in its own unconscious ground—and therefore sees more clearly where things are "already" going. Baumgarten accordingly calls the suggestiveness of perceptions saturated in this way with traces from the soul's unconscious ground *praegnantes* (pregnant with meaning)—the same term Leibniz used for the cosmic expressiveness of tiny perceptions, their abundance with traces of the future.[147]

Inspiration is, for Baumgarten, therefore not simply a "subjective" state.[148] Baumgarten's model of artistic inspiration is equidis-

---

147. The following fragment from the preface to Leibniz's *New Essays* epitomizes this conception of tiny perceptions: "These tiny perceptions ... make up those impressions the surrounding bodies make on us, which involve the infinite, and this connection that each being has with the rest of the universe. It can even be said that as a result of these tiny perceptions, the present is pregnant [*gross*] with the future and laden with the past, that everything conspires together ... and that eyes as piercing as those of God could read the whole sequence of the universe in the smallest of substances" (Leibniz, "Preface to the New Essays," 296, translation altered from "filled" to "pregnant" to reflect the common translation of French "gros"). Baumgarten likely had no access to the *New Essays*, which were not published until 1765, but was able to gather the same motifs from a number of Leibniz's writings, including the *Monadology* and the *Principles of Nature and Grace*.

148. This also runs counter to the scholarship, insofar as the scholarship has taken this topic seriously in Baumgarten at all. From Bäumler to the recent scholarship, the ground of the soul has often been seen as the realm of irrational, subjective interiority, the sum total of "sense perceptions individual to the highest degree," in the (translated) words of Victoria Niehle in *Die Poetik der Fülle*, 73.

tant from spiritualist models—the divine *enthousiasmós* of the classical artist or the *Schwärmertum* of religious enthusiasts—and from Romantic notions of a genius artist whose creations originate from the depth of subjective interiority. For Baumgarten, inspiration instead originates from the part of soul where it is least demarcated as a distinct subject, where it blends into its surroundings like the flow of indistinct tiny perceptions that grounds the life of the monad. The phenomenal dimension of the state Baumgarten has in mind is perhaps best captured by what later German aesthetics would discuss under the category of *Stimmung*: a primordial mood or atmosphere that is neither simply inside nor outside, neither "subjective" nor "objective," but registers an ambiance prior to this separation.[149] Leibniz had already claimed that tiny perceptions are individually unconscious but nevertheless "make themselves felt in the assemblage, at least confusedly," for example, in a vaguely sensed and nonlocalized "uneasiness" in contrast to the localized sensation of "pain."[150] Although the combined impact of tiny perceptions does not yield clear sensations or emotions, it nevertheless registers as a basic mood that grounds and colors conscious perception. Instead of a domain of private feelings or unconscious emotions, however, Baumgarten's ground of the soul is perhaps best described as reflecting, in the manner of a vague and usually unconscious mood, the soul's basic attunement to the mutual attunement of substances. Inspiration happens when the mind has learned through exercise to "tune into" this basic attunement and bring some share of it to

---

149. Famously difficult to render in English, the German term *Stimmung* can mean "mood," "atmosphere," "ambiance," as well as, literally, "tuning (in)" or "attunement." For recent theoretical work on *Stimmung* in the German tradition, see Gumbrecht, *Stimmungen Lesen*; Böhme, *Atmosphäre*; and Wellbery's lucid overview of the concept's history in *Ästhetische Grundbegriffe*. One of the most prominent conceptions of *Stimmung* is Heidegger's use of the term to designate a basic, immersive form of being-in-the-world. Recent work on the concept of resonance has revived many of the theorems associated with *Stimmung*, including its hybrid character "in between" a subjective and objective state.

150. Leibniz, "Preface to the New Essays," 295, 297. On the phenomenal level, tiny perceptions "make up those impressions the surrounding bodies make on us, which involve the infinite, and this connection that each being has with the rest of the universe" (296).

consciousness. In the *Aesthetica* Baumgarten accordingly introduces the various occasions that can induce inspiration with regard to the soul's perceptions *pro positu corporis*, a (Leibnizian) phrase for the soul's affectedness according to the body's position in relation to other entities in the world, or its situatedness in a specific environment.[151] Such contexts in which the mind is emphatically immersed in the world include "outward" activities of the body as much as "internal" affects: love, indignation, and other "perturbations of the soul"; dancing and listening to music; the impressions one receives from surrounding nature; the effects of being on the move and of traveling.[152] Summarizing Baumgarten, we could say that what the Romantics would misunderstand as subjective emotion and what the ancients meant by divine enthusiasm (but misattributed to the influence of some higher being) is the soul's heightened perceptiveness toward environments in which it participates and has participated. The ground of the soul is none other than the breadth of the world.

In analogy to how *indifferentia attentionis* was both a special attentional skill and the general condition of rational subjectivity for Wolff, heightened receptivity toward to the ground of the soul—the telos of Baumgarten's aesthetic exercises—marks the general condition of aesthetic subjectivity beyond the special case of artistic inspiration that constitutes its paradigm. This undermines Christoph Menke's narrative about eighteenth-century aesthetics and the modern subject, which also revolves about the concept of the "ground of the soul."[153] Menke's genealogy of modern aesthetics

---

151. Baumgarten, *Metaphysica/Metaphysik*, 272–73 (§§512–13). The recurring phrase *pro positu corporis* is Baumgarten's formula for the Leibnizian theorem that monads perceive/express/represent the world in accordance with their body. The *positio* is, in turn, defined as a thing's determination through its relation to others (84–85 [§85]).

152. See Baumgarten, *Aesthetica/Ästhetik*, 1:64–77 (§§81–95).

153. Menke has the history of modern aesthetics arising out of a debate between Descartes and Leibniz. If Descartes, in this account, gave a new definition of the sensory as the field of intractable indeterminacy opposed to the autonomous acts of the understanding, Leibniz insisted that the field of the sensory, *despite* its indeterminacy, *also* constituted a form of principled *activity*: the monad's tiny perceptions are self-produced according to an inner principle, even if this principle is unavailable to the conscious self. Aesthetics unfolds, according to Menke, in the tension between the *principled operation* of the sensory and its si-

makes a compelling case for understanding the new philosophical investigation of the senses and the arts—of what is less than fully rational—as a reflection on the conditions of subject formation. Perhaps to support his own vision of an aesthetics of force, however, he stages a polar opposition between Baumgarten's aesthetic of subjective faculties and Herder's energetic aesthetics of force that breaks down on closer inspection. According to Menke, Baumgarten's aesthetic exercises provide a blueprint for the disciplinary conversion of the mind's powers into socially useful faculties (and thus of the operation of "disciplinary" power), whereas Herder explores the anarchic play of forces in the "ground of the soul" as the pre-subjective condition of subjectivity that can never be fully integrated into the subject.

Not only does this account miss the importance of the "ground of the soul" (which Herder adopted from Baumgarten in his fragments on aesthetics) for Baumgarten's own aesthetic theory; it also misconstrues the concept's genealogy and significance based on a one-sided understanding of Leibniz's monad, which Menke, too, recognizes as the foundation of Baumgarten's aesthetics. Menke hypostatizes precisely the aspect of the monad Baumgarten deemphasized—its windowlessness—while ignoring its function as a universal mirror and metonymic "condensation" of the network of monads, which

---

multaneous *indeterminacy*; a tension that can be weighted in two different ways: On the one hand, aesthetics interprets the sensory as a field of activity that, although unavailable to immediate direction by the conscious self, can be made docile and appropriated by practice. In Menke's version of Baumgarten's aesthetics, this interpretation gave rise to a concept of the subject as bearer of faculties, both in its disciplinary dimension (faculties have to be "trained into" bodies) and its individualizing dimension (once acquired, faculties grant individual agency). On the other hand, however, the autonomous activity of the sensory can be interpreted as an unavailable ground, a play of "force" (*Kraft*) on which conscious subjectivity depends but which it can never fully integrate (this, for Menke, is Herder's understanding of aesthetics). Aesthetics thus at the same time reflects on the emergence of the subject and on its undoing. Ultimately, Menke thinks, aesthetics yields an anthropology that thinks the *difference* between the subject and what he calls the human (*qua* pre-subjective, pre-social body of forces). Aesthetic anthropology à la Menke thinks the human *as* this difference between (self-identical) subject and (pre-subjective) nonidentity, as a "being-in-between" socialized subject and a-subjective force. See Menke, *Kraft*; Menke, "Die Disziplin der Ästhetik"; Menke, "Schwerpunkt."

Baumgarten highlighted at the expense of windowlessness. From Menke's perspective, the monad's force (*vis*) therefore appears solely as the internal activity of a self-enclosed substance rather than also—as it did for Baumgarten—as a force representing the universe in accordance with the relative position of its body in the world.[154] With this, the ground of soul becomes inner life rather than living mirror, irrational depth rather than a relational breadth. In effect, Menke's view presupposes as a fait accompli the distinctness of the self from the nexus of things whose genetic logic Baumgarten explores. The human—Menke's term for the a-subjective other of the subject—remains, for him, a distinct individual self, merely one stripped of all purposive faculties, such that only sheer indeterminate force remains. Whatever the merits of Menke's account for illuminating Herder's (or Menke's own) aesthetics, it misses Baumgarten's own aesthetic interrogation of the subject. For Baumgarten, the forces at play in the ground of the soul are not contained within the individual self but traverse its deep stratum as vectors of relation to other entities within a larger interplay of forces. Drawing on his interpretation of the Leibnizian monad, Baumgarten conceives the formation of the subject as a process of dynamic decoupling from relations that precede and continue to ground it—the emergence not from an irrational "infra-self" but from a transindividual network of relations.

Aesthetic Life of the Mind

Baumgarten's commentary on the above-quoted passage on inspiration from the *Aesthetica* in his only surviving lectures on aesthetics suggests how critically important the descent of aesthetic perceptions from the obscure ground of the soul is for his overall aesthetic theory. It not only provides a genetic account of extensive clarity in the mind of the "inspired" artist but also undergirds key

---

154. Ursula Franke points out the one-sidedness of this approach when she notes (versus Menke) that Baumgarten understands *representing as an activity* (instead of, as Menke claims, as an activity *rather than* a representing) (Franke, "Sinnliche Erkenntnis," 77).

concepts like the "liveliness" of aesthetic perceptions, their affective force or "life," their semantic richness or suggestiveness, and their beauty:

> Our soul is so constituted (which was not known before the improvement of psychology) that an astounding number of representations in its ground remain obscure, yet often attain a lower degree of obscurity and come to adhere, as it were, to the realm of clarity [*sich gleichsam an das Reich der Klarheit anhängen*]. They never become strictly distinct, nor are they supposed to, but through them, all notions of the beautiful mind become livelier [*lebhafter*] and things come to mind one had already forgotten or at least thought one had forgotten.... Initially, one only considers, e.g., ten marks of a thing, and later, in the mixture the clear and the obscure, one thinks the [same] thing in perhaps a hundred and fifty. The mass of representations now wrings out tears while no one had tears on their mind upon the first representation. When the beautiful mind can look quite felicitously into the future at the time when the ground of the soul rises to a low degree of obscurity, particular beauties will be perceived in the works.[155]

In the familiar language of differential marks, Baumgarten here explains inspiration by a lowered threshold of perception that allows a subconscious fringe of obscure marks from the ground of the soul to attach themselves to conscious perceptions so that they are "carried along" into the realm of clarity and "charge" them with surplus significance. This, however, is the same psychological mechanism by which Baumgarten explained in the *Metaphysica* how the mind registers additional peripheral marks in extensive modes of attention. That Baumgarten now frames the same mechanism in a vertical topology of surface (consciousness) and depth (the soul's unconscious ground) instead of the horizontal one of center and periphery only underscores the equivalence of psychic depth and perceptual breadth in his monadological psychology. To be sure, the psychology of association by which Baumgarten describes the mechanism underlying artistic inspiration—according to which adherent marks (notes) are associated with (*angehängt*) clearer ones—is easily misread in terms of a subjective play of associations.

---

155. Poppe, "Alexander Gottlieb Baumgarten," 116 (§80).

(This is how Kant would reframe Baumgarten's idea of adherent perceptions.) For Baumgarten, such associations do have a "subjective" dimension, but only in Baumgarten's precise sense of the word: as one way the nexus of things becomes present in a subject. These associations derive from traces of tiny perceptions in which the subconscious mind registers more of the real interconnection of things because it fringes out into its context.[156] Such perceptions thus capture more of the concrete web of associations in which any one thing is embedded, including circumstances of its genesis, its history, and its consequences and effects.

Finally, the passage also suggests how the ground of the soul as a diffuse mirror of the universe underlies and conjoins what Baumgarten calls the "liveliness" (*vividitas, Lebhafftigkeit*) and the aesthetic "life" (*vita, Leben*) of cognition and representation—key concepts that have been a focus of recent scholarship on his aesthetics.[157] These concepts represent complementary explanations of the emotive power of aesthetic representations, their power to "move" or "touch" the soul. What Baumgarten calls *liveliness* explains this power (much like Breitinger does) by the internal variety and abundance of extensively clear perceptions, which rouse the powers of apperception to pleasant activity. By contrast, the aesthetic *life* of cognition (*vita cognitionis*) explains this power by the way confused representations of future goods or ills—things to attain or avoid—engage the faculty of desire.[158] In weighing these cognitive and desiderative explanations of the power to move the mind, the usually rather consistent Baumgarten seems to have undergone a rare change of heart. While the early meditations on poetry

---

156. Baumgarten, *Metaphysica/Metaphysik*, §561.

157. For the following synopsis, see the these works by Baumgarten: *Meditationes*, 83 (§cxii–cxiii); *Aesthetica/Ästhetik*, 1:25 (§22), 33 (§36), 2:607–9 (§620); *Metaphysica/Metaphysik*, 281–83 (§§531–32), 355–57 (§§669, 671); *Gedanken vom vernünftigen Beyfall*, 17–19 (§6), 26–29 (§9, esp. note 1). Baumgarten's discussion and juxtaposition of the two concepts in *Beyfall* is especially illuminating.

158. For Baumgarten's mechanical background imagery of springs—*Triebfedern*—for desire, see Torra-Mattenklott, *Metaphorologie der Rührung*, 139–47.

only knew the concept of liveliness (and filed poetry's appeal to desire as one of many contributing factors to the lively variety of extensive clarity), Baumgarten later differentiates the two categories and tends to give precedence to the "life" of cognition over a "liveliness" that, as the terminology suggests, begins to seem like the secondary and more derivative term.[159] That the "life of cognition" caps the canon of aesthetic perfections in the *Aesthetica* (the corresponding section remained tantalizingly unwritten) underscores its importance for Baumgarten's aesthetics.

The privilege Baumgarten sometimes affords to the faculty of desire has led some scholars to emphasize the ethical kernel of all of Baumgarten's thought, especially those arguing for Baumgarten's persistent Pietism.[160] Simon Grote goes as far as to argue that Baumgarten's foundation of aesthetics was motivated by an originally Pietist concern with bringing moral and theological truths to sensate "life" in order to shape the will in a virtuous way.[161] Yet this new tendency to reduce Baumgarten to the philosophical subfield of ethics is as one-sided as the focus on epistemology by an earlier generation of scholars. As the passage quoted above suggests, what Baumgarten differentiated as the theoretical and practical aspects of "living" and "lively" cognition remain linked by their shared origin in the inspired animation of the mind's powers, their "coming to life" (*lebendig werden*) through contact with an obscure ground Leibniz

---

159. For the subservient function of desire in the dissertation, see Baumgarten, *Meditationes*, 25–27 (§§xxv–xxvii). Helpful accounts of the differentiation of the two terms can be found in Berndt, *Poema/Gedicht*, 65–75; and Torra-Mattenklott, *Metaphorologie der Rührung*, 176–84. As both Mattenklott and Berndt suggest, the life/liveliness concepts reflect the complex rhetorical energeia/enargeia topos.

160. Clemens Schwaiger and Simon Grote especially have done important work to unearth Pietistic aspects of Baumgarten's thought against a simplistic "Pietism vs. Wolffian philosophy" framing prevalent in much older scholarship. See the first three chapters of Grote, *Emergence of Modern Aesthetic Theory*; and Schwaiger's reliable and lucid collection of essays, *Alexander Gottlieb Baumgarten*. The ethical aspect of Baumgarten's aesthetics is also emphasized in Mirbach, "Ingenium venustum"; by Berndt (*Facing Poetry*, 40) in her claim that Baumgarten's aesthetic aims at cultivating what she terms the "sensate will"; as well as by Guyer in *History of Modern Aesthetics*, 1:335–38.

161. Grote, *Emergence of Modern Aesthetic Theory*, 67–101.

had already characterized in vitalist terms as a "living mirror" (*miroir vivant*).¹⁶² That the power to move is borrowed from the ground of the soul is explicit in the case of "liveliness," which Baumgarten traces to the variegated multitude of adherent marks garnered from the soul's unconscious ground ("all notions ... become livelier"). Yet in evoking effusive affect (the flow of tears) and futural representations ("looking ... into the future"), the passage also explains the features distinctive of aesthetic "life" by a groundswell of the soul that surges above the threshold of perception and, as it were, inundates the conscious mind with a tearful stream of tiny perceptions.¹⁶³ Obscure perceptions are intertwined with futural images that spur desire through the same implicit logic that led Leibniz to claim that tiny perceptions go "pregnant" with the future (and led Baumgarten to adopt this term for especially emphatic representations): Obscure perceptions in the ground of the soul enfold much that is suggestive of what is yet to come and *therefore* exert a powerful pull on a faculty of desire that is set in motion by images of future perfection or imperfection.¹⁶⁴ In both cases, the powers of the mind spring to life not by withdrawing into themselves but as they branch out into the web of things past, present, and future.

Since Plato's *Ion* (and across a variegated history of metaphorical superimpositions and displacements), art's power to evoke affect

---

162. In the lecture transcript Baumgarten describes the moment of inspiration as the "lebendig werden" (becoming lively) of the soul's powers (Poppe, "Alexander Gottlieb Baumgarten," 113 (§78); Leibniz, *Monadologie*, 2002, 40 [§56]).

163. Although "life" is not mentioned explicitly in this passage, Baumgarten elsewhere uses variations of the same phrase ("looking into the future") to describe the condition for sparking desire and bring "life" into representations in order to move an audience; see Poppe, "Alexander Gottlieb Baumgarten," 87 (§31).

164. Meier would explain this connection in the following way: *because* "lively" or extensively clear perceptions are infused with many obscure marks from the ground soul, they also contain an infinite number of obscure representations of goods or evils—and thus spark passions in the soul (Meier, *Lehre von den Gemüthsbewegungen*, 86 [§51]). This does not mean that such extrapolations of future goods or evils must be correct and morally reliable. In fact, Baumgarten explains the strength of sometimes misleading sensuous desire vis-à-vis rational desire in terms of the force of powerful sensate images of things to come. The very power of sensuous desire underscores the necessity of its ethical cultivation.

was cast as the communication of "movement" from artist to audience via the work. In Baumgarten's distinctive contribution to this history, the source of this movement is neither Plato's divine "magnetism" nor subjective emotion, but—to evoke one of the more recent offshoots of this tradition—the artist's immersion into the vibrant nexus of things. This marks the decisive difference between Baumgarten's monadological vitalism and the organicist vitalism espoused by the following generation of aesthetic thinkers, who would tend to equate the "life" of the mind with self-reflexivity and self-generation. For Baumgarten, "life" is interconnection.

Truth and Semblance

In the interest of countering subjectivist readings, I have emphasized the receptive aspect of Baumgarten's aesthetic subject in the previous sections to the point that it may come to seem merely passive—a mere witness to a metaphysical order that precedes the act of artistic invention. That, however, would miss Baumgarten's conception just as completely as proto-Romantic subjectivism does. What characterizes Baumgarten's aesthetic subject is rather the middle-voiced quality of a poetic act that *reveals* something about the world by *creating* what it does not simply find there—a mode of performance that is not "midway" between passivity and activity but tends to transcend the active–passive binary altogether.[165] The kernel for Baumgarten's understanding of the creative side of artistic invention is his active account of sense perception. As we have

---

165. Émile Benveniste's reconception of the contrast between active and middle voice as that between "external" and "internal" diathesis may help avoid the reflex to think of middle-voicedness as middling or muddling somewhere between activity and passivity. According to Benveniste's historical account, the original distinguishing criterion between active voice (external diathesis) and middle voice (internal diathesis) was not whether the subject acts or is acted upon—whether it is hammer or nail—but instead whether it is (1) external to and separable from the doing, a stable agent at a safe distance from what its actions affect, or (2) implicated in a process that co-affects the subject; not because the action is "reflexive"—done to oneself—but because the subject is more participant than agent in such performances and is changed alongside the changes it effects. See Benveniste, "Actif et moyen dans le verbe."

seen, even sense perception does not take in the forms of things wholesale (like the "sensible species" of scholasticism) or intuitively grasp the basic elements of thought (like Locke's "simple ideas") but is mediated by attentional filters that are "fictional" in the sense that they are actively contributed by the mind. The question of such mediative perceptual filters is the basis for Baumgarten's outline of an elaborate theory of poetic fiction. I can discuss here only a few basic aspects of this theory as they relate to the problem of attention.

In general, Baumgarten's conception of how poetic fictions relate to the given nexus of things (the quintessence of "material" truth) involves two steps. First, poetic fictions are understood (following Breitinger's model) as representing "heterocosmic truth," a connection of things as it might exist in a different possible world.[166] The truth-value of heterocosmic fiction, though, is not identical with the represented state of affairs in another metaphysical world-edifice. It is realized in a second step, *by means* or *through the detour* of the heterocosmic fiction. Although fictions are not true in the strict sense, they can, Baumgarten argues, at times let us recognize more aspects of an "individual" (*qua* intersection of relations) and therefore reveal a *higher degree of metaphysical truth* than a corresponding general concept would.[167] Baumgarten later articulates this as a "general formula" of converting truth to verisimilitude: Whenever a fictions reveals "more material truth" than truth in the strict sense, the poet should go with fiction.[168] The truth of fictions thus consists in their power to lift into relative clarity, through "fictional" filters, perceptions of things that would otherwise remain obscure.

In this respect, the kind of truth discovered through art does not precede its presentation but is, as in Breitinger's marvelous mask, inextricably linked to and engendered by it. Baumgarten's aban-

---

166. Baumgarten, *Aesthetica/Ästhetik*, 1:418–21 (§441). In Leibniz's cosmology (and in that of his followers), God famously chooses out of an infinite number of possible worlds to actualize this world because it contains the greatest perfection. The comparison of poetic fictions with "possible worlds" is usually thought to originate in Leibniz's follower Wolff, but it actually stems from Leibniz himself, who uses this analogy quite frequently; compare *Philosophical Essays*, 28, 95, 100.
167. Baumgarten, *Aesthetica/Ästhetik*, 1:478–79 (§500).
168. Baumgarten, *Aesthetica/Ästhetik*, 1:542–45 (§565).

donment of the principle of "nature imitation" (or its reinterpretation as "thinking in accordance with one's given perceptual and intellectual capacities") further supports this notion.[169] The most explicit account of how Baumgarten understands this nonmimetic mode of truth is, however, developed in a section on "aesthetic thaumaturgy"—the art of representing (familiar) things *as* new and wondrous in order to animate attention. Again formalizing suggestions found in Breitinger, Baumgarten recommends that poets look for aspects of things that have previously gone unnoticed and "pull them out of obscurity" (*ex tenebris protrahe*) in their presentation.[170] A city, for example, will appear multiplied in perspective when looked at from different places:

> If I have seen a city a thousand times from a northerly direction and you are the first to exhibit it to me from a conveniently located lookout as one to be observed from the south, you will seem to agreeably show me a new spectacle. To then recognize the old towers, buildings, and alleys, which I already knew, but that show a new a new side and a new grouping to the eyes, will increase the pleasure rather than diminish it.[171]

This, however, is precisely Leibniz's example in the *Monadology* for the monad's singular point of view on the universe. The task of poets (and other artists) is thus to stage new monadic points of view; different "zones of clarity" or attentional prostheses that unlock perceptual possibilities. The kind of artworks his aesthetics seem to envision are thus valued as much for what can be perceived *through* them as for what can be perceived *in* them, for the perspectives they open up, quite literally: the "vistas" they disclose. Baumgarten does not share William Blake's enthusiasm that the "doors of perceptions" can ever be completely "cleansed" so that

---

169. Baumgarten, *Aesthetica/Ästhetik*, 1:84–85 (§§104–5).
170. Baumgarten, *Aesthetica/Ästhetik*, 2:844–45 (§825).
171. Baumgarten, *Aesthetica/Ästhetik*, 2:844–45 (§825). Compare §57 of *Leibniz's Monadology*: "The same town, when looked at from different places, appears quite different and is, as it were, multiplied *in perspectives*. In the same way it happens that, because of the infinite multitude of simple substances, there are just as many different universes, which are nevertheless merely perspectives of a single universe according to the different points of view of each monad" (25).

things would appear as he and Leibniz, too, think they ultimately are: infinite. But he suggests that it is possible to carve new chinks into the cavern.

In Conclusion: Baumgarten's Modernity

It may seem that we have arrived at an interpretation of Baumgarten that confirms a historical-philosophical narrative about the emergence of aesthetics first advanced by Joachim Ritter.[172] In brief, Ritter explains the rise of aesthetics by the persistence of premodern cosmological thinking in the medium of subjective experience after modern natural science had made such thought impossible in the medium of the concept. For Ritter, the emerging aesthetic sensibility for nature as a living whole, exemplified in modern landscape painting, serves as a compensatory response to the scientific objectification of nature, which was a necessary condition for the emancipation of the subject. The objectification of nature in science and its subjective reanimation in aesthetics thus form part of single historical dialectic: mathematical and analytical science grants the mastery over things on which freedom as self-determination depends, whereas aesthetics restores for the feeling subject a noninstrumental relationship that had to be sacrificed for this ideal. Aesthetic sensibility thus inherits and succeeds the noninstrumental contemplation of the cosmos that was the traditional domain of the philosophical concept.

There are certainly elements in Baumgarten's aesthetics that chime with Ritter's view. The Baumgarten who emerged in this chapter prizes aesthetic truth for sensitizing the mind to the complexity of the *nexus rerum*, which—in its twin qualities as all-encompassing and well ordered—represents the state of cosmological thinking in Baumgarten's rationalist context. Baumgarten's idea that the complexity of interrelations that constitute this nexus cannot be grasped distinctly (by philosophical or scientific concepts), but can be intimated aesthetically, would then simply spell out the conceptual logic

---

172. See Ritter, "Landschaft."

behind Ritter's historical-philosophical thesis. Yet assimilating Baumgarten to Ritter's compensation narrative (or to any kind of aesthetic holism) is possible only by forgetting the constitutive moment of technique and mediation—for us, the centrality of attention—in Baumgarten's aesthetics. Aesthetics opens up another relationship to things as another performance of *ars attendendi*, as an adjustment of a perceptual habitus that mediates any understanding of the *nexus rerum*. It is not simply the remainder of an older order (Ritter) but the discovery of a new mode of attention. Even the aesthetic mode of perception thus relies on a nonintuitive, objectifying moment. As evidence that aesthetics preserves a Ptolemaic view of the cosmos opposed to the anti-intuitiveness of Copernican science, Ritter cites Baumgarten's contrast between the sun as it appears in the aesthetic horizon of a poetic shepherd versus the sun understood as an astronomical object. This is, at best, one-sided.[173] As *one* possible way of attending to things among others, the aesthetic representation of the sun already presupposes the break with intuitive contemplation marked by reference to Copernicus. It already presupposes the adjustability of the focus—Baumgarten's metaphorical "inner lens" of the perceiving mind—even if aesthetic attention is then characterized by focusing less distinctly. In this light, Baumgarten's episode does not simply mark an aesthetic return to a Ptolemaic world but a way of acknowledging, on the far side of Copernicus, that the sun's relative movement around the earth is in fact entangled with diurnal and seasonal rhythms of terrestrial life in ways that may be evident to the poetic shepherd but lost in the astronomical abstraction of the sun as the central mass of the solar system. It is not the case, then, that the one (the astronomical sun) is true but the other (its aesthetic terrestrial manifestation) is simply subjective feeling. Both modes disclose different aspects of how things partake in the actual nexus of things.

In the bigger picture, this also means that the great critiques of the moderns from Bacon and Descartes onward—which cautioned

---

173. Ritter, "Landschaft," 155–58. It is telling that Ritter cites Baumgarten's comparison of logical truth with a perfectly rounded sphere but does not cite the parallel image of *aesthetic* truth's similarly rounded shape.

that what the scholastics took for granted as the natural order was, in fact, a smokescreen of human "prejudices" and "conventions"—remains in force. A harmonious, "cosmic" relationship to nature cannot be restored, because it never existed. One need only remember how the "great chain of being," a central concept of cosmological thought in the West, was perennially shot through with human hierarchy. The great link of all things from God to minerals was always modeled on the relationship between king and serfs on whose backs such cosmologies rested in practice. Yet Baumgarten's insistence on another possible way of relating to things does counteract any attempt to replace a nature exposed as convention with a definitive rational substitute (a tendency reflected in the common eighteenth-century equation of reason and nature). Rather than papering over the break between self and world in the mode of intuitive feeling, aesthetic practices of attention keep this openness open. Baumgarten's aesthetics should thus be understood less as a restoration *of* than a possible transcendence *toward* a nonobjectifying relationship to things.

Baumgarten does not offer a holistic aesthetics of nature, but his unredeemed foundation of aesthetics can, perhaps, be recuperated for an ecological aesthetics. If the emerging *Leitmetapher* of ecology summons ways of thinking that understand action and perception within overly complex networks of living and nonliving things, Baumgarten's metaphysics of connectivity lends a proto-ecological quality to his aesthetic thought—and it does this all the more forcefully because Baumgarten's rather austere rationalism predates all Romantic sentimentalism of nature. No doubt, such an ecological reading involves some—perhaps generative—anachronism. The Leibnizian concepts in terms of which Baumgarten articulated his insight into the all-connectedness of things—above all the doctrine of preestablished harmony—carry with it all sorts of metaphysical baggage that ecology no doubt wishes to leave behind. Yet measured by the constellation that would achieve philosophical hegemony in the generation following Baumgarten, Baumgarten's forays toward a practice of the self that realizes itself in different performances of its connectivity with things offers an alternative vision of what the "emancipation of the subject" evoked by Ritter might have meant.

Baumgarten's position between Leibniz and Kant, between preestablished harmony and the philosophy of the subject he helped engender, allowed him to articulate an aesthetics that goes beyond compensating for the loss incurred by a model of freedom premised on objectification. It instead subverts this model before it fully took hold. Perhaps the topicality of his foundation of aesthetics lies in the specific relation between what is historical in Baumgarten and our own moment—in what Walter Benjamin called the "now of recognizability," the constellation formed by Baumgarten as a transitional figure at the cusp of a period we may still recognize as our own—and the other end of that era, when the notion of a self cut off from the world is defunct beyond repair. It is because Baumgarten was engaged with problems of the subject at a time when the question as to what this subject would become was yet undecided that his reflections about subjectivity speak so eloquently to contemporary crises rooted in the sense—surely grounded more in pre-reflexive practices than in shared conscious belief—that an unbridgeable gulf separates the self from others, the human from the nonhuman world; and in a concept of freedom that is, as Kant would teach, achievable only at the price of cutting oneself loose from everything because dependence on anything threatens with heteronomy. This is the moment in Baumgarten's aesthetics we can now recognize more clearly than ever.

Epilogue

AFTERLIVES
Modulations of Attention since 1800

In the decades following the midcentury publication of Baumgarten's *Aesthetica*, the Wolffian framework that had given discussions on attention remarkable coherence for more than half a century began to fray. As Wolff's system lost its integrative power for scholarly discussions in German lands, various aspects previously negotiated under the umbrella of attention split into special problems distributed across a range of fields. In the *Sattelzeit* or transitional period around the year 1800, attention as a nomadic concept between aesthetics and science remained important for individual authors, including K. Ph. Moritz, Goethe, and Novalis, but it seemed to no longer serve as the undisputed linchpin of an entire discursive formation.[1] At least, this linchpin function was no longer readily appar-

---

1. For an overview of how the concept of attention was understood by figures like Moritz, Goethe, and Novalis, see Thums, "Aufmerksamkeit"; also Adler, "Bändigung des (Un)Möglichen."

ent: it was taken over by a Kantian subject, which was itself revealed to be a creature of attention in the preceding chapters.

In this epilogue I present three vignettes that illustrate how the link between attention and subjectivity, consolidated in the eighteenth century, has continued to surface in subsequent concerns about the formation and deformation of the self. The first highlights epistemological, poetological, and media-theoretical dimensions by reading Georg Christoph Lichtenberg's notebooks as examples of how late eighteenth-century transformations of the classical discourse on attention helped to shape a new paradigm of writing. The second revisits the issue of attention and discipline by recovering the formation of attention as an integral moment of Hegel's and Marx's conceptions of *Bildung* (education, culture) and *Arbeit* (labor). This section serves both as a recapitulation of key motifs discussed in preceding chapters and an exploration of attention's potential as a focal problem in critical theory. The final section takes a brief look at our own attentionally challenged times against the backdrop of the genealogy of modern subjectivities offered in this book. First introduced as the cornerstone of a new architecture of the mind in the eighteenth century, the faculty of attention shows no signs of losing its role as an increasingly precarious foundation of modern selves.

Lichtenberg's Antinomy of Attention

Known during his lifetime as an experimental physicist and witty satirist, Georg Christoph Lichtenberg (1742–99) achieved literary fame after the posthumous publication of personal notebooks he eventually came to call *Sudelbücher* (waste-books). Literary historians retroactively identified these notebooks as foundational texts of a tradition of German aphoristic writing running from Lichtenberg to Novalis, Nietzsche, and Adorno,[2] while a more recent strand of scholarship has situated Lichtenberg's notetaking in the history of early modern knowledge practices, such as techniques for keeping

---

2. Mautner, "Der Aphorismus"; Neumann, *Ideenparadiese*, 86–264.

commonplace books or recording scientific observations.³ Especially when highlighting the problem of attention in his notebooks, these literary and historical-epistemological perspectives need not be mutually exclusive. On the contrary, exploring the problem of "taking note" as a central concern of Lichtenberg's notebooks suggests that his grappling with epistemological quandaries about the possibility and limits of discovery generated the very features that retroactively qualified his notebooks as pioneering literary works.

In preserving material traces of particular acts of writing, notebooks generally offer a privileged place for studying how bodily gesture, writing instruments and materials—as well as mental acts of singling out what is worth noting—intersect with linguistic systems within scenes of writing.⁴ In the case of Lichtenberg's notebooks, exploring this intersection offers insight into how he assimilated and transformed techniques of attention and notetaking of the eighteenth century. In many respects, notebooks functioned as the material correlate of the epistemology of attention. In fact, Lichtenberg's own designation of his notes as *Bemerkungen* (notes) and *Anmerkungen* (remarks) strongly suggest his indebtedness to this epistemological apparatus of *Aufmerksamkeit*.⁵ If this is no longer obvious, and if Lichtenberg scholarship has largely missed this connection, this is not least because the model of cognition that considered attention a cardinal epistemic faculty was both absorbed into and replaced by the epistemological revolutions around 1800. Associated above all with Kant's critical philosophy, these shifts have continued to overshadow epistemic premises that still counted as common knowledge in Lichtenberg's time. Lichtenberg's own innovations, however—his alternative solutions to the puzzles of a

---

3. McGillen, "Wit, Bookishness," 508–19; Daston, "The Disciplines of Attention"; Daston, "Taking Note(s)."
4. Marie-Noëlle Bourget has emphasized the intertwinement of hand, eye, and mental discipline in any act of notetaking ("A Portable World," 382). Martin Stingelin has specifically explored the role of the writing instrument in Lichtenberg's notetaking scene in "'Unser Schreibzeug.'" On the analytical category of the "writing scene," see Campe, "Writing."
5. This point is convincingly made by Daston, "The Disciplines of Attention," 434–37.

faltering epistemic paradigm—only gain relief against the background of the assumptions about the role of attention in cognition recovered in the chapters of this book.

While Lichtenberg's struggles with paradoxes of attention are unusually well documented in his notebooks, he was not the only figure in the final decades of the eighteenth century who experimented with new epistemic modes by drawing on and transforming the old paradigm. Remarks on attention by Karl Philipp Moritz (1756–93) in essays such as his "Vorschlag zu einem Magazin einer Erfahrungs-Seelenkunde" (Proposal for a magazine of empirical psychology; 1782) offer a further prominent example. In this programmatic introduction to his journal project, Moritz proposed that psychological observers must cultivate "Aufmerksamkeit auf das Kleinscheinende" (attention to the seemingly small) because outwardly minor episodes can in fact mark major events in individual psychic development.[6] Such attention becomes necessary when (as in the human psyche) noticeable *marks* and essential *traits* of an object radically diverge. Ostensibly, this splintering of observability and significance is motivated by the object under observation (the elusive human mind, whose features are difficult to pin down). Moritz's analogous claims about attention in other contexts, however, suggest a more profound skepticism about the observer's ability to pick out the marks that really matter for the inner constitution of a thing. In his essays on aesthetics, for instance, he portrays the artist's task in the same terms he used to describe psychological attention. Both endeavors involve gathering details dispersed across different contexts into unities that are not at all obvious.[7] In effect, Moritz questions the symmetry of analysis and synthesis assumed in a procedure that tried to know simultaneous (spatial) wholes by submitting them to sequential (temporal) processing. About a decade earlier, Lessing had already demanded a differentiation between space-arts and time-arts based on the argument that

---

6. Moritz, "Vorschlag zu einem Magazin," 801.
7. Compare the following essays by Moritz: "Das Edelste in der Natur," 21; "Über die bildende Nachahmung des Schönen," 40–42; "Die Signatur des Schönen," 72, collected in the volume *Die Signatur des Schönen*. A similar kind of attention organizes Moritz's novel *Anton Reiser*.

descriptive poetry (as such that of Brockes) fails to evoke a sense of unity because it confuses the two dimensions.[8] Paralleling Lessing's art-theoretical reflections, Moritz's remarks on attention thus document a growing skepticism about the commensurability of marks as they register in the mind and marks as they are observable on the surface of things.

In Lichtenberg's case, the fault line at which his practice of taking note begins to diverge from the classical epistemology of attention is evident in one of his explicit engagements with this paradigm's epistemological premises. In 1769 Lichtenberg remarks in a notebook that the Haarlem Academy of Sciences had reissued its prize question on the art of observing, to which Jean Senebier had previously responded with a treatise that replicated Wolff's three stages of attention.[9] The prize question prompted a series of reflections on the subject in Lichtenberg's notebooks that were perhaps intended as sketches for his own contribution to the contest.[10] Judging from these sketches, Lichtenberg's account of the art of observation would have included a more forward-looking discussion of the pitfalls of attention than Senebier's text. Where Senebier had emphasized the capacity of expert observers to take note of all the relevant characteristics that typify a phenomenon, Lichtenberg's notes circle around the question of what escapes all notice: "What is unnoticeable [*das Unmerkliche*] in this [matter]? . . . What in this [matter] may I be overlooking because of my limited understanding[?]"[11] If there are things that structurally elude the mind's attention, lack of noticeability does not imply nonexistence or insignificance: "Silence is not silence, white not white, we only presuppose this; what we do not notice [*merken*] does not exist for us."[12] Lichtenberg's concern with what cannot be

---

8. Lessing, *Laokoon*, 124–27. Lessing, like Moritz, draws from the terminology of the very paradigm he criticizes (e.g., by referring to *Züge*, characteristic features or aspects that poets and painters convey).

9. Senebier, *Die Kunst zu Beobachten*, 1:145–50.

10. Lichtenberg, *Schriften und Briefe*, II:72 (KA 206). All quotations of Lichtenberg's work are from *Schriften und Briefe*, ed. Wolfgang Promies, hereafter cited as *SB* and referenced in accordance with the conventions of Lichtenberg scholarship (conventional abbreviation of notebook and number of entry, volume, and page number).

11. KA 86–87, *SB* II, 330, 332.

12. KA 293, *SB* II, 84.

observed may indicate emerging modes of scientific observation in which visibility and intelligibility begin to break apart, as he had occasion to notice during his own experiments with the invisible medium of electricity.[13] Yet phenomena that are inaccessible to the physical eye can only be part of the story, as his notes indicate: "What is common in this matter, that which strikes everyone's eyes, and what is uncommon, that which thousands do not see but certainly would notice if they knew that one would also have to look to things [*auf die Dinge . . . zu sehen hätte*] that do not directly strike the eye."[14] As in the remark on discovery above, the blindness at stake in this context results from not knowing how to *direct* one's vision (*sehen auf*); how to "look to" or even "watch out for" things. The invisibility Lichtenberg grapples with here lies hidden in plain sight.

Two remarks in *Sudelbuch* J suggest what it may take to "see" things well. In what can itself be understood as a writerly device for marking contrast and directing attention, the remarks are set apart in Latin cursive from the German *Kurrent* handwriting Lichtenberg usually employs in his notebooks, a distinction he seems to reserve for methodological maxims: "A new and great idea about something, even [mere] thought and hope, always stretch the mind [*Geist*] to see something better" (see figure 12).[15] Similarly, "In everything, there must be a certain spirit [*Geist*], a gaze [*Blick*] that, as it were, directs the whole in the manner of a soul."[16]

Such comments stand the classical nexus of attention and prejudice on its head. Lichtenberg probes the idea that some sort of "prejudice"—some guiding thought or idea that precedes the

---

13. See Pfannkuchen, "A Matter of Visibility," 397–400. This reading relies heavily on Jonathan Crary's *Techniques of the Observer* and Crary's claim that there was a break in the models of vision around 1800 that gave rise to the idea of "subjective vision."

14. KA 289, *SB* II, 83. The contrast between common and uncommon observation suggests that this attentional blindness might merely be the blindness of the many as opposed to the attentiveness of the few. Yet along with Lichtenberg's growing skepticism regarding the figure of the genius, whose cult seized literary Germany during his lifetime, he will eventually come to explain "uncommon," new, and original vision as being different from any sort of naturally heightened sensibility.

15. J 1435, *SB* II, 264.
16. J 1430, *SB* II, 264.

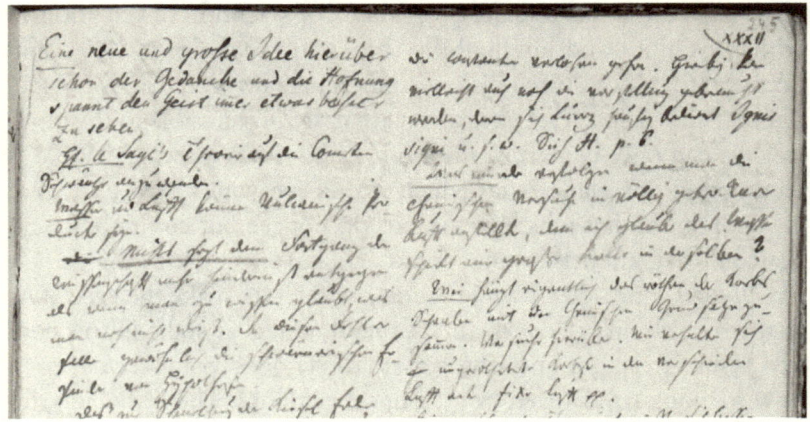

Figure 12. Detail from Lichtenberg's *Sudelbuch* J. The note in the top left corner ("Eine neue und große Idee ..."), translated in the text, stands out in Latin cursive. SUB Göttingen, Cod. Ms. Lichtenberg IV, 29 (p. xxxii).

observation—may be the condition for seeing anything well at all. Novelty is still at stake; but it is now located in novel conceptions ("new and great idea") that first make discovery possible. The evocation of "hope" as the odd third term of the series emphasizes the expectant attitude that new ideas or thoughts produce in the mind— the way a gaze animated by a new idea actively "watches out for" certain things and learns to see better in that way. As the apposition of *Geist* (spirit) and *Blick* (gaze) in the second remark suggests, the condition for good epistemic vision is no longer a neutral (or artificially neutralized) gaze purged from preconceptions that would register things directly, "firsthand," unclouded by the mist of prejudice—but a deliberately "spirited" gaze that primes the mind to notice things in places where no had cared to look.

Lichtenberg here hits upon an antinomy of attention that classical observation had ignored or hoped to circumvent by understanding artificial aids of observation as means of correcting the mind's inherent biases and prejudices. Bacon, as discussed in chapter 1, had ascribed a merely compensatory function to technology and technique by claiming that artificial "assistants to the senses" would restore a prelapsarian contact with nature. In chapter 2 we saw that Wolff addressed the problem by considering "empirical" and "rational" inquiry as complementary approaches that would compensate for each other's blind spots. For Lichtenberg, however, attention can never be the art of observing without "fictitious" preconceptions, because one cannot see ("see well," at any rate) that of which one has no preconception whatsoever. There is—there must be, Lichtenberg notes—a *spiritus rector*, an ineluctable bit of "spirit" or "theory" that guides the mind's attention. At the same time, if nothing new is registered in such acts of attention, nothing that *transcends* the guiding idea, then nothing is observed at all. This is why the problem is indeed an antinomy: already knowing what to expect appears at the same time necessary to discover things—and to defeat the purpose of discovery. The active stretching out toward something indicated in attention's etymology of *adtendere* and echoed in Lichtenberg's "stretching of the mind" appears simultaneously as the condition of possibility and impossibility of noticing anything new. What one does not know to see remains hidden in plain sight; yet if one sees only what one already knows, then nothing is seen at all in the emphatic sense of "seeing" Lichtenberg envisions: nothing new, nothing uncommon, nothing yet unnoticed.

Lichtenberg's unique notetaking strategies develop as attempts to navigate this paradox of attention. His notebooks in general read like laboratories of experimental attention in which different attentional thresholds or filters are constantly tested as enabling conditions for discovery. The outlines of Lichtenberg's strategy emerge in a series of remarks at the beginning of the second part of *Sudelbuch* J, in close proximity to those discussed above. Set apart once again in Latin cursive from the surrounding German script, the remarks solidify into a series of reflections on Lichtenberg's recurring question of how to see something new and uncommon: "to see in everything something no one has yet seen and of which no one has yet thought."[17] Directly above this familiar exhortation, however, he discusses devices that indicate how such discovery may be possible even under the constraints of an attention that discovers new

---

17. E 1363, *SB* II, 251; compare E 1254, *SB* II, 229.

things only when it knows where to look. The first is paradoxicality: "as much as possible contrary to opinion,"[18] or, as he reiterates using the Greek term, "something quite paradoxical about it, of which no one can easily have thought before."[19] The second is the use of what he calls "paradigms": "to seek out a paradigm according to which this can be declined."[20]

Lichtenberg is credited with having introduced the word "paradigm" to describe model solutions to scientific problems in a sense that prefigured the use of the term by Thomas Kuhn, who likely inherited the concept from Lichtenberg through the mediation of Wittgenstein, an avid reader of Lichtenberg's notes.[21] But Lichtenberg's use of the term for large-scale, scientific models is merely a special case of a more widespread use in his notebooks for all sorts of exemplary instances that function as heuristic devices—"heuristic pulleys [*heuristische Hebezeuge*]" that make it possible to recognize or "lift" into intelligibility what would otherwise remain unnoticed.[22] Paradigms, for Lichtenberg, are exemplary instances (however minor) that shed light on similarly situated cases *without* transcending their particularity toward the universality of a concept.[23]

Unlike classical models that promised to purge the mind of all prejudicial distortions, paradigms in Lichtenberg's sense do not evade but instead navigate the antinomy of attention by continuously readjusting, modulating, and altering patterns of attentive expectation. This might not lead to a place beyond preconception altogether, but it does offer a heuristic tool for transcending limiting preconceptions by experimentally adopting others in their place

---

18. J 1365, *SB* II, 251.
19. J 1261, *SB* II, 230.
20. J 1363, *SB* II, 251.
21. Rentsch, "Paradigma, exemplar"; Blumenberg, "Beobachtungen an Metaphern," 195–99.
22. K 312, *SB* II, 455.
23. For paradigmatic explanations of this paradigmatic logic, see Aristotle, *Rhetoric* I.2, 357b19, and Agamben, *Signature of All Things*, esp. 17. For a recent overview, see *MLN* 134, *On the Paradigmatic Force of Anomaly*, ed. Joel Lande and Jocelyn Holland. In that issue, see especially Carlina Malagon's detailed account in "A Completely New Chemistry" of how Lichtenberg used *paradigmata* to hold in abeyance phlogistonist and anti-phlogistonist approaches in eighteenth-century chemistry.

and testing what can be discovered when considering things in their "fictitious" light. By adjusting expectations, heuristic paradigms prime the mind to take note where one would not usually expect to find anything of significance. We might say that they superimpose new perceptual "filters" or "patterns of noticeability" on phenomena that catalyze discovery by changing what becomes salient in things. When Lichtenberg says that heuristic devices such as paradigms "make us attentive,"[24] he implies not that they indiscriminately heighten attentiveness, but that they bring to attention what had not yet been considered. As he puts it in another remark, such paradigms "impel" (*anstoßen*) the mind to see something new by giving attention a counterintuitive direction.[25]

In later notebooks Lichtenberg's epistemological reflections often center around his understanding of Kant's critical revolution in philosophy, on which Lichtenberg comments sometimes skeptically, sometimes sarcastically, but most often approvingly. Occasionally he articulates a sense that Kant had given explicit expression to inchoate ideas of his own, as he does in introducing the following comment on the second preface of Kant's *Critique of Pure Reason* in *Sudelbuch* J: "We only notice [*bemerken*] [in things] that which corresponds into us [*in uns herein korrespondiert*]. Wherever we look, we see only ourselves."[26] The unusual expression "corresponds 'into' us" leaves no doubt which feature of the second preface to the *Critique* Lichtenberg has in mind here: Kant's programmatic point—illustrated by the structure of a series of revolutions in philosophy and science—that we can have necessary knowledge only of those structures the mind brings to the cognition of objects. Lichtenberg's reading of Kant may have been influenced by the overly subjectively idealistic interpretation of the first *Critique* advanced by Lichtenberg's colleague in Göttingen, Christian Garve.[27] Yet what matters here is not whether Lichtenberg understands Kant correctly but how he takes Kant's project of examining the subjective conditions of all possible experience to

---

24. J 1439, *SB* II, 264.
25. K 314, *SB* II, 455.
26. J 569, *SB* I, 737; compare J 681, *SB* I, 751.
27. See Tester's introduction to Lichtenberg's *Philosophical Writings*, 15.

resonate with his own thinking: he regards Kant as engaging in an examination of the conditions under which we can *notice* (*bemerken*) anything; an examination, we might say, of "conditions of noticeability." In this perspective, Kant's project indeed resembles Lichtenberg's insights concerning the aporetic structure of attention—that we are only good at noticing what we already expect and, in that sense, only ever see in things what we bring to them. At the same time, Lichtenberg's perception of a kinship between his own project and Kant's makes it possible to compare their respective "solutions" to what Lichtenberg identifies as a shared problem. Kant set out to determine the universal conditions under which anything can become "noticeable" by examining the structure of the cognitive faculties—the a priori forms of intuition, the categories of understanding. Lichtenberg takes both a more practical and a more playful approach: that of training the mind to continuously modulate attention in order to adjust the pragmatic "conditions of noticeability" of things.

The point here is not to compare Kant and Lichtenberg on philosophical grounds but to gauge the significance of Lichtenberg's play with "conditions of noticeability" for his writing practice. While most of Lichtenberg's explicit reflections on the epistemic potential of paradigms occur in the context of his reflections on tools of scientific discovery, the most extensive application of his paradigmatic approach arguably comes in the parts of his notebooks later singled out by Lichtenberg's editors for their "literary" and "aphoristic" qualities. As a tool of scientific discovery, analogical models are instrumental in acquiring new knowledge, but they remain a preliminary step that becomes obsolete as soon as more robust explanations are established. The same does not apply to Lichtenberg's increasingly independent practice of composing witty remarks whose point is not to learn to see things "correctly" but to learn to see them "differently." Adjusting, fine-tuning, and tinkering with conditions of perceptibility thus become part of a writing practice that no longer serves the process of discovery, scientific or otherwise. Taking notes, for Lichtenberg, increasingly serves no other purpose than that of modulating attention in and through a practice of writing that matters less for what it "notes down" than for what it "makes noticeable." Like the classical "habits of attention," this mental attitude continues to strive for a paradoxical anti-routine, a routine of *attention* in an emphatic sense, yet one that is self-reflective about the possibility of circumventing the pitfalls of habit altogether. This is a habit not beyond habit but a habit of continuing to wear new habits, of adopting new routines, adjusting the parameters of noticeability. It is this dynamization of attentional routines that turned Lichtenberg's notes, which were never intended to be published, into a paradoxical paradigm of modern writing practices.

Intellectual and Manual Labors of Attention
(*Bildung, Arbeit*)

To gauge the afterlives of the eighteenth-century discourse on attention in later German philosophy, it is instructive to look ahead to discussions of attention in Hegel and Marx—conceptions that reflect earlier motifs as if in a rearview mirror and thus also offer a summative look back. The first of these comes in the *Enzyklopädie der philosophischen Wissenschaften* (Encyclopedia of the philosophical sciences; 1817/30), Hegel's attempt, in his owl-of-Minerva's flight at the dusk of the long eighteenth century, to absorb previous developments of thought into a definite philosophical system. In lectures on *Philosophie des Geistes* (Philosophy of the spirit) that were integrated into the 1830 edition of his *Encyclopedia*, Hegel ascribes to attention a catalytic role in the formation or education (*Bildung*) of subjective spirit—that of dirempting the immediate unity with things in which a merely sensing and feeling *Geist* initially finds itself enveloped:[28]

> Therefore, intelligence sublates the simplicity of sensation, determines what is sensed as a negative in relation to intelligence, and thus *detaches* it from itself, yet at the same time posits it in its *detachment* as *its own*. Only by this dual activity of *sublating* [*Aufhebens*] and *restoring* the unity between myself and the other do I get to *grasp* the content of sensation. This

---

28. This is not a primordial unity but a unity already regained at the level of "spirit," in which *Geist* already knows itself (albeit only abstractly) to be the essence of subject and object, of itself and of external reality.

happens initially in *attention*. Without attention, therefore, no apprehension of the object is possible; only by attention does mind become present in the subject-matter and obtain *cognizance* of it, though not as yet *cognition* of the subject-matter, for this requires a further development of mind. Attention constitutes, therefore, the beginning of education [*Bildung*]. . . . [I]n attention there necessarily occurs a *separation* and a *unity* of the subjective and the objective, a *self-reflection-into-itself* of free mind and at the same time an *identical direction* of mind to the object. . . . [I]t demands an effort [*Anstrengung*], since if a man wants to apprehend one specific object, he must abstract from everything else, from all the thousand and one things going round in his head, from his other interests, even from his own person. . . . The savage attends to practically nothing; he lets everything pass him by without focusing on it. Only by cultivation [*Bildung*] of the mind does attention acquire strength and fulfilment.[29]

Hegel's remarks concisely recapitulate the double move of distancing and reappropriation we encountered in philosophies of attention since Descartes: attention effects an initial separation of the subjective and the objective and simultaneously establishes a new, deliberate unity of the separated parts. The new unity achieved by attention is superior to the immediate oneness with things that the mind experiences in feeling and sensation, because it retains subject and object as distinct poles in connecting them to each other. It is not, however, a connection of symmetrical correlates: the new relation to objects established by attention has the advantage of being actively maintained and controlled, "mediated" by the subject pole of the relation. Hegel's account is precise, too, about the fine mechanics of this double process of distancing and reappropriation. The subject splits from the object by severing sensations from itself as that which is *not me* ("detaches it from itself") in order to then reclaim them all the more effectively as *mine* ("as *its own*"). In a movement that parallels Kant's transition from "empirical" to "pure" apperception, abstracting from sensations is the condition for claiming them as a possession. I can only "have" sensations once I have made sure that I "am" something categorically different from these sensations—once I have learned, that is, to treat the flux of sensations as something that has no part in me, something I can

---

29. Hegel, *Philosophy of Mind*, 179 (§448), emphases in the original.

therefore appropriate in one way or another by choosing to attend to them however I wish. Through attention, in other words, the subject achieves control over sensations and over a world of objects these sensations can now be seen as representing.

In catalyzing the switch from vague *Empfinden* (sensing) to the deliberate *Erfassen* (grasping) of objects, attention marks the transition from the spirit's passivity to its activity.[30] Attention is thus the beginning of subjective spirit's autotelic formation, education, and knowledge—the three moments united in Hegel's *Bildung*—and remains its medium, the property of the spirit that is fortified and perfected ("acquire[s] strength and fulfilment") in the course of its progressive development. This, then, is the *Anstrengung* (effort) on which all further formation of the spirit will have depended. It is also the effort and self-discipline that is said to distinguish cultivated European humanity from "savagery," though the following sentence seems to warn that a lack of discipline always entails the risk of regression: the "other" of culture Wolff marked through the figures of the infant, the beast, or the feral child has become exterritorialized in the figure of the savage, whose lack of discipline, lack of *Bildung* and self-negation, is marked by the inability to oppose things to oneself and hold them firmly in the mind's attention.[31]

---

30. To be sure, at a yet higher level, concentrated attention can again flip into an absorption in the object that lets the matter at hand "speak" (*zu Worte kommen lassen*) through the most strenuous activity of the subject, as Hegel notes in the same section (§448). Attention in this highest form coincides with Hegel's famed philosophical method of actively receptive "watching" (*bloßes Zusehen*) that transcends the division between subject and object, activity and passivity. (The logic behind this is the familiar move of negating the negation: the negation that gives rise to the subject is again negated in a self-transcendence of the subject in this highest form of attention, a conception that is a precursor of Adorno's notion of the "priority of the object.") Yet even such subsequent developments rely, like all further *Bildung* of the spirit, on the initial split, the double move of first marking off and then reappropriating the object in and through an act of attention.

31. Following Denise Ferreira da Silva, the exterritorialization implied in the reference to the uncultured savage suggests how Hegel's geographical mapping of the world-historical development or *Bildung* of the spirit toward transparent self-determination in the philosophy of history informed the grammar of modern racialization: it coded the European post-Enlightenment subject as self-transparent and "universal" while assigning to all other subjects relations of dependency and opacity. See Ferreira da Silva, *Toward a Global Idea of Race*.

To contextualize the developmental logic of subjective spirit with the historical emergence of the problem of attention we have pursued in this chapter, it is sufficient to note—as much with Hegel as against him—that a term like *Bildung* itself carries a definite historical and local index. In the *Bildungsroman* that is Hegel's *Phenomenology of Spirit*, after all, *Bildung* figures doubly, both as the logic behind the spirit's progressive formation through self-negation *and* as a historically situated phase in the development of collective consciousness—the alienated spirit of modern European "culture" (*Bildung*) that culminates in the French Revolution.[32] What is true of *Bildung* applies to the entire explanatory apparatus with which Hegel tries to capture what attention "is"; that is, which necessary step it marks in the developmental pattern of mind or spirit. As argued in chapters 1–2, the emergence of the terminological opposition between subject and object is itself based on the self-recognition of the attentive agent of perception. This genetic entanglement of *explanans* and *explanandum* invites a reversal of the explanatory direction of Hegel's remarks, a reading of them as a faithful recollection of how the object's objectivity and the subject's subjectivity are established, solidified, and maintained by incorporating the new faculty of attention into the soul. This occurs through the double move of, first, sealing the mind against things, distancing the self from the flux of sensations; and second, directing a mind thus purified and collected in itself back at things to reappropriate them in the form of a concentrated, controlled, and closely focused ray of attention. By shifting the focus from what attention *is* to what it *does*, we can frame it as the mental technique through which the world is objectified and rendered fully external: "Without attention, therefore, no apprehension of the object is possible." When thus reading the passage against the grain, attention emerges as a pragmatic condition of the absolute split between self and world that the classical philosophical systems around 1800 would first ontologize, then desperately try to overcome.

---

32. To insist on such historical resonances is not to flatten all history to a series of empirical facts but to recall, with Hegel's original anti-Kantian insight, that the transcendental schemata that fashion empirical facts are themselves subject to historical change.

Already in Hegel the concept of *Bildung* correlates with *Arbeit* (labor), the transformation of the external world with the transformation of oneself. This is what allowed Marx to read Hegel's history of the spirit's formation as a history of labor qua transformative activity. In volume 1, chapter 5, of *Capital*, where Marx temporarily abandons his internal analysis of capitalism for an excursus on the labor process as it appears independently of any historically specific social organization, Marx famously describes labor as a purposive activity through which humans regulate their metabolism with nature by setting to work the forces of the human body.[33] Yet it is not only physical forces that are exerted in the labor process; a further effort (*Anstrengung*) is equally necessary:

> He [the worker] not only effects a change of form in the material on which he works, but he also realises a purpose of his own that gives the law to his modus operandi, and to which he must subordinate his will. And this subordination is no mere momentary act. Besides the exertion [*Anstrengung*] of the bodily organs, the process demands that, during the whole operation, the workman's will be steadily in consonance with his purpose. This means close attention. The less he is attracted by [*mit sich fortreißt*] the nature of the work, and the mode in which it is carried on, and the less, therefore, he enjoys it as something which gives play to his bodily and mental powers, the more close his attention is forced to be.[34]

Marx's invocation of attention as a manifestation of the willpower required to keep the laboring organs focused on the task at hand portrays the labor process in terms that draw on the classical association of attention with an exertion the will. The same is true for the assumption that this mental exertion is inversely proportional to the intrinsic appeal of the focal phenomenon: the less the form or

---

33. Whether the labor process as portrayed in *Capital*, vol. 1, chap. 5, indeed describes a transhistorical necessity that provides an external vantage point to leverage against capitalism, or whether the ideology of labor is already a function of the capitalist mode of production, is a critical point of discussion in much contemporary Marxist theory. What can be noted here is that the *language* and the *topoi* of attention Marx invokes in this passage carry—like Hegel's supposedly transhistorical description of the role of *Aufmerksamkeit* in *Bildung*—a definite historical index.

34. Marx, *Capital*, 198; *Das Kapital*, 193 (chapter reference to the German edition).

content of work attracts attention by itself, the more such attention must be imposed by a mental effort. While the limit case at one extreme of this inverse proportion between attentional effort and intrinsic attraction is an activity whose end and reward inheres in its performance, the other extreme of the spectrum marks a case in which the purpose is entirely extrinsic to the task, and therefore needs to be continuously enforced by a watchful attention. In Marx the strain of attention required when performing a task thus functions like an indicator of the degree of alienation of the labor performed.

In Marx's reframing of these classical motifs, however, the prospect of being swept away by intrinsically appealing stimuli (suggested in the German *mit sich fortreißt*) takes on a markedly different valence than it had in earlier discussions. It no longer simply spells heteronomy but promises an alternative mode of exercising one's powers. The event that makes this new framing of attention possible is audible in Marx's evocation of aesthetic play as the counterpoint of forced attention—the ideal of an activity in which the enjoyment of one's own mental and bodily faculties becomes an end in itself. Within this new schema, the rationalist fear of becoming slave to one's passions is supplanted by the fear that the very attentional control that keeps the passions at bay reverts into a new form of enslavement—no longer to alien *impulses* but to alien *purposes*. Alienation becomes measurable against the background of the aesthetic counterimage of a different mode of activity mediated by a different mode of attention, one that implies not only a different configuration of subject and object, of reason and the senses, but ultimately also a different way of regulating the metabolism between human beings and nature.

Marx's identification of strained attention as an index of labor's estrangement raises intriguing possibilities for conceptualizing contemporary forms of labor exploitation and the potential for resistance against it. In knowledge work, focused yet adaptable attention has become a crucial exertion of the laboring powers, no longer only required to keep the physical organs on task but itself a force productive in manipulating symbolic codes. As such, however, attention is subjected to the same process of homogenization and quantification that Marx described as the effect of commodifying physical labor. In certain segments of the labor market today, what is bought and sold is above all the right to dispose of people's attention. The Marxian framework can also help us understand how attention is put to work today even when we are not working. In the digital age, leisure time has become "prolongation of work" more directly than in the Fordist era, when the culture industry offered relief from repetitive workplace tasks only by replicating them in the form of standardized entertainment.[35] The digital devices on which people today spend increasing amounts of their free time are designed to capture and measure attention in ways that feed even more directly into mechanisms of capital accumulation.[36] As ever, such "user engagement" extracted for profitable data is measured in homogeneous time, by "metrics" for attention far more fine-grained than the old-time stamp clocks at the entrance to Fordist factories. At the same time, these exertions of attention are beginning to feed visions and aspirations for societal change of the kind previously inspired by the exploitation of physical labor. If, as Anselm Rabinbach argues, the great utopias centered around labor and the body as a "human motor" are increasingly eclipsed in the digital age,[37] the vision of liberated attention may emerge as a new source of such utopian ideals, as the following section suggests.

Economies of Attention

Problems of attention resurfaced as a flashpoint of discussion at two further historical junctures: once, as Jonathan Crary has detailed, in the shocks of late nineteenth-century industrial modernity; and then again in our own time, stimulated by the pinprick shocks of digital modernity and a media environment defined by relentless competition for attention. There is much that distinguishes these

---

35. See the "Culture Industry" chapter of the *Dialectic of Enlightenment*, here: 109.
36. See Shoshanna Zuboff's *Age of Surveillance Capitalism*.
37. See the essays collected in Rabinbach, *Eclipse* (esp. chap. 7).

moments. One thing they seem to share is a dialectic of disruption and rehabituation; a confrontation with challenges that exceed established modes of perception followed by efforts to stabilize and channel this disruption into new forms of experience.

Discussions today about attention as a cultural rather than a psychological problem often revolve around the term "attention economy," a concept coined by the economist Herbert Simon, who noted in the 19070s that "in an information-rich world, the wealth of information means a dearth of something else: . . . a wealth of information creates a poverty of attention and a need to allocate that attention efficiently among the overabundance of information sources that might consume it."[38] The diagnosis of a basic mismatch between the mind's limited capacity and a world that vastly exceeds this capacity, though, is not as new as it seems, even if it has reached new dimensions in postindustrial information societies. At the threshold of a time we (sometimes still) call modernity, we found both exhilaration and terror about the idea that things are infinitely more complex than traditional categories had made us believe; that every speck of dust contains—as Leibniz speculated—more information than a finite mind can hold. This is why attention is less a new problem than a problem coeval with the new itself—with the constancy of novelty and change in a time that continues to define itself as ever-different than what came before. This is not to say or suggest that the problem of attention has remained unchanged. We may, for instance, wonder whether we have not reached a point where the pair of attention and habit has taken on a significance contrary to most eighteenth-century texts we read, so that what clouds the mind is no longer the force of habit but the force of a permanent state of attentional exception that is unable to solidify into sustainable routines. Absent the ability to settle into habitual forms, the greatest excess of perceptual possibility and stimulation becomes as blunt, repetitive, and seemingly inevitable as the idol fought by eighteenth-century writers under the name of habit.

For many practical purposes, the term "subject" coined by eighteenth-century thinkers for the agency who confronts, orders,

---

38. Simon, "Designing Organizations," 40–41.

and manages an excess of information has been eclipsed by the contemporary "user." This indicates what the modern subject of attention is up against. The economy internal to attention (that is, its relatively limited capacity) is confronted today with a digital "attention economy" that seeks to maximize "user engagement" to extract the greatest possible amount of profitable data. Far outstripping the culture industries of old, this attention economy has unparalleled power to shape the attentional habits—und ultimately, the minds and lives—of billions of people around the globe. For critics like the philosopher James Williams, the struggle over who controls attention is therefore a defining political struggle of our times.[39]

A historical study can offer to examine the conceptual armature with which such struggles are waged. The industry of self-help books meant to help overwhelmed individuals struggling with attention proves how tenacious schemata and imperatives established in the eighteenth century remain in the contemporary discourse. Consider, for instance, Nir Eyal's wonderfully titled best-seller *Indistractable: How to Control Your Attention and Choose Your Life* (2019), the most successful title of its genre. The book promises to equip readers with a "superpower" to combat the distractions of contemporary life but often continues to tread in the tracks laid by Wolff's early eighteenth-century introduction of attention as a topic of psychological inquiry.[40] Where Wolff framed attention as a capacity to shield the mind from external sense impressions and impulses that trigger internal flights of the imagination, Eyal begins by emphasizing the importance of warding off "unwanted external triggers" in the environment that "draw or pull" attention away, but also notes that it is important to "master internal triggers" that undermine one's focus.[41] The psychological formulas have changed, and the external distractions discussed now include the beeping of phones rather than the noise of tubas and the yelling of children that Wolff complained about. But the matrix of imperatives that define the subject of attention are remarkably similar: Learn to control internal

---

39. Williams, *Stand out of Our Light*, 87–96.
40. Eyal, *Indistractable*, 5.
41. Eyal, *Indistractable*, 8, 9, 19, etc.

and external triggers in order to align attention with voluntary choices ("what we really want") and thus regain control over your life, a feat the book promises to make possible through a set of "habit-forming" techniques. What is at stake in achieving or failing to achieve mastery over attention is nothing less than personal autonomy or heteronomy; the difference between "those who let their lives be controlled and coerced by others, and those who proudly call themselves 'indistractable.'"[42]

More subtle efforts to come to terms with attention in the digital age are no less circumscribed by such historical sedimentations. Conceptual artist Jenny Odell's popular manifesto *How to Do Nothing: Resisting the Attention Economy* (2019), for instance, develops a concept of art as an "attentional prosthesis" that can help sensitize us to ecological contexts that resonates strikingly (if unwittingly) with Baumgarten's inaugural vision of aesthetics. This suggests that, beyond its historical significance as what Fred Beiser has characterized as a "glorious relic,"[43] Baumgarten's approach may yet have much to offer for clarifying and theorizing contemporary art practices. And yet when it comes to "resisting the attention economy," Odell, too, falls back on individual resolve, willpower, and self-discipline as the keys to fighting distraction in order to "regain control" over attention.[44] Such appeals to individual willpower are bound to fail. From the genealogical perspective developed in this book, they merely reiterate the fraught imperative that produced the pathologies of attention in the first place. Appeals to individual discipline in fact reproduce the problem in the guise of offering a solution, because they block an understanding of the ways attention is never fully individual, never fully "inside," and therefore—as Odell also wants to insist—not simply measurable as a resource that belongs to an individual as a quantifiable property. This quantification of attention, after all, was the very conceit that made Wolff's psychology of attention possible in

---

42. See the introduction and chapters 1–2, this book; for the quotes, see Eyal, *Indistractable*, 1, 3, 177.
43. Beiser, *Diotima's Children*, 1.
44. Odell, *How to Do Nothing*, 112–18, 92–93, here: 93.

the first place, and it remains the schema underlying today's transformation of attention into a resource exploitable on a mass scale. It was also the assumption challenged by Baumgarten's differentiation between different qualities of attention as different ways of relating to one's surroundings. What this historical perspective on the subject of attention suggests is that it will remain futile to confront the problem of attention through technical fixes or individual resolve without shaping collective environments—including media ecologies—in which other forms of attention become practically possible.

Bibliography

Adams, Robert Merrihew. *Leibniz: Determinist, Theist, Idealist.* New York: Oxford University Press, 1994.
Adler, Hans. "Bändigung des (Un)Möglichen: Die ambivalente Beziehung zwischen Aufmerksamkeit und Aufklärung." In *Reiz, Imagination, Aufmerksamkeit: Erregung und Steuerung von Einbildungskraft im klassischen Zeitalter, 1680–1830,* edited by Jörn Steigerwald and Daniela Watzke. Würzburg: Königshausen & Neumann, 2003.
Adler, Hans. *Die Prägnanz des Dunklen: Gnoseologie, Ästhetik, Geschichtsphilosophie bei Johann Gottfried Herder.* Hamburg: F. Meiner, 1990.
Adorno, Theodor W. *Aesthetic Theory.* Translated by Robert Hullot-Kentor. Minneapolis: University of Minnesota Press, 1997.
Adorno, Theodor W. *Hegel: Three Studies.* Cambridge, MA: MIT Press, 1993.
Adorno, Theodor W., and Max Horkheimer. *Dialectic of Enlightenment: Philosophical Fragments.* Edited by Gunzelin Schmid Noerr. Translated by Edmund Jephcott. Stanford, CA: Stanford University Press, 2002.
Agamben, Giorgio. *The Signature of All Things: On Method.* Translated by Kevin Attell and Luca D'Isanto. New York: Zone Books, 2010.
Aichele, Alexander. "Allzuständigkeit oder Beschränkung? Alexander Gottlieb Baumgartens Kritik an Christian Wolffs Begriff der Philosophie." *Studia Leibnitiana* 42, no. 2 (2010): 162–85.

Aichele, Alexander. "Ding und Begriff: Wirklichkeit und Möglichkeit in A. G. Baumgartens Theorie ästhetischer und szientifischer Erkenntnis." In *Schönes Denken: A. G. Baumgarten im Spannungsfeld zwischen Ästhetik, Logik und Ethik*, edited by Andrea Allerkamp and Dagmar Mirbach, 117–26. Hamburg: Meiner, 2016.

Aichele, Alexander. "Wahrheit–Gewißheit–Wirklichkeit: Die systematische Ausrichtung von A.G. Baumgartens Philosophie." In *Alexander Gottlieb Baumgarten: Sinnliche Erkenntnis in der Philosophie des Rationalismus*, edited by Dagmar Mirbach and Alexander Aichele. *Aufklärung* 20 (2008): 13–35.

Alanen, Lilli. "The Second Meditation and the Nature of the Human Mind." In *The Cambridge Companion to Descartes' Meditations*, edited by David Cunningham, 88–106. New York: Cambridge University Press, 2014.

Alford, Lucy. *Forms of Poetic Attention*. New York: Columbia University Press, 2021.

Allerkamp, Andrea, and Dagmar Mirbach. "Unter produktiver Spannung: 300 Jahre Baumgarten." In *Schönes Denken: A. G. Baumgarten im Spannungsfeld zwischen Ästhetik, Logik und Ethik*, edited by Andrea Allerkamp and Dagmar Mirbach, 7–32. Hamburg: Meiner, 2016.

Andersen, Sonja M. "The Everyday in Catharina Regina von Greiffenberg's Poetics." PhD diss., Princeton University, 2023.

Arias, Francisco. *Des unerschöpffter Schatzes deren Güttern, so wir in Christo haben*. Vol. 3. Glatz: Pegen, 1685.

Asmuth, Bernhard. "Strenge Aufmerksamkeit im 18. Jahrhundert: Ihre Ausdehnung von der Rhetorik zur Ästhetik." *Rhetorik* 33, no. 1 (January 1, 2014): 1–16.

Assmann, Jan. "Die Aufmerksamkeit Gottes: Die religiöse Dimension der Aufmerksamkeit in Israel und Ägypten." In *Aufmerksamkeiten*, edited by Aleida Assmann and Jan Assmann, 69–77. Munich: Fink, 2001.

Bacon, Francis. *The New Organon*. Edited by Lisa Jardine. Translated by Michael Silverthorne. Cambridge: Cambridge University Press, 2000.

Bahr, Petra. *Darstellung des Undarstellbaren: Religionstheoretische Studien zum Darstellungsbegriff bei A. G. Baumgarten und I. Kant*. Tübingen: Mohr Siebeck, 2004.

Baisch, Martin, Andreas Degen, and Jana Lüdtke, eds. *Wie gebannt: Ästhetische Verfahren der affektiven Bindung von Aufmerksamkeit*. Freiburg: Rombach, 2013.

Balthasar, Hans Urs von. *The Glory of the Lord: A Theological Aesthetics*. San Francisco: Ignatius Press, 1990.

Barkley, Russell A., and Helmut Peters. "The Earliest Reference to ADHD in the Medical Literature? Melchior Adam Weikard's Description in 1775 of 'Attention Deficit' (Mangel Der Aufmerksamkeit, Attentio Volubilis)." *Journal of Attention Disorders* 16, no. 8 (November 2012): 623–30.

Basedow, Johann Bernhard. *Das Basedowische Elementarwerk: Ein Vorrath der besten Erkenntnisse zum Lernen, Lehren, Wiederholen und Nachdenken*. Leipzig: Crusius, 1785.

Baumgarten, Alexander Gottlieb. *Aesthetica/Ästhetik: Lateinisch-Deutsch*. Edited and translated by Dagmar Mirbach. 2 vols. Hamburg: Meiner, 2007.
Baumgarten, Alexander Gottlieb. *Ethica philosophica*. 3rd ed. Halle: Hemmerde, 1763.
Baumgarten, Alexander Gottlieb. *Gedanken vom vernünftigen Beyfall auf Akademien*. Magdeburg: Hemmerde, 1741.
Baumgarten, Alexander Gottlieb. *Meditationes philosophicae de nonnullis ad poema pertinentibus = Philosophische Betrachtungen über einige Bedingungen des Gedichtes: Lateinisch-Deutsch*. Edited and translated by Heinz Paetzold. Hamburg: Meiner, 1983.
Baumgarten, Alexander Gottlieb. *Metaphysica/Metaphysik*. Edited and translated by Lothar Kreimendahl and Günter Gawlick. Stuttgart: Frommann-Holzboog, 2011.
Baumgarten, Alexander Gottlieb. *Metaphysics: A Critical Translation with Kant's Elucidations, Selected Notes, and Related Materials*. Edited and translated by Courtney D. Fugate and John Hymers. New York: Bloomsbury, 2013.
Baumgarten, Alexander Gottlieb. "Philosophischer Briefe zweites Schreiben." In *Texte zur Grundlegung der Ästhetik: Lateinisch-Deutsch*, edited and translated by Hans Rudolf Schweizer, 67–72. Hamburg: Meiner, 1983.
Baumgarten, Alexander Gottlieb. *Reflections on Poetry. Alexander Gottlieb Baumgarten's Meditationes Philosophicae de Nonnullis Ad Poema Pertinentibus*. Edited and translated by Karl Aschenbrenner and William B. Holther. Berkeley: University of California Press, 1954.
Baumgarten, Alexander Gottlieb. *Texte zur Grundlegung der Ästhetik*. Edited and translated by Hans Rudolf Schweizer. Philosophische Bibliothek no. 351. Hamburg: Meiner, 1983.
Baumgarten, Alexander Gottlieb. *Theoretische Ästhetik*. Edited and translated by Hans Rudolf Schweizer. Hamburg: Meiner, 1983.
Bäumler, Alfred. *Das Irrationalitätsproblem in der Ästhetik und Logik des 18. Jahrhunderts bis zur Kritik der Urteilskraft*. Darmstadt: Wissenschaftliche Buchgesellschaft, 1975.
Beck, Lewis White. *Early German Philosophy: Kant and His Predecessors*. Cambridge, MA: Belknap Press of Harvard University Press, 1969.
Beiser, Frederick C. *Diotima's Children: German Aesthetic Rationalism from Leibniz to Lessing*. Oxford: Oxford University Press, 2009.
Benjamin, Walter. *Das Passagen-Werk*. Edited by Rolf Tiedemann. 2 vols. Vol. 1. Frankfurt am Main: Suhrkamp, 1983.
Benjamin, Walter. "Gewohnheit und Aufmerksamkeit." In *Gesammelte Schriften*, edited by Rexroth Tillman, 4:407–8. Frankfurt am Main: Suhrkamp, 1972.
Bennett, Jane. *Vibrant Matter: A Political Ecology of Things*. Durham, NC: Duke University Press, 2009.
Benveniste, Émile. "Actif et moyen dans le verbe." *Journal de psychologie* 43, no. 1 (1950): 121–29.
Berger, John. *Ways of Seeing*. London: BBC/Penguin, 1972.

Berndt, Frauke. *Facing Poetry: Alexander Gottlieb Baumgarten's Theory of Literature*. Berlin: De Gruyter, 2020.
Berndt, Frauke. *Poema/Gedicht: Die epistemische Konfiguration der Literatur um 1750*. Berlin: De Gruyter, 2011.
Bertino, Andrea. "'As with Bees'? Notes on Instinct and Language in Nietzsche and Herder." In *Nietzsche on Instinct and Language*, edited by João Constâncio and Maria João Mayer Branco, 3–34. Berlin: De Gruyter, 2011.
Blackwell, Richard J. "Christian Wolff's Doctrine of the Soul." *Journal of the History of Ideas* 22, no. 3 (July 1961): 339.
Blair, Ann. "The Rise of Note-Taking in Early Modern Europe." *Intellectual History Review* 20, no. 3 (September 1, 2010): 303–16.
Blumenberg, Hans. "Anthropologische Annäherung an die Aktualität der Rhetorik." In *Ästhetische und metaphorologische Schriften*, edited by Anselm Haverkamp, 406–31. Frankfurt am Main: Suhrkamp, 2001.
Blumenberg, Hans. "Beobachtungen an Metaphern." *Archiv für Begriffsgeschichte* 15 (1971): 161–214.
Blumenberg, Hans. "Das Verhältnis von Natur und Technik als philosophisches Problem." In *Ästhetische und metaphorologische Schriften*, edited by Anselm Haverkamp, 253–65. Frankfurt am Main: Suhrkamp, 2001.
Blumenberg, Hans. *Die Genesis der kopernikanischen Welt*. Frankfurt am Main: Suhrkamp, 1975.
Blumenberg, Hans. *The Legitimacy of the Modern Age*. Translated by Robert M. Wallace. Cambridge, MA: MIT Press, 1983.
Blumenberg, Hans. *Die Legitimität der Neuzeit*. Frankfurt am Main: Suhrkamp, 1996.
Blumenberg, Hans. "'Nachahmung der Natur': Zur Vorgeschichte der Idee des schöpferischen Menschen." In *Ästhetische und metaphorologische Schriften*, edited by Anselm Haverkamp, 9–46. Frankfurt am Main: Suhrkamp, 2001.
Blumenberg, Hans. *Zu den Sachen und zurück*. Edited by Manfred Sommer. Frankfurt am Main: Suhrkamp, 2002.
Böhme, Gernot. *Atmosphäre: Essays zur neuen Ästhetik*. Berlin: Suhrkamp, 2013.
Bonnet, Charles. *Essai analytique sur les facultés de l'ame*. Œuvres d'histoire naturelle et de philosophie de Charles Bonnet, no. 6. Neuchatel: S. Fauche, 1782.
Borchers, Stefan. *Die Erzeugung des 'ganzen Menschen': Zur Entstehung von Anthropologie und Ästhetik an der Universität Halle im 18. Jahrhundert*. Berlin: De Gruyter, 2011.
Borgards, Roland. *Poetik des Schmerzes: Physiologie und Literatur von Brockes bis Büchner*. Munich: W. Fink, 2007.
Bourguet, Marie-Noëlle. "A Portable World: The Notebooks of European Travellers (Eighteenth to Nineteenth Centuries)." *Intellectual History Review* 20, no. 3 (September 1, 2010): 377–400.
Braunschweiger, David. *Die Lehre von der Aufmerksamkeit in der Psychologie des 18. Jahrhunderts*. Leipzig: Hermann Haacke, 1899.
Breitinger, Johann Jakob. *Critische Dichtkunst*. 2 vols. Stuttgart: Metzler, 1966. Reprint of the Zurich 1740 edition.

Brockes, Barthold Heinrich. *Grund-Sätze der Welt-Weisheit, des Herrn Abts Genest, nebst verschiedenen theils physicalischen theils moralischen Gedichten, als des Irdischen Vergnügen in Gotts dritter Theil*. 9 vols. Vol. 3. 4th ed. Hamburg: König, 1747.
Brockes, Barthold Heinrich. *Irdisches Vergnügen in Gott, Bestehend in Physicalisch- Und Moralischen Gedichten*. 9 vols. Vol. 1. 7th ed. Hamburg: Herold, 1744.
Brockes, Barthold Heinrich. *Irdisches Vergnügen in Gott, bestehend in Physicalisch- und Moralischen Gedichten*. 9 vols. Vol. 2. Hamburg: Kißner, 1724.
Brockes, Barthold Heinrich. *Irdisches Vergnügen in Gott, bestehend in Physicalisch- und Moralischen Gedichten*. 9 vols. Vol. 4. Tübingen: Schramm, 1753.
Brockes, Barthold Heinrich. *Irdisches Vergnügen in Gott, bestehend in Physicalisch- und Moralischen Gedichten*. 9 vols. Vol. 5. Tübingen: Schramm, 1739.
Brockes, Barthold Heinrich. *Irdisches Vergnügen in Gott, bestehend in Physicalisch- und Moralischen Gedichten*. 9 vols. Vol. 6. Tübingen: Schramm, 1740.
Brockes, Barthold Heinrich. *Irdisches Vergnügen in Gott, bestehend in Physicalisch- und Moralischen Gedichten*. 9 vols. Vol. 8. Hamburg: Herold, 1746.
Brockes, Barthold Heinrich. *Land-Leben in Ritzebüttel, als des irdischen Vergnügens in Gott Siebender Theil*. 9 vols. Vol. 7. Hamburg: Herold, 1748.
Brockes, Barthold Heinrich. *Physikalische und moralische Gedanken über die drey Reiche der Natur, Nebst seinen übrigen nachgelassenen Gedichten, als des Irdischen Vergnügens in Gott Neunter und letzter Theil*. 9 vols. Vol. 9. Hamburg: Grund, 1748.
Bruck, Jan, Eckart Feldmeier, Hans Hiebel, and Karl Heinz Stahl. "Der Mimesisbegriff Gottscheds und der Schweizer: Kritische Überlegungen zu Hans Peter Herrmann, Naturnachahmung und Einbildungskraft." *Zeitschrift für deutsche Philologie* 90 (1971): 563–78.
Buchenau, Stefanie. "Die Sprache der Sinnlichkeit: Baumgartens poetische Begründung der Ästhetik in den Meditationes philosophicae." Edited by Dagmar Mirbach and Alexander Aichele. *Aufklärung* 20 (2008): 151–73.
Buchenau, Stefanie. *The Founding of Aesthetics in the German Enlightenment: The Art of Invention and the Invention of Art*. Cambridge: Cambridge University Press, 2013.
Buck-Morss, Susan. *Hegel, Haiti, and Universal History*. Pittsburgh, PA: University of Pittsburgh Press, 2009.
Campe, Joachim Heinrich. "Ueber die früheste Bildung junger Kinderseelen." In *Allgemeine Revision des gesammten Schul- und Erziehungswesens*, edited by Joachim Heinrich Campe, 3–296. Hamburg: Bohn, 1785.
Campe, Rüdiger. "Baumgartens Ästhetik: Metaphysik und Techne." In *Schönes Denken: A. G. Baumgarten im Spannungsfeld zwischen Ästhetik, Logik und Ethik*, edited by Andrea Allerkamp and Dagmar Mirbach, 149–70. Hamburg: Meiner, 2016.

Campe, Rüdiger. "Bella Evidentia: Der Begriff und die Figur der Evidenz in Baumgartens Ästhetik." In *Baumgarten-Studien: Zur Genealogie der Ästhetik*, edited by Anselm Haverkamp, Christoph Menke, and Rüdiger Campe, 49–71. Cologne: August-Verlag, 2014.

Campe, Rüdiger. "Die Schreibszene: Schreiben." In *Paradoxien, Dissonanzen, Zusammenbrüche: Situationen Offener Epistemologie*, edited by Hans Ulrich Gumbrecht and K. Ludwig Pfeiffer, 759–72. Frankfurt: Suhrkamp, 1991.

Campe, Rüdiger. "Effekt der Form: Baumgartens Ästhetik am Rande der Metaphysik." In *Baumgarten-Studien: Zur Genealogie der Ästhetik*, edited by Anselm Haverkamp, Christoph Menke, and Rüdiger Campe, 117–44. Cologne: August-Verlag, 2014.

Campe, Rüdiger. "'Ein Buch worin ich alles einschreibe': Lichtenbergs freie Rede über die Dinge im Sudelbuch." In *Lichtenberg-Jahrbuch 2019*, edited by Ulrich Joost et al., 7–31. Heidelberg: Universitätsverlag Winter, 2020.

Campe, Rüdiger. "'Improbable Probability': On Evidence in the Eighteenth Century." *The Germanic Review: Literature, Culture, Theory* 76, no. 2 (January 2001): 143–61.

Campe, Rüdiger. "Shapes and Figures—Geometry and Rhetoric in the Age of Evidence." *Monatshefte* 102, no. 3 (2010): 285–99.

Campe, Rüdiger. "Writing; The Scene of Writing." Translated by Bryan Klausmeyer and Johannes Wankhammer. *MLN* 136, no. 5 (2021): 971–83.

Campe, Rüdiger, Jocelyn Holland, and Elisabeth Strowick. "Observation in Science and Literature: Preface." *Monatshefte* 105, no. 3 (2013): 371–75.

Carboncini, Sonia. "L'Encyclopédie et Christian Wolff: À propos des quelques articles anonymes." *Les Études philosophiques*, no. 4 (1987): 489–504.

Carr, Thomas M. *Descartes and the Resilience of Rhetoric: Varieties of Cartesian Rhetorical Theory*. Carbondale: Southern Illinois University Press, 1989.

Cassirer, Ernst. *Die Philosophie der Aufklärung*. Hamburg: Meiner, 2007.

Cassirer, Ernst. *Freiheit und Form: Studien zur deutschen Geistesgeschichte*. Berlin: B. Cassirer, 1922.

Chambaud, Jean-Jacques Menuret de. "Observation." In *Encyclopédie ou dictionnaire raisonné des sciences*, edited by Jean Le Rond d'Alembert and Denis Diderot, 11:313–25. Briasson, 1765.

Chase, Michael, Stephen R. L. Clark, and Michael McGhee, eds. *Philosophy as a Way of Life: Ancients and Moderns: Essays in Honor of Pierre Hadot*. Chichester: Wiley Blackwell, 2013.

Citton, Yves. *The Ecology of Attention*. Translated by Norman Barnaby. Malden, MA: Polity, 2017.

Cottingham, John. "Philosophy and Self-Improvement: Continuity and Change in Philosophy's Self-Conception from the Classical to the Early-Modern Era." In *Philosophy as a Way of Life: Ancients and Moderns: Essays in Honor of Pierre Hadot*, edited by Michael Chase, Michael McGhee, and Stephen R. L. Clark, 148–66. Chichester: Wiley Blackwell, 2013.

Crary, Jonathan. 24/7: *Late Capitalism and the Ends of Sleep*. New York: Verso, 2014.
Crary, Jonathan. *Suspensions of Perception: Attention, Spectacle, and Modern Culture*. Cambridge, MA: MIT Press, 1999.
Crary, Jonathan. *Techniques of the Observer: On Vision and Modernity in the Nineteenth Century*. Cambridge, MA: MIT Press, 1992.
Daston, Lorraine. "Attention and the Values of Nature in the Enlightenment." In *The Moral Authority of Nature*, edited by Lorraine Daston and Fernando Vidal, 100–126. Chicago: University of Chicago Press, 2004.
Daston, Lorraine. "The Disciplines of Attention." In *A New History of German Literature*, edited by David E. Wellbery, Judith Ryan, and Hans Ulrich Gumbrecht, 434–40. Cambridge, MA: Belknap Press of Harvard University Press, 2004.
Daston, Lorraine. *Eine kurze Geschichte der wissenschaftlichen Aufmerksamkeit*. Munich: Siemens Stiftung, 2001.
Daston, Lorraine. "The Empire of Observation, 1600–1800." In *Histories of Scientific Observation*, edited by Lorraine Daston and Elizabeth Lunbeck, 81–113. Chicago: University of Chicago Press, 2011.
Daston, Lorraine. "Taking Note(s)." *Isis* 95, no. 3 (September 2004): 443–48.
Daston, Lorraine, and Peter Galison. *Objectivity*. New York: Zone Books, 2010.
Daston, Lorraine, and Elizabeth Lunbeck. *Histories of Scientific Observation*. Chicago: University of Chicago Press, 2011.
Daston, Lorraine, and Katharine Park. *Wonders and the Order of Nature, 1150–1750*. New York: Zone Books, 1998.
Deleuze, Gilles. *The Fold: Leibniz and the Baroque*. Translated by Tom Conley. Minneapolis: University of Minnesota Press, 1992.
De Man, Paul. *Aesthetic Ideology*. Edited by Andrzej Warminski. Minneapolis: University of Minnesota Press, 1996.
De Man, Paul. "Kant and Schiller." In *Aesthetic Ideology*, 129–62. Minneapolis: University of Minnesota Press, 1983.
De Man, Paul. *The Resistance to Theory*. Minneapolis: University of Minnesota Press, 1989.
Descartes, René. *L'homme*. Paris: Charles Angot, 1664.
Descartes, René. *Meditations on First Philosophy*. Edited and translated by Donald A. Cress. Indianapolis: Hackett, 1993.
Descartes, René. *Oeuvres de Descartes*. Edited by Charles Adam and Paul Tannery. 12 vols. Paris: Léopold Cerf, 1897.
Descartes, René. *The Philosophical Writings of Descartes*. Translated by John Cottingham, Robert Stoothoff, and Dugald Murdoch. 3 vols. Cambridge: Cambridge University Press, 1984.
Descartes, René. *The World and Other Writings*. Translated by Stephen Gaukroger. Cambridge: Cambridge University Press, 1998.
Disselkamp, Martin. *Barockheroismus: Konzeptionen "politischer" Größe in Literatur und Traktatistik des 17. Jahrhunderts*. Berlin: De Gruyter, 2002.

Drügh, Heinz J. *Ästhetik der Beschreibung. Poetische und kulturelle Energie deskriptiver Texte (1700–2000)*. Tübingen: Francke, 2006.

Dubos, Jean Baptiste. *Critical Reflections on Poetry and Painting*. London: J. Nourse, 1748.

Dubos, Jean Baptiste. *Réflexions critiques sur la poesie et sur la peinture*. 2 vols. Paris: Pierre-Jean Mariette, 1733.

DuCambout de Pontchâteau, Sébastien Joseph. *Der Jesuiten Christenthumb und Lebens-Wandel: Übergesetzet und vorgestellet aus einem von eyfferigen, iedoch gewissenhafften Papisten zusammengetragenem und aus Verfolgung der Jesuiten nur kürtzlich zu Pariß verbrandtem frantzösischem Wercklein La Morale Pratique des Jesuites*. Freistadt: Warner, 1670.

Dürbeck, Gabriele. *Einbildungskraft und Aufklärung: Perspektiven der Philosophie, Anthropologie und Ästhetik um 1750*. Tübingen: M. Niemeyer Verlag, 1998.

Duttlinger, Carolin. *Attention and Distraction in Modern German Literature, Thought, and Culture*. Oxford: Oxford University Press, 2022.

Eagleton, Terry. *The Ideology of the Aesthetic*. Cambridge, MA: Basil Blackwell, 1990.

Ehrenspeck-Kolasa, Yvonne. "Das Thema Aufmerksamkeit in der Pädagogik des 18. Jahrhunderts." In *Aufmerksamkeit*, edited by Sabine Reh, Kathrin Berdelmann, and Jörg Dinkelaker, 21–34. Springer: Wiesbaden, 2015.

Evans, G. "Sancta Indifferentia and Adiaphora: 'Holy Indifference' and 'Things Indifferent.'" *Common Knowledge* 15 (December 21, 2009).

Eyal, Nir. *Indistractable: How to Control Your Attention and Choose Your Life*. London: Bloomsbury, 2019.

Favaretti Camposampiero, Matteo. "Anthropology from a Logical Point of View: The Role of Inner Sense from Jungius to Kant." In *Knowledge, Morals and Practice in Kant's Anthropology*, edited by Gualtiero Lorini and Robert B. Louden, 43–61. Cham: Springer International, 2018.

Ferreira da Silva, Denise. *Toward a Global Idea of Race*. Minneapolis: University of Minnesota Press, 2007.

Feuer, Lewis S. "The Dream of Benedict de Spinoza." *American Imago* 14, no. 3 (1957): 225–42.

Finken, Karl-Heinz. *Die Wahrheit der Literatur: Studien zur Literaturtheorie des 18. Jahrhunderts*. New York: P. Lang, 1993.

Forster, Michael N. "Herder's Philosophy of Language, Interpretation, and Translation: Three Fundamental Principles." *Review of Metaphysics* 56, no. 2 (2002): 323–56.

Foucault, Michel. *Discipline and Punish: The Birth of the Prison*. Translated by Alan Sheridan. New York: Vintage, 1995.

Foucault, Michel. *The Hermeneutics of the Subject: Lectures at the Collège de France, 1981–1982*. Edited by Frédéric Gros. Translated by Graham Burchell. New York: Picador, 2006.

Foucault, Michel. *Madness and Civilization*. Translated by Richard Howard. London: Routledge, 2007.

Foucault, Michel. *The Order of Things: An Archaeology of the Human Sciences*. New York: Vintage Books, 1994.
Foucault, Michel. "Technologies of the Self." In *Technologies of the Self: A Seminar with Michel Foucault*, edited by Huck Gutman, Patrick H Hutton, and Luther H Martin, 16–49. London: Tavistock, 1988.
Foucault, Michel. "What Is Critique?" In *What Is Enlightenment? Eighteenth-Century Answers and Twentieth-Century Questions*, edited by James Schmidt, 382–98. Berkeley: University of California Press, 1996.
Foucault, Michel. "What Is Enlightenment?" In *The Foucault Reader*, edited by Paul Rabinow, 32–50. New York: Pantheon Books, 1984.
Franck, Georg. *Ökonomie der Aufmerksamkeit: Ein Entwurf*. Munich: Hanser, 1998.
Franke, Ursula. "Analogon rationis." Edited by Joachim Ritter, Gottfried Gabriel, and Karlfried Gründer. *Historisches Wörterbuch der Philosophie online*. Schwabe Verlag, 2017.
Franke, Ursula. *Baumgartens Erfindung der Ästhetik*. Münster: Menti, 2018.
Franke, Ursula. *Kunst als Erkenntnis: Die Rolle der Sinnlichkeit in der Ästhetik des Alexander Gottlieb Baumgarten*. Wiesbaden: Steiner, 1972.
Franke, Ursula. "Sinnliche Erkenntnis—Was sie ist und was sie soll: A. G. Baumgartens Ästhetik-Projekt zwischen Kunstphilosophie und Anthropologie." Edited by Alexander Aichele and Dagmar Mirbach. In *Alexander Gottlieb Baumgarten: Sinnliche Erkenntnis in der Philosophie des Rationalismus. Aufklärung* 20 (2008): 73–99.
Frey, Christiane. "Zur ästhetischen Übung: Improvisiertes und Vorbewusstes bei A. G. Baumgarten." In *Schönes Denken: A. G. Baumgarten im Spannungsfeld zwischen Ästhetik, Logik und Ethik*, edited by Andrea Allerkamp and Dagmar Mirbach, 171–81. Hamburg: Meiner, 2016.
Fried, Michael. *Absorption and Theatricality: Painting and Beholder in the Age of Diderot*. Chicago: University of Chicago Press, 1980.
Fugate, Courtney D. "Alexander Baumgarten on the Principle of Sufficient Reason." *Philosophica* 44 (2014): 127–47.
Fugate, Courtney D., and John Hymers, eds. *Baumgarten and Kant on Metaphysics*. Oxford: Oxford University Press, 2018.
Gabriel, Gottfried. "Baumgartens Begriff der 'perceptio praegnans' und seine systematische Bedeutung." Edited by Alexander Aichele and Dagmar Mirbach. *Alexander Gottlieb Baumgarten: Sinnliche Erkenntnis in der Philosophie des Rationalismus. Aufklärung* 20 (2008): 61–71.
Gasché, Rodolphe. "On Seeing Away: Attention and Abstraction in Kant." *CR: The New Centennial Review* 8, no. 3 (2008): 1–28.
Geoghegan, Bernard Dionysius. "After Kittler: On the Cultural Techniques of Recent German Media Theory." *Theory, Culture & Society* 30, no. 6 (November 1, 2013): 66–82.
Gess, Nicola. *Staunen: Eine Poetik*. Göttingen: Wallstein Verlag, 2019.
Goetschel, Willi. "Spinoza's Dream." *Cambridge Journal of Postcolonial Literary Inquiry* 3, no. 1 (January 2016): 39–54.

Gottsched, Johann Christoph. *Versuch einer critischen Dichtkunst: Erster Allgemeiner Theil.* Edited by Joachim Birke and Brigitte Birke. Ausgewählte Werke [Selected Works], VI/1. Berlin: De Gruyter, 1973.

Greenblatt, Stephen. *The Swerve: How the World Became Modern.* New York: W. W. Norton, 2011.

Grote, Simon. *The Emergence of Modern Aesthetic Theory: Religion and Morality in Enlightenment Germany and Scotland.* Cambridge: Cambridge University Press, 2019.

Gumbrecht, Hans Ulrich. *Stimmungen Lesen: Über eine verdeckte Wirklichkeit der Literatur.* Munich: Carl Hanser Verlag, 2011.

Guntermann, Georg. *Barthold Heinrich Brockes' "Irdisches Vergnügen in Gott" und die Geschichte seiner Rezeption in der deutschen Germanistik: Zum Verhältnis von Methode u. Gegenstand literaturwissenschaftl: Forschung.* Bonn: Bouvier, 1980.

Gurton-Wachter, Lily. *Watchwords: Romanticism and the Poetics of Attention.* Stanford, CA: Stanford University Press, 2016.

Guyer, Paul. "18th Century German Aesthetics." In *The Stanford Encyclopedia of Philosophy*, edited by Edward N. Zalta, 2008. http://plato.stanford.edu/archives/fall2008/entries/aesthetics-18th-german/.

Guyer, Paul. *A History of Modern Aesthetics.* 3 vols. Vol. 1. New York: Cambridge University Press, 2014.

Hacking, Ian. "Let's Not Talk about Objectivity." In *Objectivity in Science*, edited by Jonathan Tsou, Alan Richardson, and Flavia Padovani, 19–33. Springer, 2015.

Hadot, Pierre. *Philosophy as a Way of Life: Spiritual Exercises from Socrates to Foucault.* Edited by Arnold I. Davidson. Translated by Michael Chase. Malden, MA: Blackwell, 1995.

Hagner, Michael. "Aufmerksamkeit als Ausnahmezustand." In *Aufmerksamkeit*, edited by N. Haas, R. Nägele, and H.-J. Rheinberger, 273–294. Eggingen: Edition Isele, 1998.

Hagner, Michael. "Toward a History of Attention in Culture and Science." *MLN* 118, no. 3 (2003): 670–87.

Hahn, Alois. "Aufmerksamkeit." In *Aufmerksamkeiten*, edited by Aleida Assmann and Jan Assmann, 26–56. Munich: Fink, 2001.

Hatfield, Gary. "Attention in Early Scientific Psychology." In *Visual Attention*, edited by Richard D. Wright, 8:3–25. New York: Oxford University Press, 1998.

Hatfield, Gary. "L'attention chez Descartes: Aspect mental et aspect physiologique." Translated by Olivier Dubouclez. *Les Études philosophiques* 171, no. 1 (2017): 7–25.

Hatfield, Gary. "The Senses and the Fleshless Eye: The Meditations as Cognitive Exercises." In *Essays on Descartes' Meditations*, edited by Amelie Rorty, 45–76. Berkeley: University of California Press, 1986.

Hegel, Georg Wilhelm Friedrich. *Enzyklopädie der philosophischen Wissenschaften III: Die Philosophie des Geistes.* Werke 10. Frankfurt am Main: Suhrkamp, 1986.

Hegel, Georg Wilhelm Friedrich. *Phänomenologie des Geistes*. Edited by Friedrich Wessels and Heinrich Clairmont. Philosophische Bibliothek no. 414. Hamburg: Meiner, 1988.
Hegel, Georg Wilhelm Friedrich. *Philosophy of Mind*. Edited by Michael J. Inwood. Translated by W. Wallace and A. V. Miller. Oxford: Clarendon Press, 2010.
Heidegger, Martin. "Der Ursprung des Kunstwerkes." In *Holzwege*, edited by Friedrich-Wilhelm von Herrmann, 8th ed., 1–74. Frankfurt am Main: V. Klostermann, 2003.
Heidegger, Martin. "Die Zeit des Weltbildes." In *Holzwege*, edited by Friedrich-Wilhelm von Herrmann, 8th ed., 75–114. Frankfurt am Main: V. Klostermann, 2003.
Henrich, Dieter. "Die Anfänge der Theorie des Subjekts (1789)." In *Zwischenbetrachtungen*, 106–70. Frankfurt: Suhrkamp, 1989.
Herder, Johann Gottfried. "Abhandlung über den Ursprung der Sprache." In *Frühe Schriften, 1764–1772*, edited by Ulrich Gaier, 1:697–810. Johann Gottfried Herder: Werke in zehn Bänden. Frankfurt am Main: Deutscher Klassiker Verlag, 1985.
Herder, Johann Gottfried. "Herder's Notes from Kant's Metaphysics Lectures." Accessed June 24, 2021. https://users.manchester.edu/FacStaff/SSNaragon/Kant/HerderNotesComplete/MP/Texts/Text-EP531.htm.
Herder, Johann Gottfried. "Treatise on the Origin of Language." In *Philosophical Writings*, edited by Michael N. Forster, 65–164. Cambridge: Cambridge University Press, 2002.
Herrmann, Hans Peter. *Naturnachahmung und Einbildungskraft: Zur Entwicklung der deutschen Poetik von 1670 bis 1740*. Bad Homburg v.d.H.: Gehlen, 1970.
Hinske, Norbert. "Wolffs empirische Psychologie und Kants pragmatische Anthropologie: Zur Diskussion über die Anfänge der Anthropologie im 18. Jahrhundert." *Aufklärung* 11, no. 1 (1999): 97–107.
Hoffmann, Christoph. *Unter Beobachtung: Naturforschung in der Zeit der Sinnesapparate*. Göttingen: Wallstein, 2006.
Irwing, Karl Franz von. *Erfahrungen und Untersuchungen über den Menschen*. 3 vols. Vol. 2. Berlin: Verlag der Realschulbuchhandlung, 1777.
Jaeggi, Rahel. "Was Ist Ideologiekritik?" In *Was Ist Kritik?*, edited by Rahel Jaeggi and Tilo Wesche, 266–98. Frankfurt am Main: Suhrkamp, 2013.
James, William. *The Principles of Psychology*. 2 vols. Vol. 1. New York: H. Holt, 1890.
Johnson, Michael A. "The Paradox of Attention: The Action of the Self upon Itself." In *A Companion to Ricoeur's Freedom and Nature*, edited by Scott Davidson, 79–108. Lanham, MD: Lexington, 2018.
Kant, Immanuel. *Anthropology from a Pragmatic Point of View*. Edited and translated by Robert B. Louden. Cambridge: Cambridge University Press, 2006.
Kant, Immanuel. *Critique of Pure Reason*. Translated by Paul Guyer and Allen W. Wood. Cambridge: Cambridge University Press, 1998.

Kant, Immanuel. *Critique of the Power of Judgment.* Translated by Paul Guyer. Cambridge: Cambridge University Press, 2000.

Kant, Immanuel. *Gesammelte Schriften.* Edited by Königlich Preußilche Akademie der Wissenschaften. 2nd ed. 23 vols. Berlin: Vereinigung Wissenschaftlicher Verleger, 1902.

Kant, Immanuel. *Kritik der reinen Vernunft.* Edited by Jens Timmermann. Philosophische Bibliothek no. 505. Hamburg: Meiner, 1998.

Kant, Immanuel. *Kritik der Urteilskraft.* Edited by Heiner Klemme. Hamburg: Meiner, 2006.

Kant, Immanuel. "Von den verschiedenen Racen der Menschen." In *Kant's gesammelte Schriften,* edited by Königlich Preußische Akademie der Wissenschaften, 2:429–43. Berlin: Reimer, 1905.

Kircher, Athanasius. *Ars magna lucis et umbrae.* Rome: Scheus, 1645.

Kittler, Friedrich. *Optische Medien: Berliner Vorlesung 1999.* 2nd ed. Berlin: Merve, 2002.

Klein, Julie R. "Dreaming with Open Eyes: Cartesian Dreams, Spinozan Analyses." *Idealistic Studies* 33, no. 2/3 (October 1, 2003): 141–59.

Klemme, Heiner F. "How Is Moral Obligation Possible? Kant's 'Principle of Autonomy' in Historical Context." In *The Emergence of Autonomy in Kant's Moral Philosophy,* edited by Stefano Bacin and Oliver Sensen, 10–28. Cambridge: Cambridge University Press, 2018.

Knorr-Cetina, Karin, Theodore R. Schatzki, and Eike von Savigny, eds. *The Practice Turn in Contemporary Theory.* London: Routledge, 2001.

Kobusch, Theodor. "Descartes' *Meditations*: Practical Metaphysics; The Father of Rationalism in the Tradition of Spiritual Exercises." In *Philosophy as a Way of Life: Ancients and Moderns: Essays in Honor of Pierre Hadot,* edited by Michael Chase, Michael McGhee, and Stephen R. L. Clark, 167–83. Chichester: Wiley Blackwell, 2013.

Koehler, Margaret. *Poetry of Attention in the Eighteenth Century.* New York: Palgrave Macmillan, 2012.

Koyré, Alexandre. *From the Closed World to the Infinite Universe.* Baltimore: Johns Hopkins Press, 1957.

Kreienbrock, Jörg. "'Merk's! Merk's!' Aufmerksamkeit als Medium experimenteller Wahrnehmung bei Barthold Heinrich Brockes." In *Experiment und Literatur,* edited by Michael Gamper, Martina Wernli, Jörg Zimmer, and Michael Bies, 1:240–54. Göttingen: Wallstein, 2009.

Kristeva, Julia. *Powers of Horror: An Essay on Abjection.* Translated by Leon S. Roudiez. New York: Columbia University Press, 1982.

Langen, August. *Anschauungsformen in der deutschen Dichtung des 18. Jahrhunderts: Rahmenschau und Rationalismus.* Darmstadt: Wissenschaftliche Buchgesellschaft, 1965.

Laporte, Jean. *Le rationalisme de Descartes.* Paris: Presses Universitaires de France, 1945.

Largier, Niklaus. "The Plasticity of the Soul: Mystical Darkness, Touch, and Aesthetic Experience." *MLN* 125, no. 3 (April 2010): 536–551.

Lavater, Johann Caspar. *Physiognomische Fragmente: Zur Beförderung der Menschenkenntnis und Menschenliebe*. Vol. 1. Leipzig: Weidmann, 1775.
Lavater, Johann Caspar. *Physiognomische Fragmente: Zur Beförderung der Menschenkenntnis und Menschenliebe*. Vol. 4. Leipzig: Weidmann, 1778.
Le Brun, Charles. *Expressions des passions de l'Ame*. Augsburg: Martin Engelbrecht, 1732.
Le Brun, Charles. *Caracteres des passions*. Amsterdam: Picart, 1720.
Leibniz, Gottfried Wilhelm. *Leibniz's Monadology: A New Translation and Guide*. Edited and translated by Lloyd Strickland. Edinburgh: Edinburgh University Press, 2014.
Leibniz, Gottfried Wilhelm. "Meditations on Knowledge, Truth, and Ideas." In *Philosophical Essays*, edited and translated by Roger Ariew and Daniel Garber, 23–27. Indianapolis: Hackett, 1989.
Leibniz, Gottfried Wilhelm. *Monadologie: Französisch/Deutsch*. Edited and translated by Hartmut Hecht. Stuttgart: Reclam, 1998.
Leibniz, Gottfried Wilhelm. *Monadologie und andere metaphysische Schriften: Französisch - Deutsch*. Edited and translated by Ulrich Johannes Schneider. Philosophische Bibliothek no. 537. Hamburg: Meiner, 2002.
Leibniz, Gottfried Wilhelm. *Philosophical Essays*. Edited and translated by Roger Ariew and Daniel Garber. Indianapolis: Hackett, 1989.
Leibniz, Gottfried Wilhelm. "Preface to the New Essays." In *Philosophical Essays*, edited and translated by Roger Ariew and Daniel Garber, 291–306. Indianapolis: Hackett, 1989.
Leibniz, Gottfried Wilhelm. "Principles of Nature and Grace, Based on Reason." In *Philosophical Essays*, edited and translated by Roger Ariew and Daniel Garber, 206–13. Indianapolis: Hackett, 1989.
Leibniz, Gottfried Wilhelm. *Protogaea*. Edited and translated by Claudine Cohen and Andre Wakefield. Chicago: University of Chicago Press, 2008.
Lessing, Gotthold Ephraim. *Laokoon, Briefe antiquarischen Inhalts*. Edited by Wilfried Barner. Frankfurt am Main: Deutscher Klassiker Verlag, 1990.
Lessing, Gotthold Ephraim. *Werke und Briefe in zwölf Bänden*. Edited by Wilfried Barner and Klaus Bohnen. 12 vols. Vol. 6. Frankfurt am Main: Deutscher Klassiker Verlag, 1985.
Lichtenberg, Georg Christoph. *Philosophical Writings*. Edited and translated by Steven Tester. Albany: SUNY Press, 2012.
Lichtenberg, Georg Christoph. *Schriften und Briefe*. Edited by Wolfgang Promies. 5th ed. 2 vols. Frankfurt am Main: Zweitausendeins, 1994.
Lichtenberg, Georg Christoph. *The Waste Books*. Edited and translated by R. J. Hollingdale. New York: New York Review/Bloomsbury, 2001.
Liska, Vivian. "Walter Benjamins Dialektik der Aufmerksamkeit." In *Aufmerksamkeiten*, edited by Aleida Assmann and Jan Assmann, 141–49. Munich: Fink, 2001.
Lokhorst, Gert-Jan. "Descartes and the Pineal Gland." In *The Stanford Encyclopedia of Philosophy*, edited by Edward N. Zalta, Winter 2018. Metaphysics

Research Lab, Stanford University, 2018. https://plato.stanford.edu/archives/win2018/entries/pineal-gland/.

Luhmann, Niklas. *Beobachtungen der Moderne*. 2nd ed. Wiesbaden: VS Verlag für Sozialwissenschaften, 2006.

Luhmann, Niklas. *Die Kunst der Gesellschaft*. Frankfurt am Main: Suhrkamp, 1997.

Makkreel, R. A. "Baumgarten and Kant on Clarity, Distinctness, and the Differentiation of Our Mental Powers." In *Baumgarten and Kant on Metaphysics*, edited by Courtney D. Fugate and John Hymers, 94–109. Oxford: Oxford University Press, 2018.

Makropoulos, Michael. "Modernität als Kontingenzkultur: Konturen eines Konzepts." In *Kontingenz*, edited by Gerhart v. Graevenitz, Odo Marquard, Matthias Christen, and Hans Robert Jauss, 55–79. Munich: Fink, 1998.

Malagon, Carolina. "'A Completely New Chemistry': Lichtenberg's Generative Paradigmata." *MLN* 134, no. 3 (2019): 591–615.

Malebranche, Nicolas. *Oeuvres de Malebranche: Recherche de la vérité*. Edited by Jules Simon. Vol. 2. Paris: Charpentier, 1850.

Malebranche, Nicolas. *The Search after Truth*. Edited and translated by Thomas M. Lennon and Paul J. Olscamp. Cambridge: Cambridge University Press, 1997.

Marno, David. "Attention and Indifference in Ignatius's Spiritual Exercises." In *A Companion to Ignatius of Loyola*, edited by Robert Aleksander Maryks. Leiden: Brill, 2014.

Marx, Karl. *Capital: A Critique of Political Economy*. Edited by Friedrich Engels. Translated by Samuel Moore and Edward Aveling. New York: Modern Library, 1906.

Marx, Karl. *Das Kapital*. Edited by Hildegard Scheibler. Berlin: Dietz, 2005. Reprint of the 1961 edition.

Mauss, Marcel. "Techniques of the Body." *Economy and Society* 2, no. 1 (February 1, 1973): 70–88.

Mautner, Franz H. "Der Aphorismus als literarische Gattung." *Zeitschrift für Ästhetik und allgemeine Kunstwissenschaft* 27 (1933): 132–75.

McGillen, Petra. "Wit, Bookishness, and the Epistemic Impact of Note-Taking: Lichtenberg's Sudelbücher as Intellectual Tools." *Deutsche Vierteljahrsschrift für Literaturwissenschaft und Geistesgeschichte* 90, no. 4 (December 2016): 501–28.

Meier, Georg Friedrich. *Anfangsgründe aller schönen Wissenschaften*. 3 vols. Hildesheim: Olms, 1976. Reprint of the Halle 1754 edition.

Meier, Georg Friedrich. *Theoretische Lehre von den Gemüthsbewegungen überhaupt*. 2nd, improved ed. Halle: Hemmerde, 1759.

Menninghaus, Winfried. "Klopstocks Poetik der schnellen Bewegung." In *Gedanken über die Natur der Poesie: Dichtungstheoretische Schriften*, 259–361. Frankfurt am Main: Insel, 1989.

Menke, Christoph. "Die Disziplin der Ästhetik ist die Ästhetik der Disziplin: Baumgarten in der Perspektive Foucaults." In *Baumgarten-Studien: Zur Genealogie der Ästhetik*, 233–47. Cologne: August Verlag, 2014.
Menke, Christoph. *Die Souveränität der Kunst: Ästhetische Erfahrung nach Adorno und Derrida*. Frankfurt am Main: Suhrkamp, 1991.
Menke, Christoph. *Kraft: Ein Grundbegriff ästhetischer Anthropologie*. Frankfurt am Main: Suhrkamp, 2008.
Menke, Christoph. "Schwerpunkt: Zur Aktualität Der Ästhetik von Alexander G. Baumgarten." *Deutsche Zeitschrift für Philosophie* 49, no. 2 (2001): 229–32.
Menke, Christoph. "Subjektivität." In *Ästhetische Grundbegriffe*, edited by Karlheinz Barck, Martin Fontius, Dieter Schlenstedt, Burkhart Steinwachs, and Friedrich Wolfzettel. Studienausgabe, 5:734–86. Stuttgart: Metzler, 2010.
Mercer, Christia. "Descartes' Debt to Teresa of Ávila, or Why We Should Work on Women in the History of Philosophy." *Philosophical Studies* 174, no. 10 (October 1, 2017): 2539–55.
Mercer, Christia. "The Methodology of the *Meditations*: Tradition and Innovation." In *The Cambridge Companion to Descartes' Meditations*, edited by David Cunningham, 23–47. New York: Cambridge University Press, 2014.
Mirbach, Dagmar. "Ingenium venustum und magnitudo pectoris: Ethische Aspekte von Alexander Gottlieb Baumgartens 'Aesthetica.'" *Aufklärung* 20 (2008): 199–218.
Mole, Christopher. "Attention." In *The Stanford Encyclopedia of Philosophy*, edited by Edward N. Zalta. Fall 2013. http://plato.stanford.edu/entries/attention/.
Montag, Warren. *Bodies, Masses, Power: Spinoza and His Contemporaries*. New York: Verso, 1999.
Montagu, Jennifer. *The Expression of the Passions: The Origin and Influence of Charles Le Brun's "Conférence sur l'expression générale et particulière."* New Haven, CT: Yale University Press, 1994.
Montaigne, Michel de. *Essais de Michel de Montaigne*. Edited by André Tournon. Vol. 2. Paris: Nationale éditions, 1998.
Moritz, Karl Philipp. *Die Signatur des Schönen und andere Schriften zur Begründung der Autonomieästhetik*. Edited by Stefan Ripplinger. Hamburg: Philo Fine Arts, 2009.
Moritz, Karl Philipp. "Vorschlag zu einem Magazin einer Erfahrungs-Seelenkunde." In *Dichtungen und Schriften zur Erfahrungsseelenkunde*, edited by Heide Hollmer and Albert Meier. 2 vols. 1:793–809. Frankfurt am Main: Deutscher Klassiker Verlag, 1999.
Morrow, Susan. "Schematism: Poetics on the Way to Kant, 1760–1790." PhD diss., Yale University, 2019.
Mücke, Dorothea E. von. *The Practices of the Enlightenment: Aesthetics, Authorship, and the Public*. New York: Columbia University Press, 2015.
Müller, Jan-Dirk. "Evidentia und Medialität: Zur Ausdifferenzierung von Evidenz in der frühen Neuzeit." In *Evidentia: Reichweiten Visueller Wahrnehmung in*

der Frühen Neuzeit, edited by Gabriele Wimböck, Karin Leonhard, and Markus Friedrich, 57–81. Berlin: W. Hopf, 2007.

Murphy, Gardner. *Historical Introduction to Modern Psychology*. New York: Harcourt, Brace, 1949.

Nannini, Alessandro. "The Six Faces of Beauty: Baumgarten on the Perfections of Knowledge in the Context of the German Enlightenment." *Archiv für Geschichte der Philosophie* 102, no. 3 (September 1, 2020): 477–512.

Nassar, Dalia. *Romantic Empiricism: Nature, Art, and Ecology from Herder to Humboldt*. Oxford: Oxford University Press, 2022.

Neudecker, Sigismund. *Geistliche Lehr-Schuel: Das ist: Allgemeine Unterweisung Der Geistlich-Clösterlichen Jugend, Zu dem wahren Clösterlichen-Tugendsamen Leben, und sowohl inn- als äusserlicher Vollkommenheit*. Ingolstadt: De la Haye, 1740.

Neumann, Gerhard. *Ideenparadiese: Untersuchungen zur Aphoristik von Lichtenberg, Novalis, Friedrich Schlegel und Goethe*. Munich: W. Fink, 1976.

Neumann, Odmar. "Aufmerksamkeit." In *Historisches Wörterbuch der Philosophie*, edited by Joachim Ritter, 1:635–45. Basel: Schwabe, 2007.

Newman, Lex. "Attention, Voluntarism, and Liberty in Descartes's Account of Judgment." *Res Philosophica* 92, no. 1 (2015): 61–91.

Nicolai, Friedrich, ed. "Gedanken, Vorschläge und Wünsche zur Verbesserung der öffentlichen Erziehung herausgegeben von F. G. Resewitz. Zweites Stück, 1777. Drittes Stück, 1778. [Review]." In *Allgemeine deutsche Bibliothek*, Appendix to vols. 25–36, 2021–38. Berlin: Bohn, 1780.

Niehle, Victoria. *Die Poetik der Fülle: Bewältigungsstrategien ästhetischer Überschüsse, 1750–1810*. Göttingen: Vandenhoeck & Ruprecht, 2018.

Nietzsche, Friedrich Wilhelm. *Die Unschuld des Werdens*. Vol. 11 of *Sämtliche Werke*. Stuttgart: A. Kröner, 1964.

Odell, Jenny. *How to Do Nothing: Resisting the Attention Economy*. Brooklyn: Melville House, 2019.

Paetzold, Heinz. *Ästhetik des deutschen Idealismus: Zur Idee ästhetischer Rationalität bei Baumgarten, Kant, Schelling, Hegel und Schopenhauer*. Wiesbaden: F. Steiner, 1983.

Peres, Constanze. "Die Doppelfunktion der Ästhetik im philosophischen System A. G. Baumgartens." In *Schönes Denken: A. G. Baumgarten im Spannungsfeld zwischen Ästhetik, Logik und Ethik*, edited by Andrea Allerkamp and Dagmar Mirbach, 89–116. Hamburg: Meiner, 2016.

Perler, Dominik. "Suárez on the Metaphysics of Habits." In *The Ontology, Psychology and Axiology of Habits (Habitus) in Medieval Philosophy*, edited by Nicolas Faucher and Magali Roques, 7:365–84. Cham: Springer, 2018.

Pfannkuchen, Antje. "A Matter of Visibility: G. Chr. Lichtenberg's Art and Science of Observation." *Configurations* 24, no. 3 (2016): 375–400.

Phillips, Natalie M. *Distraction: Problems of Attention in Eighteenth-Century Literature*. Baltimore: Johns Hopkins University Press, 2016.

Platner, Ernst. *Anthropologie für Aerzte und Weltweise*. Leipzig: Dyck, 1772.

Pomey, François Antoine, ed. *Le grand dictionaire royal*. Frankfurt: Bencard, 1715.
Poovey, Mary. *A History of the Modern Fact: Problems of Knowledge in the Sciences of Wealth and Society*. Chicago: University of Chicago Press, 1998.
Poppe, Bernhard. "Alexander Gottlieb Baumgarten: Seine Bedeutung und Stellung in der Leibniz-Wolffischen Philosophie und seine Beziehungen zu Kant; Nebst Veröffentlichung einer bisher unbekannten Handschrift der Ästhetik Baumgartens." Diss., University of Münster, Westphalia, 1907.
Preisendanz, Wolfgang. "Naturwissenschaft als Provokation der Poesie: Das Beispiel Brockes." In *Frühaufklärung*, edited by Sebastian Neumeister, 469–94. Munich: Fink, 1994.
Rabinbach, Anson. *The Eclipse of the Utopias of Labor*. New York: Fordham University Press, 2018.
Ragland, Clyde Prescott. "Is Descartes a Libertarian?" In *Oxford Studies in Early Modern Philosophy*, edited by Daniel Garber and Steven Nadler, 57–90. Oxford: Oxford University Press, 2006.
Ravaisson, Félix. *Of Habit*. Edited and translated by Clare Carlisle and Mark Sinclair. London: Continuum, 2008.
Reckwitz, Andreas. "Grundelemente einer Theorie sozialer Praktiken." *Zeitschrift für Soziologie*, no. 4 (2003): 282–301.
Reckwitz, Andreas. "Toward a Theory of Social Practices: A Development in Culturalist Theorizing." *European Journal of Social Theory 5*, no. 2 (2002): 243–63.
Rentsch, Thomas. "Paradigma, exemplar." In *Historisches Wörterbuch der Philosophie*, edited by Joachim Ritter, 7:cols. 74–81. Basel: Schwabe, 2007.
Resewitz, Friedrich Gabriel. *Gedanken, Vorschläge und Wünsche zur Verbesserung der öffentlichen Erziehung: Als Materialien zur Pädagogik*. Vol. 2. Berlin: Nicolai, 1777.
Richards, Robert J. "Christian Wolff's Prolegomena to Empirical and Rational Psychology: Translation and Commentary." *Proceedings of the American Philosophical Society* 124, no. 3 (1980): 227–39.
Riley, Matthew. *Musical Listening in the German Enlightenment: Attention, Wonder and Astonishment*. London: Routledge, 2017.
Ritter, Joachim. "Habitus." In *Historisches Wörterbuch der Philosophie*, 3:1120–23. Basel: Schwabe, 2007.
Ritter, Joachim. "Landschaft: Zur Funktion des ästhetischen in der modernen Gesellschaft." In *Subjektivität: Sechs Aufsätze*, 141–63. Frankfurt am Main: Suhrkamp, 1989.
Ritter, Joachim. "Subjekt/Objekt; subjektiv/objektiv." In *Historisches Wörterbuch der Philosophie*, 10:407–8. Basel: Schwabe, 2007.
Rogers, K. *The Attention Complex: Media, Archeology, Method*. New York: Palgrave Macmillan, 2014.
Rorty, Richard. *Philosophy and the Mirror of Nature*. Princeton, NJ: Princeton University Press, 1979.

Rosa, Hartmut. *Resonanz: Eine Soziologie der Weltbeziehung*. Berlin: Suhrkamp, 2016.
Rössler, Reto. "Weltgebäude/Mögliche Welt: 'Gedanckenreisen' der Aufklärung." In *Versteckt—Verirrt—Verschollen: Reisen und Nichtwissen*, edited by Irina Gradinari, Dorit Müller, and Johannes Pause. Wiesbaden: Reichert, 2015.
Rousseau, Jean-Jacques. *Émile, Or, On Education: Includes Emile and Sophie, Or, The Solitaries*. Hanover, NH: University Press of New England, 2010.
Rumore, Paola. "Empirical Psychology." In *Handbuch Christian Wolff*, edited by Robert Theis and Alexander Aichele, 175–96. Wiesbaden: Springer, 2018.
Saint-Jure, Jean-Baptiste. *Erkandtnuß und Liebe Deß Sohns GOttes, unsers HErrn JESU CHRISTI, Zu vollkommener Erleuchtung, und hertzlicher Anflammung aller Christliebenden Seelen, nicht allein geist- sondern auch weltlichen Stands: Vorderst aber allen Predigern und Seelsorgern, fast nutz- und dienstlich*. Würzburg: Endters, 1692.
Sales, Francis de. *A Treatise of the Love of God*. Translated by Miles Carr. Doway: Coleyn, 1630.
Schiller, Friedrich. "Philosophie der Physiologie." In *Schiller's Werke: Kleinere prosaische Schriften*, edited by Wendelin von Maltzahn, 14:85–104. Berlin: Hempel, 1879.
Schiller, Friedrich. *Über die ästhetische Erziehung des Menschen*. Edited by Stefan Matuschek. Frankfurt am Main: Suhrkamp, 2009.
Schmidt, Gunnar. "Leeuwenhoek. Medienlogik und Wissen im 17. und frühen 18. Jahrhundert." *KulturPoetik* 2, no. 1 (2002): 1–23.
Schmidt, Siegfried J. "Aufmerksamkeit: Die Währung der Medien." In *Aufmerksamkeiten*, edited by Aleida Assmann and Jan Assmann, 183–96. Munich: Fink, 2001.
Scholz, Joachim. "Aufmerksamkeit im Schulmännerdiskurs der Sattelzeit." In *Aufmerksamkeit*, 35–54. Wiesbaden: Springer, 2015.
Schroer, Markus. "Soziologie der Aufmerksamkeit." *KZfSS: Kölner Zeitschrift für Soziologie und Sozialpsychologie* 66, no. 2 (June 13, 2014): 193–218.
Schwaiger, Clemens. *Alexander Gottlieb Baumgarten—Ein intellektuelles Porträt: Studien zur Metaphysik und Ethik von Kants Leitautor*. Stuttgart: Frommann-Holzboog, 2011.
Schwaiger, Clemens. "Wolff, Christian (Von)." In *The Dictionary of Eighteenth-Century German Philosophers*, edited by Heiner F. Klemme and Manfred Kuehn. New York: Oxford University Press, 2011. https://www.oxfordreference.com/view/10.1093/acref/9780199797097.001.0001/acref-9780199797097-e-0636.
Schweizer, Hans Rudolf. *Ästhetik als Philosophie der sinnlichen Erkenntnis*. Basel: Schwabe, 1973.
Seel, Martin. *Ästhetik des Erscheinens*. Munich: Hanser, 2000.
Seitter, Walter. "Aufmerksamkeitskorrelate auf der Ebene der Erscheiungen." In *Aufmerksamkeiten*, edited by Aleida Assmann and Jan Assmann, 171–82. Munich: Fink, 2001.

Senebier, Jean. *Die Kunst zu beobachten*. Translated by Johann Friedrich Gmelin. Vol. 1. Leipzig: Weygand, 1776.
Shields, Ross. "Zusammenhang (Nexus)." *Goethe-Lexicon of Philosophical Concepts* 1, no. 1 (January 31, 2021): 121–40.
Simon, Herbert A. "Designing Organizations for an Information-Rich World." In *Computers, Communications, and the Public Interest*, edited by Martin Greenberg, 38–52. Baltimore: Johns Hopkins University Press, 1971.
Singy, Patrick. "Huber's Eyes: The Art of Scientific Observation before the Emergence of Positivism." *Representations* 95, no. 1 (2006): 54–75.
Sluhovsky, Moshe. "Loyola's Spiritual Exercises and the Modern Self." In *A Companion to Ignatius of Loyola*, 216–31. Boston: Brill, 2014.
Solms, Friedhelm. *Disciplina aesthetica: Zur Frühgeschichte der ästhetischen Theorie bei Baumgarten und Herder*. Stuttgart: Klett-Cotta, 1990.
Spinoza, Benedictus de. *The Collected Works of Spinoza*. Edited and translated by Edwin Curley. Vol. 1. Princeton, NJ: Princeton University Press, 1985.
Spinoza, Benedictus de. *De nagelate schriften van B.D.S.: Als Zedekunst, Staatkunde, Verbetering van 't verstant, Brieven en Antwoorden*. [Amsterdam: Rieuwertsz], 1677.
Spinoza, Benedictus de. *Opera posthuma*. Amsterdam: Rieuwertsz, 1677.
Spivak, Gayatri Chakravorty. *An Aesthetic Education in the Era of Globalization*. Cambridge, MA: Harvard University Press, 2012.
Stadler, Ulrich. *Der technisierte Blick: Optische Instrumente und der Status von Literatur—Ein kulturhistorisches Museum*. Würzburg: Königshausen & Neumann, 2003.
Steigerwald, Jörn. "Die Normalisierung des Menschen: Eine anthropologiegeschichtliche Problemskizze der Mesmerdiskussion des Jahres 1784." In *Reiz, Imagination, Aufmerksamkeit: Erregung und Steuerung von Einbildungskraft im klassischen Zeitalter, 1680–1830*, edited by Jörn Steigerwald and Daniela Watzke, 13–39. Würzburg: Königshausen & Neumann, 2003.
Steigerwald, Jörn, ed. *Reiz, Imagination, Aufmerksamkeit: Erregung und Steuerung von Einbildungskraft im klassischen Zeitalter, 1680–1830*. Würzburg: Königshausen & Neumann, 2003.
Steinmann, Holger. *Absehen–Wissen–Glauben: Physikotheologie und Rhetorik, 1665–1747*. Berlin: Kadmos, 2008.
Stiegler, Bernard. *Taking Care of Youth and the Generations*. Stanford, CA: Stanford University Press, 2010.
Stingelin, Martin. "'Unser Schreibzeug arbeitet mit an unseren Gedanken.'" In *Schreiben als Kulturtechnik*, edited by Sandro Zanetti, 283–304. Frankfurt am Main: Suhrkamp, 2012.
Taylor, Dan. "Nature." In *Spinoza and the Politics of Freedom*, 40–64. Edinburgh: Edinburgh University Press, 2022.
Theis, Robert, and Alexander Aichele. *Handbuch Christian Wolff*. Wiesbaden: Springer, 2018.
Thiel, Udo. *The Early Modern Subject: Self-Consciousness and Personal Identity from Descartes to Hume*. Oxford: Oxford University Press, 2014.

Thomasius, Christian. *Ausübung der Sittenlehre.* Edited by Werner Schneiders. Hildesheim: Olms, 1968. Reprint of first edition, 1696.
Thomasius, Christian. *Liber de remedio amoris irratationalis, et praevia necessaria notitia sui, sive praxis philosophiae moralis, cum appendice, in qua Autor multiplicem usum Ethices suae ostendit, & de intellectu suo de Ethica Christiana sinceram Confessionem edit.* Halle (Saale): Renger, 1706.
Thomasius, Christian. *Von der Artzney wider die unvernünftige Liebe und der zuvorher nöthigen Erkäntniß Sein Selbst. Oder: Ausübung der Sitten-Lehre, nebt einem Beschluß, worinnen der Autor den vielfältigen Nutzen seiner Sitten-Lehre zeiget, und von seinem Begriff der Christlichen Sitten-Lehre ein auffrichtiges Bekäntniß thut.* Halle: Christoph Salfelds Wittwe und Erben, 1704.
Thums, Barbara. *Aufmerksamkeit: Wahrnehmung und Selbstbegründung von Brockes bis Nietzsche.* Munich: Fink, 2008.
Thums, Barbara. "Aufmerksamkeit: Zur Ästhetisierung eines anthropologischen Paradigmas im 18. Jahrhundert." In *Reiz, Imagination, Aufmerksamkeit: Erregung und Steuerung von Einbildungskraft im klassischen Zeitalter, 1680–1830,* edited by Jörn Steigerwald and Daniela Watzke. Würzburg: Königshausen & Neumann, 2003.
Thums, Barbara. "Die schwierige Kunst der 'Selbsterkenntnis–Selbstbeherrschung–Selbstbelebung': Aufmerksamkeit als Kulturtechnik der Moderne." In *Ästhetische Erfindung der Moderne? Perspektiven und Modelle, 1750–1850,* edited by Britta Herrmann and Barbara Thums, 139–63. Würzburg: Königshausen & Neumann, 2003.
Torra-Mattenklott, Caroline. *Metaphorologie der Rührung: Ästhetische Theorie und Mechanik im 18. Jahrhundert.* Munich: Fink, 2002.
Trop, Gabriel. "Aesthetic Askesis: Aesthetics as a Technology of the Self in the Philosophy of Alexander Baumgarten." *Das Achtzehnte Jahrhundert* 37, no. 1 (2013): 56–73.
Trop, Gabriel. *Poetry as a Way of Life: Aesthetics and Askesis in the German Eighteenth Century.* Evanston: Northwestern University Press, 2015.
Uexküll, Jakob von. *Streifzüge durch die Umwelten von Tieren und Menschen: Ein Bilderbuch unsichtbarer Welten.* Hamburg: Rowohlt, 1956.
Vidal, Fernando. *The Sciences of the Soul: The Early Modern Origins of Psychology.* Translated by Saskia Brown. Chicago: University of Chicago Press, 2011.
Vogl, Joseph. "Medien-Werden: Galileis Fernrohr." *Archiv für Mediengeschichte* 1, no. 1 (2001): 115–23.
Wagner-Egelhaaf, Martina. "Gott und die Welt im Perspektiv des Poeten: Zur Medialität der literarischen Wahrnehmung am Beispiel Barthold Heinrich Brockes." *Deutsche Vierteljahrsschrift für Literaturwissenschaft und Geistesgeschichte* 71, no. 2 (June 1997): 183–216.
Waldenfels, Bernhard. *Phänomenologie der Aufmerksamkeit.* Frankfurt am Main: Suhrkamp, 2004.
Wankhammer, Johannes. "Wurzel." In *Pflanzen: Kulturwissenschaftliches Handbuch,* edited by Joela Jacobs and Isabel Kranz. Stuttgart: Metzler, 2024 [forthcoming].

Weber, Max. "Basic Sociological Terms." In *Economy and Society*, translated by Guenther Roth and Claus Wittich, 3–62. Berkeley: University of California Press, 1968.
Weber, Max. *Soziologische Grundbegriffe*. 3rd edition. Tübingen: Mohr, 1976.
Weikard, Melchior Adam. *Der philosophische Arzt*. Vol. 3. New, expanded and improved edition. Frankfurt am Main: Andreäische Buchhandlung, 1799.
Weikard, Melchior Adam. *Der philosophische Arzt*. Vol. 4. Berlin: n.p., 1777.
Wellbery, David E. *Lessing's Laocoon: Semiotics and Aesthetics in the Age of Reason*. Cambridge: Cambridge University Press, 1984.
Wellbery, David. "Stimmung." In *Ästhetische Grundbegriffe*, edited by Karlheinz Barck, Martin Fontius, Dieter Schlenstedt, Burkhart Steinwachs, and Friedrich Wolfzettel, 5:703–33. Stuttgart: Metzler, 2010.
Welle, Florian. *Der irdische Blick durch das Fernrohr: Literarische Wahrnehmungsexperimente vom 17. bis zum 20. Jahrhundert*. Würzburg: Königshausen & Neumann, 2009.
Welsch, Wolfgang. *Ästhetisches Denken*. Stuttgart: Reclam, 1990.
Welsch, Wolfgang. "Schiller Revisited: 'Beauty Is Freedom in Appearance'—Aesthetics as a Challenge to the Modern Way of Thinking." *Contemporary Aesthetics* 12 (2014). http://hdl.handle.net/2027/spo.7523862.0012.016.
Wilczek, Markus. "Ab. Lichtenberg's Waste." *Germanic Review: Literature, Culture, Theory* 87, no. 4 (November 1, 2012): 305–24.
Williams, James. *Stand out of Our Light: Freedom and Resistance in the Attention Economy*. Cambridge: Cambridge University Press, 2018.
Williams, Mark, and Danny Penman. *Mindfulness: An Eight-Week Plan for Finding Peace in a Frantic World*. Reprint. Emmaus, PA: Rodale Books, 2012.
Wilson, Catherine. "Discourses of Vision in Seventeenth-Century Metaphysics." In *Sites of Vision: The Discursive Construction of Sight in the History of Philosophy*, edited by David Michael Levin, 117–38. Cambridge, MA: MIT Press, 1997.
Wolff, Christian. *Allerhand nützliche Versuche, dadurch zu genauer Erkäntnis der Natur und Kunst der Weg gebähnet wird*. 3 vols. Vol. 3. Hildesheim: Olms, 1982.
Wolff, Christian. *Philosophia moralis sive ethica*. Vol. 1. Halle: Renger, 1750.
Wolff, Christian. *Philosophia prima, sive ontologia, methodo scientifica pertractata, qua omnis cognitionis humanae principia continentur*. Frankfurt: Renger, 1736.
Wolff, Christian. *Philosophia rationalis, sive, Logica: Methodo scientifica pertractata et ad usum scientiarum atque vitae aptata: praemittitur discursus praeliminaris de philosophia in genere*. Frankfurt: Renger, 1732.
Wolff, Christian. *Preliminary Discourse on Philosophy in General*. Translated by Richard J. Blackwell. Indianapolis: Bobbs-Merrill, 1963.
Wolff, Christian. *Psychologia empirica*. Edited by Jean École. Hildesheim: Olms, 1968. Reprint of the 1738 edition.
Wolff, Christian. *Psychologia rationalis*. Edited by Jean École. Hildesheim: Olms, 1972. Reprint of the 1740 edition.

Wolff, Christian. *Vernünfftige Gedancken von Gott, der Welt und der Seele des Menschen, auch allen Dingen überhaupt*. Edited by Charles A. Corr. Hildesheim: Olms, 1983. Reprint of the 1751 edition. Cited as *German Metaphysics*.

Wolff, Christian. *Vernünfftige Gedancken von der Menschen Thun und Lassen: Zu Beförderung ihrer Glückseeligkeit, den Liebhabern der Wahrheit mitgetheilet*. Frankfurt and Leipzig: Renger, 1723.

Wollstonecraft, Mary. *A Vindication of the Rights of Woman: With Strictures on Political and Moral Subjects*. Vol. 1. London: J. Johnson, 1792.

Wunderlich, Falk. "Die wolffianische Schulphilosophie." In *Kant und die Bewußtseinstheorien des 18. Jahrhunderts*, 18–46. Berlin: De Gruyter, 2005.

Wunderlich, Falk. "Kant on Consciousness of Objects and Consciousness of the Self." In *Immanuel Kant: Die Einheit des Bewusstseins*, 164–80. Berlin: De Gruyter, 2017.

Youpa, Andrew. "Descartes's Virtue Theory." *Essays in Philosophy* 14, no. 2 (2013): 179–93.

Yvon, Claude and Johann Heinrich Samuel Formey. "Attention." In *Encyclopédie, ou Dictionnaire raisonné des sciences, des arts et des métiers*, edited by Denis Diderot and Jean le Rond d'Alembert, 1:840. Paris: Briasson, 1772.

Zedler, Johann Heinrich, ed. "Zusammenhang der Dinge." In *Grosses vollständiges Universal-Lexicon aller Wissenschafften und Künste*, 64:567–87. Leipzig, 1750.

Zelle, Carsten. "Das Erhabene in der deutschen Frühaufklärung: Zum Einfluss der englischen Physikotheologie auf Barthold Heinrich Brockes' Irdisches Vergnügen in Gott." *Arcadia: Internationale Zeitschrift für Literaturwissenschaft* 25, no. 3 (1990): 225–40.

Zelle, Carsten. "Experiment, Observation, Self-Observation." *Early Science and Medicine* 18, no. 4–5 (January 1, 2013): 453–70.

Zuboff, Shoshana. *The Age of Surveillance Capitalism: The Fight for a Human Future at the New Frontier of Power*. London: Profile Books, 2019.

INDEX

Note: Illustrations are indicated by page numbers in *italics*.

Abhandlung über den Ursprung der Sprache (Treatise on the origin of language) (Herder), 138
Absonderliche, 168–69, 169n40
abstraction, 147
   aesthetics and, 222–25, 227, 235–36, 238–39, 252–53, 256–57
   in Bacon, 46, 48
   in Baumgarten, 19, 148, 148n135, 209, 222–23, 235–38
   in Breitinger, 192
   in Descartes, 55–56
   in Kant, 148, 148n135, 150
   poetics and, 191, 191n87, 192
   in Wolff, 97, 121, 137, 191, 191n87, 192n88
ADHD. *See* attention-deficit/hyperactivity disorder (ADHD)

Adorno, Theodor, 253, 255–56, 279, 291n30
Aesthetica (Baumgarten), 118n66, 201–3, 204n9, 233–40, 256, 261, 264, 266
aesthetics, 37–38, 203, 211–12, 239–40
   abstraction and, 222–25, 227, 235–36, 238–39, 252–53, 256–57
   in Baumgarten, 208–16, 250–74, 276–77
   clarity and, 201–2, 207, 213, 215–16, 220. *See also* extensive clarity
   of connectivity, 250–56
   determinacy and, 239–43, 253–56
   epistemology and, 242–43
   exercises of attention, 256–60

324   Index

aesthetics (*continued*)
   freedom and, 239–40, 241n91
   indeterminacy and, 239–43, 265n153
   in Kant, 235–36, 254–55
   Leibniz and, 216–20, 243–50, 244n100
   life of mind and, 266–71
   media theory and, 210–12, 272
   morality and, 205n13, 269
   nexus-thinking and, 250–56
   perception and, 198, 221–22, 242, 251–54, 267
   power and, 204–5
   representation and, 176n57, 237
   rhetoric and, 158, 203n8, 211–12
   as science of sensate cognition, 203, 208–9, 211–12
   semblance and, 271–74
   soul and, 260–66
   truth and, 234–38, 237n86, 271–74
alienation, 48n20, 53, 122, 292, 294
Anthropology from a Pragmatic Point of View (Kant), 148
apperception, 104, 117–18, 147–48, 165, 170, 172, 196, 220n44, 235, 290
Arbeit, 279, 289–95
Aristotle, 1, 1n1, 26, 46, 65, 90, 109n45, 158n17, 168n38, 173n46, 211. *See also* scholasticism
Arndt, Johann, 108n43
art, 38, 144, *181*, 187, 193, 202–3, 204n10, 249–50, 254, 270–71
asceticism, 108n43, 109, 122n73
attention
   18th century regime of, 7–10
   active vs. passive, 22, 33, 35–36, 87, 117–19, 149–50, 154, 158, 174, 201, 209. *See also* attention, voluntary vs. involuntary
   to attention, 32, 97–104
   in Bacon, 45–50, 89
   in Baumgarten, 220, 222–27, 229–30, 232
   in Brockes, 159–67
   capacity-limitation theories of, 10–11
   as cultural technique, 9n18, 15, 24–26
   definition of things and, 19–22
   degrees of, 106–7, 120n70
   in Descartes, 54–58, 60–62, 62n44, 64–74, 76–78, 80–83, 89–91
   economies of, 295–99
   education and, 95
   education of, 86–89, 146
   emergence of, as concept, 2, 92–93
   exercises of, 106–113, 116n62, 120–21, 146, 256–60. *See also* spiritual exercises
   experience and, 3, 101
   as faculty, 28, 39, 104–13
   as gender performance, 230–33
   habit and, 14–17, 66–72, 159–67, 289
   habits of, 64–75, 166–67
   intensive and extensive, 38, 202, 224–26, 228–33, 258. *See also* extensive clarity
   intellectual labors of, 289–95
   involuntary. *See* attention, voluntary vs. involuntary
   judgment and, 67–69, 76, 209–10
   in Kant, 146–48
   in Lichtenberg, 279–89
   manual labors of, 289–95
   in Marx, 293–95
   as mediator, 102
   in Meier, 257n135
   as metahistorical device, 21n48
   in Moritz, 281
   observation and, 30–31, 93n2, 210
   proper, 6, 28
   receptive side of, 100–101, 291n30, 285
   refocusing, 42–45
   representation and, 53–64
   scientific, 21n48
   selective perception and, 9–14, 21, 28, 170–71, 196–97, 237
   sustained, 53, 106–7
   training of, 127–28, 146
   will and, 75–83. *See also* attention, voluntary vs. involuntary

in Wolff, 97–113, *107*, 298–99
wonder and, 32–35, 86–89, 158, 162–63, 213–14
voluntary vs. involuntary, 22, 32–33, 37, 77–78, 82, 87–88, 90–91, 95, *107*, 111–12, 119, 134, 145–46, 150, 154, 158, 174, 213, 222n48, 298
attention deficit, 4–7
Attention-deficit/hyperactivity disorder (ADHD), 5
Aufmerksamkeit, 10, 15, 29, 92–93, 93n2, 151, 160, 220
Ausübung der Sittenlehre (Practice of ethics) (Thomasius), 15
autocracy, 142–45
autonomy, 2–3, 37, 77, 119–24, 142–51

Bacon, Francis, 3, 13, 39–40, 45–50, 46n12, 51–53, 54n28, 89, 211, 284
Balling, Pieter, 131
Basedow, Johann Bernhard, 37, 95, 127, *128*
Baumgarten, Alexander, 3, 22, 22n49, 24, 31–32, 38, 176n57
  aesthetics in, 208–16, 250–74, 276–77
  Bacon and, 211
  Breitinger vs., 198
  clarity in, 221–30, 224n51, 233–39
  connectivity in, 250–56
  Descartes and, 199–201, 213
  gender performance and, 230–33
  genesis of aesthetics of, 208–12
  inspiration in, 260–63
  Kant and, 148n135, 202n4
  Meier and, 207–8
  morality and, 205n13, 269
  pedagogy and, 125–27
  perception in, 201–2, 211–12, 221–22, 229, 229n62, 242, 251–54, 258–59, 273–74
  soul in, 260–66, 260n143
  subject/object terminology and, 118n66, 203–4
  wonder in, 212–16

beauty, 87, 173–74, 211–12, 234, 240n89, 254n125, 257n135
Beiser, Fred, 248–49, 249n110, 298
Benjamin, Walter, 2, 15n39, 17n42, 277
Benveniste, Émile, 271n165
Beobachtung, 93n2
Berger, John, 155, 155n6
Berndt, Frauke, 203n8, 206, 206n14, 212, 212n29, 213n31, 225, 225n54
"Bewährtes Mittel für die Augen" (Brockes), 165n31
Bildung, 124–30, 289–95, 291n31
Blake, William, 173, 273–74
Blumenberg, Hans, 11, 18, 51n26, 186, 186n77, 187, 193–94
Bodmer, Johann Jakob, 156–57, 156n12, 157n13
Bonnet, Charles, 31n71, 144n128
Bourdieu, Pierre, 24n55
Boyle, Robert, 44n7, 211n26
Brecht, Bertolt, 2, 177
Breitinger, Johann Jakob, 15–16, 20, 37, 153–59, 156n12, 167–78, 173n46, 183, 188–90, 188n80, 192–98, 273
Brockes, Barthold Heinrich, 13, 13n30, 16, 16n40, 37, 152–59, 152n1, 155n8, 156n10, 161n23, 173–74, 179–87, 195–97
Buchenau, Stephanie, 206, 206n14, 234n72, 240n90
Butler, Judith, 24n55

camera obscura, 57–59, 65, 74, *81*, 164, 168, 191Campe, Joachim Heinrich, 37, 95, 127–29, 137n106
Campe, Rüdiger, 203n8, 224, 226, 256, 256n131
Capital (Marx), 293
Carr, Thomas M., 64–65
Cassirer, Ernst, 36, 59, 187–88, 193–94, 203
Chardin, Jean-Baptiste-Siméon, 62–64, *63*

Chodowiecki, Daniel, 127
clarification (of ideas), 87–88, 204, 213, 216–228, 232
clarity, 201–2, 207, 213, 215–16, 220–30, 223n49, 224n51, 233–39. *See also* extensive clarity
clear and distinct knowledge, 19, 27–31, 36, 56–59, 62, 68, 76, 114, 171, 174, 218–19, 230. *See also* clarification (of ideas)
coercion, 121n73
compatibilism, 77n71
Confucianism, 96n8
connectivity, aesthetics of, 250–56
consciousness, 117n64, 132–33, 145, 147–50, 217, 241, 245–46, 260–61
contemplation, 55, 62, 87, 93n2, 150, 274–75
contingency, 14–15, 19, 186, 260
Copernicus, Nicolaus, 51, 154, 275
Crary, Jonathan, 8–9, 9n17–9n18, 23, 58–59, 106n38, 141n122, 164n28, 197, 283n13, 295
Critique of Judgment (Kant), 150, 239, 254–55, 254n125
Critique of Pure Reason (Kant), 146–47, 287
Critische Dichtkunst (Critical poetics) (Breitinger), 15–16, 156–57, 159, 167–72, 176, 177n60, 188, 193–95, 197
culturalist theories, 24n55
cultural techniques, 9n18, 23n52, 24

d'Alembert, Jean le Rond, 31, 94, 96n8
Daston, Lorraine, 9n18, 21n48, 43–45, 43n6, 44n8, 175
De anima (Aristole), 1
decorum, 15–16, 15n35.
defamiliarization, 53, 159, 163, 172–80
deficit of attention, 4–7, 59–60
degrees, of attention, 106–7, 120n70
delight, 162–63. *See also* marvel; wonder
de Man, Paul, 166n33, 203n8, 233
de Salle, Francis, 110

Descartes, René, 3, 19, 27, 32–36, 39–41, 54–83, 55n30, 62n44, 89–91, 118, 144–45, 199–201, 213
Diderot, Denis, 94
difference, anthropological, 134–42
discipline, 44n8, 45, 119–24, 121n73, 125–26, 128–29, 204–5, 241n91, 259, 291, 298. *See also* attention, training of
Discipline and Punish (Foucault), 22, 119, 123
discovery, 162–63
disgust, 111–13
distraction, 12–13, 32, 43n4, 64, 88, 107, 108n41, 127–30, 128, 140, 148–49, 168, 224, 227
dualism, 32, 36, 40–41, 133, 220n43, 249n110
Dubos, Jean-Baptiste, 173n46

Eagleton, Terry, 203
Eckhart, Meister, 109
economy of attention, 11n24, 295–99
education. *See also* pedagogy
  of attention, 86–89
  attention and, 95
  of attentiveness, poetry as, 152–98
  discipline and, 128–29
  distraction and, 127–29, *128*, 129–30
  judgment and, 150–51
  monastic, 124, *125*
  self-discipline and, 125–26
Einleitung zu der Vernunfft-Lehre (Introduction to logic) (Thomasius), 93n3
Elisabeth of the Palatinate, 78, 78n74
enargeia, 158, 158n17, 174, 269n159
Encyclopédie, 94, 96
energeia, 158, 158n17, 174, 269n159
Enlightenment, 2, 9n18, 25, 29, 38, 145
Enzyklopädie der philosophischen Wissenschaften (Encyclopedia of the philosophical sciences) (Hegel), 289–90

epistemology, 27–28, 30, 45, 53–54, 65, 154, 156–58, 165–66, 174, 186, 242–43
Erfahrungseelenkunde (Empirical psychology) (journal), 95
Essai analytique sur les facultés de l'ame (Bonnet), 31n71
estrangement, poetic, 176–77. See also defamiliarization
evidentia, 155, 158, 158n17, 168, 176
Exercitia spiritualia (Ignatius of Loyola), 42–43, 42n4
Expression of the Passions, The (Le Brun), 33, 34
extensive clarity, 201, 207, 213, 221–30. See also clarification

fashion, 15n39
Forster, Michael, 137–38
Foucault, Michel, 22, 29, 36, 59, 73n65, 103, 104n29, 119–24, 121n73, 122n75, 164n28, 205, 256
Francke, August Hermann, 126
Franke, Ursula, 249, 266n154
freedom, 36, 77n71, 88, 144–45, 150, 239–40, 241n91, 277
Frege, Gottlob, 7
Freud, Sigmund, 38, 132n93, 133
Fried, Michael, 62–64

Garve, Christian, 287
Gasché, Rodolphe, 147–48, 147n135, 148n135
"Gedancken über ein Perspecktiv" (Thoughts on perspective) (Brockes), 179–80
gender performance, attention as, 230–33
Genest, Charles-Claude, 164
German Idealism, 183, 250
German Metaphysics (Wolff), 93, 117n64
German Romanticism, 239n87, 263
Giddens, Anthony, 24n55
Goethe, Johann Wolfgang von, 205, 278

Gottsched, Johann Christoph, 156n12, 188n80, 193n90
Greenblatt, Stephen, 14n32
Grote, Simon, 142n124, 206, 206n14, 260n142, 269, 269n160

Habermas, Jürgen, 239n87
habit, 16–17, 64–75, 71n62, 108n45, 154, 159–67, 172–73
Hadot, Pierre, 24, 42, 108n45, 122n75, 256
Hagner, Michael, 9n18, 13n29, 17, 66, 124
Haller, Albrecht von, 143, 144n128, 157
Handke, Peter, 17
Hatfield, Gary, 6, 68n58, 75n67, 223n49
Hegel, Georg Wilhelm Friedrich, 30, 134n97, 252, 253n123, 279, 289–93, 291n31, 292n32
Heidegger, Martin, 204n10, 236, 263n149
Henrich, Dieter, 116
Herder, Johann Gottfried, 95, 138–41, 138n112, 146, 205, 231, 265, 265n153
Hermann, Hans Peter, 156n12
héxis, 65, 109n45. See also habit
Hippocrates, 244
historicism, 206
horror, 112–13
How to Do Nothing: Resisting the Attention Economy (Odell), 298–99
Husserl, Edmund, 225

Idealism, German, 183, 250
idols, in Bacon, 50, 50n24
Ignatius of Loyola, 42–43, 42n4, 54, 108n43, 109
imagination, 131–33, 132n94, 133–34, 150n140, 156
imitation, of nature, 157, 172, 187–95, 273
incompatibilism, 77n71
indifference, 108–12, 116, 259, 264
innovation, 14–17

inspiration, 260–63
intermediary, attention as. 41, 50, 89–90, 102, 144
involuntary attention, 32, 37, 82, 88, 90, 119, 154, 158, 213, 222n48. *See also* attention, voluntary vs. involuntary
Ion (Plato), 270
Irdisches Vergnügen in Gott (Earthly delight in God) (Brockes), 152–53, 152n1, 153n3, 154–55, 156n10, 159–60, 180
irritability, 144n128
Irwing, Karl, 138n112

James, William, 3, 94
Jardin, Lisa, 45–46
judgment, 36, 54, 67–69, 76, 150–51, 209–10

Kafka, Franz, 136n105
Kant, Immanuel, 3, 134n97, 154, 202n4, 205
  abstraction in, 148n135
  aesthetics in, 235–36, 239, 241, 241n91, 254–55
  apperception in, 290
  Baumgarten and, 203, 230–31
  beauty in, 254n125
  de Man and, 233
  disgust in, 111
  freedom in, 277
  Lichtenberg and, 287–88
  maturity in, 230
  Menke and, 241n91
  perception in, 147–48, 268
  transcendentalism in, 150n140
  Wolff and, 94–95, 146–51
  women in, 231–32
Kircher, Athanasius, 58
Kittler, Friedrich, 184n72
Klemme, Heiner, 143
Kristeva, Julia, 112
Kuhn, Thomas, 286
"Kunst vernünftig sehen zu lernen, Die" (The art of learning to see rationally) (Brockes), 166–67

Langen, August, 154–55, 165, 165
Laporte, Jean, 65–66, 76n70, 77n72, 80n79
Late Capitalism and the Ends of Sleep (Crary), 141n122
Latour, Bruno, 24n55
Lavater, J. K., 134n97
Le Brun, Charles, 33–35, 33n76, *34*
Leibniz, Gottfried, 3, 59, 192, 194, 205, 216–20, 243–50
  aesthetics and, 216–20, 243–50, 244n100
  apperception in, 220n44, 235n75
  attention in, 19–22, 220
  Breitinger and, 187
  perception in, *165*, 170n42, 245–47, 246n103–246n104, 262n147, 263, 263n150
  perfection in, 272n166
  soul in, 114, 261–62
  Wolff and, 96, 98, 134, 189–90
lens technology, 17–19, 175n51, 210
Lessing, Gotthold Ephraim, 12, 166, 203, 281–82, 282n8
Lichtenberg, Georg Christoph, 30, 279–89
liveliness, 268–70
Locke, John, 58–59, 183, 272
Luhmann, Niklas, 13n31, 195

Makropoulos, Michael, 14
Malebranche, Nicolas, 87–88, 134
marvel, 153–54, 157, 172–79, 183, 214. *See also* wonder
Marx, Karl, 122, 140, 279, 289, 293–95, 293n33
Mauss, Marcel, 23, 23n52
meditation, 43. *See also* attention and media theory
Meditationes philosophicae de nonnullis ad poema pertinentibus (Philosophical meditations on some matters concerning the poem) (Baumgarten), 201, 212–13, 216, 240

Meditations on First Philosophy (Descartes), 54–55, 66–67, 71–72, 75, 84, 199
"Meditations on Knowledge, Truth, and Ideas" (Leibniz), 19–20, 216–17
Meier, Georg Friedrich, 9n17, 207nn15,17, 207–8, 216n37, 228n61, 231, 257n135, 270n164
Menke, Christoph, 204–5, 241, 241n91, 256, 259–60, 264–66, 264n153, 266n154
mentalisms, 24n55
Mersenne, Marin, 65
Metaphysica (Baumgarten), 118n66, 201, 204n9, 216, 220–30, 222n48, 231, 267
Mirbach, Dagmar, 211n27, 238n86, 269n160
"Mittel gegen die Unachtsamkeit" (Measures against inattention) (Brockes), 161–63, 163n27
Monadology (Leibniz), 19n46, 242n93, 243–45, 273
monads, 19, 243–47, 244n100, 245–49, 246n104, 248n109, 265–66, 273, 273n171
Montag, Warren, 132n93
Montaigne, Michel de, 182n68
moral philosophy, 142–45
Moritz, Karl Philipp, 95, 203, 278, 281
multitasking, *107*, 108

Neoplatonism, 87, 173n46, 174
New Organon (Bacon), 45–50, 89, 211
nexus rerum (nexus of things), 250–56, 251n117
Nietzsche, Friedrich, 140, 279
note, taking, 28–29
Novalis, 278–79
novelty, 15n39, 16, 175–78, 197, 284

observatio, 93n2
observation, 30–31, 108–9, 160, 186, 282–84, 283n14
observational poetry, 159–60
Odell, Jenny, 298–99

Order of Things, The (Foucault), 22, 73n65
ostranenie, 177

painting, poetic, 157, 167–68
passions, 33–35, *34*, 154, 176
Passions of the Soul (Descartes), 78–79, 82, 86–87
pedagogy, 124–30, 145
perception
 adherent, 268
 aesthetics and, 198, 221–22, 242, 251–54, 267
 apperception *vs.*, 165
 in Bacon, 47–49, 48n21
 in Baumgarten, 201–2, 211–12, 221–22, 229, 229n62, 242, 251–54, 258–59, 273–74
 in Blake, 273–74
 Brockes and, 154–55, 160
 clear and distinct. *See* clear and distinct knowledge
 complex, 229, 229n62
 confused, 217–218, 221–22, 228, 229n63, 244
 contingencies of, 179–87
 in Descartes, 67–68, 74–75, *81*, 84
 habituated attention and, 154
 in Kant, 147–48, 268
 in Leibniz, 217, 245–47, 246n103–246n104, 262n147, 263, 263n150
 poetry and, 154–55, 155n6, 160–63, *165*, 170, 177, 179–87
 representation and, 177
 seeing, 154–55, 155n6, 161–63
 selective, 10–14, 170
 in Wolff, 105–6, 113–14, 117–18
perfectibility, 134–42
Phenomenology of Spirit (Hegel), 292
Phillips, Natalie, 7n13, 9n18, 64, 108n41
Philosophia moralis (Wolff), 134–35
physicotheology, 155, 155n9
Pietists, 96n8, 118n66, 125–26, 208, 260, 260n142, 269, 269n160
pineal gland, 78–80, *79*
Platner, Ernst, 138n112, 143, 144n128

Plato, 13, 13n30, 270–71
Platonism, 87, 174
poetry and poetics, 16, 37
   apperception and, 170, 172
   in Baumgarten, 211–16, 221
   defamiliarization and, 177, 180
   didactic, 159n18
   as education of attentiveness, 152–98
   epistemology and, 157–58, 174, 186
   estrangement and, 176–77
   evidentia and, 155, 158, 168, 176
   of knowledge, 155n8
   marvel and, 153–54, 157, 172–79, 183
   novelty and, 175–78
   observational, 159–60
   perception and, 154–55, 155n6, 160–63, *165*, 170, 177, 179–87
   poetic license, 157
   poetic painting, 157, 167–68
   representation and, 168, 170–79, 187–95
   rhetoric and, 157–58
   scientific knowledge and, 45n8
   seeing and, 154–55, 161–63
   signification and, 29–30
   wonder and, 87, 162–64, 212–16
post-structuralism, 24n55, 148, 239, 239n87
Practices of Enlightenment, The (Mücke), 43n5, 108n43
practice theory, 22–27, 24n55, 26n60, 42, 71, 82–83, 241n91
pragmatism, 145–51
Preisendanz, Wolfgang, 160n21
prejudice, 13, 36, 49, 283–84
Preliminary Discourse on Philosophy in General (Wolff), 100
presence of mind, *107,* 108, 108n45, 113
Principles of Philosophy (Descartes), 77–78
Protestant Reformation, 51
Psychologia empirica (Empirical psychology) (Wolff), 94–98, 98n13, 104, *107,* 114, 114n58, 134

Psychologia rationalis (Rational psychology) (Wolff), 98, 98n11, 117
psychology, 6–7, 65, 97–100, 121, 134, 267, 281, 298
   emergence as a science, 97–104

Quintilian, 158n17

rational conduct, 31–35, 142–43
Reckwitz, Andreas, 24n55, 25n56, 26n60
reflection, 28, 113–14, 139, 141–42, 165–66, 191
Reformation, 51
religious exercises, 108–11. See also spiritual exercises
Renaissance, 45n9
representation, 29, 53–64, 168, 170–79, 187–95, 237
Resewitz, Friedrich Gabriel, 127, 129–30
revulsion, 111–12
rhetoric, 155, 157–58, 168, 168n38, 203n8Richards, Robert J., 99
Ricoeur, Paul, 77n72
Ritter, Joachim, 274–75, 275n173, 276
Romanticism, German, 239n87, 263
Rorty, Richard, 58
"Rothe Glas-Scheibe (Red glass pane)" (Brockes), 164n28, 180–87
Rousseau, Jean-Jacques, 127, 146, 209
routine, 14–17
Rules for the Direction of the Mind (Descartes), 60–61

Schiller, Friedrich, 95, 143–44, 144n128, 145, 232n69, 233, 235–36, 239
scholasticism, 40, 46–49, 53
science
   Bacon and, 45–50
   Descartes and, 32–34, 36, 39–41, 54–56, 55n30, 57–62, 62n44, 64–78, 77n71, 78–83
   focusing of attention and, 43–44, 175

natural, 44–45
observation in, 108–9, 210–211, 281–283
poetics and, 45n8, 155n8
psychology as, 97–104
scientific attention, 21n48
Search after Truth, The (Malebranche), 87–88
seeing, 154–55, 155n6, 161–63, *165*
Seel, Martin, 203n6
selective perception, 9–14, 28, 170–71, 196–97, 237
self-awareness, 147
self-consciousness, 116, 118, 149
self-control, 121–22. *See also* discipline
self-determination, 124, 145. *See also* autonomy
self-mastery, 121–22. *See also* autocracy
self-monitoring, 31–35
self-recognition, 116
self-sufficiency, 124
Senebier, Jean, 31, 282
Shklovsky, Viktor, 177
signification, 29–30
Soap Bubbles (Chardin), 62–64, *63*
soul
  aesthetics and, 260–66
  in Aristotle, 1
  in Baumgarten, 260–66, 260n143
  in Brockes, 164, 164n28
  in Descartes, 78–80, *79*, 85, 213
  ground of, 260–66
  inspiration and, 261
  in Leibniz, 114, 261–62
  shifting conceptions of, 1–2
  will and, 75–83
  in Wolff, 97–101, 101n20, 103, 114
  wonder and, 87
Spinoza, Baruch, 131–34, 133n96, 134, 244
spiritual exercises, 24, 42–43, 54n29, 71n62, 85–6, 108–9, 116n62, 122, 256
splendor, 160
Stiegler, Bernard, 2
Stimmung, 263–64, 263n149

subject, 9, 22, 36–37, 95, 89–91, 116–19, 145–51. *See also* subjectivity
  autonomous, 2, 92–151
  in Baumgarten, 203–4, 230–32, 256–266
  emergence of, as modern concept, 2, 22, 38, 234, 292
  in Hegel, 292
  knowledge and, 113–19, 117n64
  as user, 296–97
  German Idealism and, 118–19, 255
  rational, 32, 35, 37–38, 118, 154, 264
  self-consciousness and, 91, 116, 118, 149
subjectivity
  autonomous, 145
  in Baumgarten, 205, 232
  in Crary, 9
  disciplinary, 204n10
  gendered, 232
  in Herder, 265
  involuntary attention and, 32, 119.
  shifting conceptions of, 8
  Wolff and, 119, 264
surprise, 32–33
Suspensions of Perception: Attention, Spectacle, and Modern Culture (Crary), 8, 197
sustained attention, 53, 106–7
Swerve, The (Greenblatt), 14n32

"taking note," 28–29, 280
taste, 150–51
Taylor, Charles, 24n55
"Techniques of the Body" (Mauss), 23–24, 23n52
Techniques of the Observer (Crary), 23n50, 30n69, 57n36, 59n39, 59n40, 64n46, 283n13
Teresa of Ávila, 54
Thomasius, Christian, 15, 15n35, 93n3, 213–15, 213n33
Thums, Barbara, 9n18, 15, 15n39, 166
transcendentalization, 3

Treatise of Man (Descartes), 79, 80
Trop, Gabriel, 204–6, 206n14, 240n89, 256, 259

Verfremdung, 177. *See also* defamiliarization
vigilance, 92–93, 108n45
virtue ethics, 108–9
Vogl, Joseph, 179
Voltaire, 96n8
"Vorschlag zu einem Magazin einer Erfahrungs-Seelenkunde" (Proposal for a magazine of empirical psychology) (Moritz), 281

Waldenfels, Bernhard, 11n21
Weber, Max, 25–26, 25n57
Weikard, Melchior Adam, 4–7, 5n6, 6n12
Wellbery, David, 29, 136–37, 157n15, 263n149
Welsch, Wolfgang, 203n6
"*Werckstatt der Seelen, Die*" (Workshop of the soul) (Brockes), 164n28

will, 75–83, 110–11, 144
Williams, James, 297
Wolff, Christian, 3, 10–11, 17–19, 22, 28, 31–32, 36–37, 93–104, 96n8, 98n11, 98n13, 101n20, 117n64, 134–42, 135n101, 146, *165*, 169, 176n57, 183
  attention as faculty in, 104–13
  Baumgarten *vs.*, 209–10
  Breitinger *vs.*, 169–70
  Campe and, 127
  clarity in, 223n49
  essences in, 190n85–86, 190–91, 191n87
  Foucault and, 119–24
  knowledge in, 113–19
  moral philosophy and, 142–45
wonder, 32–33, 86–89, 154, 162–64, 175, 212–16. *See also* marvel
Wundt, Wilhelm, 94

Zedler, Johann Heinrich, 250–51, 251n116
Zerstreuung, 12
Zimmermann, Johann Liborius, 234n72

www.ingramcontent.com/pod-product-compliance
Lightning Source LLC
Chambersburg PA
CBHW030001240426
43672CB00007B/774